CIVIL SOCIETY AND ETHNIC CONFLICT MANAGEMENT IN NIGERIA

About AFSTRAG:

The African Strategic and Peace Research Group (AFSTRAG) was established in 1992 as an independent non-governmental, non-political, non-profit making, action-oriented research organisation. Its aim is to provide a platform for analysing strategic issues, particularly those relating to peace and security, and their effects on the political, military, socioeconomic and human conditions in Africa.

Its membership is made up of eminent scholars, senior military officers, public servants, business executives and other persons with interests and proven capacity for research and intellectual discourse on African affairs. The members are motivated by the perceived need to provide an African perspective to the search for solutions to the problems of human security, peace and stability and the social economic conditions on the continent.

Other Publications by AFSTRAG

- *Conflict Management Mechanism in West Africa*, edited by Olu Adeniji, 1997.
- *Civil Society, Good Governance and Security in Africa*, edited by R.A. Akindele, Vintage Publishers, Ibadan, 2003.
- *Civil Wars, Child Soldiers and Post-Conflict Reconstruction in Liberia and Sierra Leone* by Amadu Sesay, OAU Press, Ile-Ife, 2003.

CIVIL SOCIETY AND ETHNIC CONFLICT MANAGEMENT IN NIGERIA

Thomas A. Imobighe

Spectrum Books Limited
Ibadan
Abuja • Benin City • Lagos • Owerri

Spectrum titles can be purchased on line at
www.spectrumbooksonline.com

Published by
Spectrum Books Limited
Spectrum House
Ring Road
PMB 5612
Ibadan, Nigeria
e-mail:admin1@spectrumbooksonline.com

in association with
Safari Books (Export) Limited
1st Floor
17 Bond Street
St Helier
Jersey JE2 3NP
Channel Islands
United Kingdom

Europe and USA Distributor
African Books Collective Ltd
The Jam Factory
27 Park End Street
Oxford OX1, 1HU, UK

© AFSTRAG

First published, 2003

ISBN: 978-029-484-8

Printed by: Evi-Coleman & Co.

CONTENTS

	Page
Preface	vii
Note on Contributors	xi

PART 1

Civil Society and Ethnic Conflicts: General Overview

CHAPTER 1
Introduction: Civil Society, Ethnic Nationalism and Nation
    Building in Nigeria —Thomas A. Imobighe   3

CHAPTER 2
Ethnicity and Ethnic Conflicts in Nigeria: An Overview
    —Thomas A. Imobighe   13

CHAPTER 3
Civil Society and Alternative Approaches to Conflict
    Management in Nigeria
    —Augustine O. Ikelegbe   36

·PART 2

Case Studies from Nigeria's Six Geo-Political Zones

CHAPTER 4
Ethno-Religious Conflict in Kaduna State
    — K. Leonard Fwa   81

CHAPTER 5
Bassa-Egbura Conflict in Nassarawa State
    — Julie Sanda   106

CHAPTER 6
Hausa/Fulani-Sawaya Conflict in Bauchi State
    — K. Leonard Fwa   128

CHAPTER 7
Ife-Modakeke Conflict in Osun State
        —Babajimi Peters   148

CHAPTER 8
Aguleri-Umuleri Conflict in Anambra State
        —Okechukwu Ibeanu   167

CHAPTER 9
Urhobo-Itsekiri Conflict in Delta State
        —Agatha Eguavoen   223

PART 3

Civil Society Empowerment for Conflict Management

CHAPTER 10
Organising Civil Society for Ethnic Conflict Management
        in Nigeria
        —Ibrahim James   259

CHAPTER 11
Civil Society and Ethnic Conflict Management: Lessons
        from Other African States
        — Gane Bang Zamtato   282

CHAPTER 12
Towards Civil Society/Government Partnership in Ethnic
Conflict Management: Integrating the Traditional Democratic
Analytical Model Into Existing Conflict Management Practice
        — Thomas A. Imobighe   292

CHAPTER 13
Conclusion
        — Thomas A. Imobighe   302

Appendix   311
Index   317

PREFACE

Ever since the birth of Nigeria's Fourth Republic in May, 1999, violent communal or ethnic conflicts have become regular features of societal life in the country. We know that conflict is a normal phenomenon in the interactions between human persons, whether acting as individuals or as groups. In other words, it is not out of place for human societies to have conflictual relationship at one time or the other in the process of their regular interactions. This is obvious because when people live together, they must of necessity interact as they try to avail themselves of the necessities of life; that is, meet their physiological and other needs. In the process of doing so, they are bound to disagree and have clashes of interests from time to time as individual preferences play on their relationship and, consequently, lead them to pursue incompatible goals or use incompatible means to pursue chosen goals.

The important point to emphasize is that in order to realize their individual and collective needs, people make demands upon themselves, upon their physical environment, upon other people, upon state authority and other organizations or institutions, which are in a position to provide such needs. Whereas human beings practically always desire something, to use Abraham Maslow's analogy, the available resources to meet human desires and needs are not infinite and are usually subject to scarcity. It is due to this fact of resource scarcity that the pattern of human interactions can at times be cooperative, in which case, the parties involved are predisposed to finding common solutions to the problem of harnessing the available resources to meet their respective needs; and at times conflictual, in which case, there is disharmony or clash of interests in their struggle to harness available resources to meet their disparate needs.

The essential issue, therefore, is not that conflict should not occur within and between the different human societies, but that conflict should be managed productively any time it occurs. Thus, in this study, we do not attempt to wish away conflict. We agree that the different ethnic groups in Nigeria must of necessity compete for the available resources of land and water; as well as struggle to grasp the available economic opportunities and political positions; as a result of which conflicts are bound to occur. What is worrisome is the phenomenon of the frequency and intensity of the conflicts within and between the different ethnic groups and the fact that these conflicts have become so endemic as to threaten the survival of the country; thus indicating that these conflicts have not been productively managed.

The persistence of these conflicts and the unprecedented level of destruction to life and property they caused, clearly suggest that the formal approaches to their management have proved to be grossly inadequate. The fact that these conflicts have proliferated instead of abating is evidence that government alone cannot effectively address them and that existing formal approaches should be supplemented with informal methods in their management. This is what has informed this study, which is focused on the need for active civil society involvement in the management of these conflicts.

Until now, too much reliance has been placed on official mechanisms in the management of these conflicts. The result has been painful delays in responding to nip the conflicts in the bud and prevent the escalation of violence. Moreover, when such belated interventions come from above, they usually take the form of coercive and judicial actions, which very often do not reflect the realities on the ground or address the fundamental issues behind such conflicts. Little wonder then, as evident from the case studies presented in this volume that these conflicts keep on recurring. It is in this sense that civil society-based local arrangements have been advocated as a more creative and rewarding approach to the management of these conflicts.

Studies in civil society in Nigeria, as elsewhere in Africa, are of a recent phenomenon. And because the upsurge of civil society groups coincided with the wind of democratization that swept across the African continent in the early 1990s, most of these studies have been centred on the potentials and limitations of civil society in promoting and sustaining the democratization project. However, in Nigeria of recent, most active civil society groups have become ethnic-based. They have shifted from their initial focus as platforms for democratic advocacy and popular protest and resistance against excesses and abuses of state power; and have now become platforms for ethnic militancy against marginalisation and agitation for resource control. In short, they have become veritable platforms for violent confrontation with other groups and the state. Thus, the big challenge confronting Nigeria under the new democratic dispensation, is how to change the orientation of Nigeria's civil society groups, so that they can see their role, not merely as constituting instruments of protest and violent confrontation with the state and with other groups within the state, but also to serve as instruments for seeking common economic and political platforms and facilitating inter-group and inter-ethnic harmony within the country.

The collections in this volume represent a serious attempt to respond to the above challenge. Collectively, they serve as a vigorous exploration into an innovative civil society intervention in Nigeria's ethnic conflicts. They did not just show the need for an enhanced civil society participation in the management of the country's ethnic conflicts, they have through case studies spread across Nigeria's six geopolitical zones, documented the present level of civil society involvement in conflict management in Nigeria and proffered a range of roles civil society can play in conflict prevention, peace promotion and in the actual process of conflict resolution. This study does not claim to have found permanent solutions to all the conflicts studied. As a pioneering work in this new evolving field of civil society management of conflicts, this volume has provided a solid base for civil society's creative role in the management of Nigeria's ethnic conflicts, upon which future researchers can build.

By way of acknowledgement, it is important to explain that the data assembled in this volume are the end result of extensive fieldwork and countless interviews carried out across the six geopolitical zones of Nigeria, especially within the states and among the communities where the case studies have been selected. In this brief note of acknowledgement, it is hardly possible to mention and thank by name all those who contributed to the success of this study. We thank you all for your invaluable contributions.

The editor will like to acknowledge here the difficult circumstances under which members of this study group carried out their assignment. Many of them experienced frequent disruptions of their fieldwork, consequent to the intermittent outbreak of fresh hostilities in some of the theatres of conflict. It was under conditions of great risk to their personal safety that they carried out their fieldwork. One cannot thank them enough for this unique commitment.

Most importantly, this study could not have been possible without the generous financial support provided by the Ford Foundation. We are grateful for the interest and sustenance and, in particular, the support for AFSTRAG, the NGO under whose auspices this research has been carried out. Finally, it is left for me to say that the views expressed in this study are those of the respective authors and do not in any way represent the views of AFSTRAG or our sponsor, the Ford Foundation.

Thomas A. Imobighe
Editor

NOTE ON CONTRIBUTORS

Thomas A, Imobighe
Professor Imobighe is the director of the Centre for Strategic and Development Studies, Ambrose Alli University, Ekpoma, Nigeria. Among his recent publications, are *Conflict and Instability in the Niger Delta: The Case of Warri* (co-authored) (Ibadan: Spectrum Books, 2002) and *The OAU (AU) and OAS in Regional Conflict Management: A Comparative Assessment* (Ibadan: Spectrum Books, 2003).

Augustine O. Ikelegbe
Dr. A.O. Ikelegbe is a senior lecturer at the Department of Political Science and Public Administration, University of Benin, Nigeria.

Gane Bang Zamtato
General Zamtato is a retired general of the Chadian Army and an active member of AFSTRAG, Chad.

Julie Sanda
Ms. Julie Sanda is a research fellow at the Centre for Peace Research and Conflict Resolution, National War College, Abuja, Nigeria.

K.L. Fwa
Dr. Leonard Fwa is a senior research fellow at the National Institute for Policy and Strategic Studies, Kuru, Plateau State, Nigeria.

Babajimi Peters
Dr. Babajimi Peters is a senior research fellow at the Nigerian Institute of International Affairs, Lagos, Nigeria.

Okechukwu Ibeanu
Dr. Okechukwu Ibeanu is a senior lecturer, Department of Political Science, University of Nigeria, Nsukka. He is presently serving as programme officer, MacArthur Foundation, Abuja.

Agatha Eguavoen
Dr. (Mrs.) Eguavoen is a senior lecturer, Department of Sociology, Ambrose Alli University, Ekpoma, Edo State, Nigeria.

Ibrahim James
Professor Ibrahim James is Head of the Department of History,
University of Jos, Nigeria.

PART 1

CIVIL SOCIETY AND ETHNIC CONFLICTS: GENERAL OVERVIEW

Chapter 1

Introduction: Civil Society, Ethnic Nationalism and Nation Building in Nigeria

Thomas A. Imobighe

Ever since independence, Nigeria has tried to grapple with the problem of nation building. Since the amalgamation of Southern and Northern Nigeria in 1914, various measures have been put in place to create an integrated nation. The colonial regime created the Nigerian State, but decided to hold on to the country through a policy of divide and rule. In the process, it encouraged the separate development of the constituent ethnic units that make up Nigeria without encouraging the "Nigerianess" of the whole. As Obafemi Awolowo eloquently put it, though Nigeria was admittedly the artificial creation of the British and was "made up of a large number of small unintegrated tribal and clannish units... British policy nevertheless helped to maintain the status quo."[1] Arthur Richard made the same observation in his statement that "it is only the accident of British suzerainty which has made Nigeria one country;" and that "it is still far from being one country or one nation, socially or even economically." According to him, "socially and politically, there are deep differences between the major tribal groups—they do not speak the same language and they have highly divergent customs and ways of life and they represent different stages of culture."[2] Throughout the colonial period, Britain never bothered to encourage maximum interaction between the various groups.

The situation was further complicated by the construction of what Kalu Ezera regarded as "a tri-regional colonial federalism"[3] in which each regional unit contained one dominant ethnic group and multiple minority ethnic components. The North was dominated by Hausa-Fulani, the West by Yoruba and the East by Igbo. The structure also encouraged the emergence of regional political parties—the Northern People's Congress (NPC) in the North, the Action Group (AG) in the West, and the National Council of Nigerian Citizens (NCNC) in the East. The entire arrangement resulted in the political marginalisation, economic deprivation and social oppression of the minority ethnic groups and their consequent resentment and agitation for autonomy.

Although during the early periods of the struggle for independence the nationalists tried to create a common Nigerian identity by recruiting people from various ethnic backgrounds in the country into the anti-colonial struggle, they did not quite succeed in evolving a nation with an organic unity. Towards the end of the struggle, when the spoils of victory were to be shared, the country was to witness what James Coleman correctly described as the regionalisation of Nigerian nationalism.[4] Therefore, at independence, Nigeria was a conglomerate of numerous ethnic groups devoid of any organic unity. Instead of cultivating the feeling of national consciousness, the constituent ethnic groups remained the primary units or entities with which the people of Nigeria identified. By ethnic groups, one is referring to the various distinct socio-cultural and linguistic groups within Nigeria, each with a common set of characteristics that sets it apart from other groups.[5]

Understandably at independence, the overriding goal of the country's political elite was how to create a feeling of common belonging among Nigeria's diverse ethnic groups. In other words, national unity became a transcendent imperative to Nigeria's immediate post-independence political elite. Nigeria's first Prime Minister, Abubakar Tafawa Balewa, tried to propagate the doctrine of "unity in diversity", but the flame of national unity he thought would burn bright and strong with the construction of national symbols like the concept of Nigerian citizenship, national flag, national anthem and the practice of quota system of appointment into federal service, never materialised.[6] Indeed, the adoption of a federal constitution originated from Nigeria's search for a common bond that will unite its diverse ethnic groups. The whole idea was to establish a union without necessarily losing the identities of the various ethnic components. As the country was advancing towards independence, there were patent fears of political and economic domination. These fears and concerns took a multi-dimensional form. On the one hand, the minority ethnic groups entertained fear of domination by the larger ethnic groups. On the other hand, there was a mutual suspicion between the North and the South. The northerners feared that the southerners, by virtue of their earlier start and advancement in western education, would remain the dominant group in a fully integrated system, while the latter, on their part, expressed concern over northern domination because of their numerical strength.[7] As a direct response to these fears, Nigeria opted for a federal system to allay these fears and reflect the country's diverse social, political, cultural and economic interests.

However, when it was found that under the First Republic, the federal constitutional framework was slow in bringing about the expected national unity, the military under J.T.U. Aguiyi Ironsi tried to legislate against divisive tendencies in the country. The exercise turned out to be counter-productive as negative intents were read into Ironsi's patriotic action. It was clear that ethnic bonds and inter-ethnic suspicion were so strong that any radical measure to forge the concept of the Nigerian nation was fraught with great danger, and that such a move could even undermine the very existence of the Nigerian State.

The hostile reaction to Ironsi's move to legislate Nigeria's unity clearly demonstrated that the phenomenon of ethnic and geo-ethnic parochialism that dominated Nigeria's political landscape since the 1950s could not be wished away by a political fiat. Thus, in spite of their claim to nationalistic tendencies and a tradition of a central command structure, the military had to soft-pedal on the issue of forcing Nigerian unity. They did return the nation from the brink of total disintegration and took some progressive steps towards nation building. Among the important steps taken towards this end, were the promotion of youth mobility, interaction and national exposure through the national youth service scheme, and the development of road infrastructures. They also tried to create a more balanced federation, though in the end, what they did was to give the nation what turned out to be a distorted federal system that concentrates the control of the nation's resources at the centre, thereby making the constituent units completely dependent on the centre for resource support. This is the root of the impoverishment and the weakening of the constituent units, thereby complicating the centre-periphery dichotomy in the country.

The concentration of the control of the nation's resources at the centre meant that any group that controls the centre determines how the nation's resources can be utilised. Understandably, inter-ethnic rivalry to capture power at the centre progressively became a do or die game in which the big three ethnic groups—Hausa-Fulani, Yoruba and Igbo — became the net beneficiaries. At a time when the mainstay of the Nigerian economy was agriculture and the country's main revenue earners, like groundnuts, cocoa, rubber and oil palm, were geo-ethnically fairly well-distributed between the big three ethnic groups, the injustice of a federal character that was based primarily on the balancing of the interests of the above three ethnic groups was not so glaring. At the time, it was all right to operate a revenue allocation formula based on derivation, i.e., the arrangement, which enabled these big ethnic groups to take the plum of the resources generated in their respective zones. However, when the revenue base of the country changed from agricultural products to oil, much of which is generated outside the main concentration of the big three ethnic groups, the derivation formula was jettisoned. With this development, the injustices of operating a federal character that concentrated the control of resources at the centre that is dominated by the big three ethnic groups became too glaring to be ignored. This is the background to the cry for resource control by the minority ethnic groups from whose territory, oil, the nation's life-wire, is produced.

The decision to divide Nigeria into six geopolitical zones to ensure a fairly well-spread distribution of federal positions and the creation of more local administrative units throughout the country are measures designed to correct the above injustices. Unfortunately, these measures at creating a more ethnically balanced federal structure have not only led to stiff competition between the main ethnic groups in the country, it has also led to the tearing apart of different communities within the same ethnic groups in the desperate struggle to corner amenities to their respective sides. In fact, the situation has reached the ridiculous level whereby local communities and villages within the same ethnic group that have no kingship tradition, are now claiming separate identities and turning themselves into autonomous kingdoms in order to have a share from the national cake.

In effect, what these measures have done is to open a Pandora's box of an unending cry of marginalisation by virtually all Nigeria's ethnic groups. At one level, we have the increasing upsurge of microscopic minorities within minorities, engaged in the bitter struggle to win recognition. In effect, Nigeria's attempt to evolve an ethnically balanced federalism is generating new forms of ethnic imbalance. At the second level, because they no longer get as much of the federal plum as they used to get, the big three ethnic groups have now joined the queue of agitators against marginalisation. Under the present situation whereby Nigeria's ethnic nationalities are on each other's throat over marginalisation, it is understandable why there is an increased call for a national conference of ethnic nationalities for a renegotiation of the basis for the nation's unity.

While it is correct to say that this call for a national conference of ethnic nationalities is gaining wider acceptance among sections of the Nigerian public, it is the view here that the project will run into problem when it comes to identifying the ethnic groups to be represented. What Nigerians have failed to realise is that they have inadvertently created room for the flourishing of sub-ethnic consciousness, which the present politicians are deliberately cultivating for their selfish ends. For instance, when the idea of creating Edo State out of the then Bendel State was designed as presently constituted, we thought we were creating an ethnically homogeneous state, where individual qualities would be all that counted in the selection of people into offices. But what have the new politicians made of the state? They have now evolved, not even sub-ethnic, but mini-ethnic identities around which they are mobilising their villages and clans for selfish political gains. With the new power elite consciously promoting the cause of sub-ethnic identities, it is understandable why the attempt by one of Nigeria's foremost nationalists, Anthony Enahoro, to reconstruct the concept of one Edo People through the "Edo Opananakhin" project has failed to materialise. This observation about Edo State is what is being replicated all over the country. Everywhere politicians are carving out ethnic kingdoms for themselves. Hence, in Delta State, for instance, there are numerous autonomous kingdoms among, especially, the Urhobos. It is obvious that under the present circumstances, it would be a hell of a problem sorting out, not just the ethnic groups to be represented at the proposed national conference, but the individuals to represent them.

It is unrealistic to think that the present unending proliferation of new administrative units will solve Nigeria's ethnic problem. This is because the country's intra and inter-communal strife is traceable more to the lack of development than ethnicity. In other words, there is nothing wrong with the country's ethnic diversity. Nigerians should, therefore, not be apologetic about their country's ethnic pluralism. Rather, it is something they should be proud of because diversity enriches human relationship. What Nigeria needs are measures to turn its ethnic diversity into an asset instead of a liability, as it presently seems to represent. In other words, Nigerians must find ways of harnessing the country's numerous ethnic fingers to construct a very strong national fist to maximise the country's full potentials.

So far, too much dependence has been placed on government responses to Nigeria's problem of ethnic diversity. It is obvious that government alone cannot effectively deal with the problem. In fact, government responses, in many instances, have only helped to complicate instead of solving the problem. The situation has reached the stage where civil society must be empowered to assume a greater role in managing the problem. This study is an attempt to respond to the above challenge and explore ways civil society groups can be encouraged to play an enhanced role in the management of ethnic conflicts within the country.

Two concepts are of particular relevance in this study—"civil society" and "ethnic conflicts". The linkage we want to draw between the two in this study relates to the issue as to whether civil society can serve as a good vehicle for the management of ethnic conflicts in Nigeria. To effectively probe into this central issue, it is necessary to define precisely what constitutes civil society, and then find out whether there are in-built mechanisms within the civil society that could be harnessed to facilitate the management of ethnic conflicts in Nigeria.

Civil society can be broadly construed as representing the totality of the non-governmental functionaries within the state system who, acting individually, in groups, or through various associations, could help to promote and defend societal values and norms, organise civic action, ensure good governance and check excesses and abuses of state power. Civil society includes professional organisations, labour movements, youth, peasant, socio-cultural, civil rights and communal groups, around which the civil populace build various identities for the promotion of their various interests. Where civil society groups are effectively organised and active, they form good platforms for social protest and popular struggle against societal ills, injustice and bad government.

In Nigeria, the flourishing of civil society groups was essentially a phenomenon of the increased weakening of the legitimacy of government from the mid-1980s.[8] The period marked the beginning of organised revolt from the civil population that has been traumatised by the unbearable conditions imposed on them by the misrule and repression of successive military regimes in the country. The repressive climate of the time conditioned the character of the country's civil society groups as resistance, protest and advocacy groups for change, accountability, human rights observation and democratisation of government.

Since Nigeria's return to "democratic governance" on May 29, 1999, the focus of the civil society groups in the country has changed from a preoccupation with democratisation, to issues of marginalisation, deprivation, neglect and resource control. This is particularly so in the Niger Delta, the primary source of Nigeria's revenue base, where the situation has assumed a high level of militancy and violence unparalleled in the country's history.[9]

This shift in the focus of civil society from democratic advocacy to the issues of marginalisation and resource control has added an ethnic dimension to the activities of civil society under Nigeria's new democratic dispensation. Until now, especially during the military era, most of the active civil society groups cut across ethnic lines. Among these were the National Democratic Coalition (NADECO); Campaign for Democracy (CD); the Constitutional Rights Project (CRP); Joint Action Committee for Democracy (JACON); Organisation for the Restoration of Actual Rights of Oil Communities (ORAROC); Concerned Youths of Oil Producing States (CYOPS); and Delta Peoples Movement for Self

Determination and Environmental Protection (DPMSDEP).

Today, especially since the commencement of Nigeria's Fourth Republic, there has been an explosion of ethnic-based civil society movements and virtually all the very active civil society groups are ethnically based. Among these are the Ijaw National Congress (INC), Isoko Development Union (IDU), Urhobo Progress Union (UPU), Egbema National Congress (ENC), Movement for the Survival of Itsekiri Ethnic Nationality (MOSIEN), Movement for the Survival of Izon Nationality (MOSIN), Ijaw Youth Council (IYC), Isoko National Youth Movement (INYM), Urhobo Youth Movement (UYOMO), Egi Youth Federation (EYF), Ikwere Youth Movement (IYM), and Bayelsa Youths Federation of Nigeria (BYFN). Others include Esan Youth Movement, Egbe Afenifere, Odua People's Congress (OPC), Arewa People's Congress (APC), Ohaneze Ndigbo, Igbo Youth Movement, Igbo Salvation Front, Igbo Redemption Council, Federated Council of Igbo Youths, Igbo Peoples Council and Ndigbo Liberation Forum.

The manner in which ethnic-based organisations have taken the place of national oriented civil society groups and the violence attendant to this new transformation has reached an alarming scale. The situation is even reflected in the country's institutions of higher learning where the dominant groups in campus politics and other extra-academic activities are now ethnic and religious organisations rather than the socio-political and intellectual associations of the yesteryears. Thus, virtually in all spheres of Nigeria's societal life, the medium through which people express their grievances is either through ethnic or religious organisations. Because these ethnic and religious groups also form the basis for the violent competition for a share of the national wealth, there is such a high level of inter-ethnic and inter-religious vendetta in the country; so much so that it would seem Nigeria is now exhibiting the symptoms of a collapsing state, whose members are perpetually at war with one another.

Thus, the big challenge confronting Nigeria under the new democratic dispensation, is how to change the orientation of Nigeria's civil society groups, which have metamorphosed into ethno-religious groups, so that they can see their role, not merely as constituting instruments of protest and violent confrontation with the state and with other groups within the state, but also to serve as instruments for seeking common economic and political platforms and facilitating inter-group and inter-ethnic harmony within the country. How do we affect Nigeria's ethnic politics in such a way that Nigerians can cultivate a more positive conception of their federalism not as a hegemonic mechanism for strengthening one's ethnic group against others, but as a bargaining mechanism for resolving political differences and reconciling ethnic interests. The collections in this volume represent a serious attempt to respond to that challenge.

The book is divided into three parts. The first part deals essentially with the theoretical framework, meant to explain the concepts of civil society and ethnic conflicts within the framework of Nigeria's overall national perspective. Part two contains analyses of six case studies, one each from the six geo-political zones into· which Nigeria is divided. The third and final part concentrates on how to empower the civil society for it to play a more assertive and positive role in ethnic conflict management in Nigeria.

References

1.   Obafemi Awolowo, *Path to Nigerian Freedom* (London: Faber, 1947), 32.
2.   See Chris O. Uroh, "On the Ethics of Ethnic Balancing in Nigeria: Federal Character Reconsidered", in Kunle Amuwo et al. *Federalism and Political Restructuring in Nigeria* (Ibadan: Spectrum Books, 1998), p.191.
3.   Kalu Ezera, *Constitutional Developments in Nigeria*, Second Edition (Cambridge: Cambridge University Press, 1964), See Chapters V & X.
4.   James S. Coleman, *Nigeria: Background to Nationalism* (Benin City & Katrineholm, Broburg Wistrom, 1986), pp.319-331.
5.   See Chapter 2 for a detailed explanation of ethnic groups and the concept of ethnicity.
6.   Ehiedu E.G. Iweriebor, "Nigerian Nation-building Since Independence 1960-1990" in *Nigerian Journal of Policy and Strategy*, Vol.5, Nos.1 & 2, June/December 1990, pp.6-7.
7.   For more on this, see Kalu Ezera, *op. cit.*, pp.89-96.
8.   See M.I.M Abutudu, *The State, Civil Society and the*

Democratisation Process in Nigeria (Dakar: CODESRIA Monograph Series 1, 1995). See also B. Olukoshi, "Associational Life", in L. Diamond et. al. (eds.) *Transition Without End: Nigerian Politics and Civil Society under Babangida* (Ibadan: Vantage Press, 1996), pp.450-476.

9   See Ikelegbe, "Civil Society, Oil and Conflict in the Niger Delta of Nigeria: Ramifications of Civil Society for a Regional Resource Struggle", in *Journal of Modern African Studies*, 39, 3, 2001.

Chapter 2

Ethnicity and Ethnic Conflicts in Nigeria: An Overview

Thomas A. Imobighe

Introduction

The frequent manifestation of inter-communal violence in Nigeria has brought the issue of ethnicity and ethnic conflicts to the fore of the country's political discourse. The situation has become extremely worrisome since the beginning of the new democratic dispensation, that is, Nigeria's Fourth Republic, which was enthroned on May 29, 1999. Within the first three years of the country's return to democratic rule, Nigeria had witnessed the outbreak of not less than forty violent communal or ethnic conflicts, while some of the old ones had gained additional potency. Among the prominent recent ones are: Zango-Kataf in Kaduna State; Tiv-Jukun in Wukari, Taraba State; Ogoni-Adoni in Rivers State; Chamba-Kuteb in Taraba State; Itsekiri-Ijaw/Urhobo in Delta State; Ife-Modakeke in Osun State; Aguleri-Umuleri in Anambra State; Yoruba-Hausa community in Shagamu, Ogun State; Ijaw-Ilaje conflict in Ondo State; the intermittent clashes in Kano, Kano State; Basa-Egbura in Nassarawa State; Eleme-Okrika in Rivers State; Hausa/Fulani-Sawaya in Bauchi State; Fulani-Irigwe and Yelwa-Shendam, both in Plateau State; and the Hausa-Yoruba clashes in Idi-Araba in Lagos State.[1] Ethnic and inter-communal conflicts have

13

become so pervasive that there is hardly any part of the country that has not been affected. Some of the most recent ones are the subject of detailed study in part two of this book.

The upsurge of ethnic conflicts and their escalating level of violence are clear indications that Nigeria's post-independence efforts at nation building have so far yielded very little dividends. Three interconnected factors are mainly responsible for the increasing incidents of violent inter-ethnic conflicts in Nigeria.

The first relates to the neglect of the principle of broad public participation in public affairs management in the country and the over-concentration of the control of the country's resources at the centre. The result is the frequent cry of marginalisation by the various ethnic groups in the country and the bitter rivalry by each group to control the centre. Until recently, it was Nigeria's ethnic minorities that used to cry of marginalisation by the larger ethnic groups. Now the cry of marginalisation is loudest from the three largest ethnic groups (Igbo, Yoruba and Hausa/Fulani) who have dominated the country's political landscape since independence. In fact, the practice of the constitutional provision of federal character, by which appointments and distribution of amenities were to be based on regional spread, was primarily done to satisfy the big three ethnic groups. Until recently when Nigeria started to operate on the basis of six geo-political zones, federal character was adjudged to have been satisfied once the interest of the "big three" had been taken care of. Given the rather subjective manner in which Nigeria's political elite view the issue of marginalisation, it is now extremely difficult to determine who is marginalising whom.

Of recent, a new dimension has been added to this important issue of marginalisation, which is terribly affecting the unabating level of inter-community violence in the country. This relates to the complete marginalisation of the youths in Nigeria. The Nigerian youths are increasingly realising that the country's ruling elite have no plan for them in the scheme of things in their country. They see them as self-serving. In their desperation, they now constitute the angry brigade all over the country ready to cash in on ethnic and inter-communal conflicts, which they see as opportunities for taking their pound of flesh from a society that has compromised their future. Thus, in any small crisis, these jobless youths break into both public and private properties and cart away whatever valuables they can find. With graduate unemployment running into millions, Nigeria is perhaps the only country in modern times with so much resources and yet chosen to play with the destiny of its youth.

The second factor has to do with the emergence of ethnic militias, most of which are constituted from the youth wings of the various ethnic groups. These bands of ethnic militias usually arrogate to themselves the responsibility of promoting and defending the interests of their respective ethnic groups against the state or other groups. Most of them frequently resort to violence in the promotion of their causes. Among the noteworthy ones are the Odua People's Congress (OPC); Movement for the Actualisation of the Sovereign State of Biafra (MASSOB); Arewa People's Congress (APC); Ijaw Youth Council (IYC)—under which there are a lot of subgroups such as the Chikoko Movement and the Niger Delta Volunteer Force—also called the Egbesu Boys of Africa or the Supreme Egbesu Assembly (SEA); Isoko Youth Movement; the Bakassi Boys; the Tiv militias; and the young Turks.

The third has to do with the proliferation of small arms in the country. Small arms are being smuggled into the country through the country's porous borders. Instability and civil unrest in many countries of the West African sub-region have led to the excessive importation of arms into the sub-region, which are easily smuggled across national borders. Other sources of these arms include the unaccounted-for arms in the possession of some of the returnees from international peacekeeping or peace support operations, who smuggle such arms into the country to make quick money. Another main source of weapons for these ethnic militias is arms under the personal possession of retired military and other security personnel, some of which are distributed to their kith and kin in confrontation with other ethnic groups. Pilfering from the country's armoury by unpatriotic military personnel eager to make quick money is another source. The spread of small arms has heightened the level of violence in inter-communal or ethnic conflicts in the country.

Whether Nigeria's numerous communal conflicts could correctly be termed ethnic conflicts is, however, subject to debate. Admittedly, the conflicts highlighted here are conflicts between and within different ethnic communities. However, is that enough to regard them as ethnic conflicts? In other words, has ethnicity anything to do with the outbreak of Nigeria's numerous clashes between different communities? Will people of the same ethnic group react differently under the same circumstances faced by these so-called warring ethnic groups? How does one explain similar outbreak of violent communal conflicts within the same ethnic group? For instance, there are more inter-clan clashes among the Tivs than clashes between the Tivs and other ethnic groups. Intra-ethnic conflicts also abound among the Alagos of Nassarawa State. Besides, the Aguleri-Umuleri conflict, which is one of the cases studied in Part Two of this book, is also an intra-ethnic conflict. Flowing from the above, is it sufficient to classify conflicts as ethnic conflicts by the simple fact that they involve two or more ethnic groups without ascertaining the causality of such conflicts?

This chapter will attempt a critical analysis of the above questions and other related issues, with a view to explaining the concepts of ethnicity and conflicts in order to bring out the correlation between the two. The idea is to determine, if actually ethnicity per se is a conflict-generating phenomenon as is generally implied in some of the existing literature. In other words, does a people's recognition of their ethnic identity necessarily always lead to conflict with other groups? This line of exploration will enable us not only to present a clearer picture of the two concepts of ethnicity and conflict, but also to put the relationship between the two in its proper perspective. Ultimately, it will be possible to determine the extent to which ethnicity can be creatively cultivated in a multi-ethnic society to serve positive ends.

Conceptual Analysis

Although various attempts have been made by scholars to define and analyse the concept of ethnicity, agreeing on a precise definition has been rather problematic. A number of writers have tried to explain ethnicity through the concept of ethnic group without bothering to define the word "ethnic".[2] Nnoli, for instance, refers to ethnicity as "a social phenomenon associated with interactions among members of different ethnic groups." To him, ethnic groups are "social formations distinguished by the communal character (i.e. language and culture) of their boundaries."[3] Otite, who presents a more elaborate definition of ethnic group, turned out to present a rather restrictive and negative picture of ethnicity. According to him, ethnic groups represent "categories of people characterised by cultural criteria of symbols including language, value systems and normative behaviour, and whose members are anchored in a particular part of the new state territory."[4] He defines ethnicity as "the contextual discrimination by members of one group against others on the basis of differentiated systems of socio-cultural symbols."[5]

What seems to guide the manner ethnicity has been explained in a number of existing literature, as is obvious in the case of Otite, is the tendency to base such definitions on the dysfunctional ways ethnicity has been used to serve particularistic interests and undermine national cohesion and integration in many countries. Otite's analysis of the subject, for instance, obviously portrays the fact that he was operating within the Nigerian environment that has witnessed more of the negative than the positive aspects of ethnicity. It is a fact that Nigeria has since independence tried to combat ethnicity and mitigate its negative manifestation within the polity. As we noted in chapter one, the country even legislated against ethnicity at a time during the military era. It is therefore understandable why Otite should affirm in his book under reference, that "ethnicity has the properties of common group consciousness and identity and also group exclusiveness on the basis of which social discriminations are made."[6]

This writer does not share the negativistic view of ethnicity as portrayed in some of the existing literature. Ethnic exclusiveness is not part of the normal process of inter-communal interactions in Nigeria. If it were so, it would have been difficult for ethnic groups to welcome the arrival of other ethnic groups in their midst and provide land for them to settle; a phenomenon which has led to the intermingling of different ethnic groups within the country. Until the present wave of inter-ethnic hostilities in different parts of the country, Nigeria had enjoyed the tradition of free admixture of its diverse ethnic groups in various parts of the country. This explains why there are many ethnic Yorubas and Igbos in several of Nigeria's northern cities like Kano, Kaduna, Jos and Maiduguri. The same explains the presence of Hausa settlements in the country's southern cities like Ibadan, Lagos, Shagamu, Onitsha and Enugu. The same thing explains the multi-ethnic nature of the settlement pattern in cities like Warri, for instance, which is essentially an Itsekiri town. The same phenomenon explains the presence of large settlements of Tiv farmers in the neighbouring states of Taraba, Nassarawa and Plateau.

Even as this work is being prepared, new migrations and, hence, new ethnic settlements are springing up in places that had not experienced the phenomenon. For instance, Hausa livestock traders have started creating an ethnic enclave in Aduwawa in Benin City, capital of Edo State. Also, Igbira farmers have migrated in great numbers from Kogi State into parts of Owan West and Owan East local government areas of Edo State, just as many Hausa/Fulani cattle farmers have migrated in great numbers into parts of Esan West and Esan Central, as well as Owan West and Owan East local government areas of Edo State. These old and recent migrations are indicative of a flourishing tradition of harmonious inter-ethnic interaction in Nigeria. In essence, while socio-political stress might tend to create pockets of inter-ethnic frictions, the necessity of daily economic life continues to bring Nigeria's different ethnic groups together.

To have a clearer picture of ethnicity, there is the need to get at the root of the word "ethnic". The word "ethnic" is derived from the Greek word "ethnos", which means a group of people who share a common and distinctive culture. In its classical meaning, ethnic relates to a member of a particular ethnos. Hence, ethnicity should be seen as the feeling of belonging to a distinctive cultural or linguistic group, or a manifestation of ethnic consciousness in relation to other groups. Such a feeling of belonging to a distinctive socio-cultural group or a manifestation of ethnic consciousness cannot by itself be a bad thing just as the manifestation of national consciousness is not regarded as a bad thing within the comity of nations. The cultivation of that feeling to serve negative ends cannot be regarded as the essence of the word. After all, ethnic consciousness can also be creatively cultivated to serve positive ends in a multi-ethnic society.

Unfortunately, because of their failure to creatively apply ethnicity to serve national goals, Nigerians seem to see their ethnic diversity as a liability instead of an asset. Hence, there is a conscious official attempt to eliminate ethnicity. So far, eliminating ethnicity in Nigeria has proved an impossible mission; for the more Nigerian leaders try to eliminate ethnicity, the more ethnicity blossoms in the country. The truth is that ethnicity cannot be eliminated. You cannot eliminate the root of any particular group of people. All groups of humanity have their respective roots. Identification with one's root is part of the human existential necessity. What Nigeria's political elite should do, as we alluded to in chapter one, is to devise ways of transforming Nigeria's many ethnic fingers into a formidable national fist. The fingers of the hand have their respective distinctive features, which mark them out for the peculiar roles they play. When they are brought together, they become a formidable fist able to provide the needs of the human person.

Therefore, Nigerians should not be apologetic about their ethnic diversity. As Otite rightly observed, "over 90% of the world's independent states are plural and are in various degrees of stability at different stages of development."[7] Thus, pluralism cannot be Nigeria's critical problem when it comes to explaining the phenomenon of frequent conflict within the society. Therefore, instead of trying to kill ethnicity because of the likelihood of its being used by some people to serve negative ends, Nigerians should be proud of their country's diversity because diversity enriches human relationship. Where a people's diversity is creatively cultivated, it provides flavour, strength and vitality to the polity. Apparently, because Nigeria has all along cultivated a negative view of ethnicity, the idea of creatively applying ethnicity to serve the purpose of national integration has remained relatively unexplored.

What Nigerians need to do is to borrow a leaf from the American experience. The United States is one of the most heterogeneous countries in the world today; there is hardly any nationality that is not represented in America (U.S. and America are used interchangeably in this study to mean the United States of America). Besides, America's past history has not been a glorious one in terms of ethnic harmony or race relations. For a considerable period of its history, the country was one of the most racially divided countries on the planet. But over time, by creating opportunities for social and economic mobility, and without seeking to eliminate the manifestation of ethnic individualism, the country has been able to cultivate in every citizen the spirit of what has now become the

American dream—the aspiration to be on top in one's chosen field of human endeavour. Towards this end, the state continues to sustain those measures that guarantee individual rights and entrench the principle of equality before the law, while expanding the available opportunities for every citizen to develop and utilise his/her talent in the service of America. Thus despite the country's violent racial past, there is now a general recognition that every American life is precious and must be protected at all costs irrespective of where he resides.

Conflict in a Multi-Ethnic Society

Conflict, which represents a condition of disharmony within an interaction process, usually occurs as a result of a clash of interests between the parties involved in some form of relationship. Such a clash of interests could occur because either they are pursuing incompatible goals or they are using incompatible means to pursue their chosen goals. There is a general agreement among scholars that conflict is a normal feature in the interaction between human persons, whether acting at their respective individual capacities or in groups. Therefore, conflict can occur within a family and between families, within an ethnic group and between ethnic groups, within an organisation and between organisations, within a state and between states.

The Marxian interpretation of the laws of change, which ties conflict with societal progress, in a way, represents a more enlightened and progressive perception of conflict. According to Marxian postulation, progress occurs through conflict and struggle between opposing forces and hence, the admixture of thesis and antithesis produces synthesis. And as John Burton also points out, conflict is "an essential creative element in human relations"; it is "the means to change," and "the means by which our social values of welfare, security, justice and opportunities for personal development can be achieved."[8] John Burton believes that without conflict society would be static. Dudley Weeks has come up with a similar observation in his remark that "conflict is an inescapable part of our daily lives, an inevitable result of our highly complex, competitive and often litigious society."[9] If conflict is inevitable in all human societies, we cannot expect otherwise in a multi-ethnic society like Nigeria, especially, because if there is one thing on which conflict analysts agree, it is that conflict is an inevitable outcome of human diversity. This is why a world without conflict can hardly be desirable because it would mean a world without diversity.

The above should not be interpreted to mean that the more diversified a society is the more that society is prone to conflict, since multi-ethnicity does not by itself produce conflict.[10] What it does suggest is that if an integrated society can experience conflicts, then a pluralistic one like Nigeria's multi-ethnic society should not think that it could wish away conflict. Rather, it must plan based on the expectation of conflict and put in place effective mechanisms and absorptive institutional capacity to cope with conflict at all levels of the society. In other words, Nigeria must put in place, as is done by most of the stable pluralistic societies, what it takes to reap the full benefits of the country's diversity, among which are: an effective mechanism for power-sharing, a regime of equal opportunities; reduction of economic disparities and the construction of a non-discriminatory and all-inclusive national identity.

The point to emphasise is that while multi-ethnicity does not automatically invoke conflict, it does not also automatically insulate a society from conflict. The truth is that human persons, whether they live in a mono-ethnic or a multi-ethnic society, must struggle for the basic necessities of life, which include their physiological needs, their security needs, as well as other needs such as recognition, identity and self fulfilment or self esteem. As they strive to achieve these needs, they interrelate and make demands on one another, on their environment and on the state. In the process, conflict is bound to arise at some point, irrespective of the nature of the society or the system that is in operation within the affected society. What then determines the frequency as well as the intensity and scale of conflict within a society is the presence or absence of in-built anticipatory mechanisms and the absorptive institutional capacity to cope with the manifestation of conflict tendencies at all the levels of human interactions within the affected society. It is within this context that one can explain why a homogeneous society like Somalia has been torn apart by conflicts while some of Africa's multi-ethnic societies remain stable. The conclusion that can be drawn at this point is that even if there is a correlation between multi-ethnicity and conflict, such a correlation cannot be a straightforward one in which multi-ethnicity simply translates into conflict. Therefore, to explain the phenomenon of ethnic conflict in Nigeria, there is the need for us to reconceptualise ethnic conflict.

Redefining Ethnic Conflict

Most of the conflicts that are generally referred to as ethnic conflicts in Nigeria have little or nothing to do with ethnicity. In other words, they do not arise simply from the fact that the parties belong to different ethnic groups. Most of the conflicts are brought about by other factors, such as, religious differences, demographic explosion and struggle for· the control of state power and resources. Such struggle usually results in accusations and counter-accusations of denial of opportunities for effective participation in the political and economic affairs of the country, or what is more commonly referred to as political and economic marginalisation. Thus, depending on the mode of classification adopted, these so-called ethnic conflicts could as well go for religious, political, resource or migration conflicts. In most cases the only element, which lends credence to the claim that they are ethnic conflicts is the fact that the contestants belong to different ethnic or sub-ethnic groups. In this sense, the issue of the ethnic background of the contestants is incidental and not central to the outbreak of these conflicts. In fact, in a number of cases, individuals rather than a whole ethnic group are involved in these conflicts from the start. It is usually when escalation takes place that close ethnic members are involved.

This is usually the case in some of the conflicts between Fulani herdsmen and farming communities in different parts of the country. The conflicts usually start with clashes between individual herdsmen and local farmers. When such conflicts are not properly controlled or managed, they spread, first, involving the kith and kin of the affected individuals, and later, the whole Fulani group and a wider section of the farmers within the affected locality. The most common source of this type of conflict is crop damage by the animals of the Fulanis or the encroachment by the farmers on what the Fulanis regard as traditional grazing land; all of which usually attract violent response from the aggrieved parties.

The nature of this conflict, especially as it affects North-Eastern Nigeria, has been documented in a study by I. Williams, F. Muazu, U. Kaoje and R. Ekeh.[11] Three factors are pertinent in explaining the intensity of the conflict dynamics in the region. The first relates to the grazing pattern of the Fulanis, which is based on the conventional open access grazing system. Since they depend almost entirely on grazing from natural pastures, they are frequently on the move in search of green pastures and in the process run into problem with farmers, whose crops are often violated when the animals are not properly guided. The diminishing resource of pastoral land is another factor that has helped to reinforce the frequent migration of the Fulanis herdsmen from place to place and hence the confrontation with farming communities in the region. On this score, the Fulanis attribute the scarcity of pastoral land to the encroachment on traditional grazing land and cattle routes by farmers. Such encroachment, they claim, often inhibit their easy access to water for their cattle.

Perhaps the most troublesome factor that has helped to intensify the conflict dynamics in the region has to do with the activities of young Fulani herdsmen usually armed and unaccompanied by their older men and women, who go about at night to damage crops intentionally. These ferocious youths visit violence on any farmer that tries to prevent their nefarious activities; at times, killing such a farmer in the process.[12] The inability to identify them, which is usually complicated by their sudden migration after committing such atrocities, often lead to wide-scale attacks on their older folks.

Although the conflict between Fulani herdsmen and farmers has been particularly acute in the North-East, it is increasingly spreading to other parts of the country as the effects of desert encroachment and the diminishing resource of grazing land have led to the increasing migration of cattle rearing Fulanis to parts of southern Nigeria. Understandably, the conflict is being replicated in many parts of the country and till date, incidents of similar clashes have occurred and are still occurring between Fulani herdsmen and, particularly Hausa farmers, Tiv farmers and some farming communities in parts of Edo State. Obviously, these conflicts have nothing to do with the manifestation of ethnic hatred or ethnic sentiments. The different ethnic groups mentioned here cannot be said to hate the Fulanis neither can it be said that the Fulanis hate them. The truth is that these are conflicts between two professional groups—the agriculturists and pastoralists. It is just that in Nigeria some ethnic groups are associated with particular professions;

hence, as in this case, when there is a clash between two professional groups, the crisis assumes the nature of an ethnic confrontation. Otherwise, the conflicts are simply resource and occupational conflicts, representing part of the hazards attendant to the occupational activities of the different ethnic groups in Nigeria. The country, of necessity, must contend with these conflicts until there are effective local arrangements to regulate and harmonise the activities of the various groups living together in different parts of the country.

The point to emphasise is that this particular conflict between pastoralists and agriculturists is one that touches the economic interests of the parties—the very source of their livelihood. It is part of human nature to hold dear one's source of livelihood. That it involves the Fulani herdsman and the Hausa farmer, or the former and a Tiv farmer is immaterial. The conflict can occur within the same ethnic group. The truth is that if the roles were reversed and it is the Tiv cattle or the Hausa cattle that are destroying the Fulani farms, the latter would react in the same way as the Hausa farmer or the Tiv farmer, to protect his economic interest: either by seeking immediate redress or killing any of the cattle he could lay his hands on; a sort of tit for tat.

Another type of conflict that follows the above pattern of escalation into ethnic clashes is the type that happens in Nigeria's urban cities where quarrels between individuals of different ethnic backgrounds spread into confrontation between whole ethnic communities within the area. A good example is the February 2002 mayhem that took place between the Hausa resident community and Yorubas in Idi Araba, Lagos State. The cause of the fracas was a simple disagreement over the use of a public utility, which led to an alleged manhandling of a member of one of the ethnic groups by some individuals from the other ethnic group.[13] Translated to its logical conclusion, therefore, it is a resource conflict.

This type of conflict has become a common feature in Nigeria's urban cities because the pattern of migration and settlement tends to encourage ethnic compartmentalisation; that is, the concentration of ethnic groups in different sections of the city. There is hardly any Nigerian urban city that is not affected by this practice. The fall out is the development of ethnic enclaves in the country's main cities, thereby facilitating the mobilisation of the various groups for ethnic-motivated causes, or isolating them for physical violation or any other special treatment. This settlement pattern has been responsible for the high rate of concentrated destruction of property during clashes between members of different ethnic groups in Nigeria's big cities.

This same practice of compartmentalised settlement of the different ethnic groups in the country's big cities is often responsible for the transformation of religious conflict into ethnic confrontation. This is often the case where an ethnic group is associated with a particular religion. For instance, because the Igbos are associated with Christianity and the Hausas/Fulanis are associated with Islam, a religious disagreement between members of the two groups has often assumed the posture of an ethnic conflict. The same goes for many of the clashes between Hausa/Fulani communities and Christian communities in parts of Kaduna and Plateau States. Because ethnic and religious boundaries tend to coincide, especially between Hausa/Fulani and northern ethnic minorities, it is difficult to draw a demarcation between religious and ethnic conflicts in the affected areas. Thus, the conflicts between these two groups often take on the posture of ethno-religious conflicts. Examples include the Zango-Kataf conflict of 1992; the Kaduna mayhem of February 2000 and the Aba reprisal riot of the same month;[14] the Jos mayhem of May 2002;[15] and the Yelwa-Shendam conflagration of June 2002.[16]

Even those conflicts that seem to fall within the category of ethnic conflict proper, that is, those that involve the spontaneous rising of a whole community of one ethnic group against another, could also be traced to factors other than ethnicity. The Urhobo-Itsekiri and Ife-Modakeke conflicts, which are part of the case studies in this book, are good examples. Because the two case studies form separate chapters in this book, it will not be necessary to comment on them any further here. Another good example is the Ijaw-Itsekiri conflict in Warri, Delta State. The conflict between the Ijaws and the Itsekiris in Warri is essentially resource, territorial or land conflict, involving disagreement over the ownership of Warri. The whole quarrel centres on the question as to which group was the first to settle in Warri. However, what triggered the spontaneous clash between the two groups in 1997 was a political conflict involving disagreement over the location of the headquarters of the newly created Warri Southwest Local Government Area.[17]

The confusion, which greeted the creation of the new local government area and the location of its headquarters, was the main cause of the conflagration between the two groups. When Western Ijaw Division was carved out of Warri Division in the 1930s there was considerable reduction of the tension between the Ijaws and Itsekiris; a tension which had built up over the years arising from the desire of the Ijaws to have their own separate local administrative unit. However, because the exercise still left some Ijaw communities—Ogbe-Ijoh, Isaba, Gbaramatu and Egbeoma—within what was left of the old Warri Division, it did not completely eliminate the source of friction between the two ethnic groups. Due to what they regarded as Itsekiri marginalisation, these Ijaw communities continued with the agitation for their own separate local government.

Thus, when in December, 1996, the Delta State military administrator, Col. J.D. Dungs announced the creation of Warri Central and Warri South Local Government Areas with Ogbe-Ijoh (an Ijaw town) as the headquarters of the latter, the Ijaws greeted the announcement with great joy. They were happy that their dream of having their own separate local government council had materialized, and that, at last, they were free from the yoke of Itsekiri domination. They took steps to ensure the immediate take-off of the new Local Government Council. They raised funds to refurbish and rehabilitate old structures to serve as the temporary secretariat of the new local government council.

Later, it turned out that what Dungs announced was different from what the Federal Government actually created. What was published under the Federal Government Decree No.36 of 1996, creating new states and local government areas, was the creation of Warri Southwest Local Government with Ogidigben (an Itsekiri town) as headquarters. The Ijaws, understandably, felt betrayed. Their bitterness immediately translated into violent demonstration in which the Itsekiris became the obvious target. The violence, which erupted, soon engulfed the whole of Warri and its environ, leading to an unprecedented destruction of lives and property in the oil city.

What is obvious from our analysis here is that there is no clear-cut definition as to what constitutes an ethnic conflict beyond the nature of the stratification of the major role players. In this sense, conflicts are classified as ethnic conflicts when the active role players are stratified along ethnic lines irrespective of causality. The problem with this type of classification is that in societies where occupational, professional, religious and ethnic boundaries coincide, like in many parts of Nigeria, there is often the tendency to see an ethnic finger intruding on conflicts between individuals or groups from different ethnic backgrounds. Thus, in Nigeria today ethnicity has become a convenient term for covering up the country's societal inadequacies and the people's individual and collective failings.

Thus, in the case of the conflict between the Ijaws and the Itsekiris mentioned above, the issue of ethnicity is extolled over and above the government blunder relating to the location of the headquarters of the newly created local government. The truth is that if the same blunder is committed among communities within the same ethnic group, the affected communities would not react differently. The sorry case about government response to what has happened in Warri, as is often the case in other parts of Nigeria, is that thè tangible issues of how to improve the integrity and efficiency of government to meet the disparate needs of the people, are sidetracked in favour of issues that reinforce ethnic sentiments. Rather than respond to the developmental needs of Warri, which will benefit all its inhabitants, the responses are reinforcing the very ethnicity, which the country has been labouring to combat. For instance, the idea of creating ethnic local governments in Warri, which has been proposed, can hardly be regarded as the best approach to the problem as it could lead to the manifestation of ethnic exclusivity.[18] So also is the idea of creating new kingdoms for the ethnic groups that have no kingdoms in Warri. The argument for this is that since the Olu of Warri is Itsekiri, the Urhobo communities in Warri should also have the equivalent of an Olu. The implication of this would be the proliferation of microscopic kingdoms in places where no tradition of kingship existed.

The Warri case epitomises the manner Nigeria has abandoned its fundamental developmental problems in pursuit of ethnic trivialities. For instance, as Nigeria is moving towards the 2003 presidential election, the political parties are trading ethnic candidates instead of concentrating on a comprehensive nationwide developmental agenda that will note the past failings and present new strategies for overcoming the nation's problems. Rather than packaging and fine-tuning a developmental blueprint, which they will commit to whoever emerges as president to implement, their preoccupation is on how to continue with the present tradition of ethnic presidency; that is, whether the president should be an Igbo, Yoruba, Hausa, Fulani, or any of the other numerous ethnic groups in the country. Should the present practice of ethnic permutation in leadership choice continue, Nigeria would again have an ethnic president in 2003 without a national agenda to implement.

That the ethnic factor should be a recurring decimal in the conflicts afflicting Nigeria should not present any surprise; it is a reflection of a bias in favour of actor-based approach as against issue-based approach to conflict analysis. The actor-based approach to conflict analysis concentrates on the parties involved in the conflict and categorises conflict based on the characteristics and the extended relationship of the parties involved. In this sense, conflict can be categorised based on the number of actors involved, in which sense you could have a bilateral or multilateral conflict. It could also be categorised based on the spread of the actors, in which case you have local, regional or global conflict. Another form of classification relating to the actor-based approach to conflict analysis is the one based on the existing nature of relationship between the parties involved or their socio-cultural backgrounds. It is in this sense you have communal, inter-communal, ethnic, intramural, or adversary conflict. Flowing from this last mode of classification, once it is seen that the parties to a conflict are from two ethnic or sub-ethnic groups, the conflict is automatically adjudged an ethnic conflict. With the ethnic label clamped on a conflict, the attention of the conflict manager is focused on ethnic relations instead of focusing on the objective conditions under which they relate in order to get at the root of the conflict.

The issue-based approach to conflict analysis, on the other hand, focuses attention on the issues and the objective conditions of the environment of conflict. It is in this sense that you have resource conflict, cultural/religious conflict, system/ideological conflict, hegemonic/influence conflict, or land/boundary conflict. The issue-based approach to conflict analysis is more helpful in terms of getting at the root of conflict. It enables the conflict manager to concentrate on the substantive issues of human needs, the concerns and fears of the parties, instead of how and why the affected individuals use their various connections—family, ethnic, party, club, regional, zonal etc. —to respond to conflictual relationship. In other words, once the attention is on the issues, instead of talking vaguely, for instance, about family conflict or ethnic conflict, the focus would be on the land, resource, or any particular problem, which the two families or ethnic groups are quarrelling over. In that case, those involved in managing the conflict can concentrate on the various ramifications of the problem of land use, resource management, or the specific issue area, and work towards its comprehensive solution. It is in this sense that the issue-based approach to conflict analysis ties in with the problem-solving approach to conflict management, which most conflict analysts regard as the best answer to finding a lasting solution to any conflict; that is, a solution that is mutually satisfying to the parties.

Perhaps the reason why the problem of ethnic conflicts seems insurmountable in Nigeria has to do with the apparent neglect of the problem-solving approach in the management of these conflicts. Obviously, Nigeria is preoccupied with chasing the ethnic shadow and not the fundamental issues and the objective conditions of the Nigerian polity, which are at the root of these conflicts. Consequently, the needed regular system re-examination and correction, which are part of the vital ingredients for conflict mitigation within a given polity, are yet to form part of the Nigerian political culture. For instance, rather than address the basic issue of resource management and how to expand Nigeria's resource base by maximising the potentialities available in all the regions of the country, Nigeria's ruling elite prefer to hide in their different ethnic cocoons and quarrel over how to share the little portion of the accruable funds from their country's oil resources. Interestingly, what they quarrel over is the tiny proportion, which is given to them as the country's share by the foreign multinational corporations, who do the exploration, production and marketing of the commodity. The country's oil is got from the Niger Delta region, which is less than 15% of the total size of the country. The other 85% of the country is also blessed with abundant resources, which could be harnessed to expand the revenue base of the country's economy. In their rabid competition to consume the oil money, the Nigerian ruling elite have paid little or no attention to the expansion of the productive base of the country's economy, thereby turning the country into a hostage of its oil wealth. The immediate result of their unproductive disposition and bloated appetite for consumption, is the relegation of Nigeria to the unenviable status of a well endowed nation with the worst record of graduate unemployment in the world—not able to absorb one-tenth of the graduates from its tertiary institutions consistently for more than five years. With no unemployment benefit to mitigate the social consequences of its high rate of graduate unemployment, the country has obviously chosen to live dangerously. That these jobless youth have constituted the main source of recruits into the swelling ranks of ethnic militias that are spreading violence across the country, is perhaps one way the youth are trying to seek atonement for their apparent neglect.

Another consequence of Nigeria's failure to apply the problem-solving method relates to the over-concentration of the management of these conflicts in official hands. Since there is usually no provision for local management machinery for the resolution of these conflicts, during each emergency, the society has had to wait patiently for the solution to come from above. Of course, this usually leads to costly delays in finding solution to the conflicts. Besides, blueprints designed previously from Lagos, and now from Abuja, have often proved ineffective, obviously, because of their failure to reflect the realities on the ground. It is in this sense that civil society empowerment is being suggested in this study as a way of ensuring locally groomed formulae for handling these conflicts. As has been previously noted in this chapter, the presence or absence of such local arrangements has often made the difference as to the frequency and intensity of these conflicts. To put the problem in its proper perspective, a comparison of the way the problem has been handled in different localities will be highlighted here.

For instance, the management of the conflicts between Fulani herdsmen and farming communities in the northeastern part of the country, which was highlighted earlier on, was for many years based on the use of law enforcement agencies and the existing legal framework. So also was the handling of the Ogoni conflict with the State, the oil companies and some of its neighbours. The same thing goes for the handling of the Warri conflict, which involved the three main ethnic groups within the Oil City—the Ijaw, the Itsekiri and the Urhobo.[19] In all of these cases and many others, the over-reliance on government agencies and the use of coercive and judicial methods have proved ineffective. It has been found, as documented in various studies, that they do not always take into consideration the realities on the ground and that they usually lead to the suppression of most of the conflicts or, at best, a win-lose outcome and, hence, the undue prolongation of the conflicts since the loser would always try to reverse the outcome at some convenient time. The coercive and judicial methods have also been found to provide opportunity for the extortion of money from the parties by the police and court officials.[20]

In some areas, this extortion by security agents is having its unintended salutary effect in the sense that it is encouraging local initiatives in the management of some of these conflicts. For instance, in the case of the aforementioned conflict between Fulani herdsmen and farming communities in northeastern Nigeria, the parties have been so frustrated by the ineffectual government mechanisms to deal with their problem, that they have, on their own, established joint security committees to enforce mutually agreed local arrangements to mitigate the frequent occurrences of these conflicts. As a result of one of such initiatives, they have outlawed the unwholesome activities of the irresponsible group of young herdsmen, who have, for so long, helped to perpetuate a climate of hostilities between farmers and Fulani herdsmen in the region. Consequently, no pastoralist is allowed to move or migrate with his cattle without the members of his family.[21]

Perhaps it will be helpful to document here a good example of a typical local arrangement that has helped to ensure peace between livestock owners and local farmers among the Beron communities of Plateau State.[22] Unlike the situation in some other parts of the country where there is frequent conflict between livestock owners and farmers, the Beron communities of Plateau State have a standing rule whereby it is obligatory for livestock owners to restrict the movement of their livestock during the planting season up to the time of harvest to prevent them from destroying the crops of the local farmers. There is a specified penalty imposed, which is strictly enforced irrespective of the status or the ethnic background of those involved. Since this is a local arrangement, which does not depend on the cumbersome State apparatus to enforce, it is strictly adhered to by all concerned. Consequently, those livestock owners who cannot keep close watch on their cattle usually pin them down with pegs in open fields to graze in order to prevent them from wandering into planted fields. This local arrangement has not only prevented the outbreak of any major conflagration between the livestock owners and farmers in the affected areas, it has also enabled the farmers to plant crops even around dwelling areas without any fear of their crops being destroyed by cattle.

The usefulness of this account rests, not necessarily on the idea that other communities should apply exactly the same arrangement. Of course, it might not be possible to pin down a large herd of cattle on one spot; all the same, they can be properly guided, as often done by the Fulani herdsmen, to avoid planted fields. The idea is to emphasise the feasibility of local arrangements and the inherent benefits derivable from them. Apart from the fact that these local arrangements are more adaptable to local circumstances, they are fast and relatively inexpensive to apply and hence, they are more reliable than the conventional processes. Since the sanctions usually imposed are those that have been mutually agreed upon by the people concerned, they are usually more realistic and they tally with what the people can and are willing to pay. As long as such sanctions are in place, and enforced indiscriminately, arbitrary responses on the part of aggrieved persons, which usually lead to the escalation of these conflicts, would be discouraged.

Conclusion

What has been done in this chapter is to carry out a critical analysis of the problem of ethnicity and ethnic conflicts within the context of Nigeria's multi-ethnic society. The chapter discusses the nurturing of the country's ethnic diversity under colonial rule and its intensification in recent times by the country's new political elite who seem to find a new fascination in the whole idea of ethnic nationality. From our analysis in this chapter, it follows that the multi-ethnic composition of the Nigerian State does not automatically translate into conflict. In other words, the manifestation of ethnic consciousness by Nigerians does not automatically lead to conflict between the various groups. As

Eghosa Osaghae rightly observed, "ethnic conflict is situational"; it is a "dependent rather than an independent variable, and requires explanation beyond stating that people from different ethnic groups engage in conflict."[23] From the analysis in this chapter, it is obvious that what bring about "ethnic conflicts" in Nigeria's multi-ethnic society are the same factors that create conflictual relationship in the so-called homogeneous societies all over the world. These include competition for scarce resources, competition for the acquisition of the necessities of life, mutual intolerance, and asymmetry in resource distribution. Others include political and economic rivalry and disagreement over political and economic goals. The point to note is that while these stresses and pulls of societal life generally create these conflicts, the tendency by the parties to employ their ethnic connections to pursue their interests often makes these conflicts assume the posture of ethnic conflicts.

What has helped to sustain this conflict dynamic, in relation to the Nigerian environment, has to do with the migration and settlement pattern in the country, which has led to the development of ethnic enclaves, especially in Nigeria's big cities. Where immigrants of the same ethnic group are quartered together in different sections of the city, any small quarrel affecting two people from different ethnic quarters within the affected city quickly develops into hostility between their respective ethnic groups. This is what has contributed to the indigene/settler syndrome that has plagued the country's political landscape over the years. Therefore, in most cases what people commonly regard as ethnic conflicts in Nigeria are in fact either political, religious, resource or land conflicts involving individuals from different ethnic backgrounds who exploit their ethnic connections in their responses to the affected conflicts.

In the management of these conflicts, it has been shown that there is too much reliance on official action with minimal participation by civil society. Relying on existing knowledge, it has been demonstrated that locally groomed arrangement subscribed to and well understood by everybody within the locality, have stood the test of time over and above blueprints designed from the top. This is why this study has emphasised that a bottom-top civil society-based arrangement would be a more effective alternative to the highly centralised method of managing these conflicts. From the subsequent chapters, which deal with case studies from the six geo-political zones of the country, it will be possible to have a panoramic view of the role of civil society in the management of Nigeria's ethnic conflicts.

References

1.   For a comprehensive list of the violent conflicts Nigeria has witnessed between May, 1999, and July, 2002, see J. Isawa Elaigwu "Ethnic Militias and Democracy in Nigeria", unpublished revised version of the paper he presented at a National Workshop on Ethnic Militias, Democracy and National Security in Nigeria, organised by the National War College, Abuja, July 16-18, 2002.
2.   See, among others, Okwudiba Nnoli *Ethnic Politics in Nigeria* (Enugu: Fourth Dimension, 1980), p.5; Onigu Otite *Ethnic Pluralism and Ethnicity in Nigeria* (Ibadan: Shaneson, 1990), pp.17-19; Donald L. Horowitz *Ethnic Groups in Conflict* (Berkeley: University of California Press, 1985), pp.51-53; Sam Egwu *The Agrarian Question, Politics and Ethnicity in Rural Nigeria*, CASS Monograph No. 10, (Port Harcourt: CASS, 1999), p.49; and Samuel G. Egwu, *Ethnic and Religious Violence in Nigeria* (Abuja: African Centre for Democratic Governance, n.d.).
3.   Okwudiba Nnoli *op.cit.*, p.5.
4.   Onigu Otite, *op. cit.*, p.17.
5.   *Ibid.*, p.60.
6.   *Ibid.*, p.62
7.   Onigu Otite, *op. cit.*, p.165.
8.   John W. Burton, *World Society* (Lanham: University Press of America, 1987), pp. 137-138.
9.   Dudley Weeks, *The Eight Essential Steps to Conflict Resolution* (New York: Tarcher/Putman, 1992), p.ix.
10. W.L. Barrows shares this opinion. See "Ethnic Diversity and Political Instability in Black Africa", in *Comparative Political Studies*, Vol.9, No.2 1976.
11. See I. William et al. "Conflicts Between Pastoralists and Agriculturalists in North-Eastern Nigeria", in Onigu Otite &

Isaac Olawole Albert (eds.) *Community Conflicts in Nigeria: Management, Resolution and Transformation* (Ibadan: Spectrum Books, 1999).

12. See *ibid.*, pp.204-205.
13. For more on this, see *Insider Weekly*, Lagos, February 18, 2002.
14 See *Newswatch*, Lagos, March 6 and March 13, 2000.
15. For an account of this, see *This Day*, Abuja, May 5, 2002.
16. See *The Punch*, Lagos, June 30, 2002.
17. For a detailed analysis of the Warri conflict, see T.A. Imobighe et al. *Conflict and Instability in the Niger Delta: The Warri Case* (Ibadan: Spectrum Books, 2002).
18. For more on this, see *ibid.*, chapter 2.
19. This was the case until the present writer and others, under the auspices of Academic Associates PeaceWorks (AAPW), intervened in the management of the conflict. For a full account of AAPW's intervention in the conflict, see *ibid.*, chapter 5.
20. See Karl Maier's account of the activities of security forces in Ogoni in *This House has fallen: Nigeria in Crisis* (London: Penguin Books, 2001), pp.77-78. See also I. William et al., for the account of the activities of security and judicial officials in respect of the conflict between Fulani herdsmen and the farming communities in north-eastern Nigeria, *op. cit.*, p.205.
21. *Ibid.*, p.205.
22. This account represents a personal observation by this writer during the period 1979-1988, when he was a research staff of the National Institute for Policy and Strategic Studies, Kuru, Plateau State
23. Eghosa Osaghae, *Ethnicity and its Management in Africa: The Democratization Link,* CASS Occasional Monograph No.2, (Lagos: Malthouse for CASS, 1994), p.9.

Chapter 3

Civil Society and Alternative Approaches to Conflict Management in Nigeria

Augustine O. Ikelegbe

Introduction

Nigeria is today suffused with communal, ethnic, ethno-religious and political conflicts that often manifest in ferocious and very destructive violence. These conflicts do not only constitute the main threat to the nation's fledging democracy, national stability and security but also do consistently and stubbornly throw up the issue of the national question. Since democratization, these conflicts have become more recurring and pervasive, which indicate that hitherto repressed dissatisfaction, disillusionment and frustration are being given expression. The greatest challenge to Nigeria as a nation and a democracy is the peaceful and effective management of the conflicts and the protection of our pluralism. The pervasiveness and recycling nature of these conflicts reflect the ineffectiveness and failure of present conflict management strategies and particularly, the failure of the Nigerian state in the management of conflicts.

The management of societal conflicts has largely been a political process, in which the state plays the dominant role with international and multinational involvement in large scale conflicts. The social process which sources conflicts among groups and the state and the social arena of struggles, contestations and conjoining of interests and issues with the groups and associational pluralism that are foisted tend to be neglected. As Adejumobi has noted, little consideration has thus far been given to the civil society formation in the processes of conflict management in Africa.[1]

Yet, the associational formation is an important theatre of civil agitation, debates, education, mobilization, sensitization and action, as well as a major actor and juncture for the interaction of diverse interests, values and preferences. Civil society by its inherent situation, activities and roles, is a key player in the construction of the practice, promotion and management of peaceful pluralism. It must be oriented towards the problems of society if its social relevance is not to be dissipated. Having achieved the democratic project, in an intense, protracted and tortuous struggle of which it was the vanguard, civil society must now redirect its efforts to the issues and conflicts that undermine democratic stability.

Part of the problem is that if we look at what constitutes the present flowering of civil society groups, their direction and energy, it would be seen that western liberal ideology and donor funding dictate them. With an agenda and impetus directed from without, it is no wonder that active civil societies have only tended towards the state and democracy projects. Thus, numerous questions arise in the consideration of the constitution of civil society as an alternative platform for managing conflicts. What role can civil groups play? Which civil society groups can play such roles? What roles do civil society presently play in conflict management? What capacity do civil groups have to play such roles? How does the state impinge on civil society and its potential roles? How can that role be enlarged such that they constitute an alternative platform and agency of conflict management and resolution? How can civil society build partnership and cooperative relations for intervening in and managing social conflicts? How can civil society be strengthened and harnessed in the management of conflict?

This chapter begins by conceptualizing civil society. Attention is paid not just to the dominant conception and defining characteristics but to situating the concept in Africa. Thereafter, we categorize civil society groups and then identify their considerable organizational, ideological and material weaknesses. Thereafter, we examine the weaknesses and ineffectiveness of state management of conflicts and posit the need for alternative institutions. The probable roles of civil society are then identified followed by the contemporary status of civil society roles and activities in the management of the numerous conflicts that traverse the nation. Finally, the weaknesses of civil society as alternative institutions of conflict management as well as what can be done to strengthen them are then examined.

The Concept of Civil Society
Civil society is today not just a major analytical paradigm but a major force and factor in the politics of Africa. Its current development is regarded as "a significant milestone in the restructuring of African political life."[2] It has been associated with the wave of democratization in many countries south of the Sahara.[3] It has and is still playing a major role in the state reform project. It is being expected to play a major role in democratic consolidation.[4]

Civil society has become so central in the Africa project of the West and international donor agencies that it has become a major beneficiary of their activities and funds. It has been linked romantically and euphorically to much of the positive changes and reforms in Africa since the 1990s. As Adejumobi has noted, civil society has been associated with the "benign, progressive, developmental, democratic and everything that the state is not".[5] But while many researchers see the usage and interest in the concept as useful and justified, others see it as a vague, empty, "catch all" concept that has "cast its net too widely".[6]

We should begin our conception first by alluding to the fact that civil society comprises of certain kinds of associations or groups. It is the organization of the citizenry outside of the state.[7] It is the "realm of organised social life."[8] It encompasses the "network of institutions through which groups represent themselves both to each other and to the state".[9] Civil society typifies citizenry social activism through associational solidarity and engagement.

The second thing to note is that civil society groups are intermediate or middle level organizations situated between the family and the society on the one hand, and the state on the other. It is the private realm of the citizenry as opposed to the public realm of the state. It is also a civil realm; that of living, working and associating on the basis of decency and civility, mutual respect, fair play, civil rights, peaceful competition and tolerance of differences that is conducted on the basis of laws and conventions.[10] Because of the site of civil society, it is the composite of non-partisan institutions engaged in non-state activities and involving non-state actors.[11] Furthermore, the organizations of civil society are voluntary, non-profit, and autonomous and possess civil, public and social purposes. Giner refers to civil society as the "voluntary, non-profit, altruistic or third sector economy".[12] Further, as Ikelegbe notes, the life of civil society is distinct and relatively independent from the life of the state.[13]

The third thing to note is that civil society though is separate and distinct from the state relates to the state. This relationship could range from the complementary and co-operative to the antagonistic and hostile. However, because of the peculiar character of the post-colonial state, the nature of civil society engagement of the state has tended to be that of resistance, opposition and struggle. In fact, most conceptions of civil society are from the perspective of its countervailing, curbing and balancing the abuses and excesses of the state.

Thus Hall defines civil society as "the self organization of strong and autonomous groups that balance the state"[14] and is able to limit the "depredations of political power".[15] Gellner defines it as diverse clusters of non-governmental institutions and associations that are entered freely and that though do not prevent the performance of state roles, are able to "prevent the state from dominating and atomizing the rest of society".[16] In fact, Bayart asserts that civil society is society in "confrontation with the state", existing only in so far as there is a "self consciousness of its opposition to the state".[17]

Beneath the organisational feature, however, civil society is a theatre, a context and a means. It is a theatre of discourse, a space for the deliberation of common affairs, the arena of social relations and communication between citizens informed by law and public policy but potentially critical of them. Civil society' is the means by' which the citizenry influence the state, engage in activities to change or reform the state and its policies and seek or demand greater responsibility' and accountability'. Civil society is thus concerned with the generation of influence, as opposed to the control of power, which is the realm of political society that is directly involved in state power.

Civil society is a context within which autonomous groups emerge and interact and relate to the state, an arena where "groups organize to contest state power" and a site for "hegemonic struggle between dominant and counter hegemonic forces".[18] It is an "arena of political, social, class and ideological contestations and struggles".[19] Civil society actually constitutes the organisational framework for social forces as they engage the state in struggles for domination, accommodation and opposition.[20] The boundary between the state and civil society and the balance between them is reflective of the outcomes of and negotiated by these struggles.[21] Because of these roles and situation, particularly in relation to the state, civil society is regarded as the buttresser of the "embattled realm of citizenship", a "fount and repository of dissent" a "key brake on the state power" bulwark against state excesses and a pressure on the state from without.[22] Civil society represents a countervailing sphere that is seen as essential to freedom and democracy as opposed to the public realm of the state and public agencies.

We should note here that there are two broad streams of the conception of what constitutes civil society. The first, somewhat constrictive, conceives of civil society as voluntary intermediate organizations located between the family, locality and communities on the one hand and the state on the other, that relate to the state in the civic sphere particularly through protection of selves and struggle against the state and its excesses. The key planks of this conception are middle level organisational life and non-party political opposition.[23] The second conception sees civil society as the range of private and particular concerns and organized non-state relationship and existence. This conception comprises every organized social life of communities, groups and individuals, which would include neighbourhood, philanthropic, non-profit, non-governmental, elders, age grade, market, farmers and community development groups.[24]

Civil society is a major analytic window on the nature of interactions between the state and society in social, economic and political processes as well as an "indispensable lens", for "tracing changing political relations".[25] Therein is the major analytic advantage of the state and society interactive analysis which civil society enables. It indicates that though the central role of the state is accepted, the counterbalances of social forces is also recognized, leaving a terrain, not of state unitarism but exchanges, contestation, coalitions and conflict.[26] These constant interactions constitute the "mutually transforming dynamic" that molds and redefines the specific features, nature and dynamics of state structures, social forces, social structures and political life.[27]

Defining Characteristics of Civil Society
There is the question of what constitutes civil society. The defining base according to Harbeson is that the groups seek to define, generate support for or promote changes in the basic working rules of the game.[28] To Diamond, the defining characteristics are public purposes, non-partisan relationship to the state, pluralism, diversity and partiality.[29] Ekeh's defining character is enhancing and acting to promote individual liberties and personal freedoms.[30] To Chazan, the intermediate social groupings should coalesce into that organisational setting in which they become "separate from" but relating to the state.[31] What defines civil society, therefore, widely differs.

However, certain defining characteristics stand out. First is that they must be voluntarily constituted and must be directed at socioeconomic, political, civil and public purposes and the politics of influence on society and the state. However, they should be involved at some point in popular struggle, popular claims, civil action, resistance and contestation in relation to socio-political and economic values such as freedom, justice, equity, fairness, good governance, redress, reform and change.[32] Second, though they are non-state organisations, they must at some point or the other relate to the state. Civil society is an organisational base for affecting and contending with the state.[33] The relation to the state is not necessarily conflictual or even time-specific. The central issue is that at some point, a civil group should be engaged in the politics of counter-hegemony and possess the "potentiality of opposition" epitomized not just by overt political actions but even the rarely apparent, sometimes passive responses to state politics.[34]

Third, at a general and particularly national level, the civil groups must constitute a network or linkages between themselves and thus form a platform for responses to social trends and for relating to the state. In other words, civil society groups should represent broad platforms for relating to particular projects. There is a concertedness that qualifies a national civil society, which emerges when civil groups are transformed from civil groups in themselves to broad collective and coherent platforms in relation to certain projects.[35] Though comprised of or is actually "an aggregate of diverse interests" and diverse voices, civil society creates a consensus of "fundamental ideas among its social forces and contending groups that binds them together" in their relations to the state.[36] That is not to say that civil society is an integrative whole. It is neither "homogenous, coherent, logical, purposeful, nor ...mutually supportive".[37] Rather, as Migdal notes, it pulls in a single direction on mainly at one level, that is, as it relates to the opposition to state hegemony.[38] Otherwise, civil society may pull in different directions.

In line with our conceptions, associations that are not autonomous, are not voluntarily constituted, or are constituted and controlled by the state and are thus concerned with political or state power, are not part of civil society. Thus, state organizations and political society are not members of civil society.[39] Furthermore, associations that absolutely do not have the afore-stated purposes and do not relate or potentially relate to the state may not constitute civil society, at least, from the constrictive conception earlier mentioned. Thus, not all of the non-governmental organisations and community or ethnic groupings may constitute civil society. However, the broad conception whose major plank is organised private and particularized non-state associational life, which regards these groupings as constituting civil society, is more relevant and apposite in Africa.

The Concept of Civil Society in Africa
The concept of civil society thus far is ideologically laden with western liberalism. Its root is said to be western while its definitions have been largely influenced by the democratic project to which Africanist and western scholars have largely assigned to it. Within these frameworks, civil society in Africa is a colonial phenomenon that arose mainly out of western intervention. As such, there were no associations that intermediated between the traditional African states and their societies just as there were no associational restraints on the state and no autonomous voluntary organisations by which

the traditional societies harnessed their energies and efforts towards common public purposes.

Just as its conception thus far has had a western liberal base, so has its role been adored by international organisations and specialized development donor and financial agencies. Given this adoration, African states have been compelled to tolerate civil groups by according them differing degrees of limited activity in the socio-political space.[40] The model civil society groups indicated in liberal scholarly discourse and in line with the agenda of western donor agencies are the advocacy, civil rights and pro-democracy groups.·

The social and historical base of civil society in Africa is ignored, just as groups other than those indicated in western liberal discourse that are situated in the dynamics of African society and state–society relations. For example, most Africanist scholars exclude from civil society primordial groups. Chazan situates civil society at a "middle ground between communal groups and state structures",[41] thus, excluding communal and ethnic groups. To some others, groups that are not overtly concerned with the state and democracy projects are not part of civil society. The conceptions only embrace the urban based, formal, professional, advocacy and social engineering groups and leaves out of the organizations of civil society, the broad based, social, rural, peasant and related organisations.[42] Hearn asserts that the groups that relate to the sub-national, communities, religions and largely rural based groups more reflective of the "length and breadth of society have been ignored".[43]

There is a case for a more inclusive conception of civil society groups in Africa, not only because of the powerful and pervasive nature of the state, but also because of the centrality of the community and peculiar social issues that Africans engage in. Thus Kasfir advocates a notion that is more expansive in political space and more encompassing of groups that may be civic or not.[44] For example, communal, ethnic, cultural and sub-national groupings acquire significance in the circumstance of a bogus, looming and expansive state characterised by ineptitude, partisanship, suppression, repression, partiality and corruption. As Egwu notes, ethnicity and religion appear useful and constitute the "vehicles for mobilisation in the face of the totalising claims of an authoritarian and undemocratic state".[45] Thus, we adopt the broad conception of civil society. We agree with Ekeh when he identifies as civil society groups, deviant civic associations (secret societies, fundamentalist religious movements) primordial public associations (ethnic associations) and indigenous development associations (Farmers' unions, Development Unions).[46]

Categories of Civil Society

Civil society has been categorized based on several criteria. They could be formal (churches, schools, unions, parties, professional bodies and the mass media) or informal (voluntary groups, informal networks and social movements).[47] They could be local, relating to local issues and projects, or national based groups that relate to broad projects. They could be traditional (cultural and secret society groups) or modern (professional, labour, occupational and civic groups.[48] We could also identify groups based on issues that they address and the linkages with the national network of relations to the state based on specified projects.

Following the classification of groupings as primary, social, economic groups and network or linkage groups by Chazan et al, we could with some modifications classify groups integratedly as primary/primordial, social, economic and issue based groups and network or linkage groups. Primary associations are underlined by identities/affinity of community, ethnicity, cultural, regional and religion. They use these networks in constituting social and collective struggles and action in relation to other groups and the state.[49] Following increased social discontent and the politics of exclusion and marginalisation, ethnic, religious and regional groupings have increasingly become vehicles of mobilization, expression and alternative ideas and for challenging the state and other groupings.[50] These groups include communal, ethnic, regional, cultural groups and ecclesiastical groups. In Nigeria, these groups blossomed considerably and related quite actively to the democracy project and in the case of the Niger Delta, the oil-based environmental and resource struggle. The active groups include the Afenifere, Ohanaeze Ndigbo, Arewa Consultative Forum, Middle Belt Forum, Union of Niger Delta, Ijaw National Congress, Catholic Bishops Conference, Christian Association of Nigeria, etc.

The social, economic and issue-based groups are based on affiliation (occupational, professional, student, youth, gender, economic activities) and issues such as the environment and peace/ conflict management. In Africa, these groups have traditionally been a strong basis for involvement in socio-political concerns, public affairs, in mobilization for policy influence, opposition, protest and dissent.[51] These groups include: trade, labour and employers associations or unions, market associations, economic and consumer-related groups, professional interest groups of numerous occupational practices; media, law, academics, teaching, youths and students' groups, environmental groups, gender-based or oriented groups etc.[52] The active groups include the Nigerian Labour Congress (NLC) and its affiliate unions, Academic Staff Union of Nigerian Universities (ASUU), National Association of Nigerian Students (NANS), Nigerian Bar Association (NBA), Nigerian Medical Association (NMA), Nigerian Union of Journalists (NUJ), Manufacturers Association of Nigeria (MAN), Women in Nigeria (WIN) etc.

The network or linkage groups are more recent groups that have arisen in response to social and political crises and problems. They essentially relate to the state in respect of governance, democracy and reforms.[53] They construct or seek to construct broad platforms, social networks and national agenda for social action. It is these groups that are central to the western donor agencies and Africanist scholars and normally comprise civil rights, constitutional rights, pro-democracy and advocacy groups. Active groups in this category include the Civil Liberties Organization (CLO), Committee for the Defence of Human Rights (CDHR), Constitutional Rights Project (CRP), Campaign for Democracy (CD), United Action for Democracy, (UAD), National Liberation Council of Nigeria (NALICON) etc.

Social movements also can be regarded as part of the apex or linkage groups because of the similarities of, first, mass mobilization and participation and, second, the strategy of campaigning activity and activism in relations with the state.[54] The difference is that they are relatively informal and spontaneous. In recent times, social movements have arisen from the environmental and resource problems of the Niger Delta as indicated by numerous broad youth and regional groupings that have been in the forefront of the Niger Delta struggle and conflicts.

Organisational, Material and Ideological Strengths and Weaknesses of Civil Society

Civil society is presently seen as the master organisational network with the magic wand for resolving numerous problems pertaining to reforms, democracy and development. A robust, effective and autonomous civil society is being depended on for a high degree of accountability,[55] the setting of "the normative parameters of public behaviour",[56] inclusiveness, tolerance to pluralism and particularly the crystallization, accommodation and mediation of differences.[57] The existence of civil society and effective sharing of the public domain is said to have tremendous implications for governance particularly in terms of human rights and freedom, individual and public welfare and public policy.[58] Civil society is expected to consolidate democracy by building, promoting and strengthening citizen rights, rule of law, citizen awareness and empowerment, participation, pluralism and state responsiveness.[59]

Nevertheless, as romanticized and euphorically treated as civil society is, there are numerous weaknesses in civil society. Some of the assets of civil society such as pluralism and complexity can also constitute liabilities.[60] For example, civil society is a realm of fragmentation and consequently a source of tension, conflict and tumult, as it constitutes a site of struggle for the expression and confrontation of differences, identities and interests.[61] It is a "terrain and target" of identity politics.[62] It represents and manifests the conflict-ridden cleavages, loyalties and solidarities of the society.[63] It is, therefore, an arena for competition, contention and conflict between groups and their interests. Furthermore, civil society may also manifest the incivility, wild passions, violence, divisiveness, exclusiveness and disorder of society.[64] Thus, civil society may not actually reflect "peaceful harmony of associational pluralism".[65]

The capacity of a civil group to influence the state and society depends on their internal organization; the efficiency of hierarchies, utilization of resources, "adroitness in exploiting or generating symbols" of identity and its ability to create allies or coalitions.[66] Furthermore, civil society effectiveness partly depends on how they ensure the receptivity of the actors and institutions of economic and political society to their influence.[67]

In Africa, these attributes are particularly weak or even lacking. Civil societies are sometimes embryonic, weak, underdeveloped, divided by ethnicity, manipulated by foreign donors, suppressed by authoritarian states, unable to influence the state and to play effective roles in democratic sustenance.[68] They lack the "necessary creativity to challenge the state and its custodians" and the "necessary agenda for effective network to move the democratic project forward".[69] Civil society is not national and unified.[70] Only a few have the resources, organizational strength and experience to function at the national level. The movements are also elitist, urban-based, middle class-based and therefore lopsided. Okome notes that the untold story is that civil society in Nigeria and most of Africa is a restricted "playing field for the privileged few".[71] Being minority and consequently ineffective organizations, it is no wonder that civil society in Africa has been unable to attain broad mobilization and achieve broad platforms and has had very limited effectiveness.[72]

Juxtaposed with the large, authoritarian, patrimonial, personal, repressive and corrupt African states, civil society becomes even weaker. The state and corporate business could "penetrate and co-opt elements" of the leadership and groups of civil society such that they become conforming of the social order, legitimizing of prevailing state and corporate power and stabilizing of the status quo.[73] Thus, civil society may merely be a reflection of the "dominance of state and corporate economic power".[74] It may fall to the lure of individual gains, clientelism and opportunism extended by the state or succumb to state divisive, manipulative, repressive and corporatist prowess.[75]

Ikelegbe identifies some of the organisational and material weaknesses of civil society in Africa as, first, the lack of autonomous existence and self-sustaining capabilities which makes it fall prey to either the state or become dependent on foreign donors.[76] Second, there are problems of crippling poverty, corruption, nepotism, parochialism, opportunism, ethnicism and illiberalism.[77] Third, are internal structures and operations that denote the absence of civility, democratic values and tenets such as participation, consensus, egalitarianism and competition.[78] Consequently, they are not unified, effective and efficient democratic organisations.[79] Fourth, they reflect and articulate sectional, class and ethnic interests and loyalties. Consequently, civil society is becoming an arena of intense conflict between civil groups of organised interests along afore-stated lines. Ikelegbe notes evidence of perversion in the intense militancy and violent confrontations with other groups and the state and the loss of control over members and affiliate groups that has resulted in the Odi crisis and numerous crises in Lagos involving the Odua People's Congress.[80]

Besides these weaknesses, the context in which civil society is blossoming and is expected to perform numerous roles has been anything but positive. Two examples would suffice. Civil society groups are operating and being constituted for different projects in the context of states where there is little social and cultural infrastructures to enshrine formal liberties into actual liberties; such as respect for the laws and the spirit of independence and compromise.[81] There are many inhibiting tendencies to "liberalism, individualism, civility and self organization such as despotism, ethnic nationalism, statism and forced development and culture".[82] These tendencies situated in the character of the post-colonial state and generated by prolonged authoritarianism and repression inhibit the effective functioning and activity of civil society.

Furthermore, civil society is also emerging from an authoritarian era, which is characterized also by the heightened awakening of cultural, ethnic, communal and other primordial passions. The politics of exclusion, domination and repression characteristic of authoritarian rule has caused a flowering of both civil society and primordial passions. As Gellner notes, both are suppressed by authoritarianism. However, the flowering of primordial passions has undermined the effectiveness of civil society by injecting divisiveness, conflicts and disagreements that have precluded the formation of broad platforms for national civil struggles and action.[83] Bryant notes that in ethnic and gender issues and in what he conceptualizes as the ethnic nation, civil groups could be exclusive and intolerant or suspicious to differences and civic incorporation and thus unable to promote peaceful accommodation of pluralism. In Africa, civil groups have not only fallen prey to the intense sub-national mobilizations of the last decade but have been intensely divided and weakened by them.[84]

Development, Roles and Weaknesses of Civil Society in Nigeria
Civil society has existed in Africa since pre-colonial times. Either in the segmented or centralised societies, there were associational formations situated between the people and the state. These associations, apart from mediating the state-society relations and moderating state excesses articulated and aggregated interests, agitated on issues and constituted platforms for participation and civil actions. Thus, from the centralised states of Oyo and Benin to the segmented states of the Igbo, civil society existed. Chazan and others have rightly noted that the associational base has since the pre-colonial period constituted the avenue for participation, the channel for information and communication, the means for affecting and contending with the public realm, the basis of public opinion, the agent of socioeconomic assistance and of control of social existence and the cushion against the adverse.[85]

The interjection of colonialism into African traditional society brought in a lot of new social exchanges and dislocations that became platforms for associational activities. For the purpose of both cultural affinity and participation in the new colonial society, associations that were educational, cultural, social and ethnic were formed. The advent of nationalist agitation heightened communal, social and political consciousness and became a platform for intensified associational activities to relate to colonial policies and practices and the struggle against colonial policies and imperialism. The associational flowering of nationalist, communal, social and political associations was such that the de-colonisation period was dubbed the initial golden age of civil society.[86]

The associational effervescence was carried into the post independence era. Numerous professional, labour, cultural and sub national groups continued to emerge while some existing ones balkanised. Labour, student and media organisations continued to be active in governance and the political process. However, the state paradoxically undermined the autonomous integrity of civil society.[87] The state compromised, incorporated and circumscribed civil society groups, such that some became fractionalised, passive and apolitical.[88]

The fate of civil society became worse during the period of military rule. The military was intolerant of civil society and restricted the space of autonomous action and civil rights. While the harassment and intimidation of civil society leaders designed to weaken and undermine civil society was pervasive during the period, associational vitality persisted particularly among the media, students and labour. Paradoxically, it was this same regime of authoritarian rule and tyranny that provided the very fertile ground for the second flowering of civil society.

The intensification of state abuses, pervasive corruption and repression coupled with economic crisis and the collapse of social services and infrastructure apart from generating restiveness exposed a weak and poorly legitimated state to civil challenges by the 1980s. The opportunity for its implosion were the debates of 1985 on the International Monetary Fund loans, the imposition of structural adjustment programme in 1986 and its accompanying hardships and the numerous weaknesses, inconsistencies and impure motives of the political transition programme beginning from 1986.[89] The annulment of the June 12, 1993 presidential elections heightened the radicalisation of the civil society groups.[90] This second mass flowering has persisted in many sectors and social facets and is continuing. There is now an NGO industry with more groups emerging perhaps daily to relate to different projects such that a precise number and the present variegation are difficult to ascertain.

While a rich associational texture and activism have usually existed in Nigeria, what the nature of military rule and the ensuing struggle for democratisation brought about were the motley of civil rights and liberties and pro-democracy groups. The former included Civil Liberties Organisation (CLO), Committee for the Defence of Human Rights (CDHR) and Constitutional Rights Project (CRP) which were formed between 1987 and the early 1990s. The latter included the Campaign For Democracy (CD), Association of Democratic Lawyers (ADL), Democratic Alternative (DA), United Democratic Front of Nigeria (UDFN), National Liberation Council of Nigeria (NALICON) and United Action for Democracy (UAD) which were formed in the 1990s.

Apart from the new and albeit active entrants in civil society, the existing professional associations became more active and socially responsive. The economic and gender based groups such as Manufacturers Association of Nigeria (MAN), National Council of Women Societies (NCWS) and Women In Nigeria (WIN) also became a more visible segment of civil society. Beneath these, numerous market and trade groupings and self-help groups emerged and became active particularly among the peasants, traders, and artisans. The existing religious groupings such as the Pentecostal Fellowship of Nigeria, Christian Association of Nigeria (CAN), Catholic Bishops Conference and the Anglican Communion became more active participants in the socio-political process.

Another category of associational life that witnessed immense growth and activity relates to associations that were communal, ethnic, sectional and cultural. These largely emerged in relation to the challenge of underdevelopment and the struggle for democracy and good governance and more specifically the agitation for equity and justice among the component units of the federation. These groups are too numerous to mention but prominent among the regional and sectional groupings are the Northern Elders Forum, Arewa Consultative Forum, *Afenifere*, Yoruba Council Of Elders, Middle Belt Forum, *Ohaneze Ndigbo*, Southern Solidarity Front and Union of Niger Delta. Beneath these groups are a motley of community development associations, communal youth, age grade, cultural and self-help groups, et cetera.

Civil society has been performing numerous roles in the socio-political and economic process. The foremost role since mid-1980s has been the state and democratic projects. Since mid-1980s, civil society has constituted the platform and main protagonist for the resistance to the policies and practices of the state. The structural adjustment programme (SAP) and the transition programme were the main objects of civil society agitation and protests. The SAP deregulation and devaluation were usually opportunities for widespread civil protests against the inhuman and hard face of SAP between 1988 and 2000. State practices, particularly in respect of human rights abuses, detention of social activists and state repression were also often reasons for protests. The inconsistencies of the transition and particularly the annulment of the June 12 presidential election orchestrated widespread civil society protests. As Ikelegbe notes, the civil pressure on the state and the international community for democratisation was enormous that speedy democratisation was imperative when General A. Abubakar assumed office in June 1998.[91]

Since democratisation, civil society has kept, but in a lower scale, the pressure on the state by monitoring state practices, resisting state policies such as that on deregulation of petroleum products' prices, fighting against corruption and resisting state repression and militarisation of conflicts such as the Niger Delta and ethnic conflicts in Lagos. In particular, civil society has been active in making inputs to draft legislations and the review of the 1999 constitution. The cultural, ethnic and communal groups have, however, pursued largely a primordial agenda at some level but relates to the state at the level of the struggle for equity, justice and fairness among Nigeria's constituent units particularly through the advocacy of such issues as true federalism and constitutional reforms.

Thus, civil society groups have remained on the track of the state and democracy projects. There are several reasons for this but we shall elaborate on them later. The point to note here, however, is that since the achievement of democracy, an overarching objective of many of the civil groups, there has been a further mushrooming of the organisation of all shades of opinion and interests, particularly those that are local, communal, regional, environmental, gender, youth and others. Some of these groups have pursued primordial, local and specialised interests and agenda and some have become primordial, militant, violent and uncivil that they have constituted a perversion of the ideals and methods of civil society.[92]

Further, one central fact that the activism of the period of democratic struggle dwarfed was the organisational and other weaknesses of civil groups in Nigeria. Civil society in Nigeria has been engulfed in numerous problems. The civil rights groups were characterised by proliferation, duplication, crass opportunism, frequent squabbles and splits, factionalism, conflicts, personal differences, arrogance and ambition, ethnic, cultural and regional sentiments and identities, manipulation, treachery, regionalism and squabbles, lack of internal democracy, transparency and accountability, poor organisation and poor management.[93] These were a middle class and urban, particularly Lagos/Ibadan based phenomenon that were not self-generating and self-supporting.[94]

Thus, the problems of the civil society groups are many. However, in spite of their problems, they have continued to be relevant in socio-political events.[95] Their contemporary effervescence in different facets and sectors of the society, their previous social activism and their present activism in respect of the national question, state and democratic consolidation projects recommend roles in respect of the mediation, negotiation and resolution of the numerous cultural, ethnic, regional and religious differences, interests and conflicts that pervade Nigeria today. Particularly, they could not only monitor and moderate state roles in conflict management but complement and in fact constitute an alternative agent and platform.

State Weaknesses in Conflict Management and the Need for Alternative Institutions

The state is a major agency for resolving and managing conflicts. Fundamental issues that relate to representation and control of resources, policy and directions of the state and its constitutional and fundamental policy frameworks cause many conflicts. Since it is the source of most conflicts and given its enormous power and resources, the state is the ultimate agency for addressing these conflicts.[96] However, the unfortunate thing about the post-colonial state is that it is itself by its very nature and inherent characteristics an arena of conflict and the major source of conflicts in plural societies.

The post-colonial state has been characterized by authoritarianism, personalisation of ruler-ship, and domination by and appropriation for clientelist, patronage, prebendal and primordial purposes.[97] It has had a compulsively comprehensive, hegemonic and totalising agenda and comprehensive intrusiveness.[98] The nature of constitution and the large role and stakes of the state has made it a "purveyor of services and employment that belonged to no one", a state seen to be allocative and distributive.[99] The dominance of distributive demands of politics and policy, combined with personalisation of state resources and their disbursement, as well as clientelism and corruption, create enormous injustice and inequity that generates primordial and class conflicts.[100]

The character of the state has resulted in the expansion of the institutions of control and repression, enfeeblement of the opposition, constriction of participation, competition and dissent, personalisation of decision making and resources and subordination of the political apparatus to the executive. Furthermore, these generated the crises of the state and development, indicated first, by the ineffectiveness, unwieldy-ness, corruption, abuse of office and gross failure to meet objectives, aspirations, tasks and basic services and second, by the loss of legitimacy, support, consent and trust and a growing exasperation and challenge of the state. By the 1970s and 1980s, state repression and sheer force engendered an ever-tightening cycle of political violence.[101]

But in spite of its concentration of power, its over-bloated size, its statist developmental strategy, its comprehensiveness and extensive regulatory agencies, the Nigerian state and indeed the African states are weak. The state in Africa in its general characteristics is a paradox, possessing at once the diverse and in fact alternate properties of weakness and power, expansion and collapse, repression and feebleness, fragility and absolutism.[102] It is in decline and decaying.[103] Its weakness is indicated by a weak and poorly developed capacity for government and economic management, poor and ineffective conduct of administration, ineffective control and command over resources, poor entrenchment and lack of broad recognition of state power, decline in the authority of state institutions, "weak fragmented political authority and weak government".[104]

Besides, the exercise of state power has been characterized by predation, widespread corruption and mismanagement, profligacy, "ethical collapse in many areas of public life", politicisation and partisanship of central state institutions.[105] Prolonged exclusion of ethnic, religious, social and political groups from the political process, state repression of ethnic and religious minorities and "loyalties to community, region and section" pervade governance.[106]

The result has been the erosion and questioning of legitimacy, widespread dissatisfaction and disagreement over the distribution and uses of state power, declined authority and respect for state institutions, public distrust and progressive erosion of the nationalist sentiment.[107] There has also been de-institutionalisation of politics and regimes, constitutional erosion, the politicisation of ethnicity and other cleavages, the politics of co-optation, purge and exclusion and intense political competition, conflicts and violence.[108] Furthermore, social deterioration, political inefficacy, a weakened civic capacity, political instability, insecurity and disorder have pervaded African states.[109]

Thus, the nature of the African state has been associated with many of its ills and misfortunes. Centralization has been found to be associated with the regional and ethnic conflicts.[110] The character of the state and the activities and behaviour of its actors spawn a politics of discontent, disillusion, alienation, apathy and helplessness.[111] The competition for domination and control of the state makes it central to conflicts. For example, Nnoli has noted that the state is the target and instrument of inter-ethnic conflicts.[112] The rentier basis of some of the states, such as Nigeria, spawns intense competition by all aspirants to wealth; the bourgeois, ethnic, sectional and factional groupings, for "access to and control over state revenues and mineral wealth"; thus creating tensions, conflicts, coups and counter coups.[113] As Mandani rightly notes, the character of the post-colonial state "undermines her institutional integrity".[114]

While the weakness and inadequacies of the state generates most conflicts, they also reduce the value, status and integrity of the state to manage conflicts. Worse still, its tendencies and character such as its arrogant, insensitive, non-humane, top-down and repressive nature tend it towards exacerbating conflicts. Yet, its capacity and practices in conflict management are also very weak and ineffective.

In Nigeria, several studies indicate that the state and its key institutions and functionaries are partisan, biased and show preferences in their actions in ethnic and religious conflicts.[115] The state has had a tendency for repressive and coercive solutions and is averse to substantive dialogue and negotiations.[116] The state through inefficiency of its security and intelligence agencies and its insensitive and non-responsive character is neither proactive nor prompt in its response to conflicts. When it does respond, it is a fire brigade type of response, which is to send troops to maintain law and order or restore superficial normalcy. When the state is a party to the conflict, its vicious and devastating repressive force may be turned on its own citizenry, as has been manifested in several cases in the Niger Delta particularly Ogoni and Odi. At other times, the state resorts to helpless proselytising. Thereafter, commissions and panels are set up whose results or reports do not constitute a basis for future, remedial or even substantive resolutions. Consequently, conflicts are recurring and cyclical which abundantly indicates the failure of the state in conflict management. Thus, while the state is the ultimate instrument and platform for resolving societal conflicts, the aforementioned suggest the need to look for alternative instruments and institutions.

Civil Society As an Alternative Platform For Conflict Management
Civil society has always been and remains a vital element of our socio-political process. Its tremendous growth of numbers, variety and projects in the last 15 years or so makes it a more vital element in the socio-political concerns of addressing issues that undermine our national and democratic integrity. While civil groups have and still do address the state reform and democratic project, there is need to direct their energies to their roles in the critical areas of conflict management.

Civil society is undoubtedly well situated and fitted to perform such roles. First, its social base makes it an appropriate institution for resolving socio-political conflicts. It has citizen associations directed at socio-political purposes. Being voluntarily formed and possessing some level of autonomy, civil society constitutes a platform for harnessing citizen efforts and energies towards the overall good. More importantly it embraces and constitutes a context for the interaction of diversity of interests. Hence, it is a platform for joining issues, of deliberation and negotiation, of compromise and consensus building.

Furthermore, civil society is a context of communication where opinions are traded and molded, public policy and social actions are generated and influenced and rules of public and social responsibility and appropriateness are molded. This context is vital for not only norm setting or formation but also for setting socio-political agenda, influencing public opinion, raising public awareness and information and influencing the course of socio-political and state actions. These roles are vital to the perception and handling of issues in conflict, the behaviour of actors in conflict, the norms of conflict, the resolution of conflicts and the role and behaviour of the state in conflicts.

Civil society can perform or play considerable roles in the elimination of conflicts. First, by its very diversity and the commonalities and overlapping relations and interests that are so formed, civil groups can cut across and weaken differences and conflicts. Civil groups can deliberately promote in the juncture of socio-political communication, discourse and public opinion formation, the values of tolerance, non-violence, compromise and accommodation among different groups and interests. They can mobilise the citizenry in support of dialogue, negotiated settlements and de-emphasis of extra-legal and violent instruments of conducting conflicts.[117]

Civil society can monitor governance, identify and bring to the notice of the state issues and cases that grieve and cause disaffections and divisions and agitate for the inclusiveness of deprived and hitherto excluded groups in the distribution of state resources and actions.[118] It can identify and agitate against policies and actions that are partisan, biased, and indicative of undue preference to certain groups. They can assist in correcting anomalies of state distribution and even in the integration of hitherto excluded and marginalised groups. In so doing civil society can eliminate or reduce the reasons for and consequences of actions that source conflicts. Finally, they highlight state neglect of poor responsibility, sensitivity and attention to conflict issues and problems. Civil society can also prevent conflicts by identifying early signs of conflict or by drawing attention to simmering conflicts. They can then intervene or seek state intervention before conflict eruptions. At such early stages, civil groups can mediate in the relations between state and communities / groups and within state structures and between and within groups and communities.

Civil society can also play considerable roles in the management of conflicts. As a neutral party, it can be a platform for resolving or a mediator in the resolution of conflicts. Even when it is a party to conflict, civil groups can reach out to other groups for deliberation, negotiation, compromises and agreements on the management of the conflict. Adejumobi notes that at the local, national and international levels, civil society can assist or participate in the arrangement and management of negotiated settlements of conflicts—intervene to bring warring parties to the negotiating table, propose solutions, secure deals from the parties and ensure the implementation of agreements.[119] Particularly, civil society groups can provide neutral and informal interventions that could constitute solid bridges of understanding, trust and confidence between stakeholders in conflict.[120] They can mount pressure on parties in conflict to accept and consolidate peace. In these ways, civil society can assist in the mediation of conflicts between state and society, within the state, within and between communities, within political society and within and between political parties.

The media segment of civil society is particularly important in conflict management. The media is not just a part of civil society but a medium for its roles of communication, discourse, mobilisation and education. The media is the platform through which civil society groups and other social forces join issues, intermingle ideas and peddle influence. How this is done and particularly the manner of presentation is important to the relations between groups and the status and management of conflict. The media is, therefore, important to the understanding and appreciation of the issues and problems in conflict, the moderation of conflicting issues and actors and the nature, speed and effectiveness of their resolutions. Early reportage of conflicts and conflict issues may bring to the fore, the need for their early resolution and particularly ginger the state and civil groups into action. The manner of the presentation of conflict issues and eruptions may wound or heal the sensibilities of groups in conflict. The impartial presentation of conflict issues and situations enables objective information of the citizenry, state, and civil actors, which may facilitate their fair resolution.

The civil groups can also play considerable roles in the management of conflict situations. This is particularly in respect of the monitoring of the actors in conflict. Civil groups can provide a factual and impartial information base on conflicts. They can also monitor the conduct of state security and conflict management activities and efforts and can highlight improprieties and human rights abuses. Such monitoring can restrain the partisan tendencies, state repression and abuses by security operatives.

The other role of civil society is in post-conflict management. First, they can be involved in the provision of assistance to victims of conflicts such as relief to refugees. They can also assist in securing hostages and ameliorating hostilities. They can also raise issues relating to the roles of the state and civil groups in reconstruction, rehabilitation and resettlement of victims of conflicts. They may monitor the implementation of agreements and raise alarms at threats to the peace or signs of new conflicts.

Contemporary Status of Civil Society in Conflict Management in Nigeria

Civil society is beginning to place on its agenda and adopt as one of its manifesto, the promotion of peaceful and non-violent resolution of conflicts. This much was decided at the National Civil Society Pro-Democracy Summit in Abuja, organised with the initiative of the NLC and attended by about 22 civil society/pro-democracy/non-governmental groups.[121] Several workshops are being organised to advocate peace and non-violence and to enhance capacity for conflict management by civil society groups. The Human Rights Monitor (HRM), a Kaduna-based civil group, organised in June, 2001, a two-day advocacy workshop on conflict management for religious and community leaders as well as leaders of labour and youth organisations. At the end of the workshop, the group called on governments at all levels to, as a matter of urgency, "release the findings and implement recommendations of judicial commissions of inquiry which often probe ethnic and religious conflicts".[122] The Human Development Initiatives, a Lagos based non-governmental organisation, also organised a workshop in collaboration with the United States Agency for International Development Office of Transition Initiative, in July, 2001, for leaders of ethnic communities in Lagos State, comprising Yoruba, Ibo, Hausa and other minor tribes in the state.[123]

There are emerging specialised non-governmental organisations that are involved in conflict management. The Centre for Peace in Africa (CPA), for example, is already making general contributions on strategies for managing ethnic and ethno-religious conflicts.[124] The civil society groups have been particularly active in the realm of appeals for peace or condemnation of potentially conflicting situations. The Christian Association of Nigeria and various other ecumenical groups such as the Anglican Synods have been consistent in calling on Nigerians to exhibit religious or ethnic tolerance and particularly to "allow religious amity between Christians and Muslims to reign".[125] The Civil Liberties Organisation deplored at its 2001 annual national convention the proliferation of ethnic militias such as the Oodua People's Congress (OPC) and the Bakassi Boys, the attendant extra-judicial killing and arbitrary punishments meted out by these groups, and called for the strict control of such groups.[126]

The *Afenifere* and its Igbo counterpart, the *Ohanaeze Ndigbo,* met in Lagos in July, 2000, to resolve amicably the violent clashes between the OPC and Igbo traders in Lagos. The OPC and representatives of the Igbo traders attended.[127] The Arewa Consultative Forum (ACF) the umbrella body representing the North, and the *Afenifere* group, the Pan-Yoruba socio-cultural group, met in September, 2001, to consider a number of common issues between them among which were the Sharia episode in the North and the OPC and Hausa clashes in Lagos and other parts of Yoruba land. They resolved to come together to discuss issues that are topical in the country no matter their differences.[128].

The Arewa Consultative Forum has decided to intervene to stem the tide of violent crises in the North. It has designed a programme of action, which includes sending emissaries to trouble spots to ascertain positions and contentious issues. In respect of the Tiv/Jukun conflict, the Arewa Consultative Forum (ACF) held a meeting to broker peace between the Tiv and Jukun people. The Arewa's effort is to bring about a final resolution of the Tiv/Jukun crisis. At a meeting attended by the leaders of the ACF, the Tiv and the Jukun, they (Tiv/Jukun) indicated their intention to bury the hatchet and live together in a peaceful atmosphere.[129]

The Catholic Church has also been actively involved in reconciling opposing groups and meetings with governments and groups to iron out differences.[130] Religious groups such as the Anglican Bishops Synods and the Catholic Bishops Conference have in recent times persisted in calling for a National Conference and the restructuring of the country, "as a way to arrest the dangerous trend, regarding social and political as well as religious crises in the land".[131]

In the Niger Delta violent conflicts and militarisation between 1998 and 2000, a national civil society network existed that condemned militarisation, human rights abuses, the neglect of the region and the attitude of the state and MNCS. Following the Odi devastation and massacre, 29 civil groups visited Odi on December 8, 1999. They condemned the reckless destruction and mass killings, identified with the legitimate struggles of the Niger Delta and called for an International War Crime Tribunal to try the soldiers involved. The groups included Constitutional Rights Project (CRP), CLO, CDHR, HURILAWS, communal/ethnic/pan-regional groups such as IYC, Niger Delta Women for Justice, Oduduwa Liberation Movement and others such as Women in Nigeria.[132]

Afenifere, the pan-Yoruba socio-political group condemned the strong-arm tactics of the police in the conflict with the OPC group. Particularly, it condemned the spate of extra-judicial killing of the OPC members.[133] The *Afenifere* also condemned the 19 northern states' governors for allegedly politicising the trials and freedom of the leader of the OPC groups, Dr. Fredrick Fasehun.[134] The Campaign for Democracy (CD) condemned the shoot-on-sight order on members of the OPC, claiming "it would not solve the intrinsic problems of the country".[135] The CD also called on the Nigerian Police to ensure that the rule of law prevails in the trial and detention of the arrested leader of the militant wing of the OPC, Mr. Ganiyu Adams.[136] The National Conscience Party (NCP) led by pro-democracy activist, Chief Gani Fawehinmi (SAN) condemned the public parade of Gani Adams in chains as a violation of his dignity. Other civil groups such as the Oodua Youth Movement (OYM) and the Centre for Constitutional Rights (CCR) insisted that Gani Adams should be "given fair hearing and must not be used as a scapegoat".

The Middle Belt Forum (MBF) condemned the reaction of the 19 northern governors to ethnic clashes in Lagos between Hausa settlers and members of the Oodua People's Congress (OPC). It regarded the governors' threat to retaliate the killings of their people in the South in case of any future attack as "a clarion call for war against the South–West", which was uncalled for and not in the best interest of national harmony and integrity.[137] The Campaign for Democracy has implored the president to desist from threatening the imposition of emergency rule in states where there are crises. The group's chairman, Beko Ransome-Kuti, advised that the president should be sensitive to and resolve "the causes of disquiet and crisis all over the country rather than treat governors as his house boys".[138]

A critical analysis reveals that civil society has been involved mainly at two levels. First is the proselytising and appeal level. Civil groups have merely been appealing for restraint, peace, good neighbourliness, accommodation of differences of ethnicity and religion, respect for life, and for resolution rather than prevention of conflicts. Second, civil society groups sometimes have been monitoring and condemning practices of conflict actors, situations and management. In other words, civil groups have merely been reacting or responding to situations and circumstances of conflict and their management. Few groups have been involved in conflict resolution and post conflict management. Groups are just emerging in the area of capacity building for conflict prevention and management. Few groups have also been involved in relief and assistance of conflict victims and refugees. These indicate that the focus, efforts and activities of civil groups in conflict management is presently generally poor and weak.

Weaknesses of Civil Society as an Alternative Conflict Management Platform

There are numerous weaknesses in the institutions of civil society playing conflict management roles. The social base of civil society foists on it a dual role in the conflict management process. It can be part of the conflict; that is, an actor in the conflict and a facilitator, leader or mobilizing platform for the conflict.[139] An actor or protagonist may be immersed in the sentiments and emotions of the conflict and do not possess the neutrality and impartiality necessary to mediate conflicts.

In the Niger Delta conflict, numerous civil society groups have been actors and even protagonists. The Ijaw Youth Council (IYC), Movement for the Survival of Ogoni People (MOSOP) Chicoco Movement (CM), the Isoko National Youth Movement (INYM) and numerous youth, gender, communal and ethnic and environmental groups were actors in the Niger Delta conflict. The IYC and its affiliate groups such as the Niger Delta Volunteer Force (NDVF) and the Egbesu Boys of Africa were involved in violent confrontations with the state between 1998 and 2000. While the IYC proclaimed the Kaiama Declaration whose methodology included violent conflict, the Ijaw National Congress, the parent body of all Ijaw organisations adopted it. The INC and other groups such as the Movement for the Survival of Ijaw Ethnic Nationalities in the Niger Delta (MOSIEND), the Federated Niger Delta Izon Communities, the Nigeria Delta Oil Producing Communities Development Organisation, Ijaw Elders Forum (IEF) and the Niger Delta Women for Justice, were either involved in direct confrontations or identified with the youths.

In the Itsekiri/Ijaw conflicts in Warri, numerous civil groups in both ethnic groups were active participants. Among the Izon group, the FNDIC, NDVF, the IYC and its affiliate groups may have been involved. In the Ajegunle-Lagos conflict between OPC and IYC, both civil groups were the actors in conflict. Following numerous religious riots in which Christians were killed in northern Nigeria, the Pentecostal Fellowship of Nigeria (PFN) has stated that henceforth Christians will now use any legitimate means at their disposal to defend themselves against Muslim aggression. According to the PFN, this is an act of self-defence and preservation given the helplessness and inaction of governments and concerned authorities.[140]

Nonetheless, civil society groups in conflict can perform numerous roles if properly oriented. They can alert other groups and the state to the existence of emerging issues in conflict and threats to peace. They can reach out to similar groups on the opposing side for dialogue and resolution. They can assist in the proposition of solutions and in the monitoring of state interventions. They can assist in post-conflict management and assistance to conflict victims.

However, the role of civil groups would depend on their nature, position, credibility or integrity, capacity and resources. We have noted severally the weaknesses of civil groups organisationally, materially and ideologically. We also identified the weaknesses of civil society groups in Nigeria. Civil society is underdeveloped, feeble, undermined by the state, divided by primordial sentiments and personal differences and pervaded by opportunism, squabbles and conflicts. They are poorly organized and managed. They possess poor knowledge, skills, expertise and capacity. They lack resources and have had to depend on foreign donors even to hold seminars and run their organisations. They lack accountability and transparency in the management of their resources.

One major weakness of civil society groups in Africa is their dependency and immense difficulties in maintaining autonomy. As a result, they are unable to define their themes, focus and agenda without their donors and supporters. The inability to redefine agenda is also related to the inadequacy of resources and their dependence on foreign donor agencies. Given the need for resources, civil society groups fall prey to either the state or foreign donors.[141] In the circumstance, civil groups' relevance to their society is weakened. A focus on conflict management given its pervading and recurring character would rather depend on the foreign donors than the civil groups themselves.

These weaknesses that pervade most of the groups do not indicate that civil society is a formation with a high credibility and integrity that can be bequeathed with and trusted to effectively manage conflicts. Most of the groups do not possess the capacity and resources for effective conflict management roles. Therefore, civil groups are not presently in a position of focus and strength in relation to the management of conflicts.

There is also the problem of leadership of the civil society network. The absence of leadership creates a vacuum as to the level of activism and social action and the charting of new directions. However, the higher level of activism achieved by the Nigerian Labour Congress in relation to issues of corruption, deregulation of petroleum prices and others, indicate that a leader may be emerging. Olisa Agbakoba, the president, United Action for Democracy (UAD) has urged "organised labour to provide leadership for the civil society groups as it has the wherewithal to do so".[142]

While civil society groups can and should get involved in conflict management, they cannot take the place of the state, which must play the large role, since it alone has the resources needed to mediate conflicts and enforce peace. Besides, because many conflicts involve the state and relate to state actions, the state is the main instrument and platform for conflict management. In many cases and circumstances, civil society can only act in subsidiary and complementary roles. It does not and cannot substitute the state that constitutes such a looming, large and seemingly powerful role in the polity.[143] Furthermore, even the ability of civil society to play the subsidiary and complementary roles is predicated on the nature, character and behaviour of the state.

The governments always claim that they emphasise dialogue but avenues and fora for such are never provided and pleas for dialogue by aggrieved groups are rarely positively responded to. The state is quick to declare a state of emergency and to deploy military forces; thus, not only to militarise conflicts but fuel violence. Besides, the tendency of the state to be used or appropriated for hegemonial purposes by groups tends the state towards partisan or partial actions, which undermine its integrity as an umpire or mediator in conflicts.

In the Niger Delta conflict, the state and its corporate partners, the MNOCS, refused to dialogue in spite of several contacts and pleas by the civil protagonist. As Oronto Douglas of the Ijaw Youth Council (IYC) once put it, "all we want is dialogue. All they want is force".[144] The intention of the famous Kaiama Declaration according to the IYC leaders was discussion of the issues raised.[145] Rather than discuss, the youth groups were harassed and Bayelsa State was militarily occupied.[146] Apex groups such as the Ijaw National Congress (INC) severally sought dialogue with the state but were rebuffed.[147] Consequently, youth group resistance occurred, resulting in violent confrontations.

One reason for the violent reactions against multinational oil companies in the Niger Delta is the perception of state collaboration or support. The communities, weary of unequal relations, corporate and state arrogance, became frustrated and disillusioned. The stage was then set for youth groups who confronted state forces, which harassed and repressed the people on behalf of the oil companies. The oil companies, to protect themselves against Nigerian citizens, rallied the state security forces on their own. They did not only invite the security forces, but they supported and provided materials for them.

In the case of ethnic and communal conflicts, there are allegations also of state partisan leanings. The Tiv Progressive Movement led by Mr. Paul Unongo in a letter to President Obasanjo, alleged that the Tiv nation had resigned itself to a long war because they would not get justice from their conflict with the Chamber-Jukun that was being supported by the federal government, under the paramount influence of their big men in government.[148] In these situations, communal, ethnic and cultural groups are often compelled to become actors, supporters of groups in conflict, as well as engage in violent struggles and surreptitiously support violent conflicts. Even civic groups, rather than seek resolution sometimes become actors on the side of aggrieved groups. The character and behaviour of the state, therefore, either radicalizes or partializes groups thereby weakening them as agents of conflict management. Besides, in conflicts that involved the state such as the Niger Delta conflicts, the refusal of the state to substantively dialogue and its preference for suppression rather than resolution incapacitates civil society as agents of conflict management.

The society is used to the state and looks up to the state for the resolution of public problems and conflicts. Groups and communities in conflict seek to appropriate the state for its advantage or hopes for state's impartial but effective intervention. While the state's delayed, insensitive, ineffective and sometimes impartial interventions are well known, the society is not yet oriented to look up to and accept other agents and institutions in conflict management. While the local, communal, ethnic, women and related groups may be known, they are not yet seen generally to possess the clout, influence, resources, integrity and credibility to intervene and manage conflicts.

The rise and increasing solidity of ethnic, religious and cultural identities, their increasing solidarity and the increasing mobilisation and politicisation of these identities is a major threat to the role of civil society in the management of conflicts. The rapid proliferation of ethnic, communal, cultural and religious groupings that has resulted and the ethnic, sectional and religious basis of divisiveness and conflicts among groups further point to the possible undermining of the effectiveness of civil society as a platform for conflict management. As Wilson notes, ethnic nationalism is an enemy to civil society.[149] First, it generates dogmatism and reluctance to dialogue. Second, it does not tolerate the sphere of citizen "speaking and acting" and with capacity to "publicly choose their identities".[150] Third, it has an ambivalent relationship with violence. It is then possible to understand particularly why communal, ethnic and religious groups are often actors in conflicts, even violent conflicts.

Strengthening Civil Society for Conflict Management Issues and Prospects

The first thing to do is the creation of the awareness of the role that civil society can possibly play in conflict management. Given the spate of communal, ethnic, ethno-religious and other conflicts and the violence that has attended such conflicts, civil society groups need to know that given their intermediate positioning and their non-state roles, they constitute a viable alternative institutional platform, particularly outside the state, that can be éffective in the prevention, curtailment and management of conflicts. Rather than their present low activity and minimal involvement in conflict management, amidst the weaknesses of the state, civil society groups should be made to realize that whether they are actors and neutral bodies, they possess and occupy some advantaged social position in relation to the management of conflicts situated in our diversity and the fostering of peaceful and accommodative pluralism.

Civil society needs a conflict management project. The activities and focus of civil society groups have to be relevant to society. While the democratisation project remains important, there is need to direct attention, energies and resources to conflict management. The redirection of efforts and the conception of a conflict management project may have to be orchestrated by popular and active civil society groups. The NLC and some of the old civil rights and pro-democracy groups may have to blaze the trail of leadership in this area. Such initial activities by these groups would generate the interest of other groups in the new project.

There is need for the generation or emergence of new groups or NGOs in the area of conflict management. Such a development would enable the emergence of a quantum of specialized groups, skills, competence and capacity in conflict management. Where such groups with such competence become known, conflict actors would not only solicit their intervention but also accept them. They could, therefore, become a neutral and professional group of conflict managers that could play very effective mediation roles. We noted earlier that such groups are beginning to emerge. The trend should be encouraged.

The conflict project would require support by both foreign donors and local agencies. This is because it requires new orientations, skills, knowledge and capacity building which can be obtained or conducted through seminars and workshops. It would also require funding to acquire resources for such involvement. Just like the foreign donor agencies supported and still support civil groups in the democratization and reform projects, they should direct such to the major threat to our national and democratic survival.

There is need for partnership between the state and specified groups in the management of conflict. The state should solicit and encourage groups that play or could possibly play some roles in conflict management. In any conflict situation, the state should reach out to groups that are directly involved and urge them to mediate and intervene. Civil society groups should be encouraged to play active roles both by state recognition of their efforts and by support through state resources. This is important because the state and relevant civil society groups may have about the same interest in the effective prevention, curtailment and resolution of conflicts and both should combine efforts as partners in the now burdensome task of relieving the state from threatening conflicts. The state should particularly support specialized groups in conflict management. The state should not only partner with civil society groups involved in conflict but should accommodate or provide them social and political space, such as in the areas of conflict monitoring, where the activities of state agencies might come under scrutiny.

The role of the media segment of civil society has to be strengthened. First, this is in the creation of the awareness about the role of civil society in conflict management. Second, the press should give coverage to the activities of civil groups in the management of conflicts. Third, the press should avoid the sensational coverage of conflicts and focus more on the efforts and activities towards their resolution and the eventual resolution of the conflicts. Media personnel need training and capacity building in the coverage of conflicts such that there is a tendency towards conflict resolution rather than conflagration.

The organisational and material capacities of civil society have to be strengthened. Civil society groups cannot be effective agencies for conflict management if they are not credible, honest, accountable and transparent organisations. They have to be institutions that can be trusted and in which confidentiality can be reposed. The over-all knowledge, skills, expertise and management capacities of the groups have to be strengthened. The hitherto divisiveness, acrimonies, personal ambitions and opportunism that pervade the groups have to be countered. There should also be broad understanding, networking and coalitions such that there are no overlapping and duplication in relation to the conflict management project.

Conclusion

Nigeria is today suffused with communal, ethnic, ethno-religious and political conflicts. The recycling nature of these conflicts indicates the failure and weaknesses of the state in the management of conflicts. The state is weak because its inadequacies reduce its value, status and integrity. Its tendencies and character tends it towards exacerbating conflicts while its capacity and practices in conflict management are poor. The need to search for and strengthen non-state institutions as an effective platform for conflict management, therefore, becomes imperative.

Civil society was in the vanguard of the state reform and democracy projects. While these projects remain important, there is now a huge threat from ethnic and ethno-religious conflicts to Nigeria's democracy and existence. Though the civil society formation remains a vital, active and relevant formation in the country, it has so far not been oriented and focused on conflict management as a project. Part of the reason is the external funding and direction. Furthermore, there has been no leadership, orientation and capacity building of civil society roles in conflict management. However, civil society is a most relevant and vital formation in conflict management, which can play considerable roles in conflict prevention, management of conflict situations, conflict resolution and post conflict peace building. Particularly, as a theatre of communication, education, mobilization and influence, civil society can affect the norms of conflict, the behaviour of conflict actors and the culture of civility, accommodation, tolerance, non-violence and dialogue.

An analysis of the contemporary civil society involvement in conflict management reveals that the focus, efforts and activities are poor and weak. Besides, civil society groups are weak in relation to conflict management because, first, they are sometimes actors in conflict and second, they are organisationally and materially weak and under-developed. In addition, the character and tendencies of the Nigerian state further weakens civil society as institution for conflict management.

This chapter recommends that the awareness of the roles of civil society in conflict management be raised. A peace, non-violence and conflict management project should be created for civil society groups, while the development of specialized conflict management groups should be encouraged. The state and foreign donors need to support and even partner with civil groups to position and strengthen them. The organizational and material capacities of civil society need to be strengthened.

References

1. Said Adejumobi, "The Civil Society in Conflict Management and Peace Building in Africa", in *Development Policy Management (DPMN) Bulletin*, viii (1), July 2001, p.19.
2. M. Bratton, "Beyond the State: Civil Society and Associational Life in Africa:, in *World Politics*, Vol. 41, No. 3, 1989, pp.407-430.
3. M.J. Makumbe, "Is There a Civil Society in Africa?", in *International Affairs*, 74, 1998, pp.308-309.
4. M. Bratton, "Civil Society and Political Transition in Africa", in Harbeson et al. *Civil Society and the State in Africa* (London & Boulder: Lynne Rienner, 1992), p.76.
5. Said Adejumobi, *op. cit.*, p.19.
6. Salvador Giner, "Civil Society and its Future", in John Hall (ed.) *Civil Society: Theory, History, Comparison* (Cambridge: Polity Press, 1995), p.301.
7. L. Diamond, "Rethinking Civil society Towards Democratic Consolidation" in *Journal of Democracy*, 5 (3), 1994.
8. S. Oyovbaire, "Role of Civil Society Organisations in Enhancing Constituency Relations", in *Vanguard*, Lagos, Thursday, September 20, p.22, 2001.
9. M. Shaw, "Civil Society and Global Politics: Beyond a Social Movement's Approach", in *Millennium*, 23 (3), 1994, p.647.
10. G.A.C. Bryant, "Civic Nation, Civil Society, Civil Religion", in John Hall *op. cit.*, pp.145-149.
11. M.J. Makumbe, *op. cit.*, p.305.
12. Salvador Giner, *op. cit.*, p.319.
13. A.O. Ikelegbe, "The Perverse Manifestation of Civil Society: Evidence from Nigeria", in *Journal of Modern African Studies*, 39, 1, 2001, p.2.
14. J.A. Hall, "In Search of Civil Society", in J.A. Hall (ed.) *op. cit.*, pp15 & 25.
15. *Ibid.*

16. E. Gellner, "The Importance of Being Modular", in John Hall (ed.) *op. cit.*, pp.32 & 42.
17. J.F. Bayart, "Civil Society in Africa", in P. Chambal (ed.) *Political Domination in Africa: Reflections on the Limit of Power* (Cambridge: C.U.P., 1986), pp.111-117.
18. M. Shaw, *op. cit.*, p.649. See also M.I.M. Abutudu "The Unfinished Transition 1985-1993", in I.B. Bello-Imam (ed.) *Nigeria: Economy, Politics and Society in the Adjustment Years 1985-1995* (Ibadan: Stirling-Holden, 1997), p.158.
19. S. Adejumobi, "Reconstructing the Future: Africa and the Challenge of Democracy and good Governance in the 21st Century", *Development and Socio-Economic Progress, Issue,* No. 75, 91 & 92, pp.34-51.
20. N. Chazan, in J.S. Migdal et al. (eds.) *State Power and Social Forces: Domination and Transformation in the Third World* (Cambridge: C.U.P., 1996), p.256.
21. M. Shaw, *op. cit.*, p.649.
22. J. Keane, "Introduction" in J. Keane (ed.) *Civil Society and the State: New European Perspectives* (London: Verso, 1988), pp.1-31. See also N. Chazan *op. cit.*, p.255; M. Bratton *op. cit.*; and M.J. Makumbe *op. cit.*
23. M.W. Foley & B. Edwards, "The Paradox of Civil Society", in *Journal of Democracy,* X (x), 1997, pp.38-39
24. *Ibid.*
25. N. Chazan, *op. cit.*, pp.256-257.
26. V. Azarya & N. Chazan, "The Disengagement from the State in Africa: Reflection on the Experience of Ghana and Guinea", in *Comparative Studies in Society and History,* 19, 1, 1987, pp.106-131. See also N. Chazan et al. *Politics and Society in Contemporary Africa* (Boulder: Lynne Rienner, 1992).
27. N. Chazan, *op. cit.*, pp.256-257.
28. J.W. Harbeson, "Introduction", in J.W. Harbeson et. al. (eds.) *Civil Society and the State in Africa* (London & Boulder: Lynne Rienner, 1994), p.4.
29. L. Diamond, *op. cit.*
30. P.P. Ekeh, "The Constitution of Civil Society in African History and Politics", in B. Caron et al. (eds.) *Democratic Transition in Africa* (Ibadan: CREDU Documents in Social Sciences and Humanities, No.1, 1992), p.439.

31. N. Chazan, *op. cit.*, p.256
32. A.O. Ikelegbe, (2001B) "Civil Society, Oil and Conflict in the Niger Delta Region of Nigeria: Ramifications of Civil Society for Regional Resource Struggle", in *Journal of Modern African Studies*, 39, 3, 2001, p.439.
33. N. Chazan, et al. *op. cit.*, pp.72-77.
34. P. Chabal, *Power in·Africa: An Essay in Political Interpretation* (London: Macmillan, 1992), p.84.
35. M.I.M. Abutudu, *The State, Civil Society and the Democratisation Process in Nigeria*, (Dakar: CODESRIA Monograph Series, 1/95, 1995).
36. Joel S. Migdal, "The State in Society: An Approach to Struggles for Domination", in J.S. Migdal et al. (eds.) *State Power and Social Forces: Domination and Transformation in the Third World* (Cambridge: C.U.P., 1996), p.28.
37. P. Chabal, *op. cit.*, p.84.
38. Joel S. Migdal, *op. cit.*, pp.28-29.
39. N. Chazan, *op. cit.* p.256.
40. Said Adejumobi, *op. cit.*, p.19.
41. N. Chazan, "Engaging the State: Associational Life in Sub-Saharan Africa" in Joel S. Migdal et al. *op. cit.*, p.255.
42. A.O. Ikelegbe, p.439 (2001B), *op. cit.*,.
43. J. Hearn, "Foreign Aid, Democratisation and Civil Society in Africa: A Study of South Africa, Ghana and Uganda", *Institute of Development Studies Discussion Paper*, 386,1999, p.17
44. Banji Fajonyomi, "Civil Society and Public Accountability in Nigeria" in Iyabo Olojede & Banji Fajonyomi (eds.), *Ethics and Public Accountability in Nigeria* (Lagos: A-Trial Associates, 2001),
45. Samuel G. Egwu, *Ethnic and Religious Violence in Nigeria* (Abuja: The African Centre for Democratic Governance, 2001), p.30.
46. P.P. Ekeh, *op. cit.*, p.207.
47. M. Shaw, *op. cit.* p.648.
48. P. Chabal, *op. cit.*, p.86.
49. N. Chazan, *et al.*, *op. cit.* pp.95-97.
50. *Ibid*.
51. *Ibid.*, pp.92-93.
52. Sam Oyovbaire, *op. cit.*, p.22.

53. N. Chazan et al., *op. cit.*, p.77.
54. M. Shaw *op. cit.*, pp.652-665.
55. M. Bratton, "Micro-Democracy? The Mergers of Farmer Unions in Zimbabwe", in *African Studies Review*, Vol.37 (1), 1994, p.3.
56. D. Woods, "Civil Society in Europe and Africa: Limiting State Power Through Public Sphere", in *ibid.*, Vol.35 (2), 1992, p.96.
57. G.A.C. Bryant, *op. cit.*, pp.145-148.
58. P.P. Ekeh, "Civil Society and the Construction of Freedom in African History", in E. Onwudiwe (ed.), *African Perspective in Civil Society: Report of the Second Wilberforce Conference on Africa* (New York: Tri-Atlantic Books, 1998).
59. J. Hearn *op. cit.*, pp.14-19. See also J.W. Harbeson "Civil Society and the Study of African Politics: A Parliamentary Assessment", in J.W. Harbeson et al. (eds.) *op. cit.*, p.291.
60. Sam Oyovbaire, *op. cit.*, p.22.
61. M. Walzer, "Introduction", in M. Walzer (ed.) *Towards a Global Civil Society* (Providence: Berghahn Books, 1995), p.2.
62. J. Cohen, "Interpreting the Notion of Civil Society", in *ibid.*, p.39.
63. R. Fatton Jr., "Africa in the Age of Democratisation: The Civil Limitations of Civil Society", in *West Africa Review*, 1(1), 1999.
64. C. Young, "In Search of Civil Society", in J.W. Harbeson *op. cit.*, pp.35-50.
65. R. Fatton Jr., *op. cit.*
66. Joel S. Migdal, *op. cit.*, pp.28-29.
67. J. Cohen, *op. cit.*, pp.38-39.
68. Sam Oyovbaire, *op. cit.*, p.22.
69. J.O. Ihonvbere, "Wrong Steps to New Constitution", in *Newswatch*, Lagos, 1 February 2000.
70. International Forum for Democratic Studies (IFDS), *Nigeria's Political Crisis: Which Way Forward?* Report of One-Day Conference on the Current Political Crisis in Nigeria, 7 December 1994 (IFDS Publication, 1995).
71. M.K. Kome, "State and Civil Society in Nigeria in the Era of Structural Adjustment Programme, 1986-1993", in *West Africa Review*, 1, www.westafricareview.com
72. IFDS, *op. cit.*
73. R.W. Cox, "Civil Society at the Turn of the Millennium: Prospects for Alternative World Order", in *Review of International Studies*, 25, p.11

74. *Ibid.*, p.10.
75. IFDS, *op. cit.*
76. A.O. Ikelegbe, *op. cit* (2001).
77. M.J. Makumbe *op. cit.*, pp.309-311. See also L. Diamond "Prospects for Democratic Development in Africa", paper presented at the Democratic Governance Project, Department of Political Science and Administrative Studies, University of Zimbabwe, Harare, 1997, pp.24-25.
78. R. Fatton Jr., *op. cit.*,
79. A.S. Patterson, "A Reappraisal of Democracy in Civil Society: Evidence from Rural Senegal", in *Journal of Modern African Studies*, 36, 2, pp.423-441.
80. A.O. Ikelegbe, *op. cit.*, (2001)
81. S. Weitman, "Thinking the Revolution of 1989", in *British Journal of Sociology*, 43, 17, 1992, p.17.
82. J.A. Hall, *op. cit.*, pp.7-15.
83. E. Gellner, *op. cit.*, p.53.
84. G.A.C. Bryant, *op. cit.*, pp.145-148.
85. N. Chazan, *op. cit.*, pp.74-77.
86. C. Young, *op. cit.*, p.37.
87. A.O. Ikelegbe, *op. cit.*, p.7.
88. M.I.M. Abutudu, *op. cit.*, p.9.
89. B. Olukoshi, "Associational Life", in L. Diamond et al. (eds.) *Transition Without End: Nigerian Politics and Civil Society under Babangida* (Ibadan: Vantage Press, 1996), pp.450-476.
90. A.O. Ikelegbe, *op. cit.*, (2001) p.8.
91. *Ibid.*, p.9.
92. *Ibid.*, pp.11-22.
93. M.H. Kukah, "State of Current Actors: An Overview of Human Rights and Democratic Development in Nigeria", *Report of Proceedings of Strategic Planning Workshop on Democratic Development in Nigeria* (London: Centre for Democracy and Development, 1997). See also A.M. Jega "Organising for Popular Democratic Change in Nigeria: Options and Strategies", in *ibid*.
94. L. Diamond *op. cit.*, p.5.
95. R. Ajayi, "The State Against Civil Society in Nigeria" in *Philosophy and Social Action*, 19(4), 1993.

96. Samuel G. Egwu, *op. cit.*, p.47.
97. R.A. Joseph, *Democracy and Prebendal Politics in Nigeria: The Rise and Fall of the Second Republic* (Ibadan: Spectrum Books, 1987).
98. C. Young, *op. cit.*, p.39.
99. T. Forrest, *Politics and Economic Development in Nigeria* (Boulder & Oxford: Westview Press) pp.3-6.
100. *Ibid.* See also M.I.M. Abutudu, *op. cit.*, pp.162-166.
101. P. Chabal, "A Few Considerations on Democracy", in *African International Affairs*, (74, 92), 1998.
102. N. Chazan, et al., *op. cit.*
103. C. Young & Turner Thomas, *The Rise and Decline of the Zairian State* (Madison: University of Wisconsin Press, 1987).
104. T. Forrest, *op. cit.*, pp.251-252.
105. S. Decalo, The Process, Prospects and Constraints of Democratisation", in *African Affairs*, 91, 1992, pp.7-35. See also T. Forrest, *op. cit.*, p.254.
106. T. Forrest *op. cit.*, p.254. See also R. Sankore, "Politics of Ethnic and Religious Conflict", in *Thisday*, Lagos, 28 October 2001, p.10.
107. S. Decalo *op. cit.*, p.14. See also T. Forrest, *op. cit.*, pp.249-253.
108. J.S. Wunsch, "Centralisation and Development in Post-Independence Africa" in James S. Wunsch & Dele Olowu (eds.), *The Failure of the Centralised African States: Institutions and Self-Governance in Africa* (San Francisco: Institute of Contemporary Studies Press, 1995), p.56.
109. J.S. Wunsch & Dele Olowu, "The Failure of Centralised African States", in *ibid.*, pp.1-22.
110. M.O. Filani, "Nigeria: The Need to Modify Centre-Down Development", in W.B. Storh & D.R. Fraser-Taylor (eds.), *Development from Above or Below? The Dialectics of Regional Planning in Developing Countries* (Chicester: John Wiley, 1981), pp.283-304.
111. N. Chazan, "State and Society in Africa: Images and Challenges", in Rothchild & N. Chazan (eds.) *The Precarious Balance: The State and Society in Africa* (Boulder: Westview, 1988), p.135.
112. O. Nnoli, "Ethnic Conflicts and Democratisation in Africa", paper presented at the 8th CODESRIA General Assembly, Dakar, July, 1995.

113. T.E. Turner, Oil *Workers and Oil Communities: Counter-Planning from the Commons in Nigeria* (Ontario: University of Guelph Press, 1997).

114. M. Mandani, "A Critique of the State and Civil Society Paradigm in Africanist Studies", in Mahmood Mandani & Ernest Wamba-dia Wamba (eds.), *African Studies in Social Movement and Democracy* (Dakar: CODESRIA, 1995), pp.602-616.

115. Samuel G. Egwu, *op. cit.*

116. A.O. Ikelegbe, *op cit.*, (2001B) p.465.

117. Said Adejumobi, *op. cit.*, p.20.

118. Sam Oyovbaire, *op. cit.*, p.22.

119. Said Adejumobi, *op. cit.*, p.20.

120. Samuel G. Egwu, *op. cit.*

121. P. Egede, "NLC, NGOs Parley on How to Secure Democracy Dividends", in *The Guardian*, Lagos, March 13, 2001, p.53.

122. Agaju Madugba, "Musa Blames Ethnic Violence on Past Leadership", in *Thisday*, June 24, 2001, p.6.

123. See *Sunday Vanguard*, Lagos, July 8, 2001.

124. M.O. Ojielo, "Confronting Ethno-Religious and Other Violence in Nigeria", in *National Interest*, Lagos, November 4, 2001, p.5.

125. See O. Onabu, "Anglican Bishops Advocate Restructuring", in *Thisday*, May 27, 2000, p.3.

126. Civil Liberties Organisation (CLO), communique at the Annual National Convention", in *The Punch*, Lagos, October 30, 2001, p.21.

127. M. Adeyemi & W. Fatade, "*Afenifere*, OPC and *Ohaneze* in Historic Meeting", in *The Guardian*, Lagos, July 22, 2000, p.2.

128. C. Ochiama & C. Ajunwa, "Lessons of *Arewa, Afenifere* Parley", in *Post Express*, Lagos, September 9, 2001, pp.9-11.

129. T. Akinrinlola, "Arewa Brokers Peace Between Tiv, Jukun", in *The Punch*, Lagos, *Sunday Vanguard*, October 28, p.3.

130. D. Eze, "Catholic Church Supports Call for National Conference", in *The Post Express*, August 27, p.3.

131. See O. Onabu, *op. cit.*

132. Africa Policy Information Centre, 1999.

133. W. Adebayo & Y. Shokunbi, "Fasehun Escapes Death as Police, OPC Clash" in *The Punch*, Lagos, February 28, 2001, p.4.

134. See *The Punch*, Lagos, January 29, 2001.

135. See *The Guardian*, Lagos, January 17, 2001.
136. D. Kayode-Adedeji, "CD Calls for Fairness in Gani Adams' Trial" in *The Post Express*, Lagos, August 27, p.3.
137. Y. Garba, "Middle Belt Condemns Governors' Retaliatory Calls", in *The Punch*, Lagos, December 7, 2000, p.7.
138. *The Guardian*, Lagos, January 17, 2001.
139. Said Adejumobi, *op. cit.*, p.20.
140. W. Akinola, "Christians Will Curtail Muslims' Aggression", in *Vanguard*, Lagos, October 28, 2001, p.3.
141. Banji Fajonyomi, *op. cit.*
142. P. Egede, *op cit.*
143. Samuel G. Egwu, *op. cit.*
144. J.O. Obari & H. Oliomogbe, "Death Toll in Yenagoa Protest Now Seven", *The Guardian*, Lagos, January 1, 1999.
145. M. Osunde, *op. cit.*
146. J.O. Obari, "Government Deploys Warships in Bayelsa", in *The Guardian*, January 4, 1999, p.1.
147. J.O. Obari, "Why Niger Delta Festers by Ijaw Leaders in Lagos", *The Guardian*, Lagos, January 28, 1999.
148. Komolafe Kayode, "The Enormous Cost of Ethnic Crisis", in *Thisday*, Lagos, October 24, 2001, p.72.
149. R. Wilson, "The politics of Contemporary Ethno-Religious Conflicts" in *Nations and Nationalism*, 7 (3), p.367.
150. J. Keane, *op. cit.*, p.76.

PART 2

CASE STUDIES FROM NIGERIA'S SIX GEO-POLITICAL ZONES

MAP OF NIGERIA SHOWING THE SIX GEOPOLITICAL ZONES

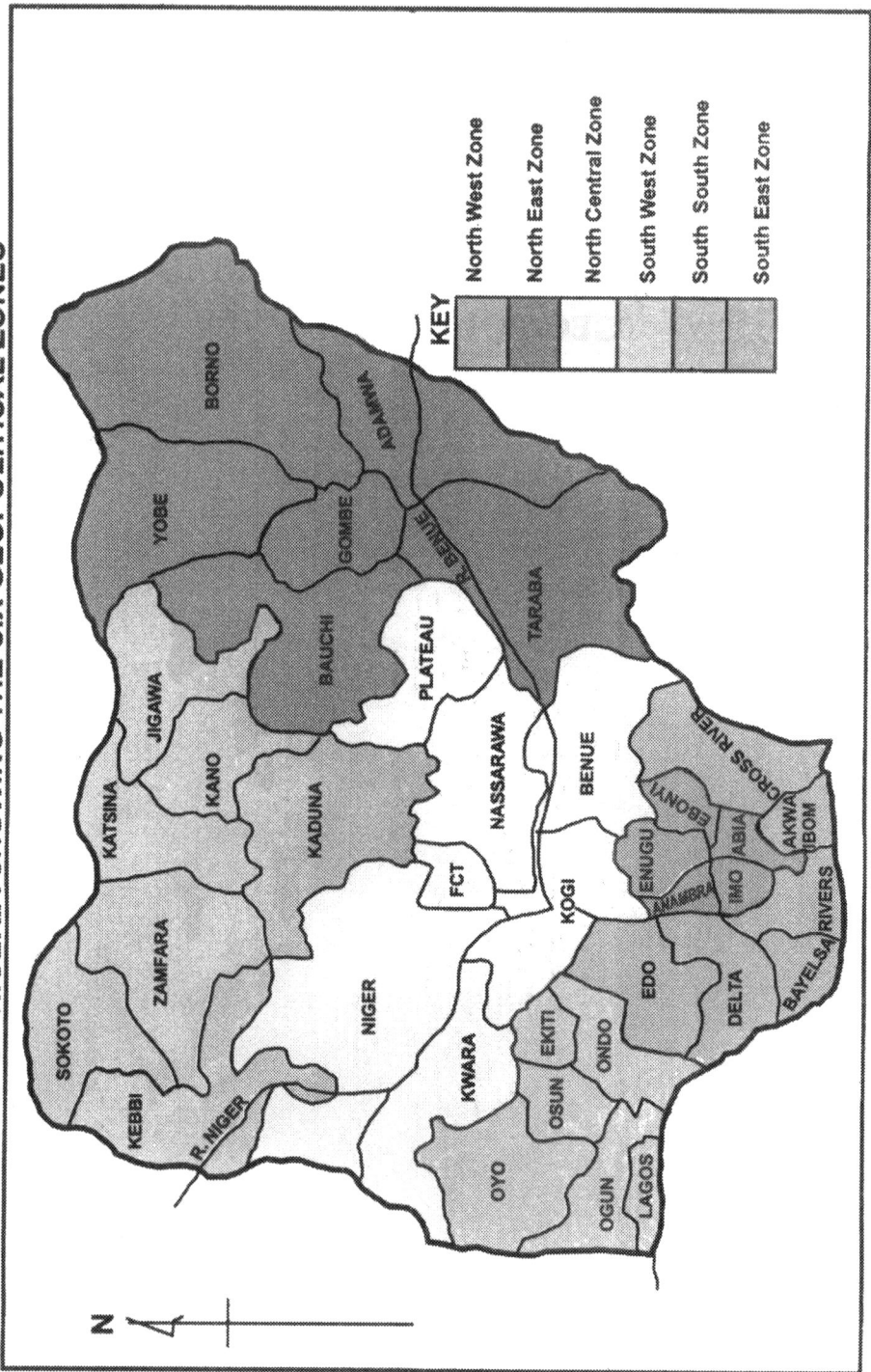

KEY

- North West Zone
- North East Zone
- North Central Zone
- South West Zone
- South South Zone
- South East Zone

Chapter Four

Ethno-Religious Conflict in Kaduna State

K. Leonard Fwa

Introduction

Conflict conducted in the name of ethnic and religious solidarity often destroys the state structure, levels entire development process and unleashes destructive violence, which can threaten the territorial integrity of a country. Recently, the successful hand-over from the military to civil democratic government on the 29 May, 1999, provided the democratic space for the expression of previously suppressed identities. A large number of actors excluded from the political process have chosen the religious stage to act out their ambitions.

This chapter examines the history and causes of the ethno-religious conflict in Kaduna and its environs. It reveals how the declaration of Sharia law in Zamfara State has created acute insecurity among Christians, and how this insecurity itself has destabilised the situation. It further discusses how both Muslims and Christians trace the failure of the formal approaches to conflict management. Finally, it advances the argument that the role of the civil society in managing ethno-religious crisis is a necessary component of any plural society with a large proportion of highly religious people.

Background

The root of the present phase of the ethno-religious conflict can be traced to January, 1986, when the military government took the controversial decision for Nigeria to join the Organisation of the Islamic Conference (OIC). The Jama'atu Nasril Islam (JNI) and the Christian Association of Nigeria (CAN) started vicious and emotional campaigns for and against the country's membership of the OIC. They paraded themselves as representative of Nigerian Muslims and Christians respectively. CAN called on Christians to rise and resist what it tagged as the march of Nigeria toward islamisation. Powerful Muslim leaders sponsored demonstrations in favour of joining the OIC and embarked on a huge propaganda campaign against the domination and marginalisation of what they called the Muslim majority in Nigeria by Christian minority. Both sides called on their faithful to rise in defence of their religious persuasion.[1] The regime, headed by both Christian and Muslim dictators, watched as religious hostility and hatred deepened in civil society. Partisan sections of the media waged a press war, while the chauvinistic elite were at each other's throats in a conflict which engulfed ordinary people.

The new malady of ethno-religious hysterics precipitated a crisis on 6th March, 1987, which led to a Muslim-Christian clash among students at Kafanchan, the biggest town in Southern Kaduna, over what were considered blasphemous remarks. The religious clash developed into a full-scale inter-ethnic confrontation between the Hausa community and the other local ethnic groups. People were killed, mosques were burnt, and a lot of property destroyed. The crisis took a serious religious dimension and spread to all the other major towns in Kaduna State. In the process, hundreds of people were killed, many churches were set ablaze, hotels were destroyed, and there was massive destruction of people. The conflict was the most spontaneous inter-ethnic religious carnage in the history of the state. As Kukah concludes, it is the poor people (who) remain the victims in the macabre dance as they are the ones that get killed; it is their relations that are destroyed.[2]

In Zango-Kataf, as in Kafanchan, there is a Muslim minority Hausa/Fulani community, which has lived in a Zango (a Hausa enclave) since the 17th Century, among a Christian Kataf (Atyab) population. The Hausa community controlled the market in this old market town, and the Kataf community, which considered itself the real indigenes, were becoming increasingly angry about this and the control of territorial administration by the Emir of Zaria.

In January, 1992, the Kataf-controlled local government council decreed that the market would be moved out of Zango on 6th February. Old grievances were unearthed and a bloody ethnic conflict ensued. What started as an inter-ethnic conflict soon widened into a national crisis with religious dimension. As the Cudjoe Report of Inquiry noted, there was a lack of decisive and prompt action by the government organs in the state to check the situation.[3] While investigations were still going on, a bigger clash broke out in May, 1992, this resulted in a massacre of Hausas. Hundreds of human lives were lost and a state of anarchy engulfed the entire state. The state finally adopted a repressive solution in a situation where it was difficult to determine guilt.

Part of the problem was the prolonged military rule, which became a major obstacle to the emergence of a democratic society.[4] Unofficially, the diffusion of power, based on a federal system of government, which still existed in theory, had been eroded. The prolonged military rule had undermined the emergence of a democratic culture. State institutions of governance, their organs and official position were used for repression and accumulation of wealth. In the new era, governance had become a question of power without responsibility.[5]

Owing to the fact that the roots of ethnic conflicts were not being tackled, cosmetic solutions such as the creation of more local government councils and chiefdoms led to the emergence of new minorities and more agitations. Even within the same ethnic group, there were class contradictions, and their primordial political game deepened conflicts along clan lines. The absence of a democratic order for so long tended to have encouraged people to compete among themselves for access to the state and for influence in policies. As Olukoshi stresses, in the course of this, ethnicity became a vital tool to be utilised (both ideological and otherwise) in the achievement of objectives.[6]

For decades, the politics of the non-Hausa elites had been increasingly organised on an ethno-religious basis. With time, peasants and other commoner strata are no longer mere victims of the virus of ethnicity. Because of indoctrination and the promotion of wrong notions of history, for which the other group was always blamed, the psyche and consciousness of the ordinary people developed increasingly along ethnic lines; with an almost pathological hatred of those perceived as their oppressors.[7] The new struggle, waged under the banner of self -determination, involved a clamour for the creation of the same feudal institutions through which many of the communities in South of Kaduna were oppressed for decades.

With the creation of chiefdoms for some of the communities in 1995 and 2001 respectively, in a situation of a normal power shift away from Hausa, the new question is: Which of the so-called indigenous ethnic groups is dominating the other? Within the same ethnic group, the battle is over local power and resources, clans are revived to support the fight. The non-Hausa groups are now turning against themselves in the struggle for appointment, control of local council and over ownership of land. In a repressive and undemocratic atmosphere, the psychology of fear of domination, real and imaginary, is great. And this could induce hatred, which could cause more conflicts. Government officials and politicians create constituencies for their support through ethno-religious propaganda.[8]

Spread of the Conflict and Level of Destruction

Kaduna state has witnessed many violent conflicts in which thousands of lives have been lost and billions of Naira worth of property looted, destroyed or burnt. Economic and social life, including internal communal relations was disrupted as a result of these crises. The Sharia question developed into a major political confrontation on 27th October, 1999 when governor Ahmed Sani Yerima of Bakura of Zamfara State inaugurated the adoption of the Sharia legal system, which took effect from 27th January, 2001. The Zamfara law extended the application of Sharia from personal law to criminal law. Following the Zamfara example, some other states in the North, such as Kano, Sokoto, Niger, Yobe, Kebbi, and Borno announced their intentions to adopt similar measures.[9] The attempt by the Kaduna State House of Assembly to pass a Sharia bill led to a series of demonstrations, first by Muslim supporters and then by Christian opponents. The anti-Sharia demonstration by Christians on 21st February, 2000 led to a major hostility between the two groups resulting in massive killing of people on both sides, the destruction of religious buildings, general arson and the destruction of property.

The scale of massacres and destruction was very high and thousands of people were reported to have been slaughtered like rams. People were said to have organised the killing of their neighbours simply because they belonged to a different religious order. This phenomenon led to a major religious restructuring of the town with people congregating in areas where majority of inhabitants had their religious faith.

What started as a peaceful demonstration resulted into violent crisis, which went on for almost three days. The crisis spread to almost everywhere in Kaduna (excluding the low density government reserved areas) and spilled over to other local governments like Kachia and Birnin-Gwari. Many lives and properties were destroyed. Women and children were displaced in their thousands. Victims were spread across about 23 different refugee camps. This crisis is reported to be the worst since the civil war in 1967-1970, and the most destructive in the history of Nigeria. It was three days of agony for the people of Kaduna and the entire nation. The nature of the crisis and its intensity was a reflection of the complex character of Kaduna city.[10]

Unlike most cities in northern Nigeria, Kaduna has its peculiarities; it was a creation of colonial government and served as the capital of the defunct Northern Nigeria. Against the exclusive nature of most old cities of Northern Nigeria, like Zaria, Sokoto, etc, where the indigenous communities are separated from "settler" communities through the "Sabon-Gari" and "Tudun Wada" system, in Kaduna there is serious interpretation across ethnic and religious lines. It is, however, possible to find places where Christians or Muslims predominate. There is also social differentiation and settlement across economic and political status: you have high density areas, with higher level of jobless youths and miscreants; and low density government reserved areas (GRA), occupied by high status elites. There are also middle class areas, popularly known as low-cost and new-extension.[11]

The crisis was more in high density areas with overwhelming presence of uneducated, unemployed youth and social miscreants like Rigasa, Tudun Wada, Sabon Tasha, Television, Kaduna, Kakuri, Barnawa, Narayi, Hayin Banki, Badarawa, Ungwar Dosa, Abakpa, etc. Incidentally, in these high density areas, some have predominance of one religious group against the other. Those found in the southern part of Kaduna metropolis are predominantly Christians, like, Kakuri, Narayi, Sabon Tasha, Ungwar Boro, Television etc. In these areas, Muslims were overwhelmed and many of them were killed and their properties destroyed. While in Northern Kaduna, like Rigasa, Tudun Wada, Abakpa, Kawo, Hayin Banki, Badarawa, etc., Christians were attacked, killed and their properties destroyed. It is, however, not our intention to state how many Christians or Muslims were slain, the essence is to capture the complexities and dynamics of the crisis.

As a result of this, many lives were destroyed in many of these high-density areas. Thousands of people who managed to escape the crisis trooped to various military and police barracks like: 44 Barracks, Airforce Base, Nigeria Defence Academy (NDA), Mobile Police Barracks, Police College and some churches and mosques and even private residents of some influential people.

On 23 March, 2000, the crisis spilled over to some local government areas, particularly, Kachia and Birnin Gwari. Unemployed youths, social miscreants and some religious fanatics led their groups to prey on their victims, hundreds of people were killed and thousands displaced. Kachia, the headquarters of Kachia Local Government, and the fourth-biggest town in Kaduna State, had been considered a relatively peaceful town because it had never experienced any crisis, particularly the recent ones of 1992 - 1999. This time hoodlums set the town ablaze destroying shops, clinics, courts, residential houses, filling stations, markets and places of worship. The crisis later spread to some neighbouring villages like Sakainu, Katul, Adadgai, Slowai, Gomal, etc. At the end of the crisis, about 350 residential houses were destroyed displacing about 25,000 people while hundreds of people were killed. Many of those displaced trooped to NASA barracks and other safe heavens. The majority of those displaced were women and children.[12]

At the end of the whole crisis in Kaduna State, about 65,000 people were displaced, while thousands of people were killed. Women and children constituted about 75% of the refugees. On the number of residential houses destroyed and other casualties, there are contradictory information from the police, the religious groups, government and members of the public. The members of the public, who were the main victims of the crisis, believed that the government and the police grossly underestimated the casualty figure. It will, therefore, be difficult to provide an acceptable figure. For instance, while the JNI claimed that 799 Muslims were killed, the police reported a total of 609 deaths. The CAN, on the other hand, provided a much higher figure for Christian victims. The official police report of the destruction that took place is as follows:

- 1944 houses including business centres and hotels destroyed;
- A total of 609 deaths recorded (corpses were picked from obscure places in various crisis spots);
- A total of 746 vehicles of various descriptions burnt;
- About 123 churches and 55 mosques burnt in various locations like Kawo, Barnawa, Sabon Tasha, Sabon Gari, Kakuri, Tudun Wada, Kurmin Mashi, Rigasa, Kachia, Birnin Gwari, Zaria, etc.;
- Police out-post at Mararaban Jos burnt; and
- Over 100 persons sustained various injuries and received treatment in hospitals.

Table 1

Estimated Houses Destroyed and Families Displaced

Crisis Areas	Houses Destroyed	No. of People Displaced
Rigasa	230	13,000
Tudun Wada	153	15,000
Kawo/Hayin Banki	74	5,350
Kachia and Environs	350	25,000
Kakuri 71	3,058	
Nassarawa	83	5,800
Barnawa/Sabo	100	2,000

Source: Compiled by researchers.

The official death toll, as far as the public is concerned and based on empirical evidence provided, is very different from the exact figure. The public believes that over 5,000 people might have died in the crisis. Table one above provides the number of houses destroyed and people displaced. Many of these displaced persons did not stay in the refugee camps beyond the period of the crisis. Many left the camps to stay with relations, neighbours and friends, while some travelled immediately out of Kaduna.

The most baffling aspect of the crisis is the free use of sophisticated weapons by both sides in the conflict. The nature of weapons used in the crisis is an indication of how loose the nation's security system is. If ex-service men could be allowed to own devastating weapons such as machine guns and other forms of arms, then the security of the nation remains threatened. The claim that only locally made weapons were used is only an undercover; eyewitness accounts had it that rifles and guns were mainly responsible for the heavy casualty.

The crisis in Kaduna demonstrated the fundamental problem posed by the adoption of the Sharia legal system. It created acute insecurity among the Christian minority groups in the affected states. They feared that the new legal regime would affect them adversely, despite claims to the contrary by the Muslims who supported the measure. Many voices on both sides called for the partition of Nigeria rather than the adoption or abandonment of the Sharia legal system. The Kaduna mayhem, which started as a religious crisis, took on an ethnic dimension and led to retaliatory killings and burning of mosques in Aba and Owerri in which Igbo youths targeted northerners, whom they accused of killing their kith and kin in the North.

The insecurity and the growing state of anarchy as a result of religious animosities, led to the conveying of a meeting of the National Council of State to discuss and seek solutions to the controversies caused by the adoption of the Sharia legal system. The president, Olusegun Obasanjo, former heads of state and state governors attended the meeting. At the end of the meeting on 29 February, it was announced that the Sharia laws being enacted would be suspended and there would be a return to status quo ante; i.e., the penal code. Shehu Shagari and Mohammadu Buhari, both members of the council and former heads of state denied that such a decision had been taken and contended that Muslims were not ready to compromise on the Sharia. Tensions mounted again and new riots were reported in Sokoto and Borno States. Non-Muslims started fleeing the Muslim dominated parts of the North.

In April, northern governors met and agreed to set up a joint Muslim-Christian Committee to align the Sharia with the penal code and to counter the threats posed by the Sharia issue to the solidarity of the North and national unity. Their communiqué, read by Governor Bafarawa of Sokoto State, announced that: "We have resolved to uphold the whole North as one indivisible geographical entity within the federation of Nigeria".

Analysis of the Survey and Assessment

What really caused that crisis? Alhaji Makarfi, the secretary of the Jama'atu Nasir Islam (JNI), Kaduna State, listed about fourteen causes of these crises. These include "lack of trust between various ethnic and religious groups as a result of deep-rooted misconception and stereotyping. Lack of tolerance, poverty and fear of socio-cultural domination, media reporting, government failure to take action in previous happenings, lack of infrastructure, excruciating poverty and manipulation of the people by retired military officers to achieve their ambitions."[13]

Most Rev. Bagobiri, by way of presenting the Christian position, posited three causes of the crises in the state. The first is the structural imbalance that disfavours the southern part of the state in terms of elections. The basis of this is what he called the "fictitious" census exercise in the state which under-counted the southern part and exaggerated the figures of the northern parts. According to him, this situation, if translated into the basis of election and representation, would show that while southern Kaduna was allocated 101 wards and 1,296 polling stations, northern Kaduna had 103 wards and 1,910 polling stations. The effect of this situation is that "northern Kaduna had a mighty advantage of 614 polling stations over the south". He observed that "when the number of polling stations is multiplied by the maximum number of 500 voters allowed per polling station it means that northern Kaduna would have 1910 x 500 = 955,000 voters, while southern Kaduna would have 1296 x 500 = 548,000.00. His conclusion is that the arrangement "gives Northern Kaduna whopping advantage of 307,000 in any electoral contest."[14]

Bagobiri then drove home his point by observing that the cumulative effect of this sham arrangement is for the people of northern Kaduna to win out-rightly any gubernatorial contest even before the race commences; "thus, condemning the people of southern Kaduna perpetually to only deputy governorship position in the state". The other reasons postulated by him included the disadvantaged position of southern Kaduna in terms of political appointments, government patronage and the appointment and posting of upper area court judges.[15]

It is clear, therefore, from both the Muslim and the Christian perspectives, that the causes of the crises concern the issue of who gets what, how and when. The issue is fundamentally that of the living conditions of the people, whether Christian or Muslim, Hausa or Bajju or Atyap. This means that it is the livelihood of the people that should be our primary concern.[16]

As Mohammed posited:

> Anybody who is interested in the promotion of the Sharia in Nigeria must first of all be concerned with the actual living conditions of Muslims, especially, talakawa, the downtrodden masses, who constitute the overwhelming majority of Muslims. For, to be a good Muslim, the talakawa needs firstly to be alive. If we are really interested in the promotion of the Sharia, we must be concerned with whether, for instance, the Muslims have food to eat and clean water to drink in order to stay alive. ...whether a Muslim woman can be examined in a hospital or .indeed whether she has access to hospital at all. We should also be concerned with whether Muslims, who live, work and pay their taxes amongst Muslims have access to education, decent housing, transportation and communication.[17]

By the testimonies of the representatives of both Christians and Muslims, it is clear that ethnicity and religion have simply provided ready tools to be used by those seeking positions, power, relevance or control of societies. This corroborates other studies which reveal that Nigerian political elite ride to power and prominence on the platitudes and promises of protecting one religion or ethnic interest;[18] only to turn round to loot the treasury and oppress the people.[19] The Sharia debate as it has been observed, has always cropped up during movements of political transition, when new power sharing arrangements are being worked out as obtained during the 1976/77 and 1985 constituent assemblies' debates. The same protagonist and antagonist quickly buried their hatchets and found common ground in the cabinets of the military government and the boardrooms of government parastatals and private companies. What, therefore, are regarded as ethnic and religious conflicts are first and foremost political. They are simply fall-outs of the politics of the elites

Beyond all the arguments about ethnic and religious crisis, the fundamental issue about Sharia now lies at the heart of politics in Nigeria and the centrality that "identity" politics has assumed. Why is this so? Kayode Fayemi argued that many of the internal contradictions of the Nigeria state have been sharpened to a point that the bare bones are now visible.[20] The failure to resolve the national question in an inclusive manner is evident in the varied responses across the country to conflicts over identity, nationality, self-determination and autonomy. These issues are, in turn, bound up with such questions as what manner of federation do Nigerians want? Unlike in the past when the government has always decreed issues like Sharia and resource control as constitutional no go areas, Nigerians are now forcing these issues in the open and the hitherto authoritarian might of the federal centre is being put to test. The above, however, does not strip bare the explanatory power of other causes which reside in the political and economic realm of the Nigerian crisis. Thus, Fayemi further stressed that:

> There can be no doubt that the Sharia issue is clearly a reaction to perceived or real loss of power by an elite stratum that is predominantly "northern" and also "Muslim". What is happening is a contest over raw political power. Who lost power, who won power, and who wants power back. The processes that threw up General Obasanjo as the candidate of this elite stratum were intimately bound up with the political crisis that has gripped the northern political class. Obasanjo, whom they had supported refused to play their game, prompting some northern political leaders like Datti Ahmed, himself a former presidential candidate, to allegedly claim the president had allowed himself to be hijacked by southwest politicians. Since General Obasanjo as a politician does not have a political base, not in the army, nor in his ethnic group, nor anywhere else, it would seem understandable that the forces in retreat dusted up the dormant Sharia issue, confident of its populist value, to challenge him, to intimidate him, to force him to back down and play things their way.[21]

For the politician in the "North", who has always been in power, the idea of getting used to powerlessness poses a huge challenge. This is a crisis for power brokers and beneficiaries of power in the North. People have to take this sea change in. And one of the ways in which the Sharia issue should be perceived is the service it offers such people to play cynical politics without alienating themselves from their communities. Limited to this course is the contest between traditional authority in the north and an emerging new political elite. Young politicians are edging out the old, but they are yet to consolidate their grip on power and Sharia offers a strong issue on the political platform. Hence, Ahmed Sani Yerima, whose position as the candidate of the All Nigerian Peoples Party (ANPP) in Zamfara State was quite precarious in a state perceived to be a Peoples' Democratic Party (PDP) stronghold, decided to play the Sharia card. Six out of the ten states that have declared Sharia in the North are ANPP controlled states.

For the remaining four states, especially those of Kano and Katsina states, popular opinion in those states had forced them to flow with the tide. There is no doubt that there is a power vacuum in northern Nigeria, and indeed at the national level. For the leading lights of the Sharia campaign, religion offered a most appropriate mechanism for winning over a largely sceptical citizenry in communities where leaders were largely perceived as dealers.

The Sharia riots can perhaps be located within the context of people who have nothing to lose in communities where they have little at stake. It is a fact that the foot soldiers of the crisis are the unemployed youths still awaiting their own democracy dividends. The problems raised by the Sharia in Nigeria go beyond religion. It is about the disillusionment of those who had been hard done by. As long as you have the unemployed, the hungry and the desperate, Sharia would always be exploited by the manipulators of differences, secure in the knowledge that there would be foot soldiers to take their war to the street. The same is true of the exploitation of other issues around the country.

The Sharia issues can be seen as a response by Islamic fundamentalism to a growing Christian population under a born again Christian president. The advent and proliferation of pentecostal Christianity as a powerful social and political force in Nigeria represents a growing concern amongst Muslims and orthodox Christian alike. The attempted introduction of the Sharia legal system by some states in the federation might, therefore, be an attempt to checkmate what they consider to be a Christian threat. Such fears have a very palpable reality in popular consciousness due to communal conflicts in the northern part of Nigeria. In sum, the issue involves problems of perceived political domination by a group considered as external or illegitimate. Hence, the tussle is over who exercises control over land and political power. What is obvious presently, is that there has been such an escalation of ethno-religious conflict in the country that the survival of Nigeria as a peaceful and corporate entity will require the active promotion of confidence-building mechanisms that will calm people's fears and encourage the difficult process of healing hate memories. To carry through this process, the role of the civil society and democracy become critical.

Formal Efforts at Managing and Resolving Conflicts
In view of the persistence of conflicts in the North-Central Zone, it is logical to review strategies that have been used to address such conflicts ·in the past, and why such efforts have not been quite successful. Lessons from this may be found useful in developing new initiatives for dealing with current problems.

Institution of Administrative and/or Judicial Commissions of Inquiry
There is hardly any crisis in this country that was not investigated by an administrative or judicial commission of inquiry, set up either by the state or federal government. Terms of reference for such commissions usually included finding the remote and immediate causes of such crisis, those involved and appropriate measures to be taken against them. It is a very sad commentary that many reports of these inquiries were never made public, let alone their recommendations implemented. Even in the few instances that the recommendations were implemented, serious allegations of·double standards and selective justice were made. The consensus is that the *political will* required to implement such recommendations was always lacking. The resultant effect is to compound the ethno-religious crisis in our hands and the feeling by some powerful individuals that they are above the law. There is also the loss of

confidence by the public who thereby resort to violence to seek redress whenever they feel aggrieved.

As an example, it may be necessary to make reference to the Willink Commission appointed in 1957 by the colonial administration to enquire into the fears of minorities and the means of allaying these fears, which may include provision of constitutional safeguards or the creation of states as may be considered absolutely necessary. From the commission's report, the following minority fears were identified.

1.   Domination of government by regional ethnic majority;
2.   Social fears and grievances, in other words, imposition of majority language, use of contemptuous phrases to describe the minority groups and non-observance of minority culture;
3.   Discrimination in economic spheres;
4.   Discrimination in recruitment into public posts and in public activities;
5.   The maintenance of public order and individual freedom;
6.   Traditional rulers and local (native authority) governments (that is, the imposition of the traditional rulers in the then southern Zaria and Ilorin); and
7.   Religious intolerance.

The increasing agitation among minority groups today for self-determination and the spate of violent conflicts experienced in recent times seem to suggest that much of these fears identified as far back as 1957 are very much with the minorities. Considering the number of years that have gone by since the commission's work, it will not be an exaggeration to state that the *political will* to decisively implement its report by successive administrations may have been lacking. This of course, is without prejudice to the creation of states and local government area that have taken place as recommended by the commission or other commissions. In addition to the Willink's Report, other reports which may be referred to include:

1.   The John Shagaya Commission on Nigeria's membership of the OIC, set up by Gen. Ibrahim B. Babangida on 3/2/86, following the OIC crisis of early 1986;

2. Federal Government Judicial Panel on the Kafanchan, Kaduna and Zaria Crises, 1987.
3. Justice Rahila Cudjoe Commission of Inquiry into the 1992 Zango-Kataf Crisis, Kaduna State.
4. Justice Benedict Okadigbo Special Tribunal on the Zango-Kataf crisis, 1992, Kaduna State.
5. The AVM Usman Mu'azu Reconciliation & Search for Lasting Peace Committee for Zango Kataf, Kaduna State, December 1994.

The Instrument of State Creation

The instrument of state creation has been used by successive administration to address identified structural imbalances in the polity. There is no doubt that this has helped a great deal to strengthen the federation and give a sense of belonging to different peoples and communities. It should be stated, however, that the same instrument has been used, consciously or unconsciously to create some other conflicts. This mainly has been due to unfair location of state capitals, local government headquarters or the arbitrary demarcation of boundaries. There are even instances where some ethnic groups have been balkanised into two or more states, which either weakens or strengthens the political and economic base of such groups. This is one of the contending issues in Bauchi State where Sayawa and the Hausa/Fulani are fighting.

The Use of Soldiers to Quell Violent Clashes

Both military and civilian administrations have relied on the use of soldiers as a crisis management strategy especially for restoration of peace and calm during violent clashes. Recent experiences, however, have shown that this strategy is fast losing credibility and efficacy. Because of the prolonged and frequent military involvement in managing these conflicts, the military is gradually being polarised along ethnic and religious lines. The use of the military, therefore, is becoming too dangerous in a complex and plural society such as Nigeria.

Peace/Reconciliatory Fora

Government and even non-governmental organisations have held various fora to promote peace and reconcile warring parties. This strategy usually aims at appealing to the conscience of people to take the path of peace and dialogue as well as respect the sanctity of life. However, its effectiveness is limited by the inability to bring the perpetrators of such conflicts to the peace fora. In addition, agreements usually reached at such fora are not sustained due to lack of legal backing. These fora, as important as they may be, only provide avenues for sermonisation rather than taking sincere and decisive action.

One may wonder why these disturbances persist. One issue that makes the incidents keep re-occurring is that the masterminds who instigate, mobilise and arm the rioters, even in cases where they are clearly identified, are never punished. Vicious masterminds of the Bauchi 1991 riots, clearly identified by the Federal Judicial Commission of Inquiry, were allowed to go scot-free. This is a great disservice to this country. The problem, to a very large extent may not be unconnected with law enforcement agents. Section 176(2) of the constitution provides that the governor of a state shall be the chief executive of that state. In matters pertaining to state security, the actions and decisions of the governor is constrained by the manner of his relationship with the law enforcement agencies. This apparent contradiction in the role assigned to the governor and his use of the law enforcement agencies places great impediment in the prosecution of perpetrators of civil disturbances.

The Role of Security Agents
The role of the security agents in the recent Kaduna crisis drew widespread criticism. When we asked our respondents what was responsible for the slow rate and ineffectiveness of the response by the police to the crisis, various interpretations were got, many of which reflected predetermined positions. The *New Nigeria* editorial blamed the violence on police who chose to ignore the crisis when the killing was going on. The paper further claimed that when the police finally came, some of them became clearly partisan, helping the assailants in their dastardly act. Some respondents ascribed the security lapse to the fact that most of the police officers during the Kaduna crisis were mainly indigenes and took sides with their people.

A retired colonel we interviewed, however, maintained that even if the assumption was correct that majority of the police officers in the Kaduna crisis took sides, the impression that they could act independently is completely erroneous. According to him, the police everywhere are a willing tool in the hand of the state and the situation is worse in Nigeria where most police officers are poor and illiterates.

On the apparent delay in the deployment of the police and army during this crisis, it was blamed on the rigorous procedure involved, especially, in bringing the soldiers to the street. However, some respondents blamed it on the influence, which some rich individuals had on the police. They also argued that even if the police were quick to respond, the police mode of operation was largely the routine duty of maintaining roadblocks, patrolling of main roads and arrest and interrogation of suspected leaders and partisans. These modes of operation were, however, generally inadequate and ineffective because they were riddled with corruption from the onset. Thus, however much the police tried, the patrols and roadblocks never acted as an effective check on the movement of rioters and dangerous weapons.

Arson and looting were the modus operandi of the rioters. Their activities lacked any cohesion, they were mob actions with churches and hotels constituting the main targets of attacks. While the main weapons of the rioters were sticks, daggers, knives, spears, cans of petrol and boxes of matches, for which the police were ill-trained and ill-equipped to handle, the introduction of sophisticated weapons into the crisis did a lot to further complicate police work. According to a military officer we interviewed, the contending groups used pistols, Franchise National (FN) Rifle, AK 47, Kalashnikov General Purpose Machine Guns (GPMG) and other automatic weapons freely.[22]

Issues and Way Out

Given the history of the ethno-religious crisis in Kaduna and the failure of the various formal management procedures which have been attempted to address it, this study was guided by the desire to elicit from respondents their own views on how to successfully manage the conflict in question.

In order to be able to elicit appropriate responses, it was necessary to ask the people their view about the causes of the problem in the first place. The overwhelming view has been that the Nigerian political elite, both military and civilian, have consistently manipulated the differences among the ethnic formations for their own selfish interests. These interests, it is believed, are fuelled by greed.

Poverty has become a persistent part of the normal life of an average Nigerian. Grinding poverty creates alienation and socioeconomic insecurity, which impel people to seek solace in primary group identity including ethnic or religious identity. Poverty and a low level of literacy and civil awareness prevent the people from fully understanding the intricacies of modern government and the real issue involved in it. Consequently, self-seeking ethnic demagogues who present ethnicity as a panacea for their economic woes can carry them away easily. Poverty generates divisive socioeconomic competition. The effect of this competition is insecurity associated with limited job opportunities and social services. Frustrated, unsuccessful competitors find it easy and convenient to blame their plight on some assured advantages possessed by members of other groups. There is usually a strong belief in ethnic group entitlement, especially, regarding the size of the national cake that should accrue to their respective ethnic groups.

The repression that characterises military rule has been a harbinger of ethnicity in Nigeria. The military has essentially been a tool of internal repression. That is why military rule is inherently a source of pervasive insecurity. Prolonged military rule in the country has done more damage to the struggle against ethnic sectarianism than any other phenomenon in Nigerian history.

Nigeria largely retains the colonial state structure, which is inherently undemocratic, because it was the repressive apparatus of an occupying power. Quite often and in the name of state building and development, the African state has oppressed individuals, ethnic groups, minorities, workers, peasants, religious groups and factions of the ruling class. The resultant hostility may be directed from one ethnic group against the government or against another ethnic group.

Globalisation reinforces the undemocratic character of the Nigerian state and its consequences for ethnic politics. In Nigeria, globalisation needs an authoritarian state capable of forcing through the fundamental restructuring of the country's domestic and international relations demanded by the world community. The history of inter-ethnic relations has been quite discordant in Nigeria.

The Igbo are still suffering over their role in the civil war, which ended thirty years ago. The Igbo and Yoruba are unable to forgive and forget the mistrust, betrayal and acrimony of their past relations, while the Hausa and Fulani are always ready to recall the history of uneven development of the country and the advantages accruing to the South as a result. Every ethnic problem is perceived from this tinted history and is reinforced by it. The failure of the formal method of conflict resolution in Nigeria necessitated the need for an alternative formula that is based on the use of civil society groups in conflict management.

The Role of Civil Society

Civil society refers to associations and institutions that enhance the prospect for individual and collective liberties by operating outside the states' control and do possess the capacity to countermine the state or any other interest when these liberties are threatened. A traditional civil organisation model exists in the form of town or village unions, community and religious organisations and age based and sex-based groups. In the more modern sector there are interest groups such as women's organisations, trade unions, chambers of commerce and farmer's associations and co-operatives, universities and human rights movements. The relative sense of justice that people in developed countries enjoy stem from the successful pressures exerted on government to act in certain ways. The NGOs, in particular, highlight issues of injustice, abuse of human rights etc., and get government to act. Unfortunately in the case of northern Nigeria, this factor is absent. It is even worsened by the absence of the media and of educated elite who would champion community causes. The result is the trampling on of rights of individuals and communities. The larger Nigerian society hardly knows or understands what is happening or even the enormity of these crises. It is, therefore, very vital to encourage both the growth of NGOs and community-based or media organisations in the area. Shedrack Best has argued that there "is the relative shortage of NGOs working in conflict management. NGOs do not necessarily provide solutions to peace-making within communities, but they do facilitate the process of peace-building and empower local groups through capacity-building. NGOs help to fill the gap and create conditions for trust and confidence-building."[23]

Civil society groups and Non-Governmental Organisations (NGOs) play vital roles in conflict. Their roles cannot become substitutes for the functions of the state. By themselves, they may be unable to bring peace, but their activities can influence public opinion through the media, which most communities cannot. Our general observation and responses elicited from the people within and outside the Kaduna environs, show that civil society played a minimal role in managing or resolving the conflict in Kaduna. Generally, the level of illiteracy among the people, coupled with prolonged military rule eroded the development of civil political culture in the country, which in turn affected the development of civil society.

The lack of democratic culture has often closed the room for meaningful debate and the flourishing of mediocrity and contrary opinions. What operates in most parts of the North are few civil society organisations, most of which tend to go along with the people in power. Hardly can you find any group actually challenging government decisions and actions because they depend essentially on government for their survival. Considering the above limitations or weaknesses, the few civil society groups operating in the state have not played any meaningful role in the management and resolution of the conflicts discussed in this chapter.

What needs to be done to stimulate the rise and growth of civil society, is to encourage and strengthen the ability of the people to consolidate democracy in Nigeria. This would in turn create the necessary political awareness in the people that would enable them to know their rights and duties and discern the options that might be open to them for the promotion of those rights. It will also encourage popular participation of the people in the development of their society and in decisions affecting their lives and communities. It is obvious from our study of the crisis that government does not lack ideas or measures to sort out long-standing problems. The experiences in Kafanchan, Zango-Kataf and Kaduna point to the fact that some powerful groups have held the state hostage. Sometimes, even when communities sit down to arrive at compromises, these are not respected by the state.

Civil society groups often work with the press to mount pressure on government. They create awareness by organising journalists to visit scenes of conflicts and report on them. Unfortunately, even the groups in Nigeria, which claim to be involved in conflict resolutions have not drawn or bothered to draw public attention to the conflicts. The atrocities committed by security agencies and even government are often hidden from the public. As long as these conflicts and the enormity of human rights violation are carefully and successfully kept away from the public, so too will the problems keep mounting. The press has been, and will continue to remain a very important instrument in fighting human rights abuses. So far, the problems and crisis in the areas studied did not receive much press attention.

Civil society groups could help them to know what is happening in good time, and the wealth of information which they have can help them to anticipate these crises, alert society and the state about them. This is because most of these conflicts do not suddenly occur. They take time and can be anticipated and early warnings could be given. Thus, one major problem of crisis minimisation is education, which the World Bank has described as the first ingredient of capacity building. The declining primary and secondary school enrolment as well as the destruction of educational infrastructure generally decrease society's ability to deal with its problems. For the Nigerian situation, the large pool of unemployed and perhaps unemployable young men and women create two major problems. First, it creates a ready army of foot soldiers. Second, and most important, it creates an army that cannot reason or understand its environment. As Obasi argues, "the starting point of any renewed effort at building capacity for the effective management of African economic, social, environmental and other crises must be to recognise the primacy of human capacity development... An enlightened citizenry can demand for its rights, hold its leaders accountable and better appreciate its situation vis-a-vis others with contradictory claims."[24] Besides the need for literacy, civic education is necessary. These responsibilities, therefore, ought to be discharged by both the state and civil society groups. These are very largely absent in the North where literacy rates have been decreasing and the number of civil society groups are few.

Conclusion
This analysis has investigated the complexity of ethno-religious

conflicts that have occurred in Kaduna and the ways in which the socioeconomic and political situation generate ethnic conflicts. The multi-ethnic nature of the North Western Zone is not the cause of the numerous and deep ethnic conflicts. The adoption of Sharia in some states of the federation has generated such developments in Kaduna. These communal and identity conflicts rapidly engulfed the zone, leading to divisions and/or unity depending on the groups or issues involved. For the process to be placed beyond harm's way, we have suggested urgent action by government to strengthen civil society, educate the people, support mediation efforts, create job opportunities for the unemployed and encourage local participation in governance.

References

1.   *Newswatch Magazine*, Lagos, 1986, pp.12-17.
2.   M.H. Kukah, "Religion and Politics of National Integration in Nigeria", in Mahdi Abdullahi, et al., *The State of the Nation and the Way Forward* (Kaduna: Arewa House, 1994), p.453.
3.   *Citizen Magazine*, Kaduna, 1992, p.15.
4.   A.O. Olukoshi & O. Agbu, "The Deepening Crisis of Nigerian Federalism and the Future of the Nation State." Paper presented at the 8th CODESRIA General Assembly, Dakar, 1995.
5.   Toure Kazah, "The Political Economy of Ethnic Conflicts and Governance in Southern Kaduna, Nigeria: Deconstructing a Contested Terrain," in *African Development*, 1999, p.136.
6.   A.O. Olukoshi & O. Agbu, *op. cit.*, p.162.
7.   T. Kazah, "The Inter-Ethnic Religious Conflict and Nationalism in Zango-Kataf Area of Northern Nigeria: Historical Origin and Contemporary Forms," CODESRIA General Assembly, Dakar, 1995.
8.   Y. Bangura, "The Pitfalls of Re-colonisation," *CODESRIA Bulletin*, No. 4, Dakar, 1995, p.23.
9.   International Idea, "Democracy in Nigeria: Continuing Dialogue for Nation Building," *Capacity Building Series*, 10, 2000, p.75.
10.   H. Abdu, "The Impact of Ethno-Religious Crisis in Women and Children in Kaduna," *Human Rights Monitor Report*, 2000,

p.13.

11. *Ibid.,* p.13

12. *Ibid.,* p.14.

13. J. Makarfi, "Ethnic and Religious Crisis, 1987-2000: Its Causes and Effects and the Role of the Government of Kaduna". Paper presented at the Workshop on Peace and Reconciliation in Kaduna, 2000, p.5.

14. Cited in Makarfi, *ibid.*

15. See S.U. Lawal, "Democratisation and Ethno-Religious Conflicts in Nigeria: Issues, Perspectives and Connotations". Paper presented at APP Conference, Kano, 2000.

16. *Ibid.*

17. S. Mohammed, "Ethnic Relations in a Multi-Cultural Setting: An X-ray of Kaduna Crisis". Paper presented at the Annual General Meeting of National Information and Public Relations (NIPR), 2000.

18. See *ibid.*

19. S.U. Lawal, *op. cit.*

20. J.K. Fayomi, "Sharia, Democracy and the Constitutional reform Agenda in Nigeria", in *Quarterly Journal of the Centre for Democracy and Development* (CDD), Vol.2, No.5, January-March 2000, p.23.

21. *Ibid.,* p.24.

22. Eyewitness Account of the Crisis from our field survey.

23. S.G. Best, "The Challenge of Peacemaking and Peace-building in the Middle Belt", in Festus Okoye, *Victims, Impact of Religious and Ethnic Conflicts on Women and Children in Northern Nigeria,* Human Rights Monitor, Nigeria, 2000.

24. N. Obasi, "Developing Capacity for Management of Africa's Socio-Economic Crisis", in Chris Garuba (ed.), *Capacity Building for Crisis Management in Africa* (Lagos: Gabumo Publishing Co., for the National War College, Abuja, 1998).

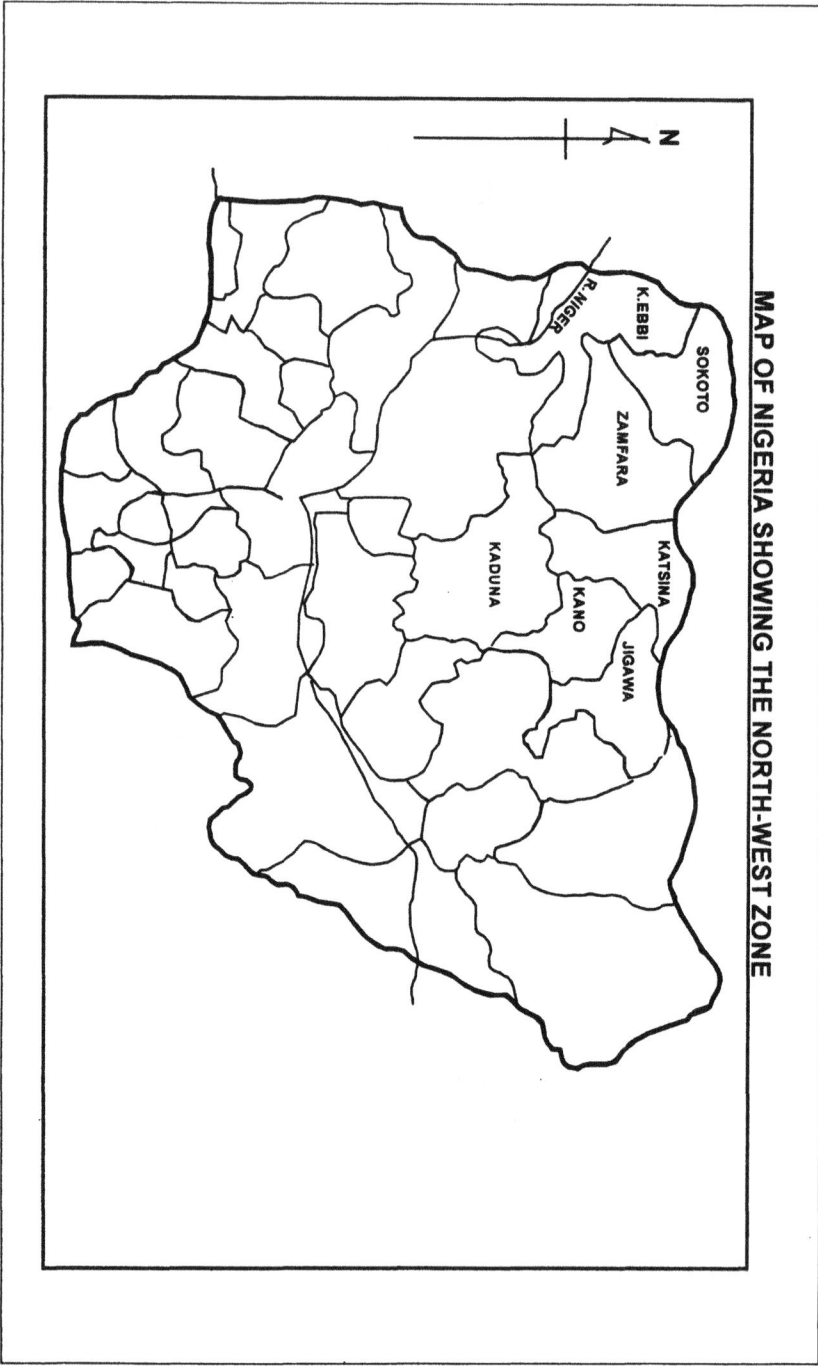

MAP OF NIGERIA SHOWING THE NORTH-WEST ZONE

MAP OF KADUNA SHOWING STUDIED AREA

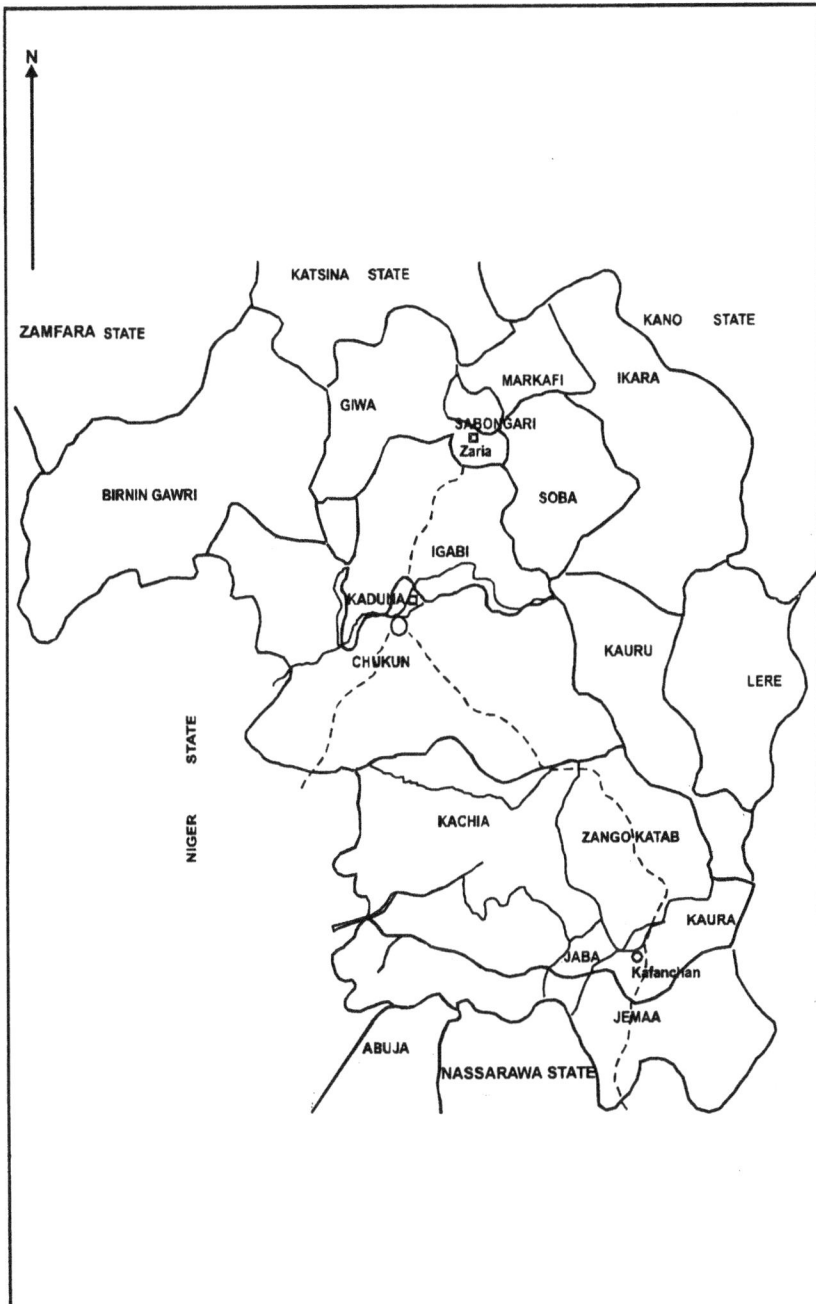

Chapter 5

Bassa-Egbura Conflict in Nassarawa State

Julie Sanda

Introduction

That Nigeria is a heterogeneous state comprising several pluralities principally ethnic and religious is not news. But that its communities, variously defined, have yet to find enduring formulae for peaceful coexistence, seems to be a major challenge to consolidating democracy and indeed nation building. This is in spite of its adoption of the federalist model for managing diversity. Of course, it can easily be argued that the military incursion into politics distorted at best, the evolution of Nigeria federalism over the three decades it lasted.

Again, while conflict is part of every human community, its nature and management determine its effect or impact on society. In Nigeria, violent conflicts have become part of the socio-political landscape since independence in 1960. The most important of these in terms of intensity, speed, and total number of casualties and overall long-term effect, has been the 1966 – 1970 Civil War. Despite the civil war experience, the state of conflict cannot be said to have changed for the better. The global trend since the end of the Cold War wherein smaller, yet hotter, conflicts have become more frequent, is reflected in Nigeria as well. In Africa today, most wars are internally generated and occur largely within state boundaries. Thus, the greater threat to security in Nigeria today may not be a full blown national conflagration but these pockets of communal conflicts erupting all over the country.

106

As localised as these conflicts have been, their effects have been felt in other parts of the country because of the multiplicity of factors that usually come to play. These local conflicts have a way of mobilising very strong primordial sentiments and thereby heightening their impact as events unfold. The intensity of violence often leaves little room for intervention beyond the application of more force by government security agents.

In a nationwide study on conflict in Nigeria conducted in 1997/98, five major conflict issue areas were identified.[1] These issues, which cut across geo-political boundaries and may overlap in any one conflict, are:

1. Land and resources management.
2. Nationalities, citizenship and national integration.
3. The federal question;
4. Local governance, traditional institutions and self-determination; and
5. Government policy and problems of implementation.

While this classification is unconventional, it avoids the trap of ascribing mono-causality to complex cases, and hence the danger of prescribing simplistic or inadequate solutions. Thus, it has both analytical usefulness and policy implications. The allocation of resources and political positions, for example, is a major area of controversy in Nigeria today and has been for a long time. A thorough discussion of this subject, for instance, would throw up land and its resources, its use and, therefore, ownership, thus questioning the Land Use Act of 1978. Ethnic communities fight each other over land but also the state over control of the resources.

The return to democracy was expected to yield a peace dividend as the prospect of the federation operating within the appropriate democratic framework gave rise to hopes of widening space for political participation. What the hopefuls did not reckon with, however, was the fact that decades of military authoritarianism; years of economic crisis and impoverishment of the citizenry would have serious implications for democratisation. Chief among those is the paradox related to the democratic deficit as alluded to earlier. While democracy has inbuilt mechanisms for managing diversity, these must be operated overtime to become popularly accepted culture and a way of life within the polity.

Crisis after crisis erupted all over the country soon after the return of democratic rule as Nigerians exercised their "freedoms" of expression, association, etc, and demanded their rights. The fledgling institutions of democracy and their practitioners were sorely tested with a mixed bag of results. While in the last three years in Nigeria, some fires of conflict have been doused, others seem to have been fanned to life or had red-hot coals added to them. The Ife-Modakeke, the Aguleri-Umuleri, the youth restiveness in the Niger Delta have taken back stage as communities in Kaduna, Kano, Lagos, Taraba, Benue, Nassarawa, etc., have experienced untold horror. While it is "true" that democracy is still struggling to take shape in Nigeria, it is also evident that multiparty politics has sharpened the cleavages in society as politicians insist on a winner-takes-all approach to politics, leaving little or no room for negotiations, bargaining, dialogue and consultation, to ensure popular participation and representation in decision-making. The spoils of office have raised the stakes even higher at every level of government. It is not uncommon, therefore, for disagreement between or within communities to take on extreme political dimensions.

Conflict Profile in the North-Central Zone

The most virulent conflict in Nigeria in recent times has been the ethnic or ethno-communal and its worst manifestations have been in the North-Central Zone commonly referred to as the "Middle Belt" region. As the name connotes, this area straddles Nigeria across from mid-North East to mid-North West or simply put is the link between northern and southern Nigeria. It comprises several ethnic communities estimated at about two thirds of Nigeria's estimated 383 ethnic nationalities and 400 linguistic groups.[2] The Middle Belt is defined variously either by geography, political aspiration, or as an expression of cultural identity. However, none of these categories is exclusive. While, for instance:

> In the First Republic, it referred to Kabba, Plateau and Benue Provinces and revolved around separation of minorities, from the North... currently, it is used to refer to the political aspiration of the indigenous people of Kogi, Kwara, Niger,

Benue, Plateau, Nassarawa, Taraba, parts of Gombe, southern
Kaduna State, the Federal Capital Territory, Abuja, and
minorities in Borno, Kebbi, Adamawa and Yobe states.[3]

This definition raises some controversy and, according to
Middle Belt scholars and activists, it is incomplete. They would
include parts of Bauchi and Kaduna states as a whole.[4] Moreover,
the issue of indigenous peoples is at the heart of the communal/
religious violence being experienced in this part of the country
whether it be Kaduna, Nassarawa, Plateau or Taraba. While most
of it revolves around "settlers" and the perceived intentions of the
Islamic North against the Middle Belt, quite a number of these
conflicts are between the minority ethnic communities themselves,
such as the Kuteb-Jukun-Chamba, the Tiv-Jukun or the Bassa-
Egbura crises.

Historical records show that the Middle Belt area has been
inhabited as far back as 40,000 years ago and its peoples are most
probably of Bantu origin.[5] Its fame lies in its sheer ethnic and
cultural diversity. The people have governed themselves both
through various centralised state systems (Jukun, Nupe, etc.) and
through clans and village democracies (Idoma, Berom, etc.).[6] They
were found to have existed largely without clear-cut territorial
boundaries, the result of "continuous migratory activities" up to
the time of colonialism.[7] Languages, culture and political
institutions were borrowed despite ethnic differences and so the
ethnic boundaries themselves became permeable.

While this chapter is not a treatise on the Middle Belt be it in
definition, history or politics, the foregoing discussion was
necessary to provide a context for understanding the case in point:
the conflict between the Bassa and Egbura communities of Toto
Local Government in Nassarawa State. Nigeria is today zoned into
geopolitical regions. Though not a constitutional demarcation, these
6 zones have been found convenient for mainly administrative and
political purposes and, therefore, are popularly accepted by a wide
spectrum of Nigerians. When the Abacha government first
introduced this zoning system in 1995, it was a response to the
ongoing restructuring debate. The areas identified were North-West,
North-East, Middle Belt, South-East, South-West and Southern
Minorities. Following protests by the southern minority ethnic

communities, that zone was renamed South-South. The Middle Belt has since become known as the North-Central Zone. Nevertheless, the North-Central Zone comprises the Federal Capital Territory, Abuja, Benue, Plateau, Nassarawa, Niger, Kogi, and Kwara states. Thus, the scope of the cultural and political Middle Belt is much wider than the present North-Central Zone. This study has adopted this zoning system, even if not constitutional, for the analytical purpose of ensuring even representation of case studies nationwide. For this purpose, therefore, our case study is located within the North-Central Zone to which Nassarawa State belongs.

To properly situate the problem, however, one has to look at the historical antecedents of the wider Middle Belt region and the dynamics of the conflicts with which it has come to be characterised. As Yoroms explains, "ethnicity and religion are two broad concepts that could be treated on their own merits. But the nature and character of political development in Nigeria has informed the symbiosis of the two concepts, especially when analysing the Middle Belt".[8]

He also posits that the character of the state is an important variable in understanding the dynamics of conflict in the region. Using Ake's typology, he explains that the state is involved either vertically wherein it facilitates "domination of independent social formations under a centralising power" or horizontally "wherein the relationship is focused on the struggle for dominion and subordination among the constituent social forces".[9] Thus, conflicts may occur in the quest to break the monopoly of the state; seek greater access to national resources and statuses; or for self-determination. This latter is expressed either in seeking local autonomy over local affairs and/or the right to cultural expression.

During colonial rule, the "indirect rule" system was employed in the northern part of Nigeria. The traditional institutions of the ethnic minorities were mutilated to fit into the emirate system with which the British had evolved a working relationship. Where there was no centralised institution, district heads were imposed. Today these institutions have grown in stature and relevance. For whatever they are worth, they have become important symbols of cultural self-determination on the one side. On the negative side, however, they have become tools in the hands of either the state or ethnic elites (or both), tools to acquire legitimacy.

As participants at a national conference in 1999 agreed:

> The traditional institution by virtue of its ascriptive qualities, namely, the ascension to power through birth rather than merit or popularity, contradicts the virtues of republicanism and democracy, vital ingredients of the next millennium.
>
> Despite the aforementioned facts, some communities in Nigeria today still have high regard 'for their traditional institutions, and the institutions have become, in the absence of any other, the signpost of ethnic identities, hence, the growing demand of communities to have their own...with all its due privileges and paraphernalia.[10]

The Kataf in southern Kaduna, for example, had consistently complained of their subordination to "alien" traditional political institutions which had often taken critical decisions affecting their means of livelihood, while at the same time excluding the participation of their own traditional institutions.[11] According to the Dasuki Committee Report, a traditional ruler is "the person who by virtue of his ancestry occupies the throne or stool of an area and who has been appointed to it in accordance with the custom and tradition of the area and has suzerainty over the people of that area.[12] Going by their historical colonial antecedents, several indigenous ethnic nationalities could never be emirs in many emirates in the general Middle Belt area. These have given rise to the "indigene" versus "settler" phenomenon in several of its communities. We will return to this problematique later.

Thus, the struggle to re-establish cultural and ethnic identity, which is linked to issues of self-determination, have become conflict generating over the years. The competition to acquire political power by those outside and the determination to hold on to it by those inside, have become fiercer as the stakes get bigger. The stakes being the due privileges and paraphernalia attached to the traditional institution, which have been increased in recent years by the military. Thus, a community which could not boast of a prominent "son or daughter" or a powerful chief virtually was not part of the powerplay that determined government action. Traditional rulers increasingly became the centres of influence and power over local governments. It has become fashionable today to find retired top military officers and public servants jostling for traditional offices and titles. Local tensions which otherwise could have been managed often escalate because of elite intervention and manipulation.

The "settler" versus "indigene" conflict type has become associated with the North-Central Zone or even the wider cultural Middle Belt. This phenomenon or syndrome, as it is variously labelled, is characterised by "the dichotomy and pathological mistrust" between those who regard themselves as indigenes on the one hand, and settlers or non-natives, on the other. According to Awa, "the problem of the indigene is one of the most intractable forces militating against national integration" yet, as he notes further, "we condemn statism while embracing warmly the value which gives rise to it."[13] While studies show that few groups can be regarded as authoctonous in Nigeria today, the fact is that certain ethnic nationalities have come to be identified with definite territorial locations. Citizenship in the Nigerian Constitution is defined biologically, not socially. So the phenomenon of indigenes versus non-indigenes has become dominant in controlling group relations, in defining identity and in acquiring greater shares of public resources and status.

Closely tied to this problem are the federal and national questions. Federalism by its very nature is a compromise mechanism that allows sub-national units to maintain their individual identities within the supra-national union. How in this context does one balance what Ochoche regards as "historical and primordial claims with citizenship rights and obligations?"[14] To what extent can the historical realities be wished away even if the position is accepted that "all migrated". As the argument goes today, the flip side says there were first arrivals. How does the state balance the dynamics and demands of nationhood with its past and internal contradictions? What is becoming increasingly evident is that integration cannot be legislated into being. There are no shortcuts, yet governments have consistently chosen this path and so conflicts keep erupting around these issues. The Jos crisis of September 7, 2001, is a good case in point. The contradictions and inconsistencies in government policies and actions have served to fuel these crises. As Ochoche noted, "many violent conflicts in Nigeria are basically protestations or rejections by people of unacceptable or unfavourable government policies"[15] We will now turn our attention fully to our case study as it is a direct fallout of the kind of governmental action noted above.

The Bassa and Egbura Communal Conflict

The Egbura and Bassa Communities occupy Toto and Doma LGAs of Nassarawa state. The Bassa and the Egbura have been living together in the past. However, the Bassa claim that the Egbura have been given chiefdoms while the Bassa and Gbagyi who are in clear majority have none. The Egbura claim that the Bassa are settlers. The Egbura are spread in areas north and east of the confluence of the Niger and Benue Rivers. They are, therefore, found in Kogi, Edo, Nassarawa, Niger and the FCT. The Bassa who also claim ownership of the area are domiciled also in the FCT, Niger and Kogi. But principally, they are found in Toto Local Government Area (LGA) of Nassarawa State and Koton-Karfe and Bassa LGAs of Kogi State. In Kogi, they are known as the Egbura-Koto and Bassa-Kwomu. Whenever conflict occurs between the groups in Nassarawa it usually spills over into their kith and kin communities in Kogi State, and vice-versa.

The first serious clash between the Egbura and Bassa occurred in 1986 and others have followed up until 1998. In 1986, there was an agitation for the change of title of the traditional head of Toto District following the death of the *Ohinoyi* of Toto by other ethnic groups who felt marginalised in the traditional arrangement. They also wanted the title to be rotated among the ethnic groups. The Bassa who are in a majority in the Toto Local Government (80%) also claim to be indigenous to the area. Yet they do not have traditional autonomy which chiefdom would have bestowed on them. The Egbura who are next to them in terms of population have the traditional stool of *Ohimege Opanda* whose occupant is paramount head of the Egbura and chairman of the Toto Traditional Council. But for the Egbura it is not a matter of numbers. According to a spokesman of the *Ohimege Opanda:*

> Traditional institutions world-wide are not essentially democratic. In fact not even in England, the homeland of civilisation. The Buckingham Palace is not run on democratic principles. This is why no matter the numerical strength of Igbo in Lagos, they cannot produce an *Oba,* so also the Hausa in Fagge cannot produce an *Obi.*[16]

At the same period (1987) disagreement over the appointment of an Egbura man to the post of *Sarkin Kasuwa* (Head of Market) to succeed another Egbura man who died, led to a bloody battle, where 72 people lost their lives. That incident occurred over the headship of a market located at Umaisha in the former Plateau State (now Nassarawa State). The head of that market was an Egbura, while his deputy was Bassa. Upon the death of the market leader, his deputy who was Bassa was disallowed from succeeding him. This was despite a previous agreement between them, which provided for rotational headship. The situation degenerated into ethnic conflict.

In August 1994, at Okpareke village in Koton-Karfe LGA, Bassa-Kwomu indigenes began to boycott the village market and others in the surrounding areas. Their action was said to be sequel to "an alleged discriminatory attitude of Egbura people towards the Bassa-Kwomu, who were regarded as second class citizens..."[17] In 1994, another incident occurred, again in Nassarawa State but with the usual spill-over effect on the ethnic groups in Kogi State. In that year, women of both ethnic tribes had a disagreement over the fetching of water at a communal pond at Ojah/Toto in Nassarawa State. It degenerated to such a level where market men and women refused to sell wares and articles to members of the "opposing" group, even in markets located throughout Koton-Karfe in Kogi. Subsequent to this and as a result of the ethnic tension already generated, a Bassa-Kwomu masquerade on an outing chased a boy right up to a mosque. An Egbura-Koto who came out to challenge the armed masquerade shot his challenger on the arm. "The situation degenerated rapidly to another confrontation that resulted in loss of lives and destruction of property. This was in Nassarawa State. However, displaced persons became refugees in Bassa and Koton-Karfe with the attendant security and socioeconomic consequences."[18]

There was a similar occurrence in 1995, this time at Oguma, headquarters of Bassa (Kogi State). A Bassa-Kwomu masquerade (*Genge*) attacked a man with his machete. The victim turned out to be an Egbura-Koto. The situation rapidly took a turn for the worse with heightened ethnic tension as the Egbura threatened armed confrontation should the victim die. Around 13 November 1997, there was another confrontation between both ethnic groups in Toto. This ostensibly was a revenge attack traceable to the Bassa claim that they sustained heavier losses during the 1995 crisis.

The 1997/98 clash was the bloodiest as it saw the introduction of sophisticated arms and the use of mercenaries. Over 3,000 people were killed and more than 100,000 Bassa displaced and eventually forced to live as refugees in at least 6 states (Oyo, Kwara, Niger, Kogi, Ondo and the Federal Capital Territory) as they still had cause to fear for their lives within the state. Their villages had been sacked and their houses razed to the ground. The villages most affected were listed as Umaisha, Ugya, Kenyehu, Shaga, Shekarnku, Kuwa, Kokulo, Shishigheneshi, Rakpani, Bakate, Dumbeku, Risagu and Shafa-Abakpa. Among the weaponry recovered at various sites were axes and daggers, dane-guns, single barrel shotguns, live cartridges, live ammunition, a bullet waist belt.[19]

Field Survey
The state government undertook a massive resettlement programme in 2000 to take the displaced Bassa back home.

In the history of Toto Local Government Area of Nassarawa State, no single ceremony has attracted as much dignitaries as the one held on July 3, to welcome home an estimated 100,000 refugees of the Bassa tribe.[20]

Barely a year later, the Bassa have again had to flee their homes. In fact, in the course of this study the present writer was strongly advised against visiting the area as the level of insecurity was very high. An "orgy of inter-ethnic violence and mindless bloodbath" was witnessed in June, 2001, as a series of sporadic ethnic crises again engulfed Nassarawa State. This time between mainly Tiv and Alago communities. As usual, this had its ripple effects throughout the state as several people were caught in the crossfire. One of these was a prominent Bassa. Given the uneasy peace and mutual suspicions between the Bassa and Egbura, the former hastily interpreted the incident to be the signal to another onslaught by their perceived enemies. In the confusion and fear prevalent in the entire state at the time, the Bassa felt insecure and again fled the camps. Their fear was reinforced by a previous experience wherein government was unable to protect them. This was the state of affairs when our field trip was undertaken. There was evidence of deep fear and suspicion on both sides.

The fresh outbreak of hostilities again turned the Bassa into internal refugees, causing a major setback to the government's resettlement efforts. They have taken refuge in mostly undisclosed locations for fear of further attacks. Indeed students interviewed at one of the higher institutions in the state still would not talk freely. Both Bassa and Egbura youths expressed fears of the investigator being linked with either ethnic group. It took two months of trying before the present writer could gain their confidence with the help of a lecturer whom they trusted. We eventually engaged an assistant, whom we made sure was from a different ethnic community, he was from Toto Local Government. Of the 50 questionnaires distributed, 23 were returned with respondents still expressing fears of being traced.

Other information was gathered from oral interviews and discussions held with the students earlier referred to, and others who had been involved in mediation efforts (both government and non-government). From the responses to the questionnaires the 4 ethnic communities that make up Toto Local Government could be identified as Gade, Bassa, Egbura and Gbagyi. Of these, the Bassa have the largest population followed by the Egbura, then the Gbagyi. In their responses, the Gade and Gbagyi held similar views to the Bassa on most points. The only distinguishing factor between their responses was the ethnic community with which respondents identified. Neither age nor occupation accounted for any difference.

Causes of the Conflict

The major issue of contention as seen by majority of respondents was land ownership and others flowed from that. The Bassa claim to be indigenous to the area and, therefore, the owners of the land. They felt the Egbura, aided by government in the creation of chiefdoms, was cheating them of their birthright. Whereas the former Plateau State government (out of which the present Nassarawa State was created) had granted the Egbura two chiefdoms, the Bassa and other communities, particularly the Gbagyi, were given none. Various government panels set up to look into the grievances of the Bassa and others recommended the creation of districts for these other groups within the local government. These were ignored.

The first major violent conflict as confirmed by most

respondents, occurred in May, 1986, while the last was 26 June, 2001. While the Bassa attributed the former incident to the creation of chiefdoms for the Egbura, the latter they attributed to the refusal of the Egbura to the resettlement programme started in July, 2000. Curiously Egbura respondents unanimously claimed that the last violent incident was recorded in February, 1988, resulting from the Bassa denying them access to their (Egbura) land. They made no mention of the 2001 incident in which the Bassa alleged armed attacks against them by the Egbura. The discrepancy in these accounts may be attributable to the deep fears the Bassa have of the Egbura through which they filter all their experiences. Independent sources link the second dispersal of the Bassa to the Tiv/Alago crisis earlier mentioned.

Effects of the Conflict
As to the effect of the conflicts on their communities, the Bassa cited the following: the scattering of their people into five states and the Federal Capital Territory; the separation of family members; and increased poverty among their people. Added to these, their people became landless, and a cheap source of labour to the communities in which they took refuge. Further research revealed the host communities to be as far-flung as Osun and Ondo states where they joined other migrant labourers to work in cocoa plantations. Further inquiries revealed that it was not uncommon to find migrant labourers from the Middle Belt on these farms. The Gade mentioned the hike in food prices and decimation of the able-bodied population, or "inadequate manpower", as one respondent put it.

The Egbura response unanimously cited inadequate food supplies, costly food prices and population decline. The Gbagyi on their part reiterated the scarcity of food and farm products, separation of communities, poverty, vandalisation of property and other assets; absence of peace, and untold deaths. The Egbura, Gade and Gbagyi communities were those left behind while the Bassa fled and this accounts for the effects they recounted like shortage of food supplies. Despite the varying shades of emphases emanating from the groups, it is clear that the overall effect of the conflicts between the Bassa and Egbura in Toto is untold destruction and devastation of lives and sources of livelihood.

Without peace, the experts say, there can be no development. This is the consequence of the repeated conflicts on the affected communities. Since 1998, there has been no developmental project undertaken in the area. The uneasy situation imposed this condition. In fact, the government took a decision to withhold the provision of social amenities and services while the crisis lasted. The area could not participate in any election as no voter registration exercise could take place there. At present, a caretaker committee runs the local council.

Government Intervention

If it is the responsibility of government to provide a secure environment, this being the milieu within which citizens can both pursue and attain the good life, then the question may be asked as to what has been the role of government in settling this conflict? In the social contract entered into between citizens and the state, the latter is responsible for providing security to lives and property and maintaining law and order. It is also to restore it in case of breach or breakdown, as is the case where violence occurs. Government is also responsible for ensuring equitable distribution of public goods and justice to aggrieved citizens. In this regard, our survey also sought to assess government involvement in our case study. The role of government is considered at the three operational levels of government in the Nigerian federation; that is, federal, state and local.

While respondents agreed that government did intervene, it fell short of expectation. Successive governments had set up several panels of inquiry (5 in all), in addition to the measures taken to restore law and order. Their recommendations were, however, either ignored or implemented in part only, and not followed through. One that stands out is the recommendation on the creation of chiefdoms in which only the Egbura benefited. When later, chiefdom was created for the Bassa, the Egbura sued the state government and the case is still pending in court. Even this move came well over a decade since the first violent outburst. The inability of the civilian government to carry through its grand resettlement programme earned it a rating of "ineffectiveness".

The state of security was one in which the two main protagonists in this conflict could not be trusted to stay together without a strong security presence to keep or enforce the peace while government implemented whatever policies it had adopted. The weaponry allegedly employed and the extent of killing, put by government sources at 3000 people,[21] had left, particularly the Bassa, in a state of fear. Some of the Gbagyi youths interviewed confirmed these fears as did Gade respondents to the questionnaires. In their view, only a strong security presence and action would be effective in managing the conflict. Indeed, they say no other alternative and no role for other agencies apart from government security organs.

Despite the fact that the resettlement programme was the initiative of the civilian government, the Bassa did not rate this effort any more higher than that of past military government. The case with which they were dislodged from their camps was, to them, a failure of the government effort. Their hope now, they say, is the federal government. The local government has not featured much in this crisis because it has been almost non-existent.

Assessment
The Nigerian State particularly under military rule has largely lost its credibility before its citizenry on several fronts whether economic, political or social. As concerns conflict management particularly, it has been implicated: "in one way or the other official governmental inquiries ... either by their content, or the manner of their implementation or non-implementation, have themselves become ready fuel for more conflicts around the country".[22] Nigerian elite has often directly or indirectly influenced policy decisions particularly in land disputes and chieftaincy matters. As democratic space shrunk under military authoritarianism, other centres of power or influence became increasingly relevant, especially the traditional institution (as discussed earlier). It, therefore, became in some cases, easy to discard the collective will of the local communities involved. The deployment of security forces or application of other legal means of redress was often tainted by these elite manipulations (both in and out of office).

In the conflict between the Bassa and Egbura, panels of inquiry seemed to serve no useful purpose in the final analysis; neither did the security apparatus of the state. In fairness, however, this does not necessarily indict the communities or the security outfits themselves but the general policy framework within which government (whether state or federal) deals with conflict. In the main, its emphasis has been on control rather than prevention, and even at that, control as crisis management. This has meant that once the emergency is over, the given conflict seems to move further down the priority agenda. This is the case with the Bassa- Egbura conflict, and it is also replicated nationwide.

Successive governments in the state have displayed what may be termed a lack of staying power or perhaps political will to carry through their policies. The 2000 resettlement programme has since collapsed; the case brought by the Egbura against government is still in court; the local government is run by a caretaker committee as democratic elections are yet to be held; no voter registration has taken place there because the displaced population is yet to return home; the ban on developmental activities is yet to be lifted. These are mostly actions which only government can expedite or implement.

Civil Society Intervention

There are steps which government either cannot undertake, or it is not best suited to undertake. The formal bureaucracy through whom government must necessarily operate is not well tailored to engage in the grassroots or community actions that sustain conflict resolution. It is not equally well organised, in the case of prevention, to monitor conflict indicators or generate early warning on a continuous basis. To what sector of the society do we turn? In the words of Kofi Annan, UN Secretary General, "there are few limits to what civil society can achieve".[23] [Jusu-Sheriff, 2001: 2]. The changes in Eastern European and the wave of democratisation in Africa are largely credited to civil society interventions. More specifically, so also to a considerable extent, the progress achieved in resolving the two major conflicts in West Africa over the past decade. In all these cases civil society moved to fill in the gaps left by the state. Civil society has also recorded numerous successes as regards developmental projects at grassroots level.

In the Bassa-Egbura conflict, civil society has made attempts to intervene with varying degrees of effectiveness. Apart from the usual and immediate humanitarian services offered by religious groups and the Red Cross, other long-term interventions have been attempted. The resettlement programme as we found out, was initiated and nurtured up to a decisive point by a Kaduna-based non-governmental outfit, Strategic Empowerment Management Agency (SEMA). As progress was made with the two communities, government then stepped up its interest to the point where an "Abuja Accord" was reached. However, ostensibly to gain maximum political mileage, government dominated the process thereafter. Perhaps this explains the rush associated with executing the programme and the elaborate reception event. After the cameras left, the communities were left to nurse the effects of broken promises. The compassion they had earlier felt evaporated as old bogeys of manipulation were raised. The·Egbura felt government was biased in favour of the Bassa while the Bassa felt let down by government.

Nevertheless, this initiative had sought out and consulted with the disputants and stakeholders at various levels, away from the public glare and the attendant pressures this brings to bear. Another third party intervention effort was undertaken in July, 2001, by a USAID/OTI-sponsored conflict resolution outfit, Centre for Peace Initiative and Development (CEPID). This offered essentially, mediation training for the stakeholders themselves. Its strength, therefore, lay in reopening channels of communication and empowering the conflicting parties to resolve their differences themselves. This is the task of post-conflict peace building which is a long-term and continuous process. It can only be sustained if the stakeholders own the process. An earlier intervention by a foreign government agency had resulted in a peace committee being formed. This group seemed to loose momentum as the state government took over the process. At present there are indications that some civil society organisations are interested in reinvigorating the committee.

Limitations
These interventions, laudable as they are, had their limitations mostly because they are externally-imposed. Apart from government interest, which is usually seen as coming to negotiations with a position, the point of entry into the conflict by civil society organisations and the distance of these organisations from the theatre of violence also affected the sustainability of commitment brought to the process. Another obstacle was funding. The costs of

overall conflict management and in particular post-conflict peace building are prohibitive even for government. The aborted resettlement was projected to cost well over two billion Naira. For reasons of credibility, non-governmental mediators have avoided government funding at least at the early stages. Most funding has, therefore, come from foreign donors. The experience in this regard indicates that foreign donors usually prefer rapid response initiatives to avoid appearing like an alternative government and to allow them the flexibility to move onto other projects.

Way Forward

All said, the strength of civil society participation in a communal clash lies in its propensity to encourage community action and ownership of the processes of reconciliation. Immediate stakeholders like community and religious leaders, elders, community-based associations, women and youth groups, are offered a non-threatening platform to work out their differences. In Toto Local Government, the Bassa are mostly the farmers while the Egbura are the traders and artisans. From a purely economic point of view, the one needs the other's market and goods. Besides, they have traditionally lived together sharing the same socio-cultural space. In Kogi State, where their kith and kin are also found, they live coterminously. So also in the Federal Capital Territory and wherever else they are found.

While civil society is being encouraged to initiate and sustain the processes of dialogue and understanding and even some measure of developmental activity, government needs to redouble its efforts in certain areas. These are law and order issues, generating good policies, and ensuring justice and equity in sharing communally owned resources and privileges. Without these, no peace building effort would be sustainable and of lasting effect. One major challenge, though yet to be seriously considered, is that in a democratic government there are communities that remain totally disenfranchised and, therefore, voiceless. This has closed up to them the avenue for non-violent conflict resolution which democracy offers. For as Zartman asserts:

> Even though an aggrieved group is not in charge of governance, the fact that it can compete for election and can

make its voice heard through representatives in coalition, or even in the opposition, transfers conflict from the violent to the political arena... Multiparty competition converts violent conflict to politics and multiparty representation gives minorities and their causes an officially recognised voice. *There is no magic in this conversion*; political competition may be almost as debilitating for national governance as military conflict... But the political process contains a potential that can long be pursued (emphasis mine).[24] [Suberu 1996: 77]

Conclusion

Nigeria seems to be in a season of crisis. If this season is not to become a permanent feature of the polity, civil society must be empowered to be more proactive in governance and public decision making processes, and more specifically, in conflict management processes. For one, government capacity in this regard is limited on intellectual and institutional fronts. Secondly, democracy is people-propelled governance and so relies for its effectiveness on citizens' initiative and participation. Unless the beleaguered and battle-weary communities of Toto Local Government are actively engaged in finding a workable solution to their problems, the cycle of violence is likely to continue. Peaceful coexistence is a process borne out of everyday choices and not the product of a one-time government action. While appropriate governmental policy and action would facilitate the process, community initiative and participation is vital to sustaining it.

References

1. S.A. Ochoche, "An Overview of Conflicts in Nigeria". Paper presented at a national workshop on Strategies for Enhancing Peaceful Coexistence in Nigeria, organised by the Centre for Peace Research and Conflict Resolution, National War College, Abuja, March 9-10, 1999.
2. International IDEA, *Democracy in Nigeria: Continuing Dialogue*, 2001, p.282.
3. *Ibid.*, p.378.
4. C.I. Logams, *The Middle Belt Movement in Nigeria's Political Development: A Study in Political Identity* (Ph.D. Thesis. University of Keele, 1985). See also Middle Belt Progressive Movement (MBPM), *Official Documents*, 2000

5. International IDEA, *op.cit.*, p.282.
6. *Ibid.*, p.282.
7. *Ibid.*
8. J.G Yoroms, "Dynamics of Ethnic and Religious Conflicts in the Middle Belt of Nigeria". Paper presented at a workshop on Ethnic and Religious Conflicts in the Middle Belt of Nigeria, organised by the Human Rights Monitor, Jos, December 15-16, 1999, p.4.
9. *Ibid.*, p.5
10. See "Report of the National Workshop on Strategies for Enhancing Peaceful Coexistence in Nigeria", organised by the Centre for Peace Research and Conflict Resolution, National War College, Abuja, March 9-10, 1999, p.4.
11. Samuel G. Egwu, "Ethnic/Communal Conflicts and Internally Displaced Population: The Case of Zango-Kataf in Southern Kaduna". Paper presented at the methodology workshop on the Study and Management of Communal Conflicts and Population Displacement in Nigeria, organised by the Pan-African Centre for Research on Peace and Conflict Resolution (PACREP), Enugu.
12. See S.A. Ochoche, *op. cit.*, .14.
13. Quoted in *ibid.*, p.9.
14. S.A. Ochoche, "Issues and Strategies in the Evolution of a National Early Warning System in Nigeria". Paper presented at a national seminar on Conflict Indicators and Early Warning Mechanism in Africa, organised by the institute for and Conflict Resolution, Abuja, July 18-19, 2001, p.18.
15. *Ibid.*, p.18.
16. Quoted in *Newswatch*, Lagos, July 17, 2000, p.14.
17. This is from a classified source.
18. *Ibid.*
19. *Security Report* (classified).
20. Reported in *Newswatch*, July 17, p.17.
21. *Ibid.*, p.21.
22. S.A. Ochoche (2001), *op. cit.*, p.
23. Yasmin Jusu-Sheriff, "The Role of West African Civil Society in Conflict Management and Peace Building". Paper presented at the conference on Towards a Pax West Africana: Building Peace in a Troubled Sub-Region. Jointly organised by the

International Peace Academy and ECOWAS, Abuja, September 27-29, 2001.

24. Quoted in Retime T. Suberu, *Ethnic Minority Conflicts and Governance in Nigeria* (Ibadan: Spectrum Books, IFRA, 1996), p.77.

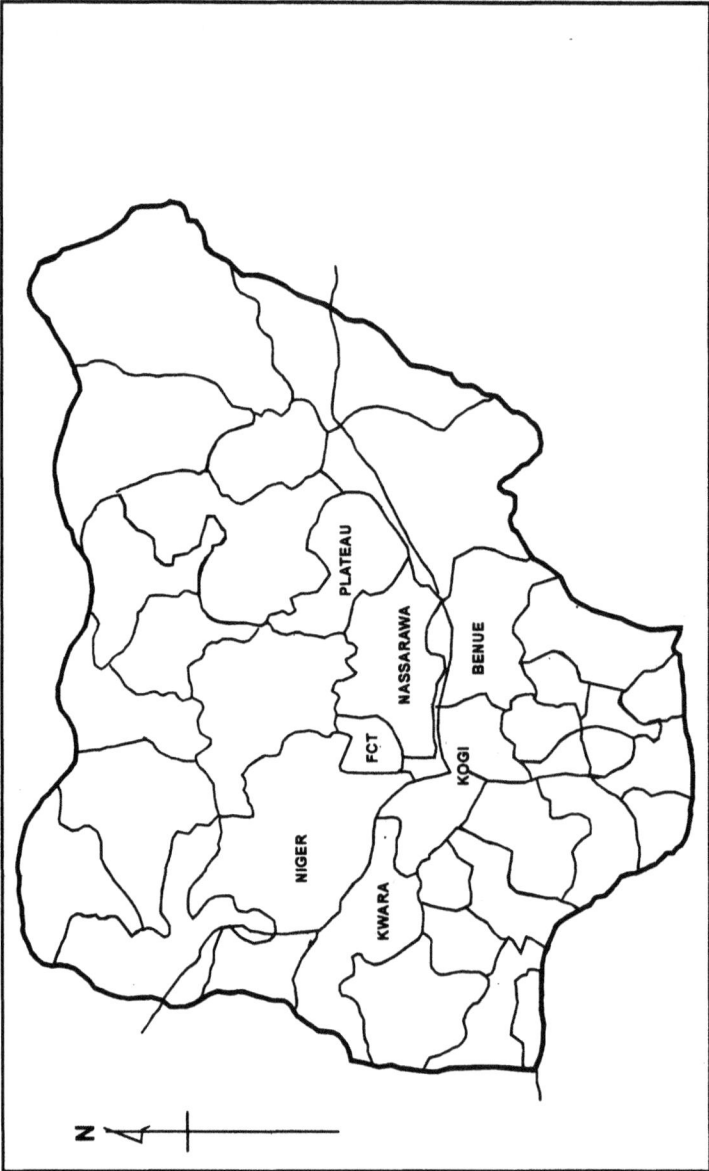

MAP OF NIGERIA SHOWING THE NORTH-CENTRAL ZONE

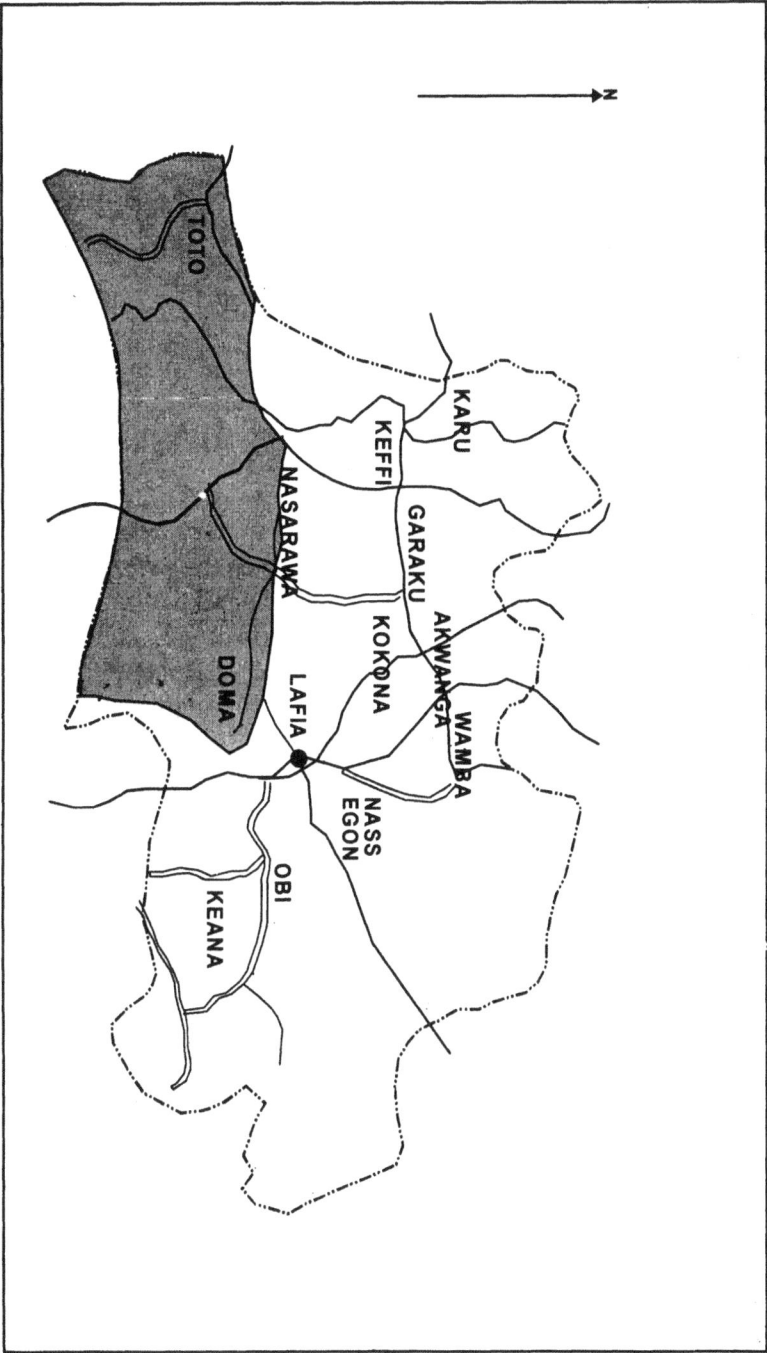

MAP OF NASARAWA STATE SHOWING THE STUDIED AREA

Chapter 6

The Hausa/Fulani-Sayawa Conflict in Bauchi State

K. Leonard Fwa

Introduction

Civil unrests of various dimensions and characters have been a recurrent factor in Nigeria's historical development before and since the attainment of independence in 1960. These unrests have expressed themselves in different forms, political, religious, communal and social. No matter their specific character, each of these crises could be described as a classic study in violence. They have exacted heavy toll on life and property (both public and private), enormously tasked the collective energies of the security forces, profoundly exposed the fragile legitimacy of successive governments while at the same time arousing understandable fear and doubts about the sustainability of Nigerian nationhood.

Three major conflicts occurred in the Tafawa Balewa Local Government Area in 1991, 1995 and 2001, which left many people dead and widespread destruction of property. The conflicts spread with ferocious intensity into the state capital, Bauchi, and other towns of the state and even beyond. This chapter will examine the nature and character of the ethno-religious crises in the Tafawa

Balewa Local Government Area of Bauchi State. It will attempt to discuss the causes of the conflict and the various responses. The paper will also advance the role of civil society as a new innovation for success in managing the conflict.

History and Background (North-East Zone)

The North-East Zone of Nigeria is very heterogeneous. It accounts for nearly half of the estimated 300 or more ethnic groups in the country. Although a plethora of religious faiths are practised in the region, the people are predominantly Christians and Muslims. There is no unanimity on what the North East region of Nigeria is. Most inhabitants of the area do not see themselves as north easterners. The confusion of identity arises from the region's ethnic heterogeneity and religious diversity. The current six states of Adamawa, Bauchi, Borno, Gombe, Taraba and Yobe that make up the North-East have a combined population of 11,907,122 (1991 census) and an area of 107,862 square miles (279,363 square kilo metres). The region shares international boundaries with the Republics of Niger, Chad, and Cameroon to the north, northeast and east, respectively.[1]

Because the North-East Zone is characterised by cultural and religious diversity, there is always the tendency for minor disagreement between individuals with different ethnic and religious background to flare up and assume a wider ethno-religious dimension. Some prominent individuals within the society usually exploit this diversity to promote their selfish interests. In most cases, minor conflicts are blown out of proportion and made unduly sensational. Some leaders and opinion moulders whip up sentiments and over-politicise issues using the media. Not only has this compounded such crises; it had led to reprisal action in other parts of the country. In dealing with any crisis in this zone, therefore, the objective must always be to achieve understanding, compromise and consensus as the best way to assuage feeling flared up by religious and ethnic considerations.

The other basic characteristic of this zone is the high rate of poverty and unemployment. The most affected segment of the population is the youth, who have become readily available materials for use as armies of destruction by disgruntled elements in the society. The presence of an army of jobless youth has raised the level of violence attendant to conflicts in this zone, as we shall see in the case study discussed in this chapter.

Bauchi State
With an estimated population of over 3.8 million (2001 projected) and total land area of 49,259 square kilometres, the state is made up of twenty local governments, among which are Alkaleri, Bauchi, Bogoro, Dambam, Darazo, Dass, Gamawa, Ganjuwa, Giade, Itas-Gadau, Jama'are, Katagum, Kirfi, Misau, Jama'are, Ningi and Dass. Though the emirates existed in history as independent entities, there was a high degree of co-operation and interrelationship among them, particularly when Bauchi State was created in 1976. Generally, the over 25 ethnic groups in the state live together peacefully. The disturbances in Tafawa Balewa and Bogoro Local Government Areas, though horrific and devastating, do not necessarily classify the state as one of the violent ones in the country. It will interest one to realise that, even in Tafawa Balewa and Bogoro Local Governments, the generality of the citizens are peace loving and law abiding.

Tafawa Balewa and Bogoro LGAs
Tafawa Balewa and Bogoro Local Government Areas are situated at the rocky southern part of the state. The total land area of the two local governments is 2,770 square kilometres. According to the 2001 population projection of the area by the National Population Commission, the population of Bogoro LGA is 62,350 while that of Tafawa Balewa LGA5 is 178,115. The two local governments are inhabited by the following ethnic groups: Fulani, Hausa, Jarawa (including Bankalawa), Sayawa, Sidawa, Tapshin (Angas/Bijin), Zaksawa and Banshawa. These ethnic groups are found in political settings referred to as village areas. The Sayawa ethnic group constitutes about 80% of the population of Bogoro Local Government, while in Tafawa Balewa Local Government Area, the Sayawa tribe constitute about 30%.

According to "Historical and Geographical Notes on the Tribes of Bauchi Province", published by W. Morgan, in a memorandum to the Secretary to the Northern Provinces, this area consists of three districts, namely, Lere, Bogoro and Bula. The people of Lere are mainly Hausa/Fulani who migrated to the area from Zaria before the Jihad of Usman Dan Fodio at the beginning of the 19th Century. When Yakubu Bauchi conquered the area he found Sarkin Lere a dependable ally and allowed him to continue administering the area. Bogoro is the head town of the Sayawa who claimed to arrive the area from Ngazargamu in old Borno Empire. They settled in Dazara, a small village in Boi area before reaching Bogoro. The people of Bula District also traced their history to the old Borno Empire. Two Fulani brothers arrived the area from Borno and settled at Wuro Mayo. The Jarawa, however, constitutes the majority tribe in Bula District.

Lere District was the most prominent district in the area. *Sarkin* Lere was allowed to administer the land, which covered a wide area spreading to the boundaries of the present Plateau State (i.e. Pankshin, Barikin Ladi, Kanam, Dengi and Jarawa District). It covered the whole area, which is today known as Tafawa Balewa and Bogoro Local Government Areas. The Chiefs of Boi and Bogoro had their appointments confirmed by *Sarkin* Lere. Initially, there was only one district in the area — the Lere District. The Bula District was excised in 1926, while Bogoro District was created in 1976. This brief history is necessary for one to understand the complexity of ethnicism in this relatively small area.

Analysis of the Survey and Assessment of the Communal Disturbances

The civil disturbances in Bogoro and Tafawa Balewa Local Government Areas, generally referred to as the Tafawa Balewa crisis were more ethnic and political than religious. The disturbances could be traced to the struggle for traditional administrative control of the area between the Sayawa who are predominantly Christians, and the Hausa/Fulani/Jarawa who are predominantly Muslims.

The agitations of the Sayawa ethnic group started as far back as 1948. A Sayawa activist, Baba Peter Gonto, masterminded the first revolt, challenging the authority of the Bauchi Emirate Council over the area. The emirate council had been exercising political control over the area through the appointment of district head for Lere. Tafawa Balewa town was a hamlet under Wai Village of the district. It never had a Sayawa man as head of the hamlet. Between 1970 and 1976, the Bauchi Emirate Council conceded to the agitation for political relevance by the Sayawa and successively appointed two Sayawa gentlemen as district heads of Lere. The last one was later posted to Bogoro to head the new district that was created in 1976.

With the creation of Tafawa Balewa Local Government in 1976, the Sayawa became more aggressive in their urge for administrative/political control of the area, particularly Tafawa Balewa town. Over the years they mobilised themselves and settled at the outskirts of the town, while also procuring plots of land and houses within the town itself. The Sayawa agitations against their marginalisation became louder. The Zar Cultural Association was the umbrella body for the Sayawa cultural and political activities. In September 1977, some Sayawas who were not satisfied with the decision of appointing a Hausa/Fulani as district head of Tafawa Balewa protested. The disagreement between the parties resulted in the death of the district head. That is what ignited the ethnic animosity in the area. The issue became more complicated with the involvement of religious organisations. Tafawa Balewa town thus became the centre of the dispute.

The 1991 Crisis

On 20 April 1991, violence broke out in Tafawa Balewa Local Government Area of Bauchi State between Muslim Hausa-Fulani and mainly Christian Sayawa peoples. The crisis produced enormous casualties and extensive damage to public and private property. The violence, which quickly spread to Bauchi metropolis, Dass and Ningi Local Government Areas, was the most intense since the Maitatsine incident in Jimeta-Yola in 1984.

To a large extent, the authorities appeared to have been caught unawares. The pervasive wave of communal violence in the 1980's had appeared to be on the wane, prompting President Ibrahim Babangida in his 1990 Christian message to describe the trend as "a matter for joy".[2] That joy turned out to be merely ephemeral for within less than four months Katsina and Bauchi were caught in the grips of widespread civil disturbances.

The Bauchi wave of the disturbances generated such degree of apprehension and anxiety in government circles that the Federal Minister of Information, Chief Alex Akinyele, desperately appealed to media houses to play down the riots. This is understandable. The Bauchi incident was coming only three days after the suppression of a similar incident in Katsina. Coming fast on the heels of the opening of the ninth National Sports Festival in Bauchi, the crisis was seen as capable of incensing collective national sensitivity. The minister's appeal was largely heeded by the government media but ignored by the private press.[3]

According to observers, the immediate cause of the unrest was a disagreement over sale of roasted beef (*Tsire*) prepared under apparently unacceptable Islamic precepts and sold by the Christian hawker to an unsuspecting Muslim customer. However, such a seemingly innocuous incident appeared insufficient to generate such a major confrontation if not for pre-existing tension between the communities in the local government area. Some of such potential issues of conflict included the joint use of the public abattoir, the sharply divided loyalties between predominantly Christian supporters and the largely Muslim sympathizers within the local government areas and worsening economic situation in the country among others.

Fighting broke out at the public abattoir on 20 April, 1991, between Sayawa and Hausa/Fulani and quickly came to involve sympathizers along religious lines as word spread round Tafawa Balewa and its environs. Throughout the day, only feeble attempts were made by the police to put down the unrest. By the following day, April 21, the orgy of violence was intensified as more and more Sayawa descended on Tafawa Balewa from the outlying villages. A security committee meeting of the local government called by the chairman on that same day had come too late to avert the catastrophe.

By the afternoon of April 22, at about 4.00pm, corpses started arriving at the Bauchi Specialist Hospital. By nightfall, thousands of Muslim sympathizers started gathering in the Emir's palace chanting *Allahu Akbar*. Before long, Muslim rioters, armed with cudgels, knives, cutlasses, containers with petrol and other dangerous weapons descended on Bauchi town in a determined feat of vengeance.

Churches were among the earliest targets. Pastor.Heman Vila, vice-chairman of the Bauchi State branch of the Christian Association of Nigeria put the estimate of burnt churches at well over thirty-five. On Hospital road alone about twenty churches were reported razed. A similar fate befell hotels, beer parlours, and residential houses belonging especially to non-indigenes. In the Bayangeri quarters alone, at least fifteen hotels were reportedly burnt down.[4]

Many non-indigenes fled to Jos to escape the mayhem. There are conflicting estimates of human casualties. According to *Citizen*, more than three hundred corpses were transported from Tafawa Balewa alone to Bauchi. *Newswatch*, quoting police sources, put the death toll at about three hundred and fifty, while mortuary sources were quoted to have recorded five hundred. The *African Concord* also quoted a figure of five hundred deaths. Official sources, however, claim total death toll to be only eighty-four.

As the crisis assumed an alarming rate, on 23 April, Governor Ali made a broadcast to the people of the state and in addition gave a separate address to traditional and religious leaders. He announced the imposition of a curfew from 7.00pm to 6.00am and assured that all those involved in the riot would be brought to book. On that same date, April 23, the federal government, anxious for the quick restoration of peace, ordered the 23 Armoured Brigade of the Nigerian Army to step in and quell the disturbances. The intervention of the army was accompanied by rumours making the rounds that policemen and soldiers deployed to curb violence were indiscriminately arresting and killing Muslims. As the rumour mounted the Emir of Bauchi, Alhaji Adamu Suleiman, was pressured to make a representation to the military governor requesting the withdrawal of all soldiers and policemen from the streets and to release those unjustifiably arrested and an assurance from the government for the guarantee of the people's safety.

Following such assurance by the governor assembled rioters made moves to disperse accordingly. The security forces mistaking such moves to be a resumption of the riot opened fire on the people. Following another security council meeting on 25 April, Police Mobile Force (PMF) Units and soldiers were withdrawn and normalcy returned soon thereafter.

According to our source, the 1991 mayhem was precipitated by the woeful performance of Hausa-Fulani candidates in the local government elections. Sensing that they had lost grip of power in the area, they decided to throw the town into confusion to create a situation of anarchy. The motive was to stop a Basayi man (Sayawa man) from heading the local government. That was the reason why they went and hired people to attack the Sayawa.

Horrendous dividends were reaped from the 1991 crisis. Determined to bring the conflict to an end or possibly to a manageable level, the federal government instituted the Justice Babalakin Commission of Inquiry. One of the highlights of the memorandum submitted by Hausa-Fulani from Tafawa Balewa was a call for the dissolution of the Local Government Executive Committee. Sayawas, on the other hand, called for the creation of chiefdom for them if lasting peace was to be guaranteed. The commission recommended the dissolution of the council and the creation of chiefdom for the Sayawas. The government council headed by Mr. Habila Lumana objected to the creation of chiefdom for the Sayawas. This unfair method of political engineering, we gathered, was the cause of carnage in Tafawa Balewa.[5]

The 1995 Conflict

The appointment of one Ibrahim Shanumwa, a Hausa resident of Tafawa Balewa as a commissioner with the Bauchi State Government, and the planned party to celebrate the appointment was the cause of this conflict. The indigenous Sayawa people saw an ulterior motive in staging the party in Tafawa Balewa town and not in the commissioner's original home area of Gukeru in Alkaleri LGA. Moreover, their anger was worsened by the Local Government Council's decision to surcharge all civil servants, through forced deductions of their salaries for the planned party, the native Sayawa then mobilised themselves to stop the party from being held.[6]

On July 1, 1995, the day of the party, women demonstrated against the party. The atmosphere became tense and the party had to be called off. As the women were dispersing, (according to some informants), the organisers of the aborted party resorted to beating and stoning the women, and many were wounded, the Sayawa reacted and then war started with several people killed.

The Hausa/Fulani in turn started killing the Sayawas in the outskirts of the town. At Zango, 17 women were killed in the church on July 3, 1995. At the secondary school of Bununu, over 30 students were killed. Many properties were destroyed. Before these two episodes, uneasy peace had existed between the Hausas and the native Sayawa in Tafawa Balewa over traditional power being held by the Hausas who had migrated and settled in the town. The Sayawa had challenged this and wanted the situation reversed, but to no avail.

The 2001 Crisis

The launching pad for this crisis was a Sayawa youth protest against the implementation of Sharia legal system in Tafawa Balewa, and it followed the same pattern as the previous crises. On 15 June, 2001, the youths under the banner of Zar (Sayawa) Youth Association had staged a demonstration in Tafawa Balewa town against the implementation of Sharia legal system in Tafawa Balewa Local Government. The youths were reported to have gone round the town chanting anti-Sharia slogans and writings on the walls of buildings. They came to the residence of the Local Government Council chairman and there, by coincidence, they met the village head of Bununu (a Bajari). They were said to have mistaken him for a Sharia court judge, molested him to the extent of tearing his gown and pulling down his turban. Later, the demonstrators dispersed, and there was peace and calm in the town. The commissioner of police dispatched half-unit of mobile police to the area. In the morning of 16 June, 2001, Hausa/Fulani Muslim youths in Tafawa Balewa town also staged a pro-Sharia demonstration in Tafawa Balewa town, which was said to have ended peacefully..

There were, however, reports that the Hausa/Fulani residents of Tafawa Balewa were moving out of the town on the rumour that the Sayawa were planning to attack them. However, on 18 June, 2001, reports came in that houses and places of worship were being burnt in Tafawa Balewa and some villages on the outskirts of the town. A number of people were killed, some inside the central mosque of Tafawa Balewa. The incident later spread to many other towns and villages of Sayawa, Hausa/Fulani and Jarawa across the local government areas of Tafawa Balewa and Bogoro. The police strength was immediately increased with reinforcement of mobile police from neighbouring states.

Although, the Sharia legal system had not come into force at the time of the Zar youth demonstration, the decision by the state government to embrace Sharia legal system in a multi-ethnic state informed the demonstration and the subsequent crises. In order to facilitate the return of normalcy in the areas, the state government constituted two reconciliation committees: Resettlement and Compensation Committee and a Relief Committee. A judicial commission of inquiry was instituted which is yet to submit its report. The process of reconciliation has been greatly facilitated by the President, Federal Republic of Nigeria during his state visit to Bauchi in September, 2001, when he met with leaders of the two disputing communities.

Spread and Level of Destruction
The history of Tafawa Balewa is a story of a people's quest for self-determination: the struggles, the travails for chiefdom separate from the Bauchi Emirate. Prior to the crisis of April 22, 1991, the name Tafawa Balewa was only associated with Nigeria's first prime minister, Alhaji (Sir) Abubakar Tafawa Balewa. The crisis of both 1995 and 2001 exposed the community as a zone of death. By whatever dimensions, the crisis has constituted a national disaster in the sense that, it resulted in the loss of lives and property, breakdown of law and order, and has also led to the heightening of religious sentiments, which has today constituted a serious form of threat to the corporate existence of the nation.

The nature of weapons used in the crisis is an indication of how loose the nations' security system is. If ex-service men could be allowed to own devastating weapons such as machine guns and other forms of arms, then the security of the nation remains threatened. The claim that only locally made weapons were used is only an undercover. Eyewitness accounts had it that rifles and guns were mainly responsible for the heavy casualty.

Closely related to this is the role played by the police and members of the armed forces. Although some people argued that the role of law enforcement agents was impartial and effective, from investigation, it was found that facts and exhibits were brought before the Justice Babalakin Commission of Inquiry showing that law enforcement agents actually contributed to the shooting of innocent civilians during the disturbances. In fact, an eyewitness and a victim actually confirmed that he narrowly escaped death after being shot by some soldiers and/or mobile policemen. This witness showed the commission the x-ray of the bullet still buried in his body and the wound of the bullet on his body. Also in 1995, traces of the machine guns and ammunition used were said to have their source from these law enforcement agents.

Whatever be the case, involvement of law enforcement agents could be described as most unfortunate, in that they should be seen as neutral, apart from being fair and firm in dealing with both parties to the conflict. The picture remains blurred on the direction the nation's security is facing. Since the state security service has a record of chronology of the events that had been occurring in Tafawa Balewa Local Government Area as far back as 1967, one would be forced to ask the question: Why is it that state security service could not detect and possibly abort the breakdown of law and order as a result of the 1995 crisis? This, on its own, shows a very big lapse in the security system of Bauchi State which automatically is a replica of the nation's security system.

Though from evidence available, the crisis is more of ethno-political than religious, but the dividing line among the Sayawas who are predominantly Christians and the Hausa/Fulani Muslim population gave the crisis religious intonations. The implication of this to the nation as a whole is the tendency to divide the country along religious lines whereby both groups see themselves as enemies of one another. This has resulted in sectional loyalties against the unifying policies of the nation. Hans Morgenthau in his book *Politics Among Nations: The Struggle for Power and Peace*, talks extensively on supra-sectional loyalties among ethnic groups within a country, their expectations for justice and some ethnic groups' overwhelming power in the society, both economically and politically. He believes that violence is associated with all societies that are advancing positively. People are supposed to learn from their mistakes and as such the 1991 crisis was supposed to have served as a lesson. Thus, the recurrence of 1995 and 2001 crises have shown that the people have not learnt from their mistakes and possibly found solutions to their problem. Regrettably, these conflicts are triggered and cemented by the ruling elite who used religion for their political gains.

One of the widespread attitudes towards these violent communal conflicts, especially in the immediate aftermath of the bloodshed, the arson and other situations, is that these are just the result of madness by those involved. It is often said, that the brutal killings of non-combatant human beings, particularly children and women, by burning them alive and cutting them up with knives and cutlasses, and gunning them down as they run away, and the destruction of vehicles, buildings, livestock, crops and all physical assets, which took place in these conflicts, are the outcome of some unleashed irrational forces, which defy logic, or, any sensible mode of explanation of human behaviour.[7]

The perpetrators of this violence, on both sides, and even the actual planners, do not appear to gain anything tangible beyond the satisfaction of eliminating an "enemy". But, in any case, this elimination has also involved the destruction of some of the key human and material assets on which the economy of the community, no matter how inequitable, rests. The dispossession, exclusion and alienation, which marked the situation of many of the perpetrators of this violence, are not brought to an end by the orgy of destruction. The wisdom in the old adage of, "everybody should be his or her neighbour's keepers", comes back to haunt the perpetrators.

Having eliminated their neighbours, they often find that it becomes much more difficult to keep their body and soul together. For, where families have lived as neighbours for years, even if not for generations, the elimination of the members of one family by members of the other, in these violent communal conflicts, leaves wounds in the psyche of those involved, which are in most cases not obvious, but are often said to be mentally and emotionally far-reaching.

Nevertheless, in spite of all these consequences of violent communal conflict, there are people always organizing and executing them. This does give some groups the view that the whole thing is a result of some irrational forces, beyond rational explanation. But when tribunals and commissions of inquiry investigate these conflicts, their findings, based on clearly stated and reliable evidence, are that these irrational forces, whatever significance they may have for particular individuals, do not provide an adequate explanation for the conflicts. The evidence shows that these conflicts are the results of calculations, planning, organisation and execution, which within the perspective of those involved, are rational and logical. That is, these people had tangible, identifiable material, political, and other non-material basis for their action and used this violence to seek to attain concrete political, economic and other goals. But, of course, we can only be sure when the federal government brings together all these reports, assesses, compiles and analyses them to see what lessons are to be learned.

Formal Efforts at Managing and Resolving Conflicts
In view of the persistence of conflicts in the North-Eastern Zone, it is logical to review strategies that have been used to address such conflicts in the past, and why such efforts have not been quite successful. Lessons from this may be found useful in developing new initiatives for dealing with current problems. The methods that are generally used have been discussed in chapter 4. These include:

1.   The institution of administrative and/or judicial commissions of inquiry;
2.   The instrument of state and local government creation;
3.   The use of soldiers to quell violent clashes; and
4.   The use of peace/reconciliatory fora

As we have indicated in chapter 4, these methods have their values and limitations. In particular, we have noted the lack of political will on the part of government to implement the recommendations of commissions of inquiry and decisions emanating from the numerous peace fora summoned to reconcile the parties in conflict. The lack of government decisiveness in the use of sanctions to ensure compliance with jointly worked-out decisions tends to perpetuate hostilities between parties in conflict.

Some of these factors have been responsible for the persistence of the disturbances in Bauchi. From our field survey, it was found that one issue that has been responsible for the recurrence of the disturbances in the state has been the fact that the masterminds who instigate, mobilise and arm the rioters, even in cases where they had been clearly identified, were never punished. For instance, the vicious masterminds of the 1991 riots, clearly identified by the Federal Judicial Commission of Inquiry, were allowed to go scot-free.

The Role of Security Agents
The intervention of government and security agents in violent communal conflicts is expected to be based on the fundamental principle of neutrality, fair play, transparency and genuine commitment to reconciliation. However, in the Tafawa Balewa disturbances, allegations of partisanship on the part of government

officials and security operatives have been rife. In fact, accusing fingers were pointed at the police officers that led the operations. The Tafawa Balewa experience tends to point to the fact that security agents are capable of taking sides with sections of the society based on their cultural or religious affinity.

The roles of the security agents in the management of the Hausa/Fulani-Sayawa conflict in Bauchi cannot be examined based on the insinuations and supposition about the alleged partisanship of the security operatives. For instance, our respondents all agreed that the police were able to bring the situation under control within the Tafawa Balewa town and its environs which was the central theatre of conflict. However, by the time the dynamics of the conflict assumed a wider proportion in Bauchi township and military response became necessary to stem the tide of hostilities, the insinuation was that the security agents used excessive force against the largely Muslim perpetrators, and this could have been interpreted as a harsher response, leading to charges of partiality and so on.

However, security agents should always be judged based on the specific objective of their intervention at each level of the conflict; their participation should be judged by the exigency of each operation as some of the issues surrounding the Tafawa Balewa crisis tend to suggest that deterrence responses in the wider interest of national security tended to have informed the role played by the military. It is normal under the constitution for the military to come to the rescue where the police had either failed to perform adequately, or proven to be grossly incapable of dealing with civil insurrection.

There is no doubt that it is the police that have the main responsibility for the maintenance of internal security. Although calling the military is not the ideal thing, it is the inability of the police to play this constitutional role for whatever reason, that has made military intervention in civil disturbances inevitable. The increasing use of sophisticated weapons in communal conflicts has further complicated the efforts of the country's internal security apparatus to cope with the incessant outbreak of communal violence. The porosity of the country's borders, a phenomenon that is particularly pronounced in the South-East Zone, has made it possible for weapons to be illegally brought into the country. The unprecedented destruction of lives and property in the Tafawa Balewa crises has been attributed to the illegal acquisition and use of weapons.

What the present situation depicts is that with increasing complexity of the communal conflicts afflicting the country, it will be increasingly difficult for the official security agents to cope with their management without the involvement of civil society. For instance, on the disturbing issue of small arms proliferation, the involvement of traditional and community leaders is necessary if we are to effectively check, not only the illegal importation but also, the massive local manufacturing of these weapons.

The Role of Civil Society

Civil society is used here to refer to the realm of organized social life that is voluntary, self-generating, (largely) self-supporting and autonomous from the state, usually bound by a legal order or set of shared rules. It is distinct from "society" in general in that it involves citizens acting collectively in a public sphere to express their interest, passions, ideas, exchange information, achieve mutual goals, make demands on the state, and hold state officials accountable. Civil society is an intermediary entity between the private sphere and the state. Thus, it excludes individual and family life, inward looking group activity e.g. for recreation, entertainment or spirituality, the profit making enterprise of individual business firms and political efforts to take control of the state.[8]

Civil society encompasses a vast array of organizations formal and informal. These include economic and productive groups and commercial associations, as well as cultural, religious, ethnic community associations. It comprises those institutions and associations that defend collective rights, values, faiths, beliefs and symbols. It also includes informational and educational organisations devoted to the production and dissemination whether for profit or not of public knowledge, ideas, news and information. In addition, civil society encompasses independent mass media as well as institutions that belong to the broader field of autonomous cultural and intellectual activity such as universities, think tanks, publishing houses, theatres, film production companies and artistic networks that are concerned with public rather than private ends. Civil society also relates to the state in some ways but does not aim to win formal power or office in the state. Rather, it seeks from the state consensus, benefits, policy changes, relief, redress or accountability.

The role of civil society in the Hausa/Fulani-Sayawa conflict in Bauchi State has been a recent phenomenon. On the whole, what could be referred to as civil society are the two religious bodies, namely, Christian Association of Nigeria and the Jama'atu Nasril Islam whose roles have been criticised by both conflict parties on the basis of partisanship. From the response we gathered, the involvement of the civil society does not translate to any meaningful role in the state.

In the fragile socio-political environment of Bauchi, the efforts of NGOs, secular and religious groups, at organising reconciliation activities, open community meetings, and other activities for free and transparent public exchanges between the parties in conflict have not met its desired goal due to illiteracy, poverty and over-reliance on the government and the power-wielding elite. Hardly are decisions of the people taken into consideration when it matters. We must emphasise that, the most desirable outcome, for a country and its people, is the prevention of conflict. Where conflict has nonetheless occurred, the work of reconciliation has to be done. Reconciliation means bringing people to have faith again in civil institutions, in justice and in the rule of law.

In addition to buttress our point, we observed with dismay that traditional rulers and the youth organisations in Bauchi and Tafawa Balewa have failed to use their positions in creating avenues for compromises and consensus-building among the people. After all, it is customary that such grave and contentions issues as those dividing the warring communities are among the issues that are generally settled in palaces of traditional rulers. Yet such good offices remained unutilised. Because the traditional rulers did not rise to the occasion, the elite who feed on these ethnic and communal conflicts as local champions had a field day.

In a recent paper presented by the governor of Bauchi State, he condemned the activities of the elite group, which composed of the vocal educated few who had exposures in different capacities in and outside governments. They generally command respect and influence in the community, and have political ambitions. They are opinion leaders who play a significant role in the information flow channel in the community. They claim to lead the community towards a struggle for political emancipation. Their roles and utterances are generally provocative, and they abound in both opposing groups in Bauchi and Tafawa Balewa Crises.

He also commented on the unfortunate role of the youth. According to him, like in other communities in the country, the youths in Bauchi and Tafawa Balewa are prone to violence. They are generally unemployed, frustrated, poverty-stricken village boys and girls. They are the instruments used to execute and perpetrate the crises to the extent desired by the elders and the elite. At times they tended to get out of control of the elite and the elders. At the end of it all, they form the majority of the casualties of the crises.

In the final analysis, lasting reconciliation must be built on forgiveness. This, therefore, underscores the role of the civil society. Revitalising civil society entails the promotion of local associations, community participation, and peer accountability. It reduces the level of individual fear, enables the collective censure of violence and promotes local security. While the role of civil society groups in the conflict studied in this chapter is minimal, the potentiality for greater civil society involvement is high and any effort towards building a strong foundation for civil society involvement in conflict management will be worth the while.

Conclusion

The magnitude/scale of destruction in the communal conflicts between Hausa/Fulani and Sayawa in Tafawa Balewa makes it very necessary and urgent for some non-formal crisis management strategies to be mapped out. The role of civil society is very important. However, the mere existence of these groups is not enough to make things work. The civil society groups need to be developed to be able to put the state activity in check. Although, there is a deluge of these groups in Nigeria, they are still weak and lack commitment. Unless they are restructured and designed to face the challenges, they may not do wonders in crises management in Nigeria.

References

1. International Idea, "Democracy in Nigeria: Continuing Dialogue for Nation Building", in *Capacity Building Series*, 10, 2000.
2. V. Elaigwu, *The Military and Management of Civil Crises in Nigeria 1960-1993*, Ph.D. Thesis submitted to the Department of History, University of Jos, March 2001, p.273.
3. *Ibid.*, p.274.
4. *Ibid.*, p.275.
5. U.O. Fabian, "Conflict, Nationalism, and the Path to Peace", in *Ethnic and Religious Rights Quarterly*, Vol.1, No.1, 1999, p.15.
6. J. Dung-Gwon, "Tafawa Balewa, Bauchi State", in *Human Rights Monitor*, Nigeria, 2000, p.44.
7. Yusuf Bala Usman, "The Violent Communal Conflicts in the Central Nigeria Uplands and the Middle Benue Basin in a Historical Perspective". Paper presented at the Presidential Retreat on "Peace and Conflict Resolution in some Central States of Nigeria", NIPSS, Kuru, 24-26 January 2002.
8. Larry Diamond, *Restructuring Civil Society Towards Democratic Consideration* (Lagos: United States Information Service, 1995).

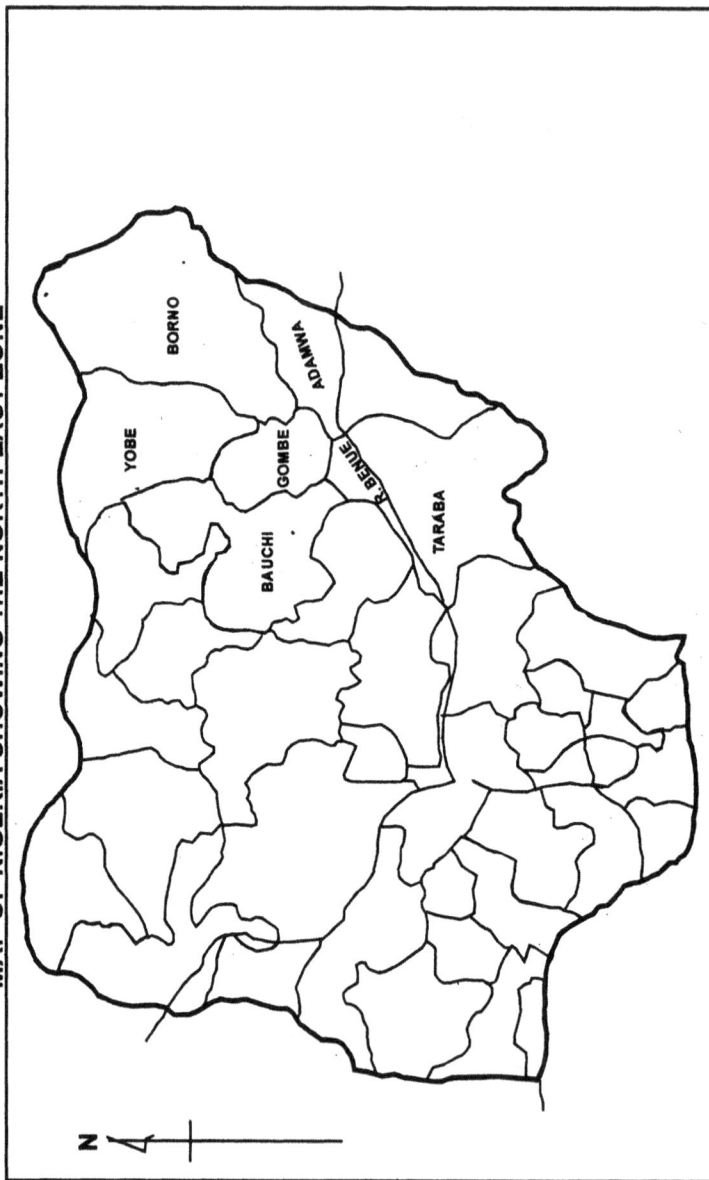

MAP OF NIGERIA SHOWING THE NORTH-EAST ZONE

MAP OF BAUCHI STATE SHOWING THE STUDIED AREA

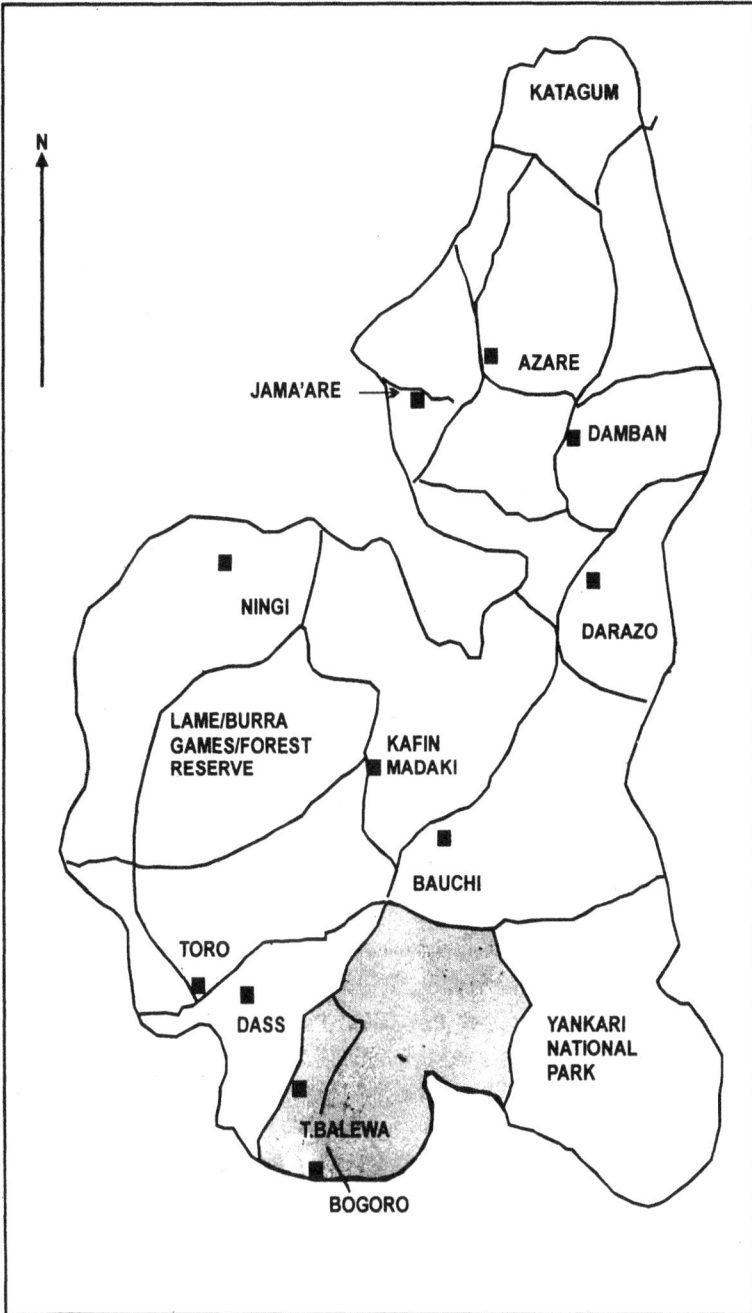

Chapter 7

Ife-Modakeke Conflict in Osun State

Babajimi Peters

> ...The Ife-Modakeke crisis is a peculiar Yoruba problem
> approximately one hundred and thirty years old since it started
> around 1893. Like a volcano, it erupts but not with any
> predictable regularity. Each particular manifestation changes
> character from some earlier forms...[1]

Introduction

Ife, which is at the centre of the communal conflict being discussed
in this chapter, is situated in Osun State in the South-West Zone of
Nigeria. The South-West Zone is made up of six states, namely,
Ekiti, Lagos, Ogun, Ondo, Osun and Oyo. The zone is traditionally
inhabited by one of Nigeria's three largest ethnic groups, the Yoruba.
The Yorubas have strong cultural affinities and beliefs. They trace
their origin to Ife, which many of them regard as their cradle and
the place where "God created man". So, Ife is very important in
Yoruba history. This strong Yoruba attachment to their culture has,
however, been tainted by the spread of Christianity and Islam into
the region. Christianity penetrated the South-West through the
coast, while Islam came in by land through present-day Kwara and
Kogi states. Among the Yoruba people, there is relative
intermingling of the people's traditional culture and the two
imported cultures of Islam and Christianity. In fact, it is not

uncommon to have adherents of the different religions within the same family. However, although the South-West Zone is said to be homogeneous, the Yorubas have been known to have fought a number of wars amongst themselves. What it means is that their homogeneity has not fully translated into harmonious relationship amongst themselves. In other words, the region does experience conflict and hostilities from time to time.

Conflict Profile in the South-West Zone
Being relatively homogeneous, the phenomenon of ethnic conflict in the South-West Zone has tended to be more of intra-ethnic than inter-ethnic. However, over the years, people of other ethnic identities have settled in the South-West, especially in such urban centres as Lagos, Ibadan, Oyo, Shagamu, Ogbomosho, etc., as to increasingly turn the region into what looks like a multi-ethnic zone. This phenomenon-has led, in recent times, to incidents of inter- ethnic hostilities in the region. Examples include the clashes between Yoruba and Hausa communities in Shagamu, Ogun State, in July 1999 and in Idi-Araba, Lagos State, in February, 2002.

Since independence in 1960, the major source of conflict in the South-West Zone has been political. The zone has had a history of violent resistance against the imposition of unpopular leaders through election rigging and other political malpractices. For this reason, the zone acquired the name "wild, wild west" during the First Republic. Operation *"wetie"*, was the popular local name given to the violence that swept through the entire zone in the 1960s. It led to an unprecedented destruction of lives and properties. The zone again in 1983, witnessed widespread post-election violence during the Second Republic, which was terminated by a military coup in December, 1983.

One other major source of conflict in the zone is chieftaincy dispute. In Yorubaland, apparently because of the high esteem in which traditional rulers are held, there is usually bitter rivalry between the so-called ruling houses to occupy vacant stools. Instances abound where the battle for succession has torn many families and communities apart. A most recent example is the Owo incident, which up to the moment of this write-up, has not abated.

Another common source of conflict within the zone is land/ boundary dispute, usually brought about by the creation of new local government areas or states. Recent pressure on available land due to population density and increasing migration of livestock herdsmen to the south in search of grazing land has led to isolated incidents of confrontation between farmers and pastoralists in this area.

While inter-ethnic conflict would remain a phenomenon of the presence of different ethnic enclaves in the urban centres, intra-ethnic conflict is likely to remain a major concern in the zone due to the steady growth in sub-ethnic consciousness. Two factors are responsible for this. First, there is a conscious effort by politicians to deliberately cultivate sub-ethnic consciousness within their communities to serve their selfish ends. Flowing from the first observation, there is now increasing clamour for separate kingdoms, where they never existed before. The case study in this chapter - Ife-Modakeke conflict appears to have some of the attributes highlighted above.

Background to Ife-Modakeke Conflict

The Ife-Modakeke conflict is a very complex conflict, which helps to explain in part, why it has proved very difficult to resolve peacefully. It has erupted under both colonial and indigenous rule, as well as during military and civilian governments. The crisis revolves around three major contending issues. These are the status of the Modakeke community itself, the request of the *Ogunsu*a of Modakeke to wear a beaded crown, and the relocation of the headquarters of the Ife East Local Government headquarters from Modakeke to Oke-Ogbo.[2]

However, both communities have their own reasons for the conflict. The Modakeke, on the one hand, have identified five major ones. These are:

1. Non-recognition of Modakeke as a separate town;
2. Relocation of the Headquarters of the Ife East Local Government to Oke-Ogbo in Ile-Ife;
3. The use of derogatory language against Modakeke such as *"Oyo pe"*;
4. Forceful ejection of Modakeke from their village and the confiscation of their farmlands by the Ifes;
5. Non payment of salaries to *Ogunsua* and his chiefs since 1997.

The Ife, on the other hand, have identified seven major causes of the conflict. These are:

1. Non-recognition of *Oluaye*, the *Ooni* of Ife by the Modakekes as the supreme and paramount ruler of Ife land;
2. Arrogating undue authority to the *Baale* of Modakeke by proclaiming him as an *Oba* and his appointment of *Baales* in Ife villages;
3. The killing of Ife landlords by the Modakekes and forceful acquisition of their land coupled with annexation of land that does not belong to them;
4. Refusal to pay tribute (*Isakole*) by the Modakekes;
5. Daily radio propaganda, jingles, and advertisement most especially on Osun Radio suggesting that all Ife areas belong to Modakeke;
6. Removal of "Ife" inscriptions from the various sign posts or boards in Modakeke;
7. Some highly placed individuals such as Chief Arisekola Alao and Alafin of Oyo as backers of Modakeke.[3]

These views were backed up by the answers provided in the questionnaire that was sent to members of both communities.

Over the years, many thousands of lives have been lost and property worth millions of naira destroyed as a result of the crisis escalating into a conflict situation. In addition, various attempts have been made, over the years, to resolve it. The government has set up commissions that include a peace committee set up by Osun State Council of Obas in 1998 and a Presidential Conflict Reconciliation Committee set up by the federal government in March, 2000. Various Non-Governmental Organisations (NGOs) have also attempted to assist in peace-building efforts. One of the most prominent in this area is Academic Associates Peace Works (AAPW).[4]

In spite of the fact that the Ife-Modakeke crisis erupts into violent conflicts ever so often, not much academic work has been done on the subject, especially on the role of civil society groups in the management of such conflicts. This study is predicated on four hypotheses. One, conflicts such as these are exacerbated because of the inability of civil society to intervene decisively at the early stages. Two, ethnic conflicts are likely to be more amenable to resolution when non-formal actors handle them. Three, civil society, if properly mobilized, can be used as a vehicle for managing ethnic conflicts in Africa. Four, civil society has far more scope in preventing conflicts and in promoting post-conflict peace-building than in the actual resolution of full blown conflicts.

According to Albert, the three possible ways of reacting when a conflict erupts in any society are: to avoid or refuse to acknowledge that the situation exists, confront the problem with the apparatus of state violence or simply to acknowledge that there is a problem and adopt a problem solving attitude. This is where NGOs and Community-Based Organisations (CBOs) can be very useful. According to Albert:

> Problem-solving refers to the situation in which the parties to the conflict, either by themselves or through the assistance of a third party find solutions to a problem in a cordial environment.[5]

In the context of the Ife-Modakeke crisis, of course, it will be unwise to adopt either the first or second option. The best way to resolve the crisis is to forge a partnership between the government and community-based organisations, on the one hand, and NGOs, on the other. It is rather obvious that the government alone cannot solve the problem because of distrust as a result of policy flip flops, especially under military regimes. NGOs do not have the same kind of credibility problem that the government suffers from. However, they lack adequate funding to carry out their activities.

The Birth of Modakeke
It is impossible to understand the crisis without a clear idea of how the Modakeke people found themselves in Ife. Two questions are therefore very central to an understanding of this issue. One, what is the relationship between Ife and Modakeke peoples? Two, what is the relationship between Ife town and Modakeke? The relationship, according to historians, began in the 19 century. J.F.A. Ajayi and S.A. Akintoye explain that "for the Yoruba people, the 19th Century was a period of intense and dramatic changes. The political troubles at old Oyo culminating in the collapse of the Oyo

Empire, the evacuation of the capital, and the mass movement of Oyo people southwards, set in motion a chain of events which came to leave its impact on every part of Yoruba land.'[6] They argue that the events of this period dramatically changed the political and demographic landscape of the region.

Although the Yorubas claim to have all descended from Oduduwa with Ile-Ife as their spiritual home, Robert Smith nevertheless argues that the Yoruba nation has never operated as one single political entity.[7] That notwithstanding, their language and their common beliefs in certain myths and legends point to their common origin and cultural heritage. It was the strength of the Oyo Empire and the spiritual leadership of Ife that provided political stability in Yoruba land. However, towards the end of the 18th Century, the authority of the *Alafin* of Oyo began to diminish with deep divisions between him and his chiefs. This led to a series of wars in Yoruba land and pressures from external powers that took advantage of the situation to make further inroads into Yoruba land. For example, the Hausa-Fulani, with Ilorin as their base, wanted to make further in-roads into Oyo Empire. They had taken over Ilorin from Afonja, who had sought assistance from them to sustain his revolt from the *Alafin* of Oyo. The Hausa/Fulani later killed him and took control of Ilorin.

These wars led to a massive displacement of peoples fleeing the carnage. Ajayi and Akintoye explain that the "dislocations caused by the pressure of this mass of people, the ambition of uprooted peoples led by their more warlike chiefs to find new homes and opportunities, provoked a series of wars in the central and southern areas of Yoruba land, with far reaching consequences".[8] Some of these refugees fled to, amongst other towns, several Ife towns; like "Ikire, Apomu, Gbongan, Ipetumodu and Ile-Ife itself". These refugees worked for Ife chiefs on their land for grants of land and some served in the army helping Ife to expand its frontiers.

However, this period of expansion was short-lived. The consequences of the revolt by Ife and Oyo peoples of Ibadan cut the ascendancy of Ife short. Ibadan, because of the influence of an Ife warrior, Okunade, was seen as an extension of Ife. In the ensuing conflict between the Ibadan and Ife, Ife came out the loser. The refugees in Ife began to be looked upon with suspicion. There was social and political unrest between the two communities. Thus, the

Oyo refugees got themselves "together in self-defence at a new settlement on the outskirts of Ife, called Modakeke".[9] The Ife tried to destroy the settlement, but did not succeed.

In 1886, after the *Kiriji* war, a peace treaty was signed between the *Alafin* of Oyo and chiefs from Ibadan, Ilesha, Ekiti, Ife, Modakeke, Ijebu and the colonial governor of Lagos. Article 5 of the treaty made provision for the relocation of Modakeke from Ife. The provision stated that:

> In order to preserve peace, the town of Modakeke shall be reconstructed on the land lying between the Osun and the Oba rivers to the north of its present situation and such of the people of Modakeke as desire to live under the rule of the *Baale* and *Balogun* of Ibadan shall withdraw from the present town to the land mentioned, at such times and in such manner as the governor his envoy or messenger shall direct after conference with the governments of the parties principally concerned, and such of the people as desire to live with the Ifes shall be permitted to do so but shall not remain in the present town of Modakeke, which shall remain the territory and under the rule of the King and chiefs of Ife, who may deal with the same as they may think expedient.[10]

However, the treaty was never implemented and, indeed, according to some reports, could never have been implemented. Apparently, the *Alafin*'s messenger, Obakosetan, had objected to this particular article, but was overruled by the colonial authority. Also, it is claimed by the Modakeke people that they did not sign the peace treaty.[11] However, Akintoye maintains that "the Modakeke, though reluctantly, endorsed the treaty in the end."[12] Olunloyo explains that there was a loophole in the clause 5 which ensured that the Modakeke people could not be forced to leave Ife. However, under the reign of *Ooni* Adelekan, *Olubuse* 1, the Ife managed to send Modakeke people out of Ife town. They left for such places as Edunabon, Apomu, Ode-Omu, Orile-Owu, and other Ife villages.[13] *Ooni, Oba* Ademiluyi later recalled these people who were seen as a source of cheap labour on the farms and also helped to swell the population of Ife so as to enhance his revenue base.[14]

The Status of Modakeke

Given the circumstance that led to the birth of Modakeke, its status and that of its people has always been a source of dispute and conflict. First, is the issue of landlord/tenant relationship. Aligned with this is the matter of *isakole* (land rent) which it is argued the Modakeke refused to pay. Second, is the issue of indigene/non-indigene and by extension the problem of citizenship. The first point to note is the fact that both the Ife and Modakeke are Yorubas who claim a common lineage from Oduduwa. In other words, as Olunloyo rightly points out, they are kith, kin and kindred.[15] But, Ife being the cradle of the Yorubas is older. Modakeke being a creation of the many wars the Yorubas waged amongst themselves in the 19th Century is, therefore, much younger.

However, as Chief Awolowo explains in his autobiography, "the Yorubas paid lip-service to a spiritual union and affinity in a common ancestor Oduduwa. But in all their long history they had waged wars against one another...the mutual hatred and acerbity which was attendant upon them lingered..."[16] Robert Smith corroborates this when he wrote that Yoruba land: "never constituted one single political entity; their very name was one not used originally by themselves but by their Hausa neighbours with reference to the northern group among them, the Oyo (from whose name it perhaps derives), and then given wider application by the Christian missionaries in the 19th century."[17] So in essence, the setting for this most protracted of conflicts in Yoruba land is provided by the very history of the Yoruba people.

It is clear that the Modakeke people came to Ife as refugees and were initially well received by their Ife hosts. According to Sabiru Biobaku, the Modakeke:

> ...came originally to Ile-Ife as refugees from the Jihadists wars of the early 19th Century, especially after the fall of the Oyo Empire in 1837. When their numbers began to swell, the *Ooni* Abewala (1839-1849) (whose mother was believed to be daughter of one of the refugees) gave them land to build a suburb of their own from lands belonging to the Iraye, Obalejugbe and Fegun families, known as Modakeke, so-called after "the cry of a nest of storks on a large tree near the site there in Iraye chanting Mo-da-ke-ke." Thus, came about the sixth quarter in Ile-Ife, along with Iremo, Okerewe, Moore, Ilode and Ilare; with its *Baale*, starting with the *Ogunsua*, who

was supported by other war chiefs of Modakeke. The *Ooni*
could create a quarter, but the ownership of the land on which
Modakeke stands remains with the Ife families of whom they
were tenants. Friction was inevitable.[18]

This position is even confirmed in the testimony given by His
Royal Highness *Oba* Adegoke Akunraledoye, the *Apetumodu* of
Ipetumodu during the sitting of the Presidential Conflict
Reconciliation Committee on Ife/Modakeke.[19]

Even the Modakeke people do not dispute the fact that they
were not the original owners of the land since they accept the fact
that they were displaced Oyo people. Barrister Goke Akinrotimi in
his presentation before the presidential committee said that: "in
1840, the *Ooni* Abewela, the reigning *Ooni* then granted the
settlement of the displaced Oyo people outside Ile-Ife. He said the
then Oyos are Modakeke".[20] What they dispute is whether
Modakeke was allowed to be a separate town or not. Historical
fact does not appear to side them on that particular point.

The Issues Surrounding the Status of the *Baale* of Modakeke
This is a very contentious issue. The Modakeke community believe
that the *Baale* of Modakeke should be given the status of an *Oba*.
They argue that under the Oranmiyan Chieftaincy Declaration of
1978 of Oyo State, the *Baale* of Modakeke is the third in rank to the
Ooni. However, they maintain, "while other *baales* had been
upgraded it was only *Baale* of Modakeke that had not been
upgraded with a beaded crown". Furthermore, they claimed in their
memorandum to the presidential committee that salaries of Ife
Chiefs in towns and villages were spelt out in a letter dated 23rd
October 1946 and Ipetumodu and Modakeke were the only two
towns in Ife area while others were regarded as villages.

Whilst the Ife argue that you cannot have two *Obas* in the same
town. They maintain some of the actions that the Modakeke people
have taken show that they do not recognize the position of the *Ooni*
of Ife. For example, they alleged that the Modakeke have illegally
installed *baales* for all the villages in Ife. Furthermore, it is alleged
that the Modakeke reject a situation whereby the *Ogunsua* would
receive his staff of office at Enuwa palace from the *Ooni* of Ife. In
1998, a peace committee was set up by the Osun State Council of
Obas to proffer solutions to the Ife/Modakeke crisis. They,

apparently, appealed to Modakeke to soft-pedal on the issue arguing that "violence cannot give *Ogunsua* any crown."[21]

The Location of Ife East Local Government Headquarters

On 17th March, 1997, the federal government announced a list of newly created local governments in the country. The old Oranmiyan Local Government was broken into three local government areas. One of the three was the Ife East Local Government Area with headquarters in Modakeke. However, the headquarters was later relocated to Oke-Ogbo. This location was supposed to be a "neutral" place between the two communities. However, the Modakeke community did not accept the new location of the headquarters because, as far as they are concerned, Oke-Ogbo is not a neutral place, but a part of Ilode ward in Ife.

The issue of a separate local government for the Modakeke community is a long-standing one. Isaac Olawale Albert explains that this agitation began in 1957, but they did not receive the support of the Action Group, which was the dominant party in the Western Region, led by Chief Awolowo. The reason he quotes Chief Awolowo as saying was because, "Ife town was one town and the request for a separate local government council for Modakeke amounted to an attempt to divide a single town."[22] It should be borne in mind, however, that Chief Awolowo was solicitor for the Ife community in their dispute with Modakeke.

The violence that followed led to the wanton destruction of property and loss of lives and it was carried out by the youths of both communities. As the *Tell* magazine of September 1, 1997 reported: "Angry youths from both sides had undoubtedly hijacked their leaders who had to toe the line in order not to be seen to be betraying 'the cause'."[23] *The News* magazine, also of September 1, 1997, corroborated the decisive role of the youths in escalation of the crisis into a conflict situation. It wrote that "the immediate cause of the violence is the counter-protest by Ife youths against the calls by the Modakekes that the headquarters of the newly created Ife East Local Government be relocated to their domain." "Ife youths", it went on, "enraged by the affront on their monarch and the bellicose attitude of the Modakekes, challenged their audacity the next day when they protested against any government plan to placate their neighbours".[24]

Various Efforts at Finding a Peaceful Solution.

All the major attempts at resolving the Ife-Modakeke crisis have been undertaken by the various governments, whether colonial or post-colonial, military or civilian. The first attempt to end the Ife-Modakeke crisis was actually linked to the peace efforts that culminated in the 1886 Peace Treaty. Akintoye explains that:

> From the very beginning of the war, attempts were made to restore the peace. These peace moves fall roughly into two periods: first, the period from 1879 to 1885, and second, the period from mid-1885 to late 1886. The former was characterised by abortive peace negotiations while the latter saw the final massing of conditions favourable to the restoration of peace. In general, intervention came from three main sources: from indigenous authorities in the interior, from missionaries and from the British administration at Lagos.[25]

The 1886 Peace Treaty sought to remove the people of Modakeke from Ife territory. However, as has been stated earlier, the treaty could not be implemented.

The Modakeke, as Akintoye explains, were not willing to honour the terms of the treaty for a number of reasons. One, they argued that Modakeke had been their home for generations and that their ancestors had been buried there. Two, they felt unsafe moving across the Osun River which "placed them too dangerously close to Ibadan, who were unreliable and might enslave them in the future." However, he went on:

> Unlike the Ekitiparapo and Ibadan camps, Modakeke was not a military camp but a town with some history. It was, therefore, a mistake to treat Modakeke like the Kiriji camps in the treaty. Perhaps if, as the Ijebu authorities had suggested, efforts had been concentrated on finding a means of making the Ife and the Modakeke live harmoniously together, the problem might have been solved. To achieve by persuasion the evacuation of a town whose citizens were not conquered but had repeatedly shown themselves superior to their opponents in war in the past, the right and wrong of the situation notwithstanding, was no easy assignment.[26]

Indeed, in December, 1882, Modakeke joined with Ibadan to take up arms against Ife. In this war, the Ifes were overwhelmingly defeated, much to their discomfort. Many Ife chiefs lamented what they felt was the ingratitude of the Modakekes. "We need not say that our guests, the Modakeke, have become too mighty for us. They have rewarded us evil for good. They have thrice dispersed us and destroyed our town. We can no longer live together with them."[27] It is, therefore, not surprising that Modakeke simply chose to ignore repeated calls for it to move to the areas designated in the 1886 Peace Treaty.

More recent attempts at finding a solution to the frequent hostilities between Ife and Modakeke communities have essentially been government inspired. In 1981, the Oyo State government, headed by Chief Bola Ige of the Unity Party of Nigeria (UPN) set up a panel of inquiry headed by Justice Ibidapo Obe to ascertain the cause of the April, 1981, violent confrontation between the two communities. As was the case in 1886, the issue of the status of Modakeke within Ife was raised not just by the representatives of the two communities, but by eminent historians invited to provide historical evidence on the issue. The panel recommended the creation of a separate local government for Modakeke. In 1983, the Oyo State government under Dr Omololu Olunloyo tried to create Oranmiyan West Local Government with headquarters in Modakeke but the idea died with the overthrow of the civilian administration in January 1, 1984.

In 1997, the Osun State Council of Traditional Rulers set up a committee to look into the issue. The National Reconciliation Committee (NARECOM) headed by Chief Alex Akinyele also looked into the problem and promised to find a lasting solution to the problem. The peace committee set up by the Osun State Council of Obas examined three issues; the request of the *Ogunsua* to wear a beaded crown, the relocation of the headquarters of the Ife East Local Government and the status of the Modakeke community. Each of these issue areas was assigned to three of the Obas constituting the committee. However, at the end of the day, all the committee could do was to appeal to the warring communities "to be patient and to honour the call of the *Obas* for peace."[28]

In March, 2000, President Obasanjo again established a 27-member peace committee under the chairmanship of Bishop Gabriel Abegunrin of Osun State's Catholic Diocese after the conflict flared up again. Soon after, the president also set up another committee, the Presidential Conflict Reconciliation Committee on Ife/Modakeke, Ife North Local Government Communities, under Commodore Olabode George (rtd.) as a subset of the earlier one, to:

1.   establish the historical right of abode for the three communities in the area;
2.   ascertain the immediate and remote causes of the conflict; and
3.   make suggestions on how to resolve the conflict with a view to ensuring permanent peace in the area.

The role of NGOs has not been widely felt by the people of both communities. In the questionnaire sent out during the course of the research for this chapter, all the respondents were of the opinion that only the federal and state governments had made attempts at resolving the crisis. However, some NGOs have tried to organise peace-building activities for the two communities. For example, Academic Associates PeaceWorks organised in 1998 "conflict resolution training workshops for some women and secondary school teachers drawn from Ife and Modakeke".[29] The activities of the NGOs are too insignificant since these require funding which they lack.

In terms of effectiveness of some of the actions taken, the majority of the respondents to my questionnaire believe that the measures taken by the various governments, especially under civilian rule, have been quite effective. For example, many are happy with the response of the Obasanjo government to the crisis that erupted in 2000. On the other hand, when the 1997 crisis broke out, many believe that the reaction of the Colonel Obi-led state government further fuelled the crisis.

Options for Resolving the Conflict

What are the chances of this long-standing conflict between Ife and Modakeke communities being peacefully resolved? Indeed, what options are available for arriving at an amicable solution? What role should the different tiers of government play in the efforts at finding a solution that both sides will accept? What role do non-governmental organisations (NGOs) and community based organisations (CBOs) have to play and how do the people perceive them? What options do the actors themselves think are available and what input do they think they can make into the whole process?

The first step in resolving any conflict is understanding the perceptions of the actors themselves and what they think needs to be done. Dialogue with the youths was an important initiative of the Presidential Reconciliation Committee because they are the ones that perpetrate the acts of violence and.destruction. Indeed, any effort at reconciliation must target them for it to have any chance of success.

Again, both communities proffered different solutions since they hold different views on the causes of the conflict. The Modakeke community felt that the following needs to take place for there to be lasting peace in the area:

1.   Genuine reconciliation between the leaders of the two communities especially *Kabiyesi Oluaye* the *Ooni* of Ife, *Oba* Okunade Sijuade II, and the *Baale* of Modakeke, Francis Adedoyin, on the one part, and the Modakeke Progressive Union and the Ife Action Council and the youths of the two communities, on the other;
2.·   Police security to be beefed up in all the border areas;
3.   Sanitization of the police contingent sent to the area;
4.   That policemen should be stationed in both Ile-Ife and Modakeke to maintain peace as against the present situation whereby the police are only stationed in Ile-Ife;
5.   That the headquarters of the Ife East Local Government should be relocated to Modakeke as contained in the Federal Government Gazette which contained the list of local governments created in 1996;
6.   That all recruitment made recently into the Federal Civil Service, State Civil Service, Teaching Service, the Nigerian Police and the Nigerian Army that eluded Modakeke should be redressed.

Ife youths, on the other hand, were of the opinion that the following measures would bring about a solution to the long standing problem:

1.   Historically, Ile-Ife is the custodian of tradition and the *Ooni*

is the supreme head that must be accorded his deserved respect by all and sundry, including Modakeke;

2. The maintenance of the status quo ante of the *Baale* of Modakeke as there cannot be two *Obas* in a town

3. The Modakekes should be ready to pay *isakole*;

4. They must be ready to pay tax regularly;

5. They should stop their forceful acquisition of Ife land;

6. They should not carve a separate entity for themselves as they cannot stand as an island;

7. All radio announcements/advertisements portraying Modakeke as a separate town should stop;

8. All illegal appointments of village *baales* by the *Baale* of Modakeke should be declared a nullity;

9. A separate state should be created wherein Ile-Ife would be made the capital so as to stop the problem of land ownership once and for all;

10. Curbing the activities of some highly placed individuals that are aiding Modakeke.

Recent developments do however suggest that the conflict between the two communities is far from over. In March, 2002, the Modakeke community proclaimed its own local government (Ife East) and named an interim chairman. This was in response to what they felt was foot dragging on the part of the federal government to implement some of the recommendations of the peace panel it set up under Olabode George. One of the recommendations of the panel was the creation of a separate local government as part of the measures to ensure lasting peace in the area.

But the approach of the Modakeke community is clearly a recipe for further crisis and bloodshed. The response of the Osun State government, whose responsibility it is to create new local government councils was to say that "there cannot be sovereignty within sovereignty". The Ife community made it clear that the announcement of self government by the Modakekes was a "declaration of war and an invitation to another bloodbath."

Clearly, NGOs and CBOs will find it difficult to play a very effective role in this kind of environment. The solution to the crisis is political, linked to the larger issue of the unresolved national question. The most effective target for NGOs and CBOs is to train negotiators and educate the youths on the need for reconciliation and hope that in the medium term such can begin to have an impact on the situation.

References

1. Omololu Olunloyo, "Ife-Modakeke, Yoruba Problem: Insights (II)" , *Nigerian Tribune* (Ibadan) Monday 6 October, 1997, p.18.
2. See "Ife-Modakeke: Let There Be Peace", *Tribune-on-Saturday*, 7 February 1998, p.17. See also *Report of the Meeting of the Presidential Conflict Reconciliation Committee on Ife-Modakeke, Ife North Local Government Communities*, June 2000, (hereafter referred to simply as Presidential Committee Report).
3. *Ibid.*, pp.30-32
4. For more on their activities, see Isaac Olawale Albert, "New Directions in the Management of Community Conflicts in Nigeria: Insights from the Activities of AAPW", in Onigu Otite & Isaac Olawale Albert (eds), *Community Conflicts in Nigeria* (Ibadan, Spectrum Books, 1999) pp34-63
5. *Ibid*, p.34
6. J.F.A. Ajayi & S.A. Akintoye, "Yoruba land in the Nineteenth Century" in Obaro Ikime (ed.), *Groundwork of Nigerian History* (Ibadan: Heinemann Educational Books (Nig.) Ltd, 1980) p.280.
7. Robert S. Smith, *Kingdoms of the Yoruba* (London: James Curry, 1988) p.7.
8. Ajayi & Akintoye, *op. cit.* p.283.
9. *Ibid*, p.285.
10. See Appendix II, S.A. Akintoye, *Revolution and Power Politics in Yorubaland 1840-1893* (London: Longman, 1971) pp.236-240.
11. See Presidential Committee Report *op.cit.*, p.21.
12. S.A. Akintoye, *op. cit.*, p.179.
13. Omololu Olunloyo, *op. cit.*, p.18.
14. *Ibid.* See also Saburi Biobaku, "Re: Ife-Modakeke Problem: Insights (VI)", *Nigerian Tribune* 2 December, 1997, p.8.
15. Omololu Olunloyo, "Of Solutions to the Ife-Modakeke Problem: Finale," *Nigerian Tribune*, 24 November, 1997, p.18.

16. Quoted in Omololu Olunloyo, "Ife-Modakeke, Yoruba Problem: Insights (V)", *Nigerian Tribune*, 27 October ,1997, p.18.
17. Robert S. Smith, *op.cit.*, p.7.
18. Saburi Biobaku, *op.cit.*, p.8.
19. Presidential Committee Report, *op.cit.*, pp.16-17.
20. Presidential Committee Report, *op.cit.*, p.21.
21. "Ife-Modakeke: Let There be Peace", *Tribune-on-Saturday*, 7 February, 1998, p.17.
22. Isaac Olawale Albert, "Ife-Modakeke Crisis" in Onigu Otite & Isaac Olawale Albert (eds.), *op. cit.*, p.153.
23. *Tell*, September 1, 1997, p.22.
24. *The News*, September 1, 1997, p.18.
25. Akintoye, *op.cit.*, p.152.
26. *Ibid.*, p.182.
27. Parliamentary Papers: Account and Paper 12 vol. LX of February, 1887. Quoted in Isaac Olawale Albert, *Ife-Modakeke Crisis, op.cit.*, p.147.
28. "Ife-Modakeke: Let There be Peace", *Tribune-on-Saturday, op. cit.*, 7 February, 1998, p.17.
29. See Appendix 2 "The Peace-Building Activities of AAPW in Ife and Modakeke."

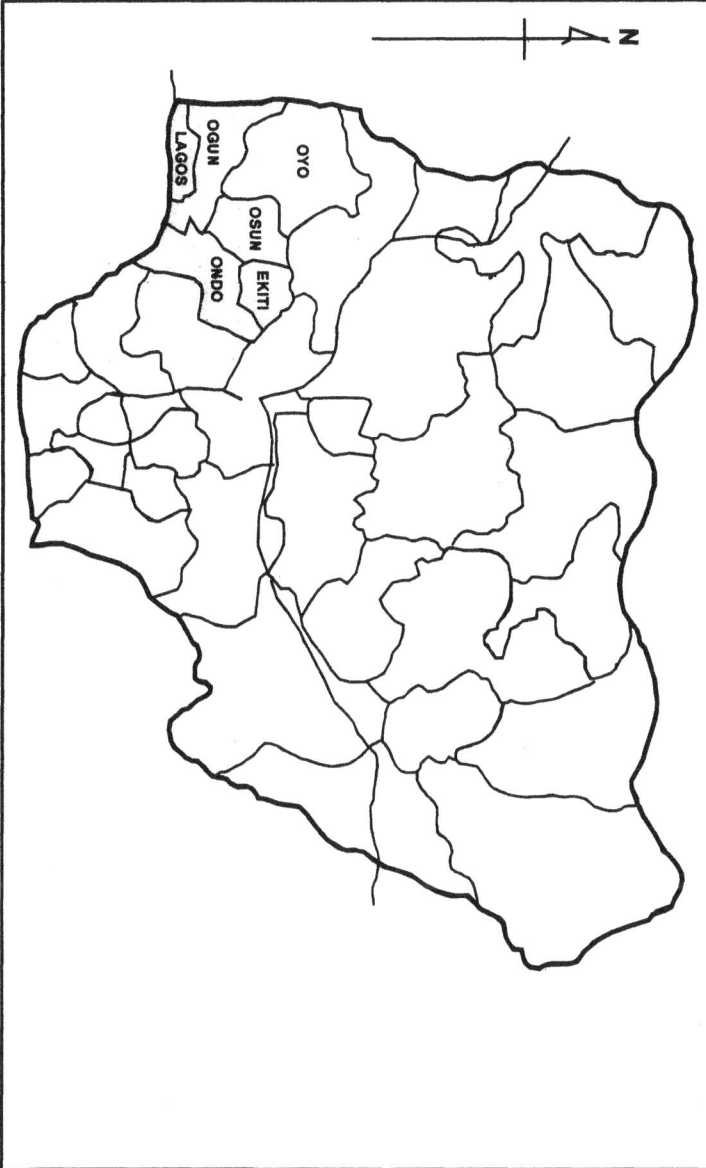

MAP OF NIGERIA SHOWING THE SOUTH-WEST ZONE

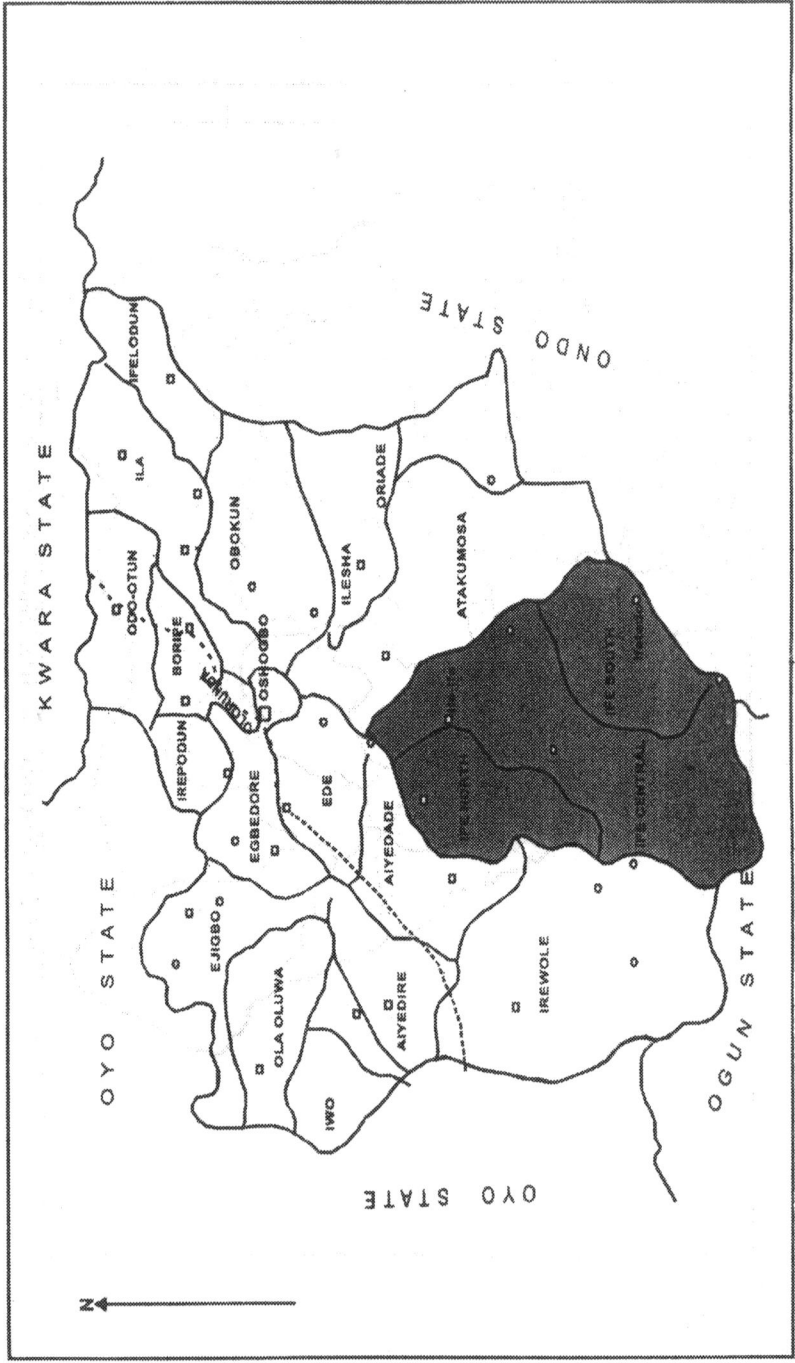

MAP OF OSUN STATE SHOWING THE STUDIED AREA

Chapter 8

Aguleri-Umuleri Conflict in Anambra State

Okechukwu Ibeanu

> Our elders say that a brother's anger should touch the flesh
> and not the bone. Aguleri and Umuleri are the same people
> because we all trace our descent from Eri. This blood letting
> is a sickness caused by greed and hate.
> — *An elderly villager at Umuleri*

> ... there was in the history of Aguleri and Umuleri, a period
> of prevailing peaceful coexistence when everyone was friendly
> with one another. It was from the time of Agulu Eri up to the
> advent of the white man.
> — *Aguleri Community*[1]

Introduction
The rising tide of communal conflicts in Nigeria continues to pose
challenges of analysis and policy to academics and government
officials. Often, inter-ethnic conflicts have particularly caught
attention because of their implications for national unity and
stability. All too often, intra-ethnic conflicts, such as that between
the two Igbo communities of Aguleri and Umuleri in Anambra
State, have only received fleeting considerations. Yet, such conflicts
raise very crucial academic, social and political questions. For one
thing, the profundity of the violence and destruction that
accompany them would suggest that explanatory variables more
fundamental than cultural or linguistic differences are at play in

communal conflicts. For another thing, they point to the importance of more nuanced analysis of communal conflicts, focusing more closely on the unique characteristics of each conflict. This is not to deny the possibility of applying covering laws; instead, it is to suggest the need to eschew hasty generalizations.

Initially, the rash of contemporary communal conflicts in Nigeria were widely thought to be directly linked to "grey areas" resulting from the many state creation exercises, in which the country has now been split into thirty-six states from the four that existed before 1967. Consequently, government engaged in a series of boundary adjustment and boundary demarcation exercises. Yet, the conflicts have persisted and worsened, not only among communities in different states, but also among those in the same state. Ethnic difference then emerged as a popular explanatory variable, drawing from the old "interaction thesis" which explained ethnicity as the result of interaction among people of different ethnic groups, especially in contexts of scarcity.[2] State creation was then thought to heighten ethnic differences and to unearth latent ones as it created new contexts for interaction among different ethnic groups within and between states.

Conflict Profile in the South-East Zone

The South-East Zone of Nigeria consists of the five states of Abia, Anambra, Ebonyi, Enugu and Imo. In terms of ethnic composition, the zone is almost totally homogenous since this area is the heartland of the Igbo ethnic group. However, the zone is becoming increasingly multi-ethnic with increasing settlement of people of other ethnic identities, especially in urban centres like Enugu, Owerri, Aba and Onitsha.[3] Although ethnic heterogeneity in the zone is predominantly an urban phenomenon, curiously it has had a long history in the rural areas of northern Igbo land, especially in the Nsukka environs. For instance, the village of Ibagwa in the outskirts of Nsukka has had a long history of settlement of the Igala, Hausa, Nupe and Yoruba. In addition, a substantial proportion of the Igbo inhabitants of the village are Muslim, in spite of the predominantly Christian religious affiliation of the Igbo.[4] This unique case of rural multiculturalism has been attributed to the historical interaction between northern Igbos and the Igala.[5]

As a result of the near ethnic homogeneity of the South-East, conflicts have tended to be less inter-ethnic and more intra-ethnic. However, increasingly, conflicts between ethnic minority settlers and indigenous Igbo people in Ibagwa and between Igbos and Fulani herdsmen in villages and cattle markets have been reported.[6] Still, the predominant basis for identity conflict in the zone is sub-ethnic. Sub-ethnic identities in the zone are numerous, taking their origins variously from dialects of the Igbo language, clans, administrative districts and even towns. Some of the popular sub-ethnic identities in the South-East Zone include Ado, Wawa, Jookwa, Ohuhu and Ijekebe. Although these sub-identities often have cultural, linguistic and geographical origins, they are subsequently cultivated and nurtured politically. Take the example of the Wawa in the Enugu and Ebonyi areas of the zone. It has been noted that the word Wawa "has no more significance than its occurrence in many dialects in the area. Initially, it had no cultural connotation. However, careful cultivation of the identity by prominent politicians from the area, particularly Chief C. Onoh, has raised it into a sub-ethnic identity accepted across the area."[7] This tendency to cultivate sub-ethnic identities and to mobilize grievances behind them for political and economic purposes, especially through the work of town and clan associations, has been very important in intra-ethnic conflicts in the South-East Zone.

A major pivotal factor in conflicts in the South-East Zone is land (*ana*). The popular view is that this is because of the spirituality of land in Igbo culture as expressed in the prominence of the deity *Ana* and the importance of the yam crop. It is also expressed in the general view that the land is the spiritual connector of the living, the dead and the unborn. Consequently, land is a very serious issue among the Igbo since it touches both the material and the spiritual, the very essence of Igbo ontology. Thus, land is something that is worth dying for.

Nevertheless, this spiritual thesis affords a limited explanation of the violence that attends land disputes in the South-East Zone today. We think that the explanation lies in the increasing commercialization of land, population density, collapse of traditional structures for gaining access to land and managing conflicts therefrom and government rural development policies. Related to land is the growing conflict between farmers and pastoralists, usually Fulani herdsmen, over livestock grazing on farm crops. Other sources of conflict in the zone include chieftaincy disputes, political differences, citing of administrative headquarters of local governments and inter-confessional differences among religious groups.

However, by far the most important cause of conflict remains land. Table 1 shows the findings of a recent study of the South-East in which respondents were asked the most important causal factor in conflicts in their communities. Table 1 confirms that land is the central issue in most conflicts in the zone. The table shows that out of a total of 75 major conflicts of varying degrees of violence, 49 or 65% involved land. The table also shows that most of the land conflicts involved violence. The tendency of land conflicts in the South-East Zone to be violent is brought into bold relief in the Aguleri-Umuleri conflict, which is the subject of this chapter.

Table 1: Profile of Major Conflicts in the South-East Zone in the Last Ten Years

Conflict	Pivotal Factor	Level of Violence
Igbere vs Ozuabam	Land	Very violent
Unubi vs Uga	Land	Violent
Eluoma vs Amamba	Land	Non-violent
Odekpe vs Oshalu	Land	Non-violent
Abba vs Ukpo	Land	Non-violent
Onitsha Ngwa vs Ikot Abasi	Land	Very violent
Ufuma vs Nanka	Land	Non-violent
Abriba vs Ebem	Land	Violent
Umunwala Nsulu vs Umuode Nsulu	Land	Non-violent
Ekwulumili vs Amichi	Land	Non-violent
Amokwe Item vs Apanu	Kingship	Non-violent
Igboukwu vs Uga	Land	Very violent
Eluoma vs Ngwu Uzuakoli	Land	Non-violent
Enugwu-Ukwu vs Abagana	Land	Non-violent
Aguleri vs Umuleri	Land	Very violent
Ogidi vs Abatete	Land	Violent
Nkpor vs Ogidi	Land	Very violent
Ogidi vs Ogbunike	Land	Violent
Nkpor vs Obosi	Land	Violent
Ogidi vs Umudioka	Land	Violent
Nnewi vs Nnobi	Land	Non-violent
Ajali vs Akpu	Land	Very violent
Ogbunike vs Ogidi	Land	Violent

Omor vs Anaku	Land	Very violent
Oba vs Obosi	Land	Violent
Uga vs Amesi	Land	Violent
Onitsha vs Obosi	Land	Violent
Ezira vs Umuomaku	Land	Very violent
Nibo vs Awka	Land	Non-violent
Awka vs Amawbia	Land	Very violent
Obosi vs Ozze	Land	Violent
Nenwe vs Ngbo	Stream with mineral deposits	Violent
Obosi vs Ogbaru	Land	Violent
Abagana vs Eziowelle	Land	Violent
Ugwuoba vs Achalla	Land	Non-violent
Abagana vs Ukpo	Land	Violent
Nise vs Mbukwu	Land	Non-violent
Ukpo vs Abba	Land	Violent
Nkpor vs Umuoji	Land	Non-violent
Abba vs Awkuzu	Market	Non-violent
Adazi Nnukwu vs Nri	Land on shores of Agulu Lake	Non-violent
Nkpor Uno vs Nkpor Agu	Market	Very violent
Akpo vs Achina	Land and market	Non-violent
Awka	Chieftaincy	Non-violent
Nimo vs Abatete	Land	Violent
Uke	Chieftaincy	Non-violent
Agulu	Religion	Non-violent
Abagana	Chieftaincy	Violent
Awkuzu vs Ifitedunu	Land	Very violent
Agukwu Nri	Chieftaincy	Violent
Nkwere Ezunaka vs Onitsha	Land	Very violent
Ezinifitte	Chieftaincy	Violent
Ogidi	Religion	Violent
Nanka	Religion	Very violent
Omo vs Igbakwu	Land	Very violent
Nawfia	Chieftaincy	Non-violent
Nkwere Ezunaka vs Ozze	Land	Non-violent
Ukpo	Chieftaincy	Non-violent
Agulu	Chieftaincy/ Religion	Non-violent
Nawgu	Chieftaincy	Non-violent
Owerre Ezukala	Chieftaincy	Violent
Uke	Chieftaincy	Non-violent
Ozubulu	Chieftaincy	Violent
Akpuoga Nike vs Owo	Land	Very violent
Orifite	Chieftaincy	Violent
Ekwegbe vs Ugwogo Nike	Land	Violent
Umunze	Chieftaincy	Non-violent

Ezza Agu vs Mgbaleze	Land	Violent
Awkuzu	Chieftaincy	Non-violent
Mgbowo vs Nenwe	Land	Very violent
Awka-Etiti	Chieftaincy	Very violent
Umabi vs Ama Owelle	Land	Violent
Omor	Chieftaincy	Non-violent
Ezi Anam	Chieftaincy	Non-violent
Isu-Ofia	Chieftaincy	Non-violent

Source: *Adapted From Ibeanu & Onu, 2001, pp. 51-54.*

The study of the Aguleri-Umuleri conflict is significant first because it could serve as an experimental control for testing some assumptions underlying the study of ethnic conflicts in Nigeria, particularly those positing a link between ethnic/cultural differences and conflicts. The two communities belong to the same ethnic group (Igbo) and to the same clan (Eri). They also belong to the same state (Anambra) and the same local government area (Anambra East). Secondly, Aguleri-Umuleri conflict focuses attention on intra-ethnic conflicts, which have not received adequate attention among research scholars of communal conflicts in Nigeria. Consequently, sub-ethnic identity has not featured very much in the study of ethnicity in Nigeria. Yet, such identity could become a strong basis for political mobilization and ferocious communal conflicts.

In recent times, researchers have pointed out the surge of rural ethnicity in Nigeria.[8] Hitherto, ethnicity was formulated as a predominantly urban phenomenon. Thus, Nnoli argues that the colonial urban centre with its insecurities and uncertainties for the migrant, was the cradle of ethnicity in Nigeria.[9] While the urban areas are the cradles of ethnicity, the rural areas are now its hotbed. At the heart of rural communal conflicts is the land question. Pressure on land resulting from a combination of expropriation, monetisation, rising population density, degradation and resurgence of precolonial communal competition has raised land into a *primal casus belli* in rural communities. This is taking place in contexts in which formal, modern demarcation of boundaries remains unfashionable. Attempts by government to demarcate boundaries to keep warring communities apart have, almost as a rule, failed to bring a lasting solution to violence. So have other approaches such as litigation, commissions of inquiry and/or reconciliation and creation of local government areas. In fact, in many cases, warring parties considered government to be biased, and its interventions have only served to worsen the conflicts. This persistent failure of government to solve many of these conflicts has led to discussion of alternative means of communal conflict management in Nigeria. Civil society, as that mediatory space between the state and the private citizen, has emerged as a possible vehicle for filling this role. This is the focus of this study. The study seeks to analyse the Aguleri-Umuleri conflict and explore the role of civil society in its management.

Theorizing the Aguleri-Umuleri Conflict
The Aguleri-Umuleri conflict, like most rural communal conflicts in Nigeria, has to do with land. Always at issue is the question of boundaries, which define the extent of control inherent in each community. According to Prescott, the general term boundary conflict consists of four different types of disputes between political units having some measure of autonomy. Taking note that boundary disputes occur over the whole range of international and internal boundaries, he divides them into international, extra-national, federal and intra-national.[10]

Early observers explained boundary disputes in terms of the military power of states, in the context of international relations. For them, it was a geo-political matter. Observers like Ratzel and Huashofer, regarded as the founders of geo-politics, argue that the state is akin to a living organism, its boundaries representing its skin. Like all living organisms, it is in the nature of states to grow and expand.[11] As such, boundaries are not rigid. They only express the strength of states. Therefore, they are in a constant state of flux. As the strength of a state increases, so too does its need for "good" boundaries. Haushofer notes that a dynamic state is entitled to organic boundaries; that is, boundaries that correspond to its geo-political structure. It has the rights to claim a territory if it has the capability to exploit and if the possessing state lacks such capability. These geo-political ideas were later incorporated into Nazi ideology and policy, and were at the roots of German claim to *Lebensraum* (living space) in the 1930s and 1940s.

This geo-political conception of the boundary question,

especially the general idea of the power of states has remained the dominant explanation of boundary conflicts among liberal political scientists. It can be found variously expressed in Holdich,[12] Spykman and Rollins,[13] and the works of many power theorists in International Relations. The implication of these ideas is that boundary conflicts are natural. They are part of the very nature of states, which is expansionist, conditioned only by their relative strength in relation to one another. Thus, Spykman and Rollins, refer to states as "power struggle organizations" which have an inherent tendency to expand. On a general basis, these observers argue that boundary conflicts mirror power struggles among states. These struggles could be political, economic or military. According to Prescott, sudden changes in the power of states in the international environment result in the proliferation of territorial claims. This is because states rarely choose to negotiate from a position of weakness.[14] That is why the international environment is replete with such claims at the conclusion of major wars or serious systemic changes.

Nevertheless, many of these writers recognize that not all boundaries are equally significant. The more significant a boundary is, the more crisis-prone it becomes. In their view, the significance of a boundary is related to the power of a state. A border becomes significant if it is capable of enhancing the power of a state. For instance, an area containing useful natural and material resources is likely to induce conflicts. As such, disputes could be reduced not by recurrent re-delimitation of boundaries, as we see at the end of the major wars, but by diminishing boundary significance. This can be achieved through integration and the formation of regional economic organisations.[15] In short, a boundary loses its significance if it ceases to hinder the free interaction of people on both sides. Echoing Boggs, Jones insists that the main evil is nationalism or national feelings, which implies a lack of identification with others.[16] Nationalism inhibits the free interaction of people across boundaries. In the same vein, Strassoldo calls for the reduction of the importance of boundaries by diminishing the "... economic, cultural and psychological disadvantages of dividing people from one another".[17] Of course, the most evil part of nationalism is the attempt by nation-states to dominate others.

Boggs and others are correct to the extent that they recognize the centrality of resources to boundary conflicts and how exclusivist claims fuel them. However, most classical works on boundary conflicts are flawed for a number of reasons. First, one characteristic shared by most of them is their state-centric orientation. Dominated by the billiard-board perception of international relations, they assume states to be the predominant, if not exclusive, actors in the international environment. The interaction of these actors constitutes a struggle for power. Consequently, boundary conflicts are seen as one dimension of the struggle. Yet, by focusing exclusively on state actors and international boundaries, these works overlook a myriad of domestic non-state processes useful in understanding boundary conflict in its various ramifications. Moreover, internal boundaries are rarely studied. Yet, the survival of a state as an international actor could depend on domestic boundary conflict. For example, secessionist and irredentist claims could arise directly from problems with internal boundaries. To illustrate, in situations in which ethnic communities live astride an international boundary, which is common across Africa, a dissatisfactory boundary demarcation within one country is likely to generate either secessionist demands from inside or irredentist pressures from outside. In fact, internal boundaries could be very central because as Prescott points out, "People are more aware of the influence on their lives of federal and internal boundaries than of international boundaries".[18]

Second, this state-centric orientation blurs a myriad of social processes within the international environment such as the interaction of classes and other social forces. We think that it is the interaction of social forces, rather than any natural expansionist tendency in states, that is the most fundamental explanation of boundary conflicts. In fact, to say that boundary conflicts are natural does not tell us anything. Finally, these works have concentrated on international boundaries, again because of their state-centric orientation. Consequently, little attention has been given to boundary conflicts within countries. These include boundaries between politico-administrative units like states, districts and councils; and between communities like villages, towns, clans and ethnic groups. Conflicts arising from communal boundaries in countries like Nigeria call for particular attention. Prescott traces this neglect to the fact that internal boundaries are ephemeral and subject to rapid change.[19] In addition, according to him, they are often not demarcated in contrast with international boundaries. Obviously, the reason adduced by Prescott for the neglect of internal boundaries by hitherto existing works are, to say the least, unsatisfactory. It is evident that this lacuna in the literature results because internal boundaries and conflicts do not fit neatly into the dominant liberal conceptual frameworks of power and decision-making.

How then do we explain boundary/land conflicts, especially in their domestic and inter-communal dimensions? It should be noted right away that boundaries represent territorial points of difference among social forces in distinct social formations. The differences and the social forces around which they are built could be class, religion, country, nation, ethnicity, clan or other communal considerations, depending on the concrete situation. It is in this light that we argue that boundary conflicts arise from the conflicting material interests of social forces. Boundary conflicts like that between Aguleri and Umuleri are not gratuitous, atavistic incidents as some observers think. Neither are they the result of inherent expansionist tendencies in communities. Instead, they result from clearly identifiable material interests of these communities, particularly land. It is the material undercurrents that explain the persistence and animosity that attend these conflicts. These material undercurrents become sharpened over time, thereby deepening the conflict and bitterness. Accordingly, many of these conflicts pre-date colonial times, they were deepened over the period of colonial rule and they have become violently resurgent in the post-colonial period.

The centrality of land to pre-colonial Nigerian societies, especially those occupying the equatorial rain forests, cannot be in doubt. They were essentially farming societies. Animal husbandry was minimal compared to the Savanna region. So also was long distance trade. The climate and the vegetation made these two endeavours, which would have reduced dependence on the land, difficult to pursue. Apart from farming, land also served variously the payment of bride price, wealth, reparation for murder and other serious crimes and as a means of exchange. Land came to be the symbol of wealth and social standing in these societies. This importance of the land is recreated in myths connecting members of the society to the land. The land became sacred and central to numerous rites and rituals in these societies. It is not surprising that this area has historically seen constant conflict over land, predating contact with Europeans. Consequently, the impression sometimes created by African scholars and Africanists that colonialism met a calm and serene Africa is inaccurate. To the contrary, colonialism met societies in ferment, in which a distinct class of warlords had emerged and become entrenched. In fact, that is why colonialism met stiff opposition in most parts of Africa. This class of warlords is very important in the history of boundary clashes in southeastern Nigeria. The importance of this class of social agents lay in the fact that wars were inextricably linked with the very survival of these societies, namely, control of land.

This materialist perspective on pre-colonial land conflicts is more plausible than the usual reference to the absence of clearly demarcated boundaries between pre-colonial communities. For one thing, it should be remembered that boundaries make sense if they are enforceable. Where largely independent communities that recognize no single enforcing authority are involved, location of boundaries depends on a balance of coercive forces among them. So, it is less a question of whether boundaries existed in pre-colonial times as it is a question of where the communities think the boundaries should be, based on their ability to back up a claim. This ability depended largely on the development of a class of warriors in a position not only to defend the land already in their possession, but also to capture more land. For another thing, the "no-clear-boundary" hypothesis cannot explain why within the same community, in which case boundaries are clearly demarcated employing traditional/cultural means, serious clashes among villages, kin groups and families still occur. But even if we assume that this hypothesis is right about the pre-capitalist/pre-colonial societies, the persistence of territorial disputes under the subsequent dominance of colonial and neo-colonial capital undermines its plausibility.

If the view that Europeans met a serene Africa is inaccurate, the opposing view that they pacified a Hobbesian Africa is even more incorrect. To claim that colonialism brought order to Africa could not be farther from the truth. What it did was to alter existing contradictions, giving them a new meaning and force. First, in the early days of contact with European capital, the principal aim of inter-communal wars, which was principally to gain more land took a new turn. The hunting of slaves for sale to Europeans on the coast became the central objective because slaves were not taken in wars before the contact with Europeans. However, the taking of slaves was incidental and secondary to the aim of territorial gains and the capture of livestock. In fact, before this new trade in slaves, captives were only taken for doing farm and domestic work for the privileged strata of society. The numbers of such slaves were very limited. Also, insofar as slaves had certain rights in the captive communities, taking very large numbers could become counter productive. The arrival of Europeans not only exploded the demand for slaves, but also appreciated their value immensely. Thus, clashes among communities, ostensibly over territory, became even more frequent and violent.

Second, European capital and later colonial rule worsened the contradictions among communities by backing some against others. This support was initially military by arming warring communities. The interest was mutual. While the communities with European support extended their boundaries, the Europeans picked up more slaves at cheaper prices. These wars later became part of "Pax Britannica" as some communities were used to wage the colonial war of conquest on others. Apart from military support, colonial administrators gave legal and political backing to some communities against their adversaries. The district officers and court clerks gained notoriety for this. Their kangaroo courts transferred territory to favoured communities. The district officers and the court clerks came to represent the immense venality and injustice of European rule among the Igbo. It is common knowledge that court clerks accepted bribes to decide cases in favour of some communities. The point is that such questionable decisions led to a substantial loss of faith in the colonial legal system, and this loss of faith has rubbed off the post-colonial judiciary. Igbo communities became widely cynical of the justice dispensed by colonial courts. This is because the people saw it as not only an alien system imposed on them, but also because of the conduct of those who administered the system. As a result, the colonial legal system could not intervene decisively to check conflicts.

Third, the acquisition of land by European traders, missionaries and the colonial government for various purposes served to create and exacerbate land conflicts. European companies needed land for trading and residence, Christian missions for churches, schools and farms, and the government for residential quarters and other administrative infrastructure. Such land was often located at border areas between communities, in areas either not yet brought under use or were thought to be the abode of evil and malevolent spirit. This arose out of the general suspicion and trepidation with which pre-colonial Igbo societies treated Europeans. It was unacceptable to grant land to Europeans in the heart of the community. The point, however, is that plots of land either granted to or forcefully taken by Europeans often became a source of conflict among neighbouring communities. This was worsened by competition among Europeans themselves, particularly among Christian denominations and Levantine companies. A clear example is the competition between the Church Missionary Society (CMS) and the Roman Catholic Mission. In many places, neighbouring communities became divided among the two missions. A grant of land to one meant a grant to the other. Where disputed territory was involved, a spiral of conflict was immediately unleashed.

Finally, colonialism created a new economy and class structure, which invariably were conducive to the escalation of land conflicts. For one thing, the growing urban population required increased food production, which fell on the peasantry. At the same time, the replacement of the slave trade by legitimate trade meant increased production of cash crops for export. All these meant the need to increasingly bring more land under cultivation by the peasantry. Invariably, unused land became a cause of disagreement among peasants of neighbouring communities. For another thing, the new colonial dispensation created a local class of petty-bourgeois elements who sought property in land for various reasons. In addition, this group of social agents became the champions of interests of their communities chiefly for economic and political ends. The burgeoning of town and ethnic unions, which became a veritable instrument for petty-bourgeois political aspiration, is a remarkable feature of this era. Excluded politically and economically by colonialism, communal mobilization became a useful platform readily open to this rising class of young, educated professionals, particularly lawyers. They became the vanguard of their communities in the various land disputes. In essence, nationalism was reproduced as communalism at the local level.

Post-colonial Nigeria has seen the worsening of land conflicts in the rural areas. There is no doubt that to a large extent these conflicts were carried over from the colonial era. However, a great deal of them is to be located in the very nature of the post-colonial society. This is particularly so with regards to the intensification of these disputes. It is true that because of the overall undemocratic nature of the colonial society, many communities were not in a position to express the grievances they may have had over the land question before independence. As such, self-government provided an opportunity for them to do so. Thus, the rising tide of conflicts may be seen as part of the explosion of expectations and the inevitable self-assertion that goes with independence. But this does not explain the situation very much. For one thing, it has since become unclear whether independence gave Nigerians that much freedom. In fact, many Nigerians would today doubt that the post-colonial society is more democratic than the colonial society it replaced. For another thing, the rising tide of communal conflict may well represent the frustration and privations of the post-colonial society. Indeed, the post-colonial society seems to be conducive to conflicts for various reasons. First is the growing importance of land to the economic interest of various classes. This is so even for the working class, which classically lives out its exploitation in the industry. As a result of the persistence of communal ties and sentiments, concept of the indigene has become very important in Nigeria. At birth, Nigerians in addition to being members of ethnic groups, are indigenes of particular villages, towns, clans, local governments and states. It does not matter if they spend their entire life outside those "indigenous homes". In fact, if they happen to do so, at death they must be returned to their indigenous homes for burial. Even an urban worker living thousands of miles from "home" is expected to have a house and land in his indigenous home. More importantly, because of the highly exploitative character of the formation, Nigerian workers have always augmented their income by maintaining small farms. This has become even more so with the deteriorating economic conditions of the last two decades.

The peasantry on its part has always made a living from the land. As such, every piece of land controlled by a peasant is a priced possession. This is particularly so in areas like Anambra State where historically, the population density has been relatively high. Land has become even more critical to the survival of peasants in the dire economic conditions of the post-colonial society. Nevertheless, in the process, the peasantry is caught in a serious contradiction, which is important in understanding the rising tide of land conflicts. On the one hand, the rising cost of their non-food expenditure means that ever increasing areas of land must be brought under cultivation. This is the only way out in the face of stagnant technology and an overall low level of development of productive forces, low output, out-migration of labour from the rural areas and low prices of peasant products. On the other hand, peasants are now most willing to sell land to meet the increasing economic pressure. This, in conjunction with the agricultural policies of successive Nigerian governments that emphasized large-scale farming, has unleashed an unprecedented land-grabbing spree by capitalist farmers and petty-bourgeois elements in the rural areas. So we observe a contradiction: survival for the peasant means, at one and the same time, increasing land under cultivation and selling-off land. As they are squeezed-off land it becomes even of greater material significance for the peasantry. In the circumstance, hitherto unused land, which usually lies in the border areas between communities, becomes very significant. The ownership of such boundary areas, which in many cases had never been on the agenda (or had been but never seriously addressed), must now be addressed and resolved.

A second reason for the rising tide of land disputes in post-colonial Nigeria is the persistence of communal sentiments. This variously manifests as clannishness, ethnicity and other atavistic sentiments. Such sentiments have attracted the interest of observers of Nigerian politics over the years. Two major explanations of their persistence have been put forward. While the right sees them mainly as natural, innate, primordial and inevitable, the left has often portrayed them as constructed and manipulated by the ruling classes. Communal identity is, therefore, false consciousness. However, while the view that these sentiments are natural is highly presumptuous and ahistorical, the view that they constitute false consciousness, which is instrumentalised by ruling classes is too voluntaristic to be fundamental. Ake tries to move the debate further. He attributes the persistence of ethnic consciousness in post-colonial Nigeria to what he calls the limited penetration of capitalism and commodity relations. Therefore, he argues, that where there is a limited atomization of society the market ethic does not rule the lives of a vast majority of Nigerians, especially in the rural areas.[20] It is these factors, which are characteristic of capitalism that can destroy such sentiments. Ake's formulation without doubt advances our understanding of the persistence of ethnic and other communal sentiments. But there are two major problems with his formulation. First is that in those areas of the formation where we could rightly say that capitalism has substantially penetrated (e.g. the urban areas), such sentiments remain quite strong. Second and more fundamental is that Ake describes only one form of capitalist commodity relations, namely, the free market/competitive type. While this may be conducive to the atomization of society and the growth of individualism, other forms of capitalist commodity relations such as monopoly and oligopoly may, in fact, hamper these processes.

The general point then is that while land and other material interests are the major immediate *casus belli* in communal conflicts, they do not explain the identities that form around them and how these identities acquire specificity and become the basis of intensification of conflict. For instance, although both the Aguleris and Umuleris agree that they are descended from Eri, their common descent has receded almost completely and they see themselves as distinct. It is paradoxical that the two communities at one and the same time claim common descent and yet different identities. This irony calls for an understanding of the character of identity formation and persistence.[21] This could be done effectively by reconciling the primordial/innate and constructions/instrumentalist viewpoints. We need to transcend the portrayal of the two as opposing. In fact, they are two dimensions of a historical process of emergence and development of ethnic or sub-ethnic identities. To begin with, an ethnic identity exists where there is a large group of people defined by:

1. Their collective consciousness of belonging to a cultural, linguistic or other communal ensemble;
2. Their collective attachment to a specific geographical homeland; and
3. Their collective engagement in the propagation and transmission of that identity over a relatively long period of time.

On the other hand, a sub-ethnic identity exists where some members of an ethnic identity perceive the existence of distinct cultural, linguistic or other communal characteristics that they and/ or others believe are uniquely possessed by them and not shared by all members of the larger ethnic identity.

All ethno-communal identities are in a sense constructed. However, the construction is not an event, as we perceive in many constructionist writings, but a long historical process. When communal traits arise, through both conscious and unintended actions of both group members and outsiders, and persist over a long historical period, they acquire primordiality and appear as rudiments of the existence of the communal identity. We may describe this as the primordialisation of these traits. Primordialisation is usually achieved through conscious propagation of these traits as the unique possession of the group. These traits may include language, myth of common ancestry, collective history, possession of a common geographical space or homeland, staple food, dance steps or dressing mode. Once these traits acquire primordiality, they become the basis of intensification of the identity and future construction/reconstruction and primordialisation of the identity. This set of quadrangular activities, namely, construction of trait propagation, primordialisation and intensification are fraught with conflict as they are designed to exclude others, while maximizing benefits for the in-group. This is worsened in contexts of scarce resources as land, markets and job opportunities, which necessitate competition between the in-group and out-group. As we shall show shortly, the two related factors of Eri ancestry and ownership of Otuocha land lie at the roots of construction, propagation, primordialisation and intensification of different identities between Aguleri and Umuleri and, therefore, central to the conflict.

A Note on Methodology

Aguleri and Umuleri are two rural communities inhabiting the Anambra River escarpment. They are both located in the Anambra East Local Government Area of Anambra State. The capital of the Local Government Area is at Otuocha, the area bitterly contested by the two communities. Although there has been rapid urbanization at Otuocha with the growing presence of government offices, financial institutions and private sector activities, the rest of Aguleri and Umuleri are still rural. The concentration of habitation of the two communities is on the eastern bank of River Anambra (Map 1). They share boundaries with communities like Nsugbe and Nteje to the south, Nando to the east and Anaku to the northeast. To the west, across the river, are communities like Anam and Umuoba, which are in Anambra West Local Government Area.

Our research design was multifaceted. Firstly, it was meant to elicit usable information from a cross-section of the population of both communities. Secondly, a lot of first-hand information was gathered through observation. Thirdly, we amassed a sizable amount of secondary materials in the process, as a means of supplementing data from primary sources. Based on this design, primary data came from a semi-structured self-report questionnaire as well as interviews. Sampling for both were purposive. However, we tried to reach a number of important elements in the communities particularly public servants, religious leaders, youth/students, community leaders and women. It was our estimation that coverage of these groups will help our sample approach representativeness, even if the sampling process was non-probabilistic. Table 2 shows the distribution of questionnaire among these groups and the selection of interviewees in each community.

Table 2: Selection of Respondents and Interviewees

Questionnaire

Category	Total Questionnaire	Female	Male
Public servants including teachers	20	10	10
Religious leaders	10	5	5
Youth and students	20	10	10
Community/Town union leaders	10	5	5
General public	40	20	20
Total	**100**	**50**	**50**

Interviews

Category	Total interviews	Female	Male
School teacher	2	1	1
Elected official	1	-	1
Religious leader	1	-	1
Title holder or town union official	2	1	1
Youth leader	2	1	1
Women	2	2	-
Total	**10**	**5**	**5**

In analyzing the data from our questionnaire, we principally employed counts and percentages, which were in some cases cumulated for grouped and rank order questions. For such rank order questions, we produced a rank coefficient from a strategy analogous to the Likert method. For instance, where respondents were asked to rank an issue as very important, important, not important, not applicable, "weightings" of 3,2,1 and zero were applied respectively. These were cumulated after cross multiplication and a mean derived the cumulative score by total number of people responding to the question. This means became the rank coefficient R, which is defined as:

Where r is rank weighting and n_i is the number of respondents choosing a specific option.

$$R = \frac{\sum_i r_i n_i}{N}$$

N is the sum of n_i

Although these statistical techniques, especially percentages may seem rudimentary, they are adequate for the data under consideration and particularly so because of the non-probabilistic design we adopted.

Eri Genealogy and the Aguleri-Umuleri Conflict

Solomon, a 20-year-old man from Aguleri is still in Senior Secondary II. He participated with other youths from his community in fighting the Umuleris in 1999. Yet, Solomon informed us that folktale in his community holds that both Aguleri and Umuleri are descendants of *Eri*. He said that he constantly wondered why the two communities fought with so much bitterness and hatred if they were of common ancestry. Eri ethnography or more correctly Eri mythology is widely canvassed in the Anambra River valley. Indeed, it goes further eastwards to Agukwu in Njikoka Local Government Area, westwards as far as Ibuzo in Delta State and northwards to Idah in Kogi State. In fact, some people even claim that "Eri is the progenitor of the Igbo, Edo and Igala races".[22] Eri genealogy has become a central factor in the Aguleri-Umuleri conflict. Paradoxically, rather than serve as a unifying force for the communities in forging a common identity, it has become a very divisive one. This is not difficult to understand. Eri mythology predates the conflict. Consequently, each side tries to show that it is the authentic direct descendant of Eri. The reasoning is that applying the rule of primogeniture, the direct descendant of Eri must be the original occupier of the land. Yet, neither side denies that the other is part of the Eri ancestry. However, what is contested is which of the two communities is primogenial in the Eri heritage. For the Umuleri community, there is the head of the Eri clan. In recent times, they have chosen to be called Umueri rather than Umuleri, the former translating into "the children of Eri". According to the Umuleri interpretation of genealogy, the patriarch, Eri was a great hunter, medicine man and polygamist. He married many wives, among them Iguedo. This union begot Ogbunike, Awkuzu, Umuleli and Nando (Fig.1). Aguleri hotly contests this claim. Their interpretation is that Umuleri are the descendants of Ulueri, the product of an illicit love affair between Okebo, an itinerant Arochukwu trader and Iguedo, the pretty daughter of Aguleri. Consequently, Umuleri actually is Umu Ulueri, which translates into "the children of Ulueri" (Fig. 2). The claim that they are Umueri is, therefore, untenable.[23]

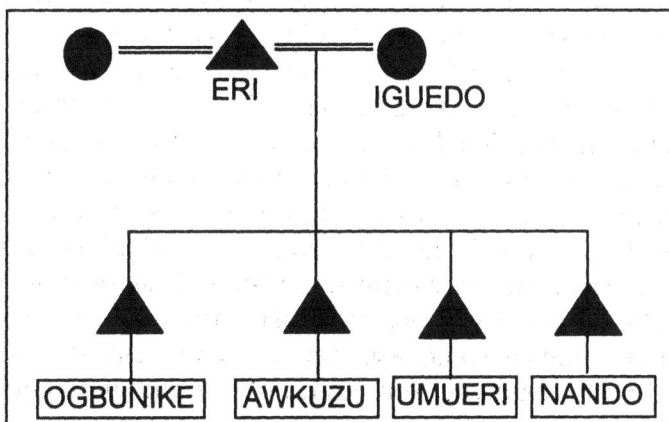

Fig. 1:Eri Genealogy-Umuleri Interpretation

Adiele Afigbo, the renowned professor of History, provides yet another interpretation (Fig. 3). He suggests that Nri genealogical chart presents three tribal segments. In the primary segment, Eri and his first wife had four male children namely, Nri, Aguleri, Igbariam and Amanuke. The secondary tribal segment is linked to Nri, the eldest son of Eri. He had five sons and one daughter, but only four of these sons were able to found communities that have survived to date. These are Agukwu, Enugu-ukwu, Nawfia and Enugu-Agidi. Finally, the tertiary tribal segment arises from the only daughter of Nri, Iguedo. She married and had four sons each of which was able to found a viable community. These are Awkuzu, Umuleri, and Umunya – they were mentioned in this "tribal fraternity", but were not properly fitted in this genealogical chart.[24]

Most pre-colonial anthropologists in Nigeria propagated one myth/folktale of origin or another. Colonial anthropologists and historians, in the absence of other convenient methods of gathering historical data, often employed oral tradition in their work. Concerned principally with the ethnography of the communities, it became inevitable that myths of origin would feature greatly in their work. While this method served very important scientific purpose, it has also been manipulated to prove untenable pet theses of the anthropologists and, historians. These included various notions about the history, ethnography, migratory patterns and defining features of pre-colonial societies. Among other things, these pet theses served the purpose of dividing and ruling these societies as well as making "scientific sense" of many things in these societies, which the western background of these colonial administrators and anthropologists considered "unorthodox". Unfortunately, the limits of these oral traditions as a basis of ethnographic and historical research are rarely addressed. Sponsored, sanctioned and propagated by colonial rule, the stereotypes embedded in these myths became a veritable instrument for subordination of societies and elevating others. In the postcolonial environment, these myths and folklore, which in some cases have been perniciously elevated to the status of science, became a central factor in intercommunal conflicts.

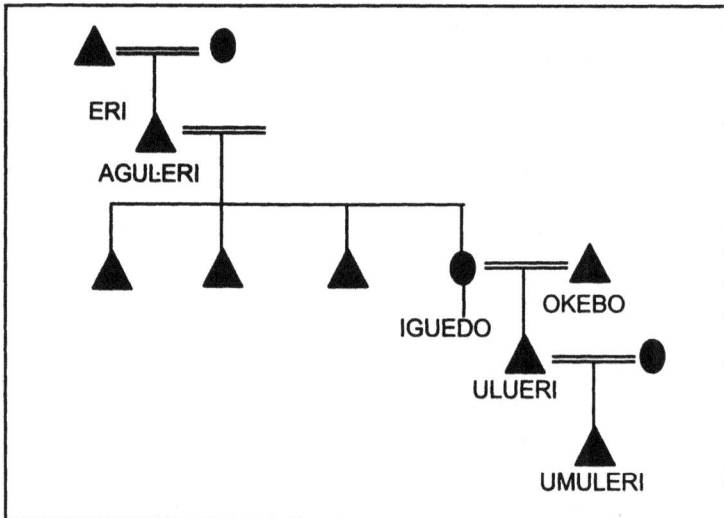

Fig 2: Eri Genealogy-Aguleri Interpretation

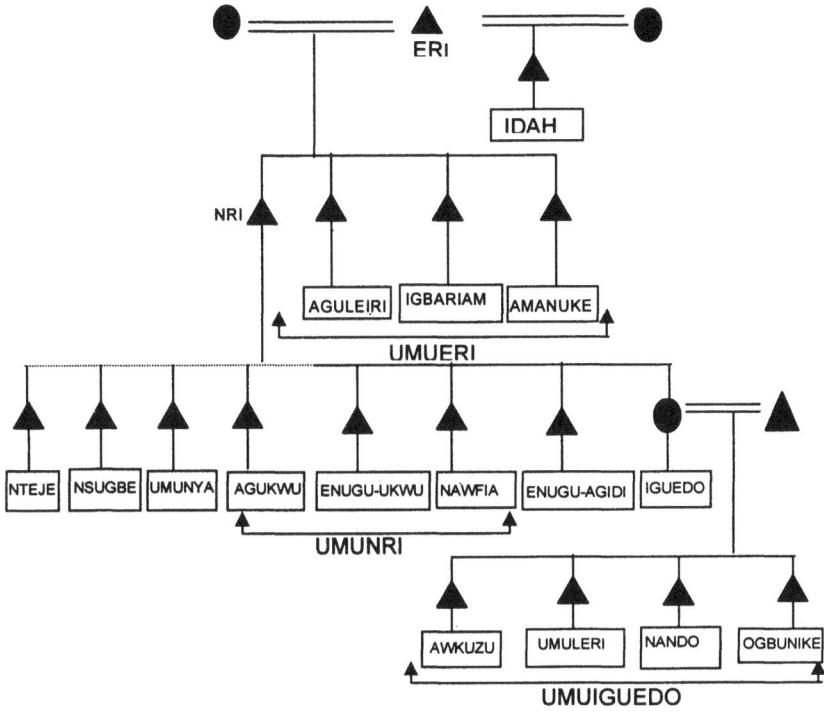

Fig. 3 Nri Genealogical Chart (A. Afigbo)

From Resource Conflict to Animosity Conflict: A Historical Overview of the Conflict

The oldest living member of Umuleri community today was born around 1906. In an interview, he informed us that no man living today knows when the conflict began. What is, however, clear is that it has been intermittent. In fact, as Fig. 4 shows, the conflict erupts violently every thirty years (one generation). We derived the graph from responses to a question in our questionnaire about the dates conflicts occurred in the past. The frequency of dates provided by respondents when plotted yielded this pattern. The sequence shown in the graph is quite interesting. The cycle of conflict consists of ten years of peace. In other words, there is a tension phase, eruption phase and a hiatus phase (T-E-H) (Fig. 5). The pattern has become so recurrent and virtually permanent that most members of the community when asked the rationale for the conflict simply said that they were born into it. It is this seeming "naturalness" of the conflict that has made it intractable.

The first recorded violent conflict occurred around 1904. Evidence suggests that it was a culmination of disaffection expressed by each community over the way the other sold or leased Otuocha land to Levantine companies and other organisations. Otuocha, which is the central *casus belli* in the Aguleri-Umuleri conflict, is a river beach on the eastern side of the Anambra River, a tributary of the River Niger. It stretches about 92 meters inland. It became a popular port of call for white traders and missionaries as they intensified their drive into the Igbo hinterland in the 19th Century.

Occurrence of the Conflict

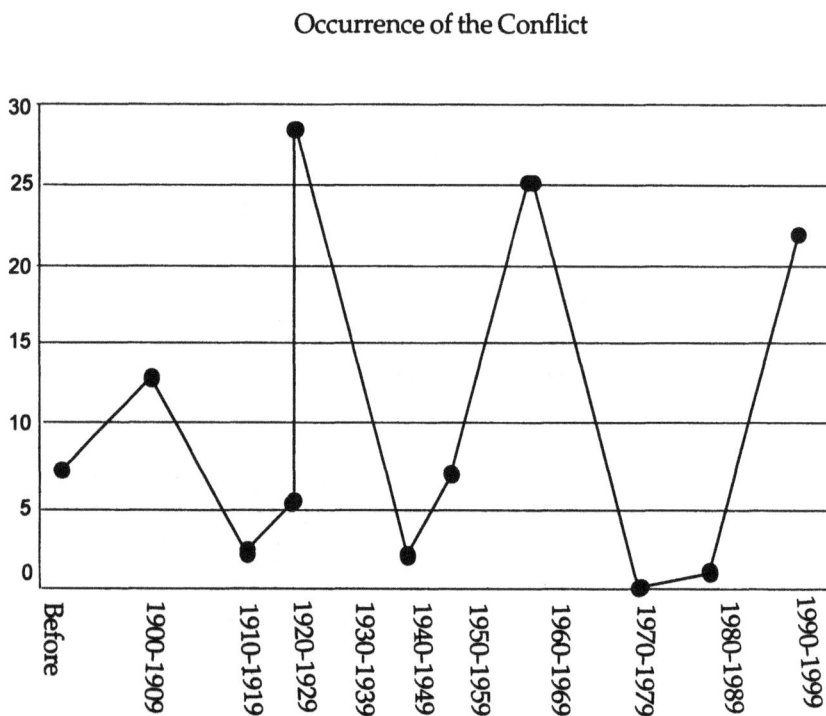

Fig. 4: Pattern of Occurrence of the Aguleri-Umuleri Conflict

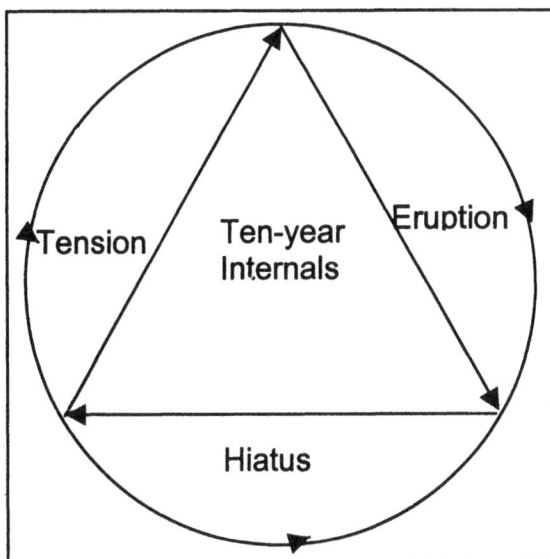

Fig. 5: Cycle of the Aguleri-Umuleri conflict

Understandably, the Royal Niger Company, now a chartered and limited liability company led the way. Towards the end of the 19th Century, the two communities, which together with the neighbours such as Nsugbe and Umuoba had used the beach amicably, began to compete to grant land to the arriving Europeans. It was a case of grant and counter grant, sale and counter sale to Europeans, of land that historically was used commonly without problems. The Idigos, who became the ruling family in. Aguleri, made the first grant to the Roman Catholic Mission (RCM) in 1894 and renewed it in 1898. The land was later abandoned by the RCM in 1903 when it was given another land in Nkponwofia just outside Otuocha land. In 1891, Aguleri granted portions of Otuocha, known as Aguleri Igbo, to the Royal Niger Company. The company finding it difficult to pronounce Aguleri called the area "Gloria Ibo". Not wishing to be left out of the benefits of giving land to Europeans, Umuleri, led by another ruling family called the Umuchezis, on 4th January, 1898, sold a very large chunk of Otuocha to the Royal Niger Company. Other European groups that acquired parts of Otuocha included the Church Missionary Society in 1920 to build a church, John Holt in 1926 and CFAO in 1931.

There is no doubt that behind this frenzy to sell or lease land was a calculation of material benefits. One group of settlers on the land, the Umuoba Anam, at one point paid seven cows, eight hundred yams, and eight hundred fishes to Aguleri. In his 1955 judgment in one of nearly a dozen court cases over the Otuocha land, J. Hurely, the trial judge remarked:

> When at last the Umuleris took exception to these dealings with the land and instituted the 1933 action, it was, as they then said, because they wanted rents which Aguleri was getting ....Perhaps they had not realized the value of leases to commercial firms before their own grant to Royal Niger Company in 1898 had been made in exchange for a few cases of gunpowder and matches (*sic*) and some guns.[25]

Clearly, the upsurge in the value of Otuocha land with the arrival of Europeans on River Anambra was a central causal factor in the conflict. Over one century later, Otuocha remains the central bone of contention. 85.5% of respondents to our questionnaire, rated struggle over Otuocha land as a very important causal factor in the conflict. Only 2.8% of respondents thought that it was not important (Table 3). The importance of Otuocha is confirmed by the rank coefficient (Table 4), which weights the various responses and cumulates them. From the Table, we observe that Otuocha has the highest rank coefficient of 2.75 out of a maximum of 3. The closest to this is "fear and hatred by communities" with a coefficient of 1.13. This is a substantial margin.

Table 3: Causes of Aguleri-Umuleri Conflicts (% of Row)

	Very Important	Important	Not Important	No Response	Did Not Apply	Total
Struggle for Otuocha land	85.47%	7.82%	2.79%	0.0%	3.91%	100.00%
Political competition & intrigues	3.91%	4.47%	21.23%	17.88%	52.51%	100.00%
Instigation by wealthy people	9.50%	10.61%	15.08%	17.88%	46.93%	100.00%
Struggle for political office	2.79%	7.26%	21.79%	18.99%	49.16%	100.00%
Increasing scarcity of land	5.03%	12.29%	21.23%	17.88%	43.58%	100.00%

Rising economic hardship	5.59%	2.79%	27.37%	15.08%	49.16%	100.00%
Fear and hatred by communities	15.08%	16.20%	17.32%	15.64%	35.75%	100.00%
Lack of confidence in the judiciary	12.29%	11.73%	15.08%	18.99%	41.90%	100.00%
Partiality of government	16.20%	10.61%	13.97%	21.23%	37.99%	100.0%
Creation of local government	10.61%	6.70%	21.79%	18.44%	42.46%	100.00%

However, a very central pointer from Table 4 is that the Aguleri-Umuleri conflict, which started as a resource conflict over material interest in Otuocha land, is now an animosity conflict. An animosity conflict is one in which memories of past conflicts acquire a relative autonomy, and become significant in renewing and intensifying conflict. Animosity conflicts are likely to be very prolonged conflicts in which the protagonists have memories of loss, hurt or humiliation. An animosity conflict often begins as resource conflict. However, over time the original cause of the conflict becomes only apparent, while bitter memories become the immediate cause of new conflict. At the same time, fears of pre-emptory attacks by the opponent provide a very short fuse that ignites new rounds of conflict. In fact, the situation becomes so combustible that a minor issue is sufficient to renew the conflict. In the Aguleri-Umuleri conflict, mere rumours that the Aguleri community was planning to use the head of an Umuleri person for the burial of Mike Edozie, a former chairman of Anambra East Local Government Area, was enough to call Umuleri to arms in 1999. Four years earlier, singing and dancing by Umuleri people chanting "Aguleri *ipo*", which means Aguleri weaklings, was said to be one of the immediate causes of the 1995 conflagration. Our respondents rated persistent fears and hatred generated by the conflict as the second most important causal variable after the struggle for Otuocha. A further demonstration of the transformation from a resource conflict to an animosity one is that issues such as land scarcity and poverty were ranked relatively low as causes of the conflict. In Table 4, we find that land scarcity has a coefficient of 0.74, while rising economic hardship and poverty has a coefficient of only 0.59. If the conflict was still over resources per se, it should be expected that these two issues, which are generally pivotal in resource conflicts, should have had high rank coefficients.

Table 4: Causes of Aguleri-Umuleri Conflict (Rank Coefficient)

	Did Not Apply r=1	Not Important r=0	Important r=2	Very Important r=3	Total N	Rank Coeffi-ent
Struggle for Otuocah land	7	5	14	153	179	2.75
Political competition & Intrigues	94	38	8	7	147	0.51
Instigation by wealthy people	84	27	19	17	147	0.79
Struggle for political offices	88	39	13	5	145	0.55
Increasing scarcity of land	78	38	22	9	147	0.74
Rising economic hardship	88	49	5	10	152	0.59
Fear and hatred by communities	64	31·	29	27	151	1.13
Lack of confidence in the judiciary	75	27	21	22	145	0.93
Partiality of government	68	25	19	29	141	1.06
Creation of local government	76	39	12	19	146	0.82

Table 5 provides further confirmatory evidence. We asked respondents to our questionnaire to identify the next most important cause of the conflict after Otuocha land. Over 38% believed that fear and hatred existing between the two communities because of Otuocha conflicts is the next most important factor. This was followed by instigation by wealthy people in the communities (12.3%) and partially of government in handling the conflicts (11.7%). Incidentally, indicators of resource conflict like rising economic hardship (0.56%) and land scarcity (6.7%) did not feature strongly.

Table 5: Next Most Important Cause of Conflict after Otuocha

	FREQUENCY	RELATIVE
Creation of local government	7	3.91%
Fear and hatred by communities	69	38.55%
Increasing scarcity of land	12	6.70%
Instigation by wealthy people	22	12.29%'
Lack of confidence in the judiciary	4	2.23%
Partiality of government	21	11.73%
Political Competition & Intrigues	4	2.23%
Rising economic hardship & poverty	1	0.56%
Struggle for Political Offices	2	1.12%
None of these	24	13.41%
No response	13	7.26%
Total	**179**	**99.99%**

Immediate Causes and Effects of the 1995 and 1999 Conflicts
The 1995 and 1999 flare-ups are located in the fourth peak of the ten-year cycle of the conflict. Those two break-outs demonstrate the increasing importance of animosity in the Aguleri-Umuleri conflict. An attempt by one Chief Dan Ekwevi, alias *Okwu oto ekene Eze*, a native of Umuleri, to build a petrol station in the contested Agu-akor land ostensibly triggered the violence on 30 September, 1995. A group of Aguleri youths had engaged some construction workers and Umuleri youths in a battle at the site. After the initial skirmish, Umuleri youths were said to have marched around Otuocha chanting "Aguleri *ipo*" (Aguleri weaklings). Later in the night, the violence escalated as Aguleri youths attacked Our Lady of Victory Catholic Church and the Umuleri Town Hall among others. The violence soon spread as youths from the two communities engaged each other in a counter-value four-day war in which public and private properties worth billions of naira were destroyed.

By the end of the week, the two communities reached a cease-fire agreement at the Nkisi Palace Hotel, Onitsha, following the personal intervention of Colonel Mike Attah, the military governor of Anambra State. Colonel Attah had visited Otuocha on 2 October, at the height of the mayhem. Three weeks later, on 25 October, he empanelled a three-man judicial commission of inquiry into the violence under the chairmanship of retired Justice Moses O. Nweje.

The government White Paper on the commission's report, which was released in February, 1997, found among other things that Chief Ekwevi's filling station was only used by Aguleri as "an excuse to attack Umuleri, when their earlier baits had failed to provoke an armed conflict with Umuleri".[26] According to the commission, the two communities had built up animosities against each other since the landmark Supreme Court case in 1984 practically sealed the hopes of either side establishing exclusive ownership of Otuocha. The Nweje Commission particularly blamed the Aguleri community for various acts suggestive of war-mongering. These included the attack on Our Lady of Victory Church construction workers, destruction of the statue of the Blessed Virgin Mary at Agu-akor in 1994, destruction of signposts bearing Umuleri at Otuocha, establishment of a market/motor park at Agu-akor and brazen defiance of repeated appeals by the State Boundary Adjustment Committee to suspend development projects on the disputed land pending the demarcation of boundary between the two communities. In fact, the Nweje Commission noted that Aguleri would have attacked Umuleri in December, 1994, had mobile policemen not been drafted to the area to maintain peace. Finally, the commission underscored the ill will that lay at the foundation of the conflict. According to the commission:

> ... the animosity between Aguleri and Umuleri was as a result of mutual suspicion, mistrust and jealousy and that any action by one side was immediately misconstrued by the other side as directed towards it. That syndrome made it impossible for the two parties to dialogue and resolve their differences amicably.[27]

Expectedly, the Aguleri community rejected these claims, describing the Nweje Commission findings as "one sided (sic) and, therefore, incapable of solving the Aguleri/Umuleri crisis particularly as the findings and recommendations did not, repeat did not, reflect the proceedings of the panel of inquiry".[28] However, many people we spoke to in both towns suggested that hopes had been high in Aguleri that the 1984 Supreme Court judgment would be in their favour, having won a preceding appeal at the Court of Appeal. That this did not materialize appears to have annoyed the Aguleri community, especially since many Umuleri people had misconstrued this as a victory and sought to fortify their steady expansion into parts of the disputed territory since the end of the civil war in 1970.

Partly as a result of its rejection by the Aguleri community and partly as a result of political dynamics, including the replacements of Colonel Attah by Wing Commander Emmanuel Ukaegbu, the many recommendations of the Nweje Commission were not implemented. These were as follows:[29]

1. Constitution of Otuocha into a Local Government Area all by itself.
2. That the Otuocha Local Government Area, when constituted, be divided into 20 to 24 wards numbered as Otuocha Ward I, Otuocha Ward II, etc. in order to avoid either of the two communities claiming the wards.
3. The traditional rulers (*Igwe*) of Aguleri and Umuleri should relocate from Otuocha to their various inland towns, *Ime Obodo* or *Enu Obodo*, where they should observe their festivals *Ofala* and all civic and public functions.
4. That the celebration of "Aguleri Day" or "Umuleri Day" should be moved out of Otuocha to the various "*Ime Obodo*" or "*Enu Obodo*".
5. Institutions located at Otuocha should be identified as being situated at Otuocha and not Aguleri or Umuleri. For instance, St. Peter's Church, Otuocha. Institutions which "because of similarity in names are only identified by the community to whom they belong e.g. banks and post offices, should elect either to change their names and drop their community or transfer their business premises to their parent inland towns".
6. Buildings such as Town Halls should drop the word "town" and become designated as being located at Otuocha. For instance, Aguleri Town Hall becomes Aguleri Hall, Otuocha.
7. A law should be promulgated making it an offence punishable with three years imprisonment to put up any sign indicating that Otuocha belongs to any particular community.
8. Constitution of a body to demarcate with "heavy concrete beacons reinforced with rods" the boundary between Aguleri and Umuleri.

The government accepted most of these recommendations. However, they were not implemented before Colonel Attah was replaced. His successor, Wing Commander Ukaegbu, considered the Aguleri-Umuleri conflict either inconsequential or too hot politically to handle.

On Good Friday, April 2, 1999, the peace of the graveyard that prevailed in Otuocha was broken. In Aguleri, Easter preparations were rather subdued as the community prepared for the funeral rites of Chief Mike Edozie, former chairman, Anambra Local Government Caretaker Committee. Umuleri community regarded Chief Edozie as the brain behind the attack against them by Aguleri in 1995. They accused him of using his office as caretaker committee chairman to arm Aguleri and ensure that the Divisional Police Command did nothing to stop the attacks. In fact, the Nweje panel roundly indicted Chief Edozie in its report. According to the government White Paper, "the commission found that Chief Mike Edozie, chairman, Anambra Local Government Caretaker Committee 'was fully aware' of the planned attack on Umuleri by Aguleri on 30th September, 1995 and could have stopped the attack, if he were not an Aguleri man".[30] The non-implementation of the White Paper of the Nweje panel did not go down well with the Umuleri community. They became even more unhappy because Aguleri increasingly portrayed this non-implementation as a victory and humiliation of Umuleri. Consequently, Chief Edozie, who was indicted in the White Paper, became a hero in Aguleri. By contrast, he became a hate figure in Umuleri.

The funeral of Chief Edozie provided a good opportunity for the two communities to renew hostilities. The funeral procession marched through Otuocha and there were allegations that Aguleri youths in the cortege threatened to bury Chief Edozie with the head of an Umuleri man. This is a long-abandoned practice common among the Igbo in the olden days. It was a practice reserved for the burial of great warriors. In effect, Aguleri youths insinuated that Chief Edozie was a great warrior in the "defeat" of Umuleri in 1995. Umuleri resented this, and just as the "Aguleri *ipo*" song was the match in the tinder box in 1995, the threats to use an Umuleri head for the burial of Chief Edozie, however unlikely, served as a short fuse for the dynamite in 1999.

The socio-political environment at the time could not have been·
more conducive to the renewal of conflict. The military government
was on its way out and showed little interest in intervening in a
very politically charged issue. The police at Otuocha was very
cautious, having been heavily criticized for its role in 1995. There
was a general atmosphere of insecurity in Anambra State at the
time, with the vigilante Bakassi Boys waging a relentless war with
criminals around Onitsha and Nnewï. Moreover, there was free
flow of small arms and political thugs used by politicians and their
military patrons to prosecute the 1999 elections. In fact, it is widely
held in the two communities that political thugs and criminals from
Onitsha served as mercenaries in the violence. Thus, Aguleri version
of events holds that a notorious criminal from Umuleri, one
Obanyeli Ikeli, organized and attacked people observing a night
vigil for Chief Edozie on the night of 2nd April, 1999. Above all,
because government did not implement its own White Paper on
the 1995 crisis, which included the issue of sources of ammunition
used in the conflict, many guns and equipment used in prosecuting
the 1995 violence were still largely available in 1999. Incidentally,
the Nweje Commission had found that most of the arms used by
Aguleri in 1995 "were amassed by Aguleri from the time of their
conflict with Obale in Kogi State".[31]

This conjuncture of events foreboded a long and bloody war
between the two communities. The war lasted from early April to
the end of July 1999, probably the longest round of violence in the
long history of the conflict. The 1999 violence was also characterized
by involvement in the conflict of Umuoba Anam, a neighbouring
community, on the side of Aguleri. Over the years, the Umuoba
people have been largely neutral in the conflict. Their involvement
has been given two different interpretations. The first, which is
mainly offered by Umuoba people, is that they attached Umuleri
because their rampaging youth had murdered two of their people
at Chief Edozie's vigil. The second interpretation, which is prevalent
in Umuleri, is that, Umuoba being settlers, were jealous of their
achievements over the years. In addition, the Umuoba being settlers,
were promised a share of the land to be taken in the conflict by
Aguleri, if they assisted the latter in sacking Umuleri.

The 1995 and 1999 conflicts were devastating in terms of their
material and human cost. In the 1995 conflict, our respondents

estimate that at least 200 people died on both sides. The 1999 conflict was even more extensive in human toll. Some estimates put the numbers of deaths as high as 1,000. Some reports hold that half a million people were displaced. It is difficult to confirm these figures. Still, our respondents overwhelmingly agreed that the 1999 conflict was unprecedented in its human cost. Generally, official figures of casualties are much lower. The police, through the area commander, Onitsha, in 1995 reported that they found only one body burnt beyond recognition. On its part, the Nweje panel found that four persons were killed during the armed conflict. However, our respondents suggest that both communities intentionally under-report casualties in order not to appear to have been defeated. Moreover, because the warriors put forward a façade of invincibility, it was necessary to report minimal casualties in order to maintain that image. Some of the youths that said they participated in the conflict told us that they took part in rituals that were meant to protect them from gunshots. The notice of *odi eshi* (impenetrable), which has now become popular across Igboland, gained prominence in the 1995 and 1999 conflicts. It is the motif of the human body that is impenetrable to gunshots or machete cuts.

Apart from the human cost, the material cost of the conflicts has also been staggering. The Nweje panel estimates that private houses and properties destroyed in the 1995 conflict were to the tune of ₦3 billion, most of them on the Umuleri side. Table 6 shows that damage to major public buildings was in excess of ₦232 million. Informed estimates of material destruction in the 1999 conflict are yet to emerge. The Araka Commission set up by the Anambra State government to look into the crisis is yet to submit its report. However, our interviewers reckon that the material cost of the 1999 conflict was unprecedented in the history of Aguleri-Umuleri conflict. Looting was also said to be widespread, unlike in previous conflicts. Our interviewees also suggest that the extensive loss of property in the conflict was partly due to the fact that the 1999 conflict war involved the three communities of Aguleri, Umuleri and Umuoba, unlike the twosome it used to be. Table 7 shows how respondents to our questionnaire estimated the losses of their communities in the 1999 conflict. It shows that deaths, injuries, destruction of social facilities and reduction in

economic well being have very high coefficients. Each of them has
a rank coefficient above two on a scale of three. However,
destruction of social facilities, injuries and deaths ranked highest.

Table 6: Public Property Destroyed in the 1995 Conflict

PROPERTY	ESTIMATED COST (Naira)
Technical College, Umuleri (Boy's High School)	172,000,000
Girls' Secondary School, Umuleri	15,809,463
Umuleri Community Bank	4,818,450
Our Lady of Victory Church, Umuleri (Rev. Father's House)	30,000,000
St. Gabriel's Anglican Church Umuleri (Building with Parsonage)	4,899,942
Umuleri Town Hall	5,000,000
Total	232,527,855

Source: Government of Anambra State White Paper on the Justice Nweje Panel Report. p. 18.

Table 7: Respondents' Estimates of Loss in 1999 Conflict

	Not Applicable r =0	Minimal r=1	Serious r=2	Very Serious r =3	Grand Total	Rank coef-ficient
Deaths	1	31	59	83	174	2.22
Injuries	1	28	61	82	172	22.1
Homes	38	7	126	1	172	1.46
Social Facilities	8	18	36	107	169	2.30
Economic Well-being	7	27	39	89	162	2.08

Growing Problem of Firearms

One issue that continues to worry observers of communal conflicts
in Nigeria is the growing sophistication of the firearms used in
prosecuting the conflicts. This new trend was clearly manifested in
the last two major Aguleri-Umuleri wars of 1995 and 1999. The
Nweje Commission of Inquiry found that "double and single barrel
short guns and pump-action short guns both local and foreign"

were used.[32] Even the protagonists agree that the firepower has been on the increase. One elderly villager in Aguleri, who claimed that he experienced the 1933 war, told the investigators that many years back, the conflict was a "machete and stick fight", but these days frightening weapons are freely used. Interviewees on both sides consistently say that sophisticated assault rifles, rocket launchers and grenades were freely used in the last two conflicts. Rumours even have it that mortars were used to bring down whole buildings. The extent of damage to buildings in Otuocha, for instance, suggests that this may not be very far from the truth.

The Nweje Commission identified two major sources of weapons. First, the commission found that Aguleri Community had a lot of weapons carried over from their earlier conflict with the Obale of Kogi State. Second, both legal and illegal weapons were freely available from the Onitsha main market.[33] We think that what the conclusion of the commission raises is the ready availability of small arms in local communities. In a sense, this is paradoxical considering the rising level of rural poverty. The picture becomes clearer, however, if we bring a number of other issues into context. For one thing, the rising militarisation of social relations in Anambra State in the past few years, especially following the rise of vigilante groups like the Bakassi Boys, who were initially armed by wealthy people around the commercial town of Onitsha and, later, by the Mbadinuju government, contributed immensely to the flow of weapons.

For another thing, rich members of warring communities provided arms for youth to prosecute the conflict. As the principal of a local secondary school, who is not from any of the two warring communities, told the investigators, "the rich men of these communities are the problem. Do you know that during the war, they freely provided mercenaries and weapons for their communities?" Other independent observers confirm this. The investigators were told that a rich business man from a nearby town, who was well connected in the past military governments and who has strong family connections in Umuleri, was the chief procurer of weapons for Umuleri during the conflict. Unfortunately, government has not given this issue the attention it deserves. The Nweje Commission simply recommended that the police trace and prosecute owners of licensed weapons that were registered as exhibits. Government reaction was as tame as ever. According to the White Paper on the report of the commission, "government notes the recommendation and advises the police to ensure that all those who have guns renew their licenses".[34]

Mediation and Mistrust: Assessment of State Intervention in the Conflict

The Nigerian state has intervened in various ways in an attempt to check communal land conflicts across the country. Usually, each time violence erupts the starting point is for government to set up a panel of inquiry to trace the causes and proffer solutions. The communities sometimes contest the composition of such panels. However, the major sticky wicket is how the communities will view the product of the inquiry. Often, communities contest the reports and government White Papers and the panels are accused of bias. In the aftermath of the 1995 eruption of the Aguleri-Umuleri conflict, the Anambra State government set up a judicial commission to look into the matter. The commission's members were:

1. Moses O. Nweje, a retired High Court judge as chairman;
2. Chief D.C. Odenigbo, a retired permanent secretary (member);
3. Mr. S.S.C. Oguagha, a retired director-general (member);
4. Mrs. M.C. Emengo, a chief legal officer, Ministry of Justice (counsel); and
5. Mr. Eric O.Uchendu, a director in the Office of the Military Administrator (secretary)

The terms of reference of the panel included inquiring into the circumstances of the conflict and ascertaining the degree of involvement of persons or groups in it. The panel was also asked to ascertain the extent of loss of lives and property, the sources and types of arms used in the conflict and examine ways of enhancing peace and progress in the two communities.

One common solution that government panels of inquiry into communal land conflicts put forward is boundary demarcation between the warring communities. Often this has been done in cases involving communities in different states of the country. For example, after the creation of new states in 1976, the Justice Nasir Committee was established by the federal government to look into the problem of state boundaries. Apart from this nationwide exercise, other attempts at boundary demarcation have been made, especially following serious interstate boundary disputes. In the Aguleri-Umuleri case, government has made no serious attempt at boundary demarcation, notwithstanding the constant clamour for that by both communities. Still, the possibility of creating such a boundary is remote because of attendant difficulties. Boundary demarcation exercises in cases like this have usually been problematic because they attempt to create boundaries where historically there hardly was any. Often, they have relied on definition of boundaries conducted by the colonial government. But for the communities involved, these boundaries have never been recognized and so they are considered "government boundaries". They are even more loathsome if the colonialists created them. For instance, Aguleri has contested the boundary of the land sold by Umuleri to the Royal Niger Company, Chartered and Limited in 1898 for over 100 years. In a memorandum to the National Boundary Commission, the Aguleri community claimed that the same land the Umuleris were said to have sold to the Royal Niger Company (RNC) in 1898 was partly leased by Aguleri to a number of agencies, including the Royal Niger Company itself. The leases included the Roman Catholic Mission (1894), Hausa, Ijaw, Yoruba and Nupe communities (1915-1917), UAC (1922), Royal Niger Company (1924), John Holt (1926) and CFAO (1913).[35] Consequently, they consider the boundary in the agreement between the Umutchezi family of Umuleri and the RNC of no effect. Of course, the Umuleris insist that the boundary is legitimate.

The situation is worsened by government attempts to create boundaries by fiat, which often attracts accusations of bias by "disfavoured" communities. In 1964, Public Notice E.N.L.G.138 signed by the regional minister of local government, Chief J.U. Nwodo, was published by the Eastern Regional Government. The Notice changed the name Otuocha to "Otuocha Aguleri". The Umuleri community accused the minister and the Eastern Nigerian government of supporting Aguleri. The disaffection culminated in the Otuocha riots of that year. Subsequently, Umuleri community took the minister to court to challenge the legality of the change of name. Although they lost the case, perhaps the seeming injustice of such a rash decision compelled the East Central State Government to reverse the change after the civil war.

It is not surprising that the Justice Nweje Commission made profound recommendations on boundary adjustment in the area. The commission recommended that:

> Otuocha be constituted a local government area all by itself, be slightly expanded on the eastern side by taking the boundary beyond the Onitsha-Adani Road to bring the Dan Ekwevi filling station site within the Urban Area and be enlarged on the southern side to "flush" with Akor River and across the Onitsha-Adani Road up to Esisike Drinking Place.[36]

The state government accepted the principle of this recommendation. However, it noted that in the light of difficulties of getting the federal government to create a separate local government, Otuocha, as redefined by the panel, should be administered as a township or urban area based on Statutory Right of Occupancy rather than Customary Right of Occupancy. However, in their reaction to the government White Paper, the Aguleri community rejected these decisions. They accused the panel of bias, claiming among other things that the extension of Otuocha Urban was recommended solely to protect Chief Dan Ekwevi's filling station by including it in Otuocha Urban. The Aguleri community also claimed that one Mr. Henry Jidani, an Umuleri man who was also the director-general for lands at the time, masterminded the extension of the boundaries of Otuocha. According to them, Mr. Jidani "unduly included Aguleri ancestral homelands, which ought not to be included if he had been a neutral person. We, therefore, request that such extension be excluded".[37]

Again, after the 1999 flare-up the governor of Anambra State set up a commission to look into the conflict. The chairman of the Commission was named as Justice Emmanuel Araka, a retired High Court judge. However, the 1999 Commission was based on a slightly different approach. Unlike the Nweje Commission, the government named this. Some members were drawn from each of the three warring communities of Aguleri, Umuleri and Umuoba Anam. The members were Chief Barrister S.A.G. Umeadi (vice-chairman), Chief Igwah (secretary), Chief Emma Egwuoba (member), Chief V.M. Nwasi (member), Chief Ignatius Udalor (member) and Reverend Emma Mmuoba (member). Expectedly, the terms of reference of this commission read almost like that of the Nweje Panel. They include investigation of the remote and immediate causes of the conflict, investigation of the factors that sustained the conflict, sourcing of funds and materials for the rehabilitation of the victims, and recommending measures to bring about sustained peace. The report of the commission is still awaited. However, during our fieldwork in Aguleri we picked up skepticism about the commission. We were told that as a young lawyer in the 1950s, Araka represented Umuleri in one of the court cases. As one interviewee put it, Aguleri people are waiting to see if his role in the peace committee would be another case of the voice of Jacob and the hands of Esau.

It is hoped that the peace commission strategy will work better than the previous judicial one. This is because it is expected that the reconciliation and consensus principles behind peace commissions could provide a more lasting solution than the principles of retribution and remediation behind judicial commissions. Still, the difficulties that are likely to confront the peace panel should not be overlooked. First, its emphasis on consensus means that it is likely to be time-consuming, tardy and expensive. Second, it is difficult to see how the animosities of one century could recede so quickly in favour of consensus building. Third, devoid of the capacity of sanction, it is difficult to see how the peace commission could compel long-standing combatants to accept its decisions. Finally, reconciliation is irrelevant without justice. But, justice in this case is a tall order. The persistence of age-old animosities and exclusive claims to Otuocha by the communities will be intractable issues for the commission to solve. Yet, any long-lasting solution to the Aguleri-Umuleri conflict must resolve these issues.

The most frequent intervention of the state in the Aguleri-Umuleri conflict has manifested through the law courts.[38] Records show that between 1920 there were at least 12 cases over Otuocha land in which both Aguleri and Umuleri sought exclusive ownership of the land (Table 8). In 1933, Umuleri sued Aguleri at the Native Court and got a declaration from Captain Dermont O'Connor, the divisional officer, who ruled that Aguleri was late in challenging the sale of Otuocha land to the Royal Niger Company by Umuleri. In his ruling on the appeal brought by Aguleri, Justice Graham Paul held that Umuleri could not prove ownership of the land having sold it to the Royal Niger Company. In 1935, Umuleri again sued for the rest of Otuocha outside the limits sold to the Royal Niger Company. Following admission by both sides that they used the land in common, Umuleri was non-suited, that is ordered to return to the status quo before the suit.[39] Following the order to the Crown abandoning Otuocha land, Umuleri once more sued Aguleri for exclusive ownership of the land in 1950 at the Umuiguedo Native Court. Umuleri retained the services of Mr. Daddy Onyeama, while Aguleri briefed L. N. Mbanefo. Both lawyers later became acclaimed names in legal circles in Nigeria and internationally with Onyeama becoming a justice of the International Court at the Hague. In December, 1950, the case was transferred to the Onitsha Supreme (High) Court. In his 1955 ruling, Justice W.H. Hurley ruled in favour of Aguleri because the plaintiffs could not establish exclusive ownership. Umuleri went on to appeal both to the West African Court of Appeal (WACA) and the Privy Council in London and lost.

On 15 October, 1964, by a Public Notice signed by Chief J.U. Nwodo, who was the regional minister of local government, the Eastern Regional Government amended the Instrument that constituted Anambra County Council by replacing the word "Otu-Ocha" with "Otu-Ocha Aguleri". This attracted a lawsuit from Umuleri against the minister of local government. Umuleri lost the suit and possibility of an appeal was overtaken by the civil war. However, after the civil war the East Central State government reverted to the original name of Otuocha. Then in 1975, Aguleri sued Umuleri for exclusive ownership of the land. Justice T.C. Umezinwa at Onitsha heard the case. In what has become a visionary ruling, Justice Umezinwa ruled that neither community could establish exclusive ownership of Otuocha. On appeal against Umezinwa's ruling to the Appeal Court in Enugu, Aguleri got a ruling in 1978 granting it ownership of Otuocha land. Six years later the case was ruled on by the Supreme Court in an appeal brought by Umuleri against the Enugu Court of Appeal ruling. The two communities were represented by an array of renowned Nigerian lawyers including Chief F.R.A. Williams and G.C.M. Onyiuke for Umuleri, and G.N.A. Okafor and Chief O.B. Onyali for Aguleri. The case was heard by some of the best justices of the Supreme Court, namely, Ayo Irikefe, Mohammed Bello, Andrews

Obaseki, Kayode Eso and Augustine Nnamani. Their historic ruling put paid to the long battle of Aguleri and Umuleri for exclusive ownership of Otuocha. Justice Nnamani has summarized it all:

> I would wish particularly to associate myself with this hope that the Aguleris and Umuleris, after 60 years of litigation which has largely confirmed each community as owners of a portion of the area in dispute, would now seek a rapprochement and allow the spirit of communal harmony and accommodation to prevail.

Table 8: Court Cases Over Otuocha Land, 1920-1984

Year	Place	Plaintiff/Appellant /Lawyers	Defendant /Lawyer	Ruling
1920	Native Court	Umuleri	Aguleri	Not available
1933	Native Court	Umuleri	Aguleri	Captain O'Connor ruled in favour of Umuleri
1933	Onitsha High Court	Aguleri (Appeal against 1933 case)	Umuleri	Justice Graham Paul reversed O'Connor's ruling
1935	Onitsha High Court	Umuleri	Aguleri	Umuleri was non-suited (directed to return to status quo before the suit)
1950	Umuiguedo Native Court	Umuleri (Onyeama; Soetan & Osadebay)	Aguleri (L.N Mbanefo)	Case was transferred to Onitsha Supreme (High) Court
1951	Onitsha Supreme Court	Umuleri (Messrs. Soetan & Araka)	Aguleri (Mr. Balonwu)	Justice W.H. Hurley ruled in favour of defendants in 1955
1955	West African Court of Appeal	Umuleri (Mr. Dingle Foot, QC)	Aguleri (Mr. Pheneas Quass, QC)	Justice Cyril Hubbard and Foster Sutton ruled in favour of the defendants
1958	Privy Council	Umuleri (Appeal against WACA ruling)	Aguleri	WACA ruled in favour of Aguleri

1964	Onitsha High Court	Umuleri	Minister of local government	Suit was overtaken by the civil war
1975	Onitsha High Court	Aguleri	Umuleri	Justice Umezinwa ruled in favour of defendants
1978	Appeal Court, Enugu	Aguleri (Appeal against High Court ruling)	Umuleri	Appeal court reversed Umezinwa's ruling
1984	Supreme Court	Umuleri (Appeal against Appeal Court ruling)	Aguleri	Supreme Court restored Umezinwa's ruling

Role of Civil Society in the Management of the Conflict

The court cases over Otuocha must stand out as some of the most vigorously contested in the legal history of Nigeria. The names that have been associated with the court cases sound like the legal "who is who" of Nigeria. They include T.C. Umezinwa, Alfa Belgore, Phil-Ebosie, O. Olatawura, Sir Louis Mbanefo, Chief F.R.A. Williams, Chief G.C.M. Onyiuke, Chief D.C. Osadebe, Chike Ofodile, Soetan, Emmanuel Araka, Chief Fani-Kayode, F.O. Nwokedi, Dove Edwin, and Balonwu among many others. However, that the conflict has persisted points to the inadequacy of settling such communal disputes in the law courts. Indeed, the entire system of state interventions in the conflict has failed to resolve it. This has led to increasing calls for alternative conflict management strategies. It is in this context that civil society has increasingly emerged as an alternative platform to the state for managing the conflict. Still, this is not to say that state intervention is either unnecessary or irrelevant. In fact, local people in the communities still value government intervention in the conflict in various ways. Indeed, there remains a strong feeling that it is only government that is capable of resolving the conflict and backing it up with action, if it so wishes. To confirm this point, we asked respondents to our questionnaire what agencies have been involved in conflict management and how successful they have been. Their responses are illustrated in Fig. 6. The chart shows that the warring communities rank the federal government high in attempts to resolve the conflict. This is not unrelated to the visit by President Obasanjo to the area in August, 1999, and the provision of some relief materials by the federal government some months later.

However, the chart also shows a consistent high ranking of non-governmental processes in the management of the conflict. For instance, community leadership and organizations like *Ohaneze Ndigbo* were rated highly as active agents of conflict management. It will be recalled that *Ohaneze* intervened in the conflict on April 20, 1999, calling for cessation of hostilities. Non-governmental organisations, churches, kindred meetings, women's groups and youth organisations were also ranked highly as active participants in the conflict management process.

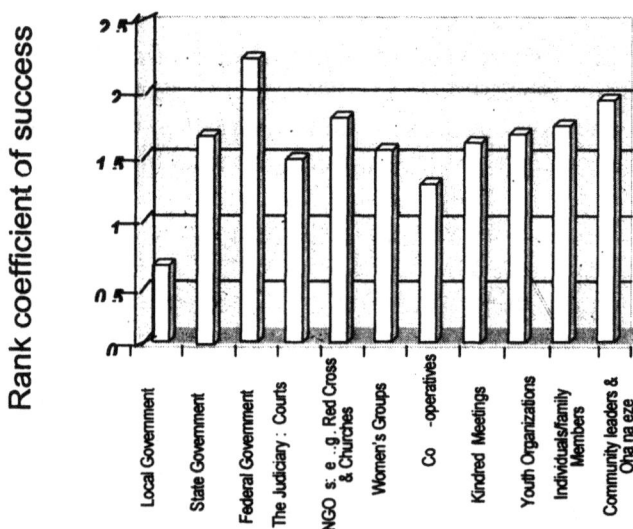

Fig. 6: Respondents Ranking of Conflict Resolution Agents

The main form of assistance provided to victims of the conflict was food relief, as shown in Table 9. However, it does seem that the general level of assistance given to people was low. Apart from food assistance, which about 70% of our respondents said was provided, all other forms of assistance recorded low frequencies. For instance, 85% of respondents said that people were not relocated from conflict areas, 77% said that assistance with shelter was not provided and 73.7% said that financial assistance was not given. In fact, we found that during the conflict people were assisted more by family member/relations and non-governmental organizations, than by government, especially local government. This is worrisome because the local government is meant to be the closest tier of government to local people. Explanations given to us by local people for this poor showing of local government vary. Some argued that the poor relationship between the warring communities makes it difficult for the Anambra East Local Government to function effectively. Officials are readily accused of taking sides in the conflict, whenever they act. This, they say, derives partly from past experience with some officials who sought to use the local government machinery to further the interest of one community or another. Other people we interviewed said that the local government is not properly resourced to take care of such problems. Because of poor funding, local councils are not in a position to deal with complex emergencies such as befell the communities during the conflicts. They called for increased capacity for local councils to deal with such situations in future.

Table 9: Forms of Assistance Provided to Victims of Conflict

	YES	NO	NO RESPONSE	TOTAL
Provision of food relief	125	40	14	179
	69.83%	22.35%	7.82%	100.00%
Relocation of people	17	152	10	179
	9.50%	84.92%	5.59%	100.00%
Provision of shelter	31	138	10	179
	17.32%	77.09%	5.59%	100.00%
Provision of legal aid	7	162	10	179
	3.91%	90.50%	5.59%	100.00%
Provision of scholarship	11	158	10	179
	6.15%	88.27%	5.59%	100.00%
Provision of other financial aid	30	132	17	179
	16.76%	73.74%	9.50%	100.00%

The ineffectiveness of the local government in caring for victims of the conflict is simply shown in Table 10. Compared to the federal government that had a rank coefficient of 2.02 and the state government which had a rank of 1.3, the local government only recorded a coefficient of 0.48, the lowest in the table. On the other hand, NGOs did very well as did families and individuals in providing care for victims. Surely, the role of NGOs in the conflict was not limited to provision of care for victims. They were also heavily involved in finding new ways of conflict management. This is in the light of the shortcomings of standard approaches to conflict management adopted by the state. In fact, 90.8% of respondents to our questionnaire thought that civil society and community-based organizations such as religious groups, elders, town unions, cooperatives, and family/kindred meetings have important roles to play in the management of the conflict. Even more so, majority of respondents expressed high confidence in non-government organisations' ability to effectively manage or solve the issues behind the conflict. Table 11 gives the ranked responses to the question in our questionnaire which is, "What level of confidence do people in your community have in the ability of the following to effectively manage or solve the issues creating the conflict?"

Again, the table shows that the federal government was ranked highest. Religious organizations, non-governmental organizations and community-based organizations were also highly ranked. It is, however, interesting that youth organizations were ranked as high as third. In all the questions involving the ranking of various agencies, this was the highest ranking received by youth organizations. Our worry is that youth organizations are actually the phalanxes used by the communities in these conflicts. To rank them this high could mean either of two things, on the one hand, it could mean that being the foot soldiers in the conflicts, youths are in a position to change the course of events if they embrace peace. On the other hand, however, it could mean that the communities look forward to future conflicts in which the leadership of youth organizations will be central to "victory".

Table 10: Ranking of Effectiveness of Care Provided to Victims of Conflict

	Very effective	Effective	Not effective	Not involved	Total	Rank Coefficient
Local Government	3	14	30	92	139	0.48
State Government	23	52	21	53	149	1.30
Federal Government	72	43	17	26	158	2.02
Religious						

Groups (e.g) churches	97	34	18	12	161	2.34
NGOs e.g Red Cross	72	40	12	32	156	1.97
Women's Groups	40	35	17	53	145	1.43
Co-operative Societies	25	32	29	57	143	1.17
Kindred Meetings	65	25	20	42	152	1.74
Youth Organisations	45	40	10	48	143	1.57
Individuals/ immediate Family	48	50	13	40	151	1.70
Community Elders/ Traditional Council	62	41	16	34	153	1.86

Civil Society Conflict Management Initiatives

Ohanaeze Ndi Igbo Initiative
The first civil society initiative to resolve the Aguleri-Umuleri conflict in recent times is to be credited to *Oha na Eze Ndi Igbo*. This is a pan-Igbo cultural-political organisation founded by renowned Igbo political, intellectual, business and cultural elite as a platform for redefining the Igbo position in national affairs. Unhappy with the lack of response by the outgoing military government at the state and federal levels to the plight of innocent citizens in the violence, the *Ohanaeze* met in Enugu in April, 1999, on the conflict. On 20 April 1999, they issued a communiqué signed by Chief K. Onyioba, Professor Ben Nwabueze, Chief Austin Ezenwa, Chief Desmond Oguguo, Chief L. Ejinkonye and Chekwas Okorie. While calling for an immediate cessation of violence, they criticized the government for being insensitive and not decisively responsive to finding a lasting solution to the problem. Particularly, *Ohanaeze* criticized the state government under Wing Commander Ukaegbu for its failure to implement the recommendations contained in "its own White Paper" on the report of the Nweje Panel, which was published in February, 1997, almost two years before the resurgence

of violence. Subsequently, *Ohanaeze* organized several peace meetings with the communities at Awka and visited the communities. The *Ohanaeze* initiative was able to secure a temporary truce in the fighting, for about two weeks. Unfortunately, the process was not consolidated and the violence resumed soon after.

Table 11: Ranking of Level of Confidence in Conflict Management Agencies

	Very Confident	Confident	Little Confident	Total	Rank Coefficient
Local Government	7	21	119	147	1.24
State Government	21	79	51	151	1.80
Federal Government	66	51	36	153	2.20
Religious Groups e.g churches	22	30	91	143	1.52
NGOs e.g Red Cross	63	39	48	150	2.10
Women's Groups	36	42	69	147	1.78
Co-operative Societies	34	38	72	144	1.74
Kindred Meetings	34	36	77	147	1.71
Youth Organisations	55	38	54	147	2.01
Community Elders /Traditional Council	40	47	57	144	1.88

Anambra East Peace Council
The second initiative was under the auspices of the Anambra East Council of Traditional Rulers and Leaders of Thought. The chairman of the Anambra East Council of Traditional Rulers, Chief (Dr.) Kelly Nzekwesi, who is also the traditional ruler (*Igwe*) of Igbariam, initiated the process. The process began in mid July 1999, with an inaugural meeting at the Onitsha North Local Government headquarters. In addition to *Igwe* Kelly Nzekwesi, other leaders of the initiative were the traditional rulers of Nsugbe, Nando, Aguleri, Umuleri and Umuoba, as well as some prominent members of the three feuding communities and their neighbours. The group became known as the Anambra East Peace Council.

The thrust of the Anambra East Peace Council initiative was to return to traditional means of settling disputes. After a series of meetings, the council announced a number of steps to ensure the return of peace. They pledged co-operation with the Araka

Committee. At the same time, they called for immediate end to hostilities and return of persons displaced in the conflicts to their homes. Finally, they set up a process of traditional oath taking and covenant to end the feuding and shedding of blood. Oath taking (*nghu iyi*) and blood covenant (*iko mme*) are common traditional practices in the Anambra River basin. The first involves swearing to powerful community deities and pledging a specified course of behaviour. Oath taking was a very powerful mechanism for behavioural change in traditional Igbo societies. The second arises in situations where there has been shedding of blood. It is a means of appeasing the *Ana* deity, which abhors the spilling of blood. *Iko mme* involves sacrifices and may also involve reparations taking the form of exchange of human beings to replace the dead (*nkechi mmadu*) or mere exchange of valuables and/or services. That these practices, which had previously been widely abandoned, were re-invented in spite of the tremendous progress of Christianity in the area, including the recent beatification of Father Iwene Tansi of Aguleri, points to the desperate desire of the communities to find a lasting solution to the conflict. Many Christians in the community and beyond have criticized the resort to "fetish practices" by the communities. However, the traditional leaders challenge critics to find better solutions to the century old conflict.

The first attempt at effecting the oath taking and covenant was made in the beginning of 2000 and involved five communities namely, Aguleri, Umuleri, Igbariam, Nando and Nsugbe. The communities came with their various deities to be sworn to. These included *Aro Olome Nkilisi* (Aguleri), *Isi mkpume* (Umuleri), *Udude onu ogwu* (Igbariam) *Isi Ogwugwu* (Nando) and *Iyi Oji* (Nsugbe). However, this attempt failed because of petition from the Umuoba community, as well as faction of the Aguleri community. The Aguleri faction arose out of conflicts over the traditional stool of the community following the death of *Igwe* Idigo. The state government intervened by asking the council to ensure that the process was inclusive. The exclusion of Umuoba was partly at the instance of Umuleri. They had argued that the process could not commence between Umuleri and Umuoba because the attack of Umuoba on Umuleri violated an earlier oath between the two communities in the dry season of 1910. Also, unlike Aguleri, Umuleri, Igbariam, Nsugbe and Nando, the Umuoba are not regarded as descendants of Eri. Apart from these issues, there was the thorny issue of participation of Christians in the process. To proceed without the participation of the large population of Christians would have undermined legitimacy of the process. It took about three months to resolve these problems. Finally, on 4 April, 2000, the ceremony took place at Otuocha. All the communities came with their deities, while the Christians participated by inviting priests to pray. While the traditionalists swore to the deities, Christians also swore on the Bible. The communities through their representatives swore never to wage war against each other and to use dialogue to resolve disputes. They also asked the deities to punish violators of the oath. Thereafter, Christians did the same with Catholic and Anglican priests presiding.

Eri Brothers Association

At the same time that process led by the Anambra East Council of Traditional Rulers and Leaders of Thought was on, a parallel move under the aegis of what later became known as the Eri Brothers Association was also on. Many observers have wondered how Aguleri and Umuleri could have sustained such a fratricidal conflict in the midst of strong bonds of blood and marriage that link the two communities together. In fact, it is said that there is scarcely an Aguleri person who does not have relations in Umuleri and vice-versa. In fact, for a long time there have existed people from the two communities who supported a peaceful resolution of the conflict using traditional methods, which draw extensively on such bonds. The *umudiana* and *umuokpu* are well-established traditional structures that interface marriage and blood relationships. That the Aguleri-Umuleri conflict has lasted this long is even more surprising because the two communities even believe in their common descent from Eri. This means that there is even a stronger basis to exploit such cross-community bonds. It is this challenge that the group, which later called itself Eri Brothers, sought to take up. This group, which included individuals from Aguleri, Umuleri, Nsugbe, Nando and Igbariam, were active in the first oath taking in 2000. One problem, however, was the division within the Aguleri community itself. The rift between the *Udedibia* group and the *Obukezie* group is not unconnected with the struggle for the vacant stool of the traditional ruler of Aguleri, following the death of *Igwe* Idigo. The exclusion of Umuoba Anam from the oath taking at the beginning of 2000 led to a walkout by the *Obukezie* group. In their petition to the state government, which led the government to order the cancellation of the oath taking, the Umuoba Anam community described the process as a conspiracy under the guise of a new found Eri brotherhood and threatened to disregard the earlier cease-fire agreement.[40]

Role of the Churches
Christian churches have also been a very active part of civil society seeking to end the bloodletting between Aguleri and Umuleri. The Catholic, Anglican and Pentecostal churches have been widely involved. As a matter of fact, the conflict has affected the churches adversely. Apart from the general disruption of church activities, the churches have also lost properties each time the conflict erupted. For instance, both the Our Lady of Victory Catholic Church and St. Gabriel's Anglican Church lost properties worth nearly 35 million Naira during the 1995 crisis.[41] In addition, the persistence of the conflict has cast a very negative image on the Christian churches in the area. Many people feel that the clergy have not done enough to broker peace. Above all, there is a feeling that the conflict may not have seriously undermined the long expected Catholic sainthood of late Reverend Father Iwene Tansi, a native of Aguleri. During the 1999 crisis and in its aftermath, the churches were more actively involved. Prayers were said for the safety of people and many displaced people took refuge in churches. In the aftermath of the conflict, the churches were also actively involved in the process of peacemaking. Priests of both the Anglican and Catholic churches were said to have prayed for Christians during the antiwar oath taking in April, 2000, crusades were organized at Otuocha to pray for an end to the conflicts and lasting peace.

Conclusion
This chapter set out to analyse the Aguleri-Umuleri conflict and the role of civil society in its management. Its central thesis is that there is need to re-evaluate the notion linking cultural differences and communal conflicts against the backdrop of intra-ethnic communal conflicts. In addition, the chapter set this re-evaluation

in the context of rural land conflicts. It began with a critique of classical theories of boundary conflicts, especially those that link conflicts to inherent expansionism of political entities. To the contrary, it is argued that land conflicts are linked to the material interests of social forces in interaction.

The history of the Aguleri-Umuleri conflict shows that the struggle for the ownership of Otuocha, a beach along the River Anambra, has been the central *casus belli*. The arrival of Europeans in the area transformed not only the economic value of land, but social relations among communities, which had used the land in common until that time. Competition to sell or lease land for profit to Levantine organisations, rather than for farming and other communal uses, became the central motive force behind land property. This transformation was conducive to conflict. Over time, the conflict itself was transformed from a resource conflict into an animosity conflict because of the long years of struggle, particularly the court cases that spanned almost sixty-five years.

The limited success recorded by conflict management strategies adopted by government increasingly led to calls for alternative means of conflict management. Still, the role of government has to be nuanced. The study found that consistently the role of the federal and state governments in the conflict was highly rated by respondents to our questionnaire. However, this may well be a rating of particular governments at the time of the study rather than a general assessment of the intervention of government over the years. Also, particular forms of government intervention at specific times created more problems than they solved. This was particularly the case with court cases and commissions of inquiry. The attempt of these interventions to be retributive and remedial rather than to build consensus, increased the sense of loss, deepened grievances and prolonged animosities. The change that civil society interventions seem to have introduced into the management of this conflict, which could be helpful in similar situations in future, relates to the building of broad-based consensus drawing on traditional approaches to conflict management. It is in this light that the oath taking and blood covenant strategies adopted by the Anambra East Council of Traditional Rulers and Leaders of Thought are to be seen.

References

1. Aguleri Community, "A Memorandum Submitted to the National Boundary Commission, Abuja, by the Aguleri Community in Respect of Aguleri-Umuleri Boundary Dispute", November 14, 1999 (mimeo), p.3.
2. See Okwudiba Nnoli, *Ethnic Politics in Nigeria* (Enugu: Fourth Dimension, 1978). See also Samuel Egwu, *Ethnic and Religious Violence in Nigeria* (Abuja: African Centre for Democratic Governance, 2001), p.11.
3. O. Ibeanu and G. Onu, "Ethnic Groups and Conflicts in Nigeria, Volume 2: The Southeast Zone of Nigeria" (Ibadan: Programme On Ethnic and Federal Studies, 2001).
4. O. Ibeanu, "Religious Pluralism and Democratic Governance in Southeastern Nigeria", *Research Report No.1*, (Kano: Centre for Research and Documentation, 2002).
5. A. Afigbo, *Ropes of Sand: Studies in Igbo History and Culture* (Nsukka: U.N.N. Press, 1981), pp.90-93.
6. *Ibid.*, p.20. See also O. Ibeanu & G. Onu *op. cit.*, p.49.
7. Ibeanu & Onu, *ibid.*, p.33.
8. Samuel Egwu, "Agrarian Question, Politics and Ethnic Conflicts in Rural Nigeria", *CASS Monograph Series*, No.10 (Port Harcourt: Centre for Advanced Social Science, 1999), p.11.
9. O. Nnoli, *op. cit.*
10. J. Prescott, *The Geography of Frontiers and Boundaries* (Chicago: Adline Publishing Co., 1965).
11. S. Tagil et al., *Studying Boundary Conflicts: A Theoretical Framework* (Lund, Sweden: Scandinavian University Books, 1977), p.151.
12. T. Holdich, *Political Frontiers and Boundary Making* (London: Macmillan, 1916).
13. N. Spykman & A. Rollins, "Geographic Objectives in Foreign Policy", in *American Political Science Review*, Vol.33, 1939.
14. J. Prescott, *op. cit.*, p.114.
15. S. Boggs, *International Boundaries: A Study of Boundary Functions and Problems* (New York: Columbia University Press, 1940).
16. S. Jones, *Boundary Making: A Handbook for Statesmen, Treaty Editors and Boundary Commissioners* (Washington, D.C. Carnegie Endowment for International Peace, 1945).

17. S. Tagil, et. al. *op. cit.*, p.159.
18. J. Prescott, *op. cit.*
19. *Ibid.*, p.153.
20. Claude Ake "The Future of the State in Africa", in *International Political Science Review*, Vol.6, No.1, 1985
21. O. Ibeanu & G. Onu, "Ethnic Mapping of the Southeast Zone of Nigeria" (Ibadan: University of Ibadan Programme on Ethnic and Federal Studies (PEFS), 2001).
22. Aguleri Community, *op. cit.*, p.2.
23. *Ibid.*
24. A: Afigbo, *op. cit.*, pp.36-37.
25. Federal Court of Appeal, *Otuocha Land Case: Judgement of the Federal Court of Appeal, Enugu Judicial Division Holden at Enugu* (Enugu: Thompson and Group Printers, 1981), p.13.
26. Government of Anambra State, *Government White Paper on the Report of the Aguleri and Umuleri Disturbances Commission of Inquiry* (Awka: Government Printer, 1997), p.4.
27. *Ibid.*, p.17.
28. Aguleri Community, *op. cit.*, p.15.
29. Government of Anambra State, *op. cit.*, pp.4-5.
30. *Ibid.*, p.7.
31. *Ibid.*, p.16.
32. *Ibid.*
33. *Ibid.*
34. *Ibid.*
35. Aguleri Community, *op. cit.*, pp.14-15.
36. Government of Anambra State, *op. cit.*, p.4.
37. Aguleri Community *op. cit.*, p.20.
38. R. Chinwuba, *Legal Essay on the Otu-Ocha Land Case* (Enugu: Star Printing and Publishing Co., 1981).
39. Government of Anambra State, *op. cit.*, p.3.
40. C. Ifediora, *Odera's First Role in Anambra State: Casting the Devil out of Aguleri/Umuleri and Umuoba Anam* (Onitsha: Creative Forum Publishers, 2000), p.31.
41. Government of Anambra State, *op. cit.*, p.18.

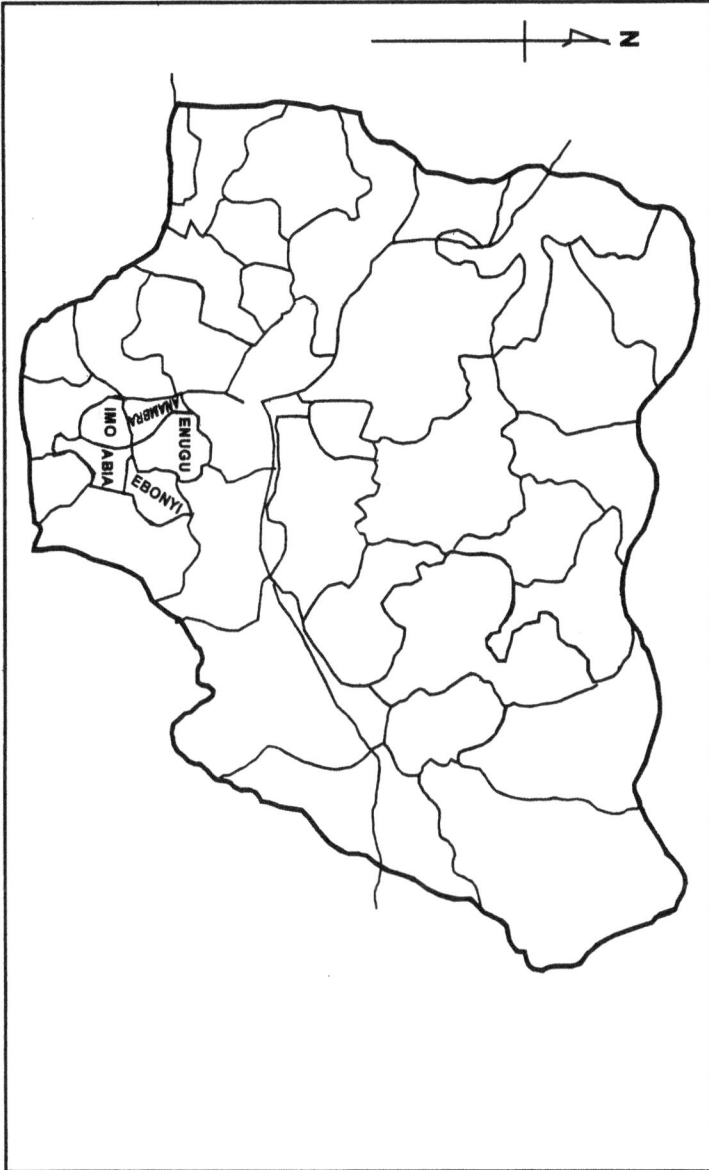

MAP OF NIGERIA SHOWING THE SOUTH-EAST ZONE

MAP OF ANAMBRA STATE SHOWING STUDIED AREA

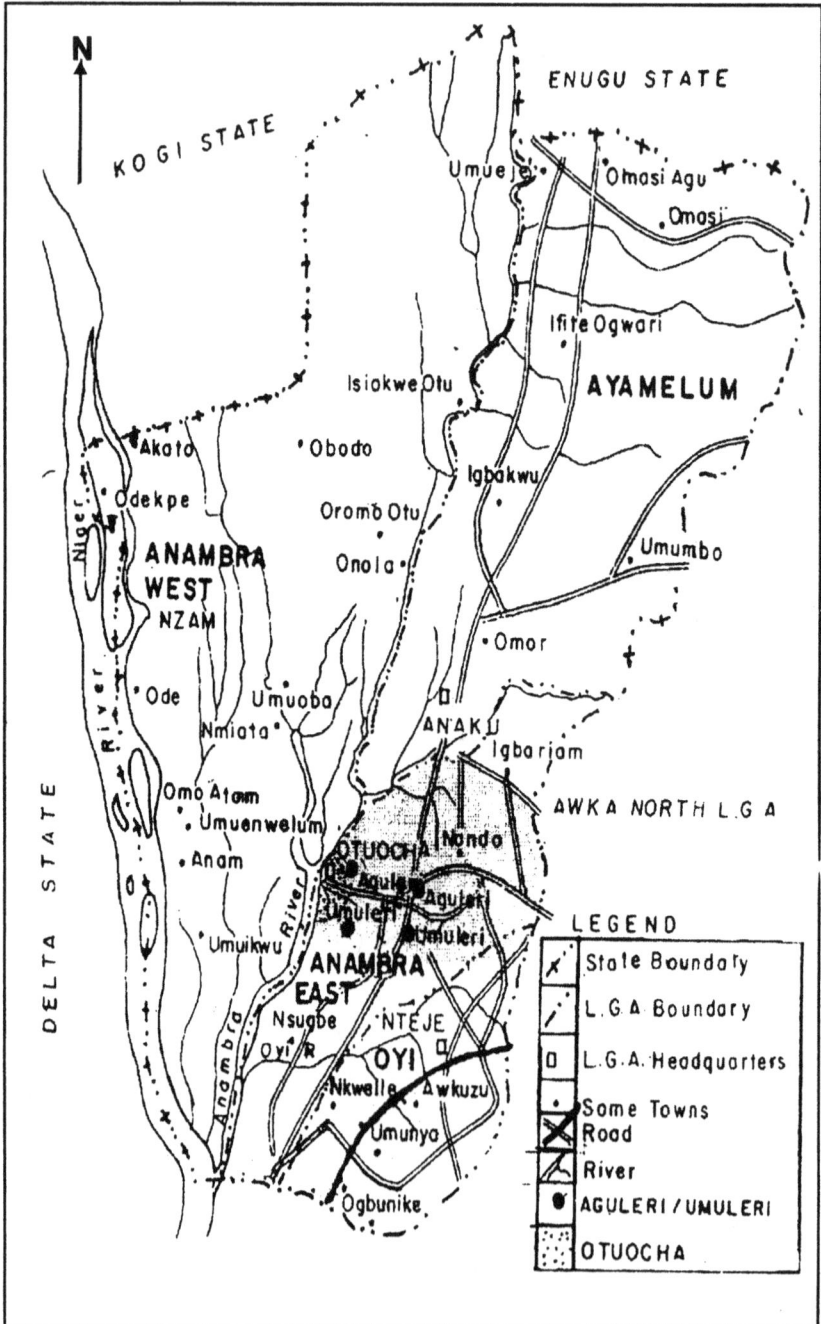

Chapter 9

Urhobo-Itsekiri Conflict in Delta State

Agatha Eguavoen

Introduction

Conflict management and resolution became an important phenomenon or concept because of the magnitude of conflict taking place in our societies. In any settlement or social formation, where there are two or more divergent views, interests, or goals and aspirations by individuals or groups, conflict is bound to arise. The magnitude and dimension such a conflict eventually takes depends on the value placed on the contentious issues by the parties involved and the methods adopted to resolve such issues. Most conflicts, especially in Nigeria, have ethnic or religious undertone and their origin predates the colonial era. The coming of the white man did not in any way help matters because, the colonial masters were more interested in administrative convenience than in addressing the issues involved in ethnic conflicts. This trend has left its mark all over the places colonised by the whites. Even the intractable middle-east crisis is traceable to the activities of the colonial masters in the region.

Coser defined conflict as a struggle over values and claims of scarce status, power and resources, in which the aims of the opponents are to neutralise, injure or eliminate their rivals.[1] To Donohue and Kolt, conflict involves situation in which differences are expressed by interdependent peoples in the process of achieving their needs and goals.[2] Onigu Otite has identified seven likely

sources of conflict in our communities. They are:
1. The struggle for land space and the resources available;
2. Disputed jurisdiction of certain traditional rulers and chiefs, where a king of one ethnic or sub-ethnic group claims rulership over people belonging to another ethnic group;
3. Creation of new local government councils and the location of their headquarters;
4. Ethnic and individual or sectional competition over access to scarce political and economic resources;
5. The micro and macro social structures in Nigeria;
6. Population growth and expansionist tendencies to sustain ethnic-bound occupations—a type of conflict popular amongst users of land resources; and
7. The perception or disregard for cultural symbols and the "pollution" of cultural practices.[3]

All these are veritable sources, of conflict in our Nigerian society. Sources 1 – 4 are all present in our case study and will be discussed in details. Conflicts, especially ethnic conflicts, have taken very serious dimension in Nigeria. The mayhem always associated with such conflicts has heightened the anxiety and sense of insecurity in the country. The high sense of insecurity has given birth to all types of para-military organisations from different ethnic groups, who claim to be helping the law enforcement agents in maintaining peace and order in their environment. They come under different disguises: some as youth organisations, some as vigilante groups and some as militant groups of one ethnic group or the other. The apparent helplessness of the populace in the face of increased violence and insecurity in the country has given a tacit approval and support to these ethnic militant groups and their likes. There is, therefore, the need to address the issues of ethnic conflicts in all zones or areas where they exist in order to find a lasting solution in either managing the situation or resolving the issues in dispute.

The Study Area
This chapter is primarily concerned with the complex conflict in the Niger Delta Region, involving three of the main ethnic groups in the area, namely Urhobo, Itsekiri and Ijaw. The conflict is being played out in the oil city of Warri in Delta State. Delta State is located

in the South-South Zone of the six geo-political zones into which Nigeria has been divided. The South-South Zone comprises the states within the Niger Delta region, where the bulk of Nigeria's crude oil is produced. Crude oil is the greatest export revenue-yielding venture in Nigeria. It accounts for about 95% of the country's foreign exchange earnings. The South-South Zone accounts for about 90% of the country's crude oil production. Hence, the zone is the most strategic region of Nigeria, where the country's economic life-wire is concentrated.

The South-South Zone is made up of six states, namely, Akwa Ibom, Bayelsa, Cross River, Delta, Edo and Rivers. These states are usually referred to as the Southern Minority States because they are inhabited by the minority ethnic groups in the southern part of Nigeria. The zone is home to not less than 55 out of Nigeria's over 300 different ethnic and sub-ethnic groups.[4] The major ethnic groups in the region include Edo (Bini), Igbo, Efik, Urhobo, Isoko, Itsekiri, Izon (Ijaw), Ibibio, Calabari, Ikwere, Okrika, Gokana, Eleme, Andoni, Anang and Ogoni. Despite the tremendous wealth in the South-South Zone, there is incessant crisis in the area and cries of political marginalisation, economic pauperization and environmental degradation. The zone is, therefore, a hotbed of protest and conflict.

Conflict Profile in the South-South Zone
The South-South zone is a region with high conflict quotient, as a result of which it has suffered a lot of devastation. Examples include the Ogoni episode, the Odi massacre and the mayhem in Warri. The most prevalent conflicts in the zone are inter-ethnic conflicts, that is, conflicts between the various communities and conflicts between the latter, especially the youth, and the oil companies and, by extension, the government. The reason for the high conflict quotient is not far-fetched. The nation's wealth is mainly derived from this area, yet it is the least developed in the country. Environmental degradation of the area due to the activities of oil companies has virtually destroyed the people's means of livelihood. Aquatic life and fish stock are diminishing due to environmental pollution. The various communities are hardly at peace with one another. Cost of living is high in the Niger Delta, as river transportation is cumbersome and quite expensive. The poverty

level is high in most if not in all the oil producing communities. The people have no access to clean water or electricity; educational opportunities are low, while the level of unemployment is very high. The result is the presence of an army of jobless youths who are easily mobilized and ready to go on rampage at the slightest provocation.

There is virtually a running battle between the youth and the oil companies and by extension the government. Oil employees, both Nigerians and expatriates, are regularly abducted for ransom. Because the South-South Zone holds the key to the country's economic prosperity, the government is particularly sensitive to the outbreak of conflicts that have the potentiality of disrupting the exploitation of the country's strategic minerals, oil and gas, in the area. This sensitivity has led to the frequent deployment of security forces to the area; thereby creating the impression of a region permanently under military occupation.

The Case Study
As we remarked earlier, this chapter is concerned with the deep-rooted conflict between the Urhobo, Itsekiri and Ijaw ethnic groups in Delta State. The main objective of the study is to explore ways of bringing about a lasting solution to the conflict that has led to a lot of devastation in Warri. To this end, we shall look into the causes of the conflict, its spread and effect on the people and the nation at large, past efforts at managing it, as well as the means of arriving at an amicable resolution of the conflict. The resolution of the conflict will aim at

1. fostering peaceful co-existence among the three different ethnic groups in Warri;
2. seeking alternative mode of ethnic conflict management in the area; and
3. empowering the non-governmental organisations or any other organisations, which thrive in civil society, in the management of ethnic conflicts in the area.

Method of Study
The study area consists of Warri town, and the totality of the warring three ethnic groups, namely, Itsekiris, Urhobos and the Ijaws. Given the fund and time available for this study, we definitely could not

cover the total population. Therefore, we had to adopt a sampling strategy. A multi-system sampling method was adopted; first, through clusters in the different communities and then through a systematic random sampling to arrive at our final elements of study. One thousand respondents were chosen from each ethnic community. And at the end of the day, 900 were found worthy of analysis.

Techniques of Data Collection
In this study, a combination of methods was used in generating data given the nature of the study. Both primary and secondary data were very vital. The primary sources included interview and questionnaire administration. Both methods were used because of the literacy level in the community. Our respondents include both literate and illiterate population.

Questionnaire schedule was administered to the literate population while the same schedule served as interview schedule for the illiterate community. Focus group discussion was also part of the primary sources of data collection. Six sessions of two in each community were conducted. Information gathered from key informants from the three communities was of great importance. A focus interview approach was adopted in generating information from these categories of persons. This requires that the interview takes place with person(s) known to be involved with particular concrete experiences. Applied to situations analysed before, the interview emphasises major areas of inquiry and elicits the subjective reactions of respondents.[5] Secondary sources such as documentary record, literature review etc. were also utilized in information gathering.

Historical Background to the Ethnic Conflict in Warri
The Itsekiris and the Urhobos are two neighbouring peoples who inhabit part of the Delta region of Nigeria. Ikime observes that the relation between these two people has been quite uneasy.[6] Yet they had for a long time been known to be socially interrelated, with high frequency of intermarriage amongst themselves, live together in the same community, commercially interdependent and remain very much so up till date. The conflict between the Urhobos and the Itsekiris predates the coming of the colonial masters. The conflict

between these two ethnic groups is historical in origin, thereby making it difficult to access who actually is presenting the real facts. The Urhobos claim that they are the original owners and settlers in Warri, and only gave tenancy lease to Itsekiri people to farm since they were mostly occupying swampy areas of Delta and as such had no dry land to farm. They perceive the Itsekiris as migrants whom they helped to overcome their occupational crisis at a given point in time in the history of their existence, and when their leasing period was over, instead of handing over the occupied area, they cashed in on their privileged position with the colonial masters to engage in a tussle with them over the ownership of Warri. The Urhobos contend that Ode-Itsekiri is the ancestral home of the Itsekiris and there stops their land ownership and control. To support this viewpoint, they cited the fact that the Itsekiris refer to Ode-Itsekiri as "big Warri" while Warri town the area in contest they call "small Warri". They, therefore, reasoned how one could leave big Warri and make small Warri the seat of their traditional ruler if not for the social and economic benefits that are associated with small Warri. According to them, they have more stakes in big Warri than in small Warri, and an ancestral home of a people should be the seat of their traditional ruler.

Amongst the Urhobos, there seems to be a division about the conflict in Warri. Some of the people (Urhobos) are of the view that the conflict in Warri essentially is concerned with only a particular family lineage and the Itsekiris. And the family, the others perceive, are fighting for their own selfish end; and not for the whole Urhobo clan. This school of thought believes that the family in question sold the disputed area to the Itsekiris long ago without knowing the implications of what they were doing, but with the oil boom and the subsequent benefits arising from the position of Warri being central in an area of many oil wells, development of infrastructure and the like, the quest and tussle of ownership of the area became a major crisis.

The Itsekiris, on their part, claimed the ownership of Warri town. They argued that they are the original occupants of the area referred to as both small and big Warri, and that they only gave the area in contest now to their slaves (the Urhobos) to be farming since they (the Itsekiri) are mainly fishermen and middlemen traders. The distinction between the big and small Warri was made because of the river that separates the same community into two. They see the Urhobos as the intruders into their community.

This tussle over ownership of land gave rise to yet another serious problem that helped to complicate further the issue in that area, and that is the position of *Olu* of Warri. The argument amongst the non-Itsekiris (Ijaws and Urhobos), mostly the Urhobos, is that since Itsekiris are not the original owners of Warri, and the fact that there are other ethnic groups inhabiting the place, one of the ethnic groups cannot lay claim to the traditional stool of the place, and then lord it over the other ethnic groups. They, therefore, suggest that the stool be referred to as *Olu* of Itsekiri, an appellation that automatically delineates the jurisdiction of the *Olu*, and defines the limitations and extent of his powers. *Olu* of Warri indicates that he is the paramount ruler of all the ethnic groups resident in Warri and that the title carries some air of supremacy with it. That, to the Urhobos is unacceptable. To the Itsekiris, the *Olu* of Warri institution has been in existence as far back as 1480 AD, and as such no one can change it now on grounds that 'migrants' have come to stay with them. These two major issues, according to history, laid the foundation of the conflict in the Warri Delta Zone and became the sources of incessant conflict amongst the two communities.

As the place became more developed, especially with increasing activities of oil companies, a new dimension was added to the crisis in that area. The Ijaws, who also occupy the place along with the Urhobos and the Itsekiri, started agitating against the marginalisation of their ethnic group. They demanded for their own local government council where they could be heard and recognised. So, the new dimension now is between the Ijaws and the Itsekiris in that zone. This new dimension to the conflict in Warri has further helped in complicating an already complex situation. At any little provocation the crisis takes a dramatic turn, resulting in great casualties and loss of properties and human lives. At one time, it is between the original parties to the conflict—the Itsekiris and the Urhobos; at another time, it is between the Itsekiris and the Ijaws and at another time, the Urhobos will team up with the Ijaws to fight the Itsekiris, since the two groups (Ijaws and Urhobos) share a common sense of marginalisation and oppression.

The Ijaw/Itsekiri conflict started with the citing of the Warri South Local Government Area headquarters at Ogbe-Ijoh, an area predominantly occupied by the Ijaws. The Itsekiris protested it, arguing that they were the one who requested for the creation of a new local government area and as such the headquarters should be in Ogidigben an enclave of the Itsekiris. More importantly, they argued that the gazette announcing the local government creation named Ogidigben as the local government headquarters not Ogbe-Ijoh. They attributed the mix-up to the then military administrator of Delta State, Col. David Dung, and the attempt to correct the mix-up resulted in a mayhem. Human beings were slaughtered, houses were burnt, in fact the affected area was left desolate. The Urhobos cashed in on their standing grievances against the Itsekiris to give a tacit support to the Ijaws and that helped to widen the scope of the conflict. Until date, the conflict is yet to be resolved. These historical and structural setting, therefore, laid the foundation and context for the violent and ever unending conflict in Warri.

Socioeconomic Characteristics of Study Population

In this section, we present the socioeconomic characteristics of the study population.

Table 1: Age Distribution of Respondents

Age Distribution	Itsekiri Community Freq.	Percentage	Urhobo Community Freq.	Percentage	Ijaw Community Freq.	Percentage
Less than 31 yrs	119	13.2	101	11.2	150	16.7
31-40	104	11.6	242	26.9	202	22.4
41-50	310	34.4	431	47.9	221	24.6
51-60	225	25	92	10.2	197	21.9
Over 60 yrs.	80	8.9	22	2.4	92	10.2
No Idea of Age	62	6.9	12	1.3	38	4.2
Total	900	100.00	900	100.00	900	100.0

Source: Fieldwork, 2001

Table 2: Religious Affiliation of Respondents

Religious Affiliation	Itsekiri Community		Urhobo Community		Ijaw Community	
	Freq.	Percentage	Freq.	Percentage	Freq.	Percentage
Christianity	608	67.6	538	59.8	502	55.7
Muslim	4	0.4	17	1.9	2	0.2
African Traditional Practitioners	227	25.2	255	28.3	349	38.7
Others	49	5.4	58	6.4	37	4.1
No Response	12	1.3	32	3.6	10	1.1
Total	900	100	900	100	900	100

Source: Fieldwork, 2001

Table 3: Occupational Distribution of Respondents

Occupational Distribution	Itsekiri Community		Urhobo Community		Ijaw Community	
	Freq.	Percentage	Freq.	Percentage	Freq.	percentage
Farming(crop)	381	42.3	62	6.9	128	14.2
Farming (fishing)	118	13.1	328	36.4	250	27.8
Trading/ Business	90	10	216	24	131	14.6
Govt. Workers (including teachers)	183	20.3	145	16.1	201	22.3
Small Scale Cottage Industry	125	13.9	98	10.9	110	12.2
Manufacturing	3	0.3	51	5.7	80	8.9
Total	900	100	900	100	900	100

Source: Fieldwork, 2001

Table 4: Marital Status of Respondents

Marital status	Itsekiri Community		Urhobo Community		Ijaw Community	
	Freq.	Percentage	Freq.	Percentage	Freq.	Percentage
Married	598	66.4	442	49.1	422	46.9
Single	135	15	222	24.7	158	17.6
Separated	5	0.6	38	4.2	91	10.1
Divorced	5	0.6	38	4.2	119	13.2
Widowed	56	6.2	72	8	106	11.8
No Response	101	11.2	88	9.8	4	0.4
Total	900	100.0	900	100.0	900	100.0

Source: Fieldwork, 2001

Table 5: Sex Distribution of Respondents

Sex	Itsekiri Community		Urhobo community		Ijaw community	
	Freq.	Percentage	Freq.	Percentage	Freq.	Percentage
Male	585	65	625	69.4	620	68.9
Female	315	35	275	30.6	280	31.1
Total	900	100.00	900	100.00	900	100.00

Source: Fieldwork, 2001

Table 6: Educational Qualification of Respondents

Education Qualification	Itsekiri Community		Urhobo Community		Ijaw Community	
	Freq	Percentage	Freq.	Percentage	Freq.	Percentage
No Education	257	28.6	139	15.4	215	23.9
Primary School	92	10.2	74	8.2	112	12.4
Secondary School	121	13.4	107	11.9	160	17.8
Teacher Training	68	7.6	81	9	50	5.6
NCE/OND	142	15.8	122	13.6	164	18.2
University Education	185	20.6	321	35.7	193	21.4
Others (pls. specify)	35	3.8	56	6.2	6	0.7
Total	900	100	900	100	900	100

Source: Fieldwork, 2001

Causes of the Conflict

Apart from the historical documentation of the cause(s) of the conflict in Warri, we tried to find out from our respondents what they think are the major causes of the Warri crisis. Specifically, they were asked to list in order of importance the five major causes of the Warri crisis. Tables 7A, 7B and 7C below represent the·views expressed by our various respondents in the three ethnic groups involved.

Table 7A: Itsekiri Community Respondents

S/n	Responses	Freq.	%
1.	The inability of the other ethnic groups (Ijaws and Urhobos) to accept their migrant status in Warri	756	84
2.	The Ijaws and the Urhobos want to share in a heritage that does not belong to them – the claim to the *Olu* of Warri dynasty	620	68
3.	The Ijaws want a local government headquarters in an area that they do not even have enough wards to win any reasonable election	540	60
4.	The inability of the government both at state and federal levels to deal decisively with the contentious issues.	485	53.8
5.	The cry of marginalisation by the Urhobos and Ijaws is mere envy. They are envious of the Itsekiris, right from the colonial period because of the friendly disposition of the whites to the Itsekiris.	225	25

Table 7B: Ijaw Community Respondents

S/n	Responses	Freq.	%
1.	The claim of the Itsekiris and their show of supremacy and arrogance over the other ethnic groups in Warri.	821	91.2
2.	Marginalisation of the Ijaws by the Itsekiris and attempt to dispose them of their political and economic share of the national resources	720	80

3.	The inability of the three ethnic groups to appreciate one another and exhibit some sense of fair play and equity	341	37.8
4.	Warri should be understood to belong to all the three ethnic groups living there and as such should have equal share of all benefits accruing from the land in terms of job opportunities, royalties and all other associated benefits	684	76
5.	The unenviable role played by government at both state and federal levels. The government appears to be taking sides with the Itsekiris, because they are close to the corridors of power and good at petition writing	525	58.3

Table 7C: Urhobos Community Respondents

S/n	Responses	Freq.	%
1.	The Itsekiris are migrants in Warri and they should accept that and should be so treated	824	91.5
2.	The presence of *Olu* of Warri as a paramount traditional ruler of our people is unacceptable to the Urhobos. He should be called *Olu* of Itsekiri not *Olu* of Warri	788	87.5
3.	The oil wells money accruing from their land is not equitably distributed amongst the different stakeholders, rather, a greater percentage of it goes to the migrants (Itsekiris)	620	68.8
4.	High level of unemployment amongst the Urhobo youths (youths' demand).	558	62
5.	The inability of the government both at state and federal levels to deal with the Itsekiri people	482	53.5

The result of the survey indicates that ownership of Warri town is the main contentious issue in the conflict. There are claims and counter claims by each group as to who is a migrant in Warri and who should be in control of the town, 84 percent of the Itsekiri respondents think that the main cause of the Warri conflict is the inability of the other ethnic groups, namely, Ijaw and Urhobos to accept their migrant status in Warri. The Ijaws and the Urhobos with 76 and 91.5 percent respectively identified the Itsekiris' claim and domination of Warri as the main cause of the conflict. The issue of the legitimate owner of Warri remains central to the Warri crisis. All other issues are fallouts of this main issue.

The next most important issue is the institution of the *Olu* of Warri. 96.2% percent of our Ijaw respondents feel that the institution and coronation of *Olu* of Itsekiri as *Olu* of Warri creates an air of superiority and supremacy around the Itsekiris; and this act in turn creates room for arrogance on the part of the Itsekiris as if they were better than other ethnic groups, according to one of our Ijaw respondents. The Urhobos consider it unacceptable that the *Olu* should be referred to as *Olu* of Warri instead of *Olu* of Itsekiri.

> I found it strange and unacceptable that a stranger in our land should be coronated in our land as a traditional ruler when he is not a son of the soil.
> Warri is not for the Itsekiris, Ode-Itsekiri is their place. How can they now come to boss it over us here. The *Olu* should be referred to as the *Olu* of Itsekiri and not *Olu* of Warri.

This is the type of remark and question we were confronted with all through the fieldwork. The general consensus from the Urhobos and the Ijaws was that the coronation of the *Olu* of Warri instead of *Olu* of Itsekiri in a community that is shared by three different ethnic groups is an affront on the other two groups, and until that is resolved, according to one of our discussants "peace cannot return to Warri." The implication of this is that, first, the issue of who is the legitimate occupant and who is the migrant must be resolved before addressing the issue of the jurisdiction of the *Olu*.

Our Itsekiri respondents (68%) on their part, find it ridiculous that the Ijaws and the Urhobos want to share in a heritage that does not belong to them. As they refer to the other ethnic groups:

> ...they are migrants, they are foreigners, they can never in the history of this town be coronated as *Olu* of Warri. It has never happened and I cannot see it come to pass. The institution of *Olu* in this place dates as far back as 1480. How can we change it overnight because some people want to share in a heritage they do not belong to?

Thus, each party in the dispute feels strongly about his own position and does not see why there should be a shifting of ground to accommodate the others' views and feelings.

The third contentious issue is the creation of more local government areas to identify with the different ethnic groups and the location of the headquarters in areas where each of the three ethnic groups considers an area of high concentration of their people. In addition, the Ijaws are requesting for the creation of more wards in such local governments, as is the case with the turbulent Ogbe Ijoh/Ogidigben situation, so that their chances of winning reasonable positions during elections can be guaranteed. With the present configuration of the local government in that area as it stands now, an Ijaw man can never have the opportunity of being elected as a chairman. So, the Ijaws are demanding that they have the same number of wards with the Itsekiri or even more to make for a control of the area. This demand is yet another source of tension in that community. Although this particular point does not concern the Urhobos directly, they have found it convenient to team up with the Ijaws, since they all share a common sentiment and enemy — the Itsekiris. The Urhobos and the Ijaws share a common sense of marginalisation and oppression from the Itsekiris and, as such, are always willing to join forces in fighting the Itsekiris.

The most disheartening revelation of the survey is that all the three groups involved in this crisis have no confidence in the ability of the government, both at state and federal levels, to settle the matter. The Itsekiris hold the government of Col. D. Dung, former military administrator of Delta State, responsible for the Ogbe-Ijoh and Ogidigben crisis. 53.8 percent of the Itsekiri respondents think that the government position is not helping matters. They think the federal and state governments should come out and take a decisive step towards solving the matter. The decisive step, to them, is for the government to call the Urhobos and the Ijaws to order. The Urhobos (53.5%) on their part think that the government is not doing enough to cut down on the excesses of the Itsekiris while the Ijaws are bemoaning the unenviable role the government at all levels are playing. They feel strongly that the government is taking sides with the Itsekiris, because the Itsekiris are close to the corridors of power and are good at petition writing.

One of the Ijaw discussants observed that:

> ...the government cannot talk to the Itsekiris, because the Itsekiris are helping them to defraud our people through the oil companies. If they talk to the Itsekiris, they will expose them, that is why they cannot do anything to them.

The Ijaws and the Urhobos contended that the Itsekiris were always in the act of manipulating decisions and policies to suit them. They cited readily the Itsekiri/Ijaw Local Government headquarter's location as an example and their (Itsekiris) manipulation of the reports of the various commissions of inquiry to suit them; be it military or civilian administration. They alleged that when they sensed that government or any commission of inquiry position did not favour them, they would ensure that such a report did not see the light of the day. This is why almost all the reports of the panels set up by government on this Warri crisis remained unpublished. "We want the previous government commissions' reports released".

The other reasons they adduced (Urhobos and Ijaws) are what they classified as "youths' demands", which include:

1. Providing the youths with jobs;
2. Provision of good roads for the communities; and
3. Creation of more local government areas;

These demands appear to be a very recent inclusion to the causes of the crisis, to help in mobilising more of the youths to join in the perpetration of the existing animosity amongst the communities.

From our fieldwork experience and interaction with the different ethnic groups in Warri, the Urhobos and the Ijaws appear to be the most aggrieved of the parties. The two communities nurse a deep feeling of bitterness arising from a sense of being oppressed and marginalised. Their feeling and expression give one the impression that the problem of Warri crisis is intractable.

The Degree of Violence and Sources of Arms Used

The degree of violence attendant to the conflict any time it erupts has been such that the material and non-material losses, including lives, have always been on the high side.   There   is   obvious evidence that the warring factions in the Niger-Delta crisis have a reasonable quantity of sophisticated arms and ammunition available to them. The question that remains unresolved, which is yet to be addressed, is how they come about these arms and ammunition. During the fieldwork, we tried to address the issue to see if we could gather reliable information as to how these arms used in most of these violent clashes are acquired.

Each of the groups claims that they receive their arms from their leaders who encourage them to fight for their cause, a cause they think is a just cause. The interesting thing is that the Itsekiris would give you names of prominent Urhobos and Ijaws who, they claimed, supplied arms to the youths, but they would not mention anyone from their side. Similarly, the Urhobos and Ijaws would mention prominent Itsekiris who, they claimed, made guns available to their youths without mentioning anybody on their own side also. No one was ready to mention names from his own side as being responsible for the act of supplying arms. What is obvious, however, is that the elites within the three communities were involved in the supply of arms and ammunition to their respective youths, which has led to the escalation of violence in the region.

Another question which arises is how these arms come into the country with all the security and intelligence networks spread throughout the country. Our respondents identified three sources:

1.   Through the waterways;
2.   Through the airstrips in the zone; and
3.   Through hiring of guns from security operatives and individuals licensed to keep guns.

We were informed that the airstrips in the Delta region, mostly intended for use by the oil workers for transportation of staff and equipment, were sometimes used to transport and conceal arms and ammunition being smuggled into the Niger Delta region. This is easy to do because there are no security operatives at these airstrips to ensure that the goods brought into the country through these routes are thoroughly screened. The same thing applies to transportation through the waterways. The numerous creeks that crisscross the Niger Delta region of Nigeria provide easy access for smugglers to smuggle in arms and ammunition into the region without being apprehended. The third source, we were informed, is through hiring of arms from security operatives or individuals licensed to keep guns who are willing to give it out during crisis period for a fee.

Of course, they did not fail to mention or display their prowess at the use of traditional medicine or charms (*Egbesu* charm) which is exclusive to the Ijaws. *Egbesu* is believed to neutralize the effect of gunshots and machete cuts. Their elders and medicine men were highly acknowledged in this regard for their unflinching support.

The easy access and apparent availability of these arms is one major reason why the Niger-Delta crisis is always associated with high incidence of violence and death. The ease with which they are ready to confront even the law enforcement agents (police, mobile police and soldiers) attest to the fact that they are combat ready with a high level of confidence at all times. The latest violent outbreak of the conflict, which occurred in March, 2003, is believed to·be the worst ever in terms of the level of destruction. So far, the number of civilians killed is yet to be known. Six soldiers, one policeman, a contractor with one of the oil companies, and three employees of the oil companies in that region were killed during one of the recent clashes.[7] A number of Itsekiri villages were razed down to rubbles and in one brazen incident, the youths shot at one of the oil company aircraft which was evacuating oil employees and displaced villagers in an attempt to bring it down.

Clearly, the situation in Warri, as in the other parts of the Niger-Delta region and the other troubled zones of the country is a clear indication of the failure of the country's intelligence agencies. The over-concentration of arms and ammunition in private hands is creating problem for national security nationwide. The March, 2003, Warri crisis is also a pointer that all steps taken so far to resolve the problem have failed to achieve the desired result. The situation calls for an intensified and concerted effort by all concerned, government and civil society groups to solve the problem.

The law enforcement agents and our intelligence operatives should live up to their responsibility in tracking down the arms smugglers and peddlers. It will go a long way to help in reducing the level of violence that occurs anytime the conflict escalates into open hostility.

Effects of the Conflict

In assessing the effects of the conflict on the communities concerned, we asked the questions below:

1.   What are the effects of this conflict on your community?
2.   Estimate the material and non-material losses as a result of the conflict.

(Responses from the three ethnic groups are ranked in their order of intensity as recorded from the respondents).

3.   High incidence of death, including death as a result of shooting or machete cuts, death resulting from rape, and death resulting from accidents during the course of finding an escape route from the crisis, this mostly takes the form of drowning and stampede due to panic;
4.   Destruction of properties, including looting, burning of houses, and household items, hijacking and destroying of fishing boats and market boats. Burning down of business centres and buildings;
5.   Raping of women and female children;
6.   Starvation; and
7.   Molestation of people especially women and girls by law enforcement agents.

From the responses from the three ethnic groups, death amongst them appears to be the highest concern for all the parties. Of course, this could easily be explained because of the finality associated with death. It is an irreversible process. All the three ethnic groups ranked death through killing from the opponents or loss of life while attempting an escape as the most serious effect of the crisis. The Ijaws (85%), the Urhobos (72%) and the Itsekiris (92%) say death is the most serious consequence of the conflict. Next in the ranking, is destruction of properties; this includes burning of houses and household items, destroying fishing boats, business centres, etc. This is closely followed by sporadic fighting and raping of women. The Itsekiris claim that they suffer this effect more from the Ijaws, whenever they attack suddenly or hijack the boats of women on their way to the market. Starvation was next on the list of the effects of the crisis, as people will want to either remain indoors to avoid molestation or seek refuge in some hideout without adequate provision for feeding, waiting for the conflict to subside. As long as the conflict lasts, they are faced with the problem of surviving with whatever their host can provide or with nothing if they are in the bush.

Finally, all parties decry the molestation received from security agencies, such as police, mobile police and soldiers sent to quell the crisis. In one of the Focus Group Discussion (FGD) it was observed that the women appear to feel more concerned about the harassment they receive from security·agencies who are supposed to come and help them in their moment of distress. One of the women observed that:

> The police and army people are worse than our enemies (Ijaw and Urhobo). They come to make all sorts of request from us, ask for money, and take away our things while pretending to be helping us. The most annoying thing is that they will be touching our daughters anyhow. We don't like it at all.

Another discussant remarked that, "one of the mobile policemen,.took·away my trinket set, as I made attempt to raise alarm, he shot into the air and I ran away. What can I do?" she asked.

They all dread the effects of the conflict, men and women alike, from the three ethnic groups. However, it is the women and children, especially female children that are worse hit. Women and children, who were able to escape death, do not only suffer from material losses, but also from molestation, harassment and assault on their womanhood, from both the warring groups and the law enforcement agents. The threats, in most cases, are real while some are perceived. Consequently, women and their children especially the female children are always the first to take to their heels anytime there is a threat to the peace and tranquillity of their communities.

The activities of the so called "area boys" were not left out. Most of the looting that took place were associated with the area boys. One of our male discussants observed that:

> It is not our youths who came to fight for their legitimate rights, that are looting, it is the area boys, all these jobless people who came to Warri to seek jobs that are not here, that are looting, they always cash in on the situation to provide for themselves

Another discussant summarizes the whole idea of the crisis and the associated loss or effect as simply "madness". According to him:

> ...nobody or group of persons can assess adequately the amount of loss incurred whenever this crisis occurs. In terms of lives lost, you never get the exact figures, in terms of materials loss, the estimate ranges into several millions if not billions of naira. You can imagine what happened during the Ogbe-Ijoh and Ogidigben tussle, a whole community was razed down. How do you estimate that? In terms of the psychological effect, it is unquantifiable. Most people who were killed by either gunshot or machete cuts, died of shock, especially those that have history of heart problem. Some just slump and die at the sight of the destruction of their properties. That is why I call it madness; and the madness just has to stop.

From the presentation above, it is obvious that none of the parties involved enjoys the effect of the conflict and neither can put a price tag on its fallout. The degree and level of violence is always on the high side and the consequences are very unpleasant. There is a consensus by all concerned that there is a need for a truce, not just a temporary one but a lasting solution.

Allport did suggest that social contact and acquaintance make for friendliness, that is to say, contact and acquaintance may lead to social distance, reduce social conflict, increase cooperation and of course accommodation among various social groups.[8] The Urhobos, Itsekiris, and the Ijaws for centuries have been living together, have inter-married and have engaged in commercial activities amongst themselves on a daily basis. So there is really no need for the high level of animosity exhibited amongst them because the social contact and acquaintance among them is on the high side.

During the FGD sessions, one question I consistently asked in all sessions was how they were able to cope, bearing in mind that during the crisis a brother can kill a brother or cause the death and destruction of another brother given the high level of social interaction and inter-marriages amongst them. All parties agreed that incidents of that nature were not only possible but had actually taken place a number of times. One of the discussants vehemently remarked, that:

> ...there is no pure Itsekiri or Urhobo amongst us; almost all of
> us have either Itsekiri and Urhobo blood in us. An Itsekiri
> man who doesn't have an Urhobo mother, has Urhobo wife,
> or the daughter or sister or auntie is married to Urhobo and so
> have a relation amongst the Urhobos, the same applies to an
> Urhobo man. So why are we fighting ourselves over land? It
> is very bad. The matter should be resolved.

The Itsekiri found the Urhobos more accommodating than the
Ijaws. The Ijaws go after their nieces and nephews and kill them
during any crisis simply because their father is Itsekiri, not minding
how their sister would feel.

The recent outbursts of violence, first between the Urhobos and
the Itsekiris and next between the Ijaws and the Itsekiris exhibited
the usual trend of mayhem and violence. The clashes led to the
razing down of many villages and the disruption of oil exploration
in the region by rampaging youths. Some of the oil companies
suffered human losses in the mayhem. Even the efforts of the oil
companies at helping displaced villagers were frustrated by the
youths. Because of the incident, the oil companies in that locality,
notably Chevron, Texaco, Shell, Elf, were forced to close down
several of their flow station, as well as suspend flights into the
affected areas. A number of law enforcement agents, with unknown
numbers of civilians were also killed.

The nation suffered huge economic losses as Total Fina Elf shut
its facilities in Escravos as a result of the outburst of hostilities;
amounting to the loss of 440,000 barrels of oil per day and 285
cubic feet of gas. Shell alone lost 76,000 barrels per day as a result
of the fracas. In totality, 20% of Nigeria's crude oil export was
affected. All these losses are not inclusive of that of all other
economic activities outside the oil sector ceased to function or were
disrupted. What attempt, therefore, has been made by government
at all levels, individuals and non-governmental organisations to
bring a lasting truce to this troubled zone?

The cruelty and mayhem always associated with the conflict
brings us to the most important aspect of this study. How best can
this conflict be managed or resolved through the involvement of
civil society since the efforts of government have so far failed to
achieve the desired result?

Management and Resolution of the Conflict

Who will manage or resolve the conflict? From the result in Tables 9A, B and C, it is obvious that the people have no confidence in the ability of the government, whether military or civilian, to resolve the conflict. All the parties involved seem not to be ready to do business with government officials any longer, since the end products of government panels are not made public neither are decisions implemented or enforced. All the groups seem to be skeptical about the role of the government both at state and federal levels. Even the presence of law enforcement agents especially the mobile police and soldiers portends another season of terrorism and harassment for the people. Their presence is usually welcomed with some reservation. The question then is: How can the conflict be handled? Who will handle the situation and how can the problem be resolved to make for a lasting peace in the area?

The different communities suggested ways in which they think the crisis can be resolved, and all the suggestions are directed at addressing the central issue in dispute. The responses are hereby summarized in the tables below.

Table 8A: Itsekiri Respondents

S/n	Responses	Freq.	%
1.	Violence should not be rewarded by any group or government. The government should evolve a policy of ignoring any group that thinks it can hold the government to ransom or attract attention to itself	721	80
2.	Dialogue with all parties involved should be encouraged especially with non-governmental bodies, youths and religious bodies or organisations	640	71.1
3.	Non-indigenes, and unbiased third parties possibly from outside this environment (Edo and Delta States) should be party to the settlement team	318	35.3
4.	Prayers can do wonders – so we encourage all concerned parties to pray for the return of peace in our communities. Let everyone accept his/her God given position and location with a thankful heart	824	91.5

Table 8B: Urhobo Respondents

S/n	Responses	Freq.	%
1.	Change of *Olu* of Warri title to *Olu* of Itsekiri, or make the *Olu* stool to rotate amongst the three ethnic groups resident in Warri	860	95.5
2.	All government panels of inquiry and commission reports should be released, and the findings implemented	611	67.8
3.	All the other ethnic groups in Warri should have their traditional ruler who should have the same status as *Olu* of Warri with their areas of jurisdiction properly delineated	841	93.4
4.	More local government areas should be created with corresponding wards and constituencies to accommodate the various ethnic interests in Warri	735	81.6
5.	Job opportunities and social infrastructures should be created to keep the youths occupied at all times.	673	74.7

Table 8C: Ijaw Respondents

S/n	Responses	Freq.	%
1.	The permanent return of the local government headquarters to Ogbe-Ijoh without further delay, and the creation of more wards for all stakeholders of the community to accommodate a meaningful election in that area.	809	89.8
2.	Creation of more local government areas to reflect all the various ethnic interests in Warri	716	79.5
3.	Abolition of *Olu* of Warri title to *Olu* of Itsekiri and creating a traditional position that all ethnic groups in Warri will benefit from.	662	73.5
4.	Creation of more jobs for the youths of our community	418	46.4

Suggestions on Methods/Groups that Can Help in Resolving the Conflict

Table 9A: Ijaw Respondents

S/n	Responses	Freq.	%
1.	Dialogue with youths and our elders especially those residing with us here	552	61.3
2	Non-governmental organisations outside these communities with religious bodies operating also outside here	818	90.8

Table 9B: Urhobo Respondents

S/n	Responses	Freq.	%
1.	The use of government and its agencies is unavoidable as bad and uncooperative as they might appear	321	35.6
2.	Non-governmental agencies to initiate dialogue with all interested parties. Such non-governmental agents must not have any vested interest in this area	740	82.2
3.	Women bodies can serve a useful purpose, given that they are the greatest losers any time the crisis erupts	719	79.8

Table 9C: Itsekiri Respondents

S/n	Responses	Freq.	%
1.	Religious bodies and non-governmental organisations to engage in dialogue with all interested groups	714	79.3
2.	Intervention groups must not be interested parties whether within or outside these communities	466	51.7

Previous Attempts at Resolving the Conflict

From one administration to the other, both military and civilian, there has been an obvious inability to decisively address the Niger-

Delta crisis as a whole and the conflict in Warri in particular in order to find a lasting solution to the problem. Thomas Imobighe observed that efforts had been made but the efforts were not holistic or integrated.[9] In his integrated conflict management theory,[10] Imobighe advocated three levels of conflict management, which include, conflict prevention and peace promotion, conflict control and abatement, and conflict resolution. These three levels, Imobighe observed, are not mutually exclusive. One level of the conflict management leads to the order, until it eventually gets to the point of resolution of the conflict. In the Nigerian situation and Warri conflict in particular, the second level of conflict management seems to be quite popular with the government in its conflict management efforts, while the first and the third levels seem to suffer relative neglect.

Government seems to provoke the crisis by making some careless mistakes or pronouncement or by failing to mete out equal treatment to all the parties involved. As soon as crisis erupts, government moves to suppress the conflict through the drafting of military and paramilitary personnel to the affected areas. When the situation appears to calm down, the actual resolution of the crisis is forgotten. The implication of this is that the calm achieved through suppression is not followed up by actual and intense negotiation by the parties involved and the mediator, which in this case is the Nigerian government.

Since the conflict in Warri started, various methods have been adopted in an attempt to resolve it. Apparently, because of the failure of government attempts to resolve the conflict, the parties seem to have been attracted to the judicial method. Documented evidence shows that over twenty court rulings have been given on the Warri land dispute. Some of the cases went as far as the Supreme Court of Nigeria, West African Court of Appeal and the Privy Council in London.

Majority of the judgments conferred and established ownership of most Warri land to the Itsekiris, while others established Urhobo or Ijaw ownership of certain portions of land in Warri.[11] For example, in 1926, there was a case of Ometan on behalf of *Agbassa Urhobo* v. *Chief Dore Numa* on behalf of the Itsekiris. Agbassa in the said suit was challenging the Itsekiris' right of ownership of Agbassa area of Warri. The lower court upheld the position of the Itsekiris.

In 1931, the Urhobos challenged the ruling of the lower court in the Supreme Court, and the Supreme Court upheld the decision of the lower court. In 1933, the same case went to the Privy Council which also confirmed and upheld the decision of the two earlier courts and took a step further to apportion one pound (£1.00) as an annual tribute to the *Olu* by the Urhobos. The Urhobos, apparently not satisfied and unhappy with the court ruling, resurfaced the case again in 1949 and 1957 pushing it to the Supreme Court in 1973 where the earlier rulings on the matter were still upheld. In 1934, Sabo village community in Ogbe-Ijoh went to court against Ogbe-Sobo (Aladja) over a disputed parcel of land. They won the case on the evidence that their ancestors got permission to settle in the place from the *Olu*.

In 1973, Okere-Urhobo got a judgment against Itsekiri, which was confirmed by the Supreme Court, that Okere-Urhobo was never part of the *Olu*'s kingdom. From the above documentation it is clear that the judicial avenue at resolving this crisis has been explored to it's logical end. The question that remains unanswered then, is why the parties involved in the dispute cannot abide by the court rulings and why the government on it's part cannot enforce the court rulings.

In doing so, conscious effort should be made in delineating boundaries so that none of the three parties would trespass the others' boundary in strictly administrative and political matters, while in social and economic interactions they could crisscross boundaries. How possible this idea is in practical terms, one cannot really know until an attempt at practising it is made.

The judicial method described above employed in resolving the perennial Warri crisis is that adopted by the individual parties involved in the matter. The judicial technique popular with the government is that of setting up of tribunals, commissions and panels of inquiry to look into the crisis soon after the eruption of crisis and the suppression of violence with the aid of military force. Most of the commissions set up by government end up at the inaugural and sitting sessions, the outcome of their sittings are never made public neither are their recommendations, if any, implemented. The eventual outcome is a situation where the parties in the dispute are left in suspense and with speculations of possible outcomes. All through the fieldwork, the agitation by the three parties has been that the federal government should release the findings of the various commissions. Some members of the parties in the dispute expressed confidence that the result of the panel would be in their favour, while some felt that the others had either manipulated the outcome or forestalled the release because the outcome would not be in their favour. So the judicial method of setting up panels of inquiry and commissions seems to have failed completely. As much as it is true that there have been agitations for the release of the findings, the people have also expressed their lack of confidence in the outcome of the findings. It is not expected that communities that did not obey Supreme Court ruling would have any respect for the outcome of a panel of inquiry or the findings of judicial commissions. It is, therefore, not surprising that the Niger-Delta crisis is not abating. Obviously, the management methods adopted by both government and the parties in conflict have produced results that are not mutually satisfactory to the latter.

The Role of Civil Society

There has not been much civil society participation in the management of the conflict in Warri. Third-party intervention in the conflict had all along been monopolised by government. The first known active civil society intervention in the conflict was carried out by the Academic Associates PeaceWorks (AAPW), a non-governmental organisation. The approach of AAPW took a different stance from what the government had been doing.[12] AAPW's approach, which took a social dimension, appeared more holistic; the main idea being to bring the warring factions together, on a neutral ground, create a friendly atmosphere and bring them into dialogue outside the influence and reach of the elites of the warring communities. Along this line, AAPW organized training and seminar programmes for different categories of persons. These include:

1. Training of mediators;
2. Training for Warri youth leaders (the youths of all parties in dispute);
3. Training for community leaders;
4. Peace education training; and
5. Training of elders; and

6.   Training of local government officials.

The central theme in all these training exercises is to educate and enlighten all the parties involved in the dispute on the need to embrace peace and to emphasize more those things that bind them together rather than those things that separate them. It was during these training programmes that the concept of "Warri Our Land" was developed and sold to them. The concept or idea was meant to give a sense of belonging to all the parties involved. The concept was expected to help reduce the fears and anxiety expressed by some of the youth leaders, including fears of marginalisation, negative images of extinction, domination, exclusion, oppression etc., which underline their reactions to the conflict and which have also been exploited by the elites in their communities to serve selfish ends.

At the end of the day, AAPW was happy that there was a change in the mindset of the trainees as they collectively accepted the concept of 'Warri Our Land'. This appears to be a remarkable milestone in the history of the management of the conflict in Warri.. After the training programmes, various other follow-up and enlightenment visits were made by AAPW, all in an attempt to keep up the spirit and momentum gathered at the training sessions and also to carry their message to the wider community. The attempt seemed to be quite successful and a breakthrough in the right direction. It is, therefore, quite surprising that there was fresh outbreak of violence in February/March , 2003. Could it be that the youths have jettisoned all they had achieved during the peace and confidence-building workshops? As disheartening as it may appear, we must accept that peacemaking process is a very long and tasking endeavour. It is more tasking in a situation were the stakes involved are quite high as it is in the present conflict.

The Case for Encouraging the Intervention of Women NGOs
At this point, it might be necessary to highlight an aspect that has been left unexplored by the previous efforts at managing the conflict, including AAPW's intervention. This relates to the role the womenfolk can play in the peace and confidence-building process. It would seem the input of women have been neglected in the peace process. The mere fact that they did not play any combatant role is

not enough to exclude them from the peace process. Women groups at all levels, in the church, market associations, clubs etc., should be mobilised and sensitised to enter into negotiations with their sons, husbands, friends and in-laws within the three warring ethnic groups. At the home front women are known to be major agents of socialization; they should be enlightened to help in debriefing and in the enlightenment of the young adults to imbibe in them peace-promoting concepts, such as the concept of "Warri Our Land".

In the biblical documentation, it was recorded that Jesus performed His first miracle at the instance of his mother at a wedding in Cana. Although He remarked that His time had not yet come, He still went ahead to obey His mother.[13] It is an example of the hold women have on their children and, to some extent, men in general when they (women) occupy any significant position in the men's life. This special attribute can be exploited in resolving the conflict in Warri. This very attribute is being exploited by some other groups of persons but in a very negative way. Some time in December, 2002/January, 2003, some groups of women were mobilised to demonstrate at oil installations in the Niger Delta. The same group of persons brainwashing the youths of the area, are again diverting their brainwashing exercise to the uneducated and vulnerable women in the community. This is the time to move fast to forestall a major damage in this direction. Women are instruments of peace, they hate losing their children or spouses in whatever manner. During the fieldwork, these views were strongly canvassed by the women that they would want to be an integral part of the peacemaking process because in the long run according to them "they are the greatest losers".

The omission of women's groups of all age grades, including the unmarried ones, was an oversight in AAPW programmes and we suggest that future attempts at peace making in the zone should necessarily involve the women at all levels.

Conclusion

An attempt has been made in this chapter to critically examine the intractable conflict involving the Itsekiris, the Urhobos and Ijaws in Delta State. It is observed that third-party involvement at managing the conflict had been monopolised by government. The case has been made for greater civil society involvement in its management. To this end, interventions, as those carried out by Academic Associates PeaceWorks should be encouraged. In particular, the involvement of women groups has been particularly emphasised.

The focused group discussion sessions gave a better insight on how best to handle the conflict, and the views emanating from them, especially those relating to the role of women, are incorporated in this brief conclusion. It is remarkable that the womenfolk in all the three ethnic groups seem to agree that the bloody war is uncalled for. That the womenfolk seem to demonstrate a genuine concern for peace is understandable. After all, they are the ones who lose their husbands, sons and daughters any time hostilities break out. They are of the view that their sons and daughters (the elite amongst them) living outside Warri are not helping matters because they are not receiving the heat directly whenever there are open hostilities. Most of the suggestions arising from the FGD focused attention on awareness programmes for the youths, starting from the primary school level up to the tertiary institutions, with the objective of:

1. Changing the negative mindset of the youth and children of the parties to the conflict;
2. De-emphasising those things or issues that are contentious in favour of things that are common and unite the three ethnic groups; and
3. Minimising the disposition of the youth towards violent behaviour.

For the purpose of this awareness campaign, it is suggested that government and other interested parties should try to use the leaders at the grassroots, rather than the so-called "big men" who directly or indirectly sponsor the conflict and benefit from it. Finally, it is suggested that women NGOs should be fully represented in all the negotiating teams and dialogue sessions, so that they can influence the deliberations on the side of peace rather than war. To this end, efforts should be made in any future peace process to involve such groups as the associations of market women, other women organisations and associations from the three ethnic groups, as well as religious bodies and organisations made up of women. The idea behind this emphasis on women NGOs from the three ethnic groups is based on the fact that, at the end of the day, they are the greatest losers — apart from commercial and material losses, their children, in-laws, grand children, nieces and nephews have always formed the bulk of the human casualties.

References

1. L.A. Coser, *The Functions of Social Conflict* (Glencoe III: The Free Press, 1956).
2. W.A. Donohue & R. Kolt, *Managing Interpersonal Conflict* (Newbury: 1992), p.3.
3. O. Otite, *Ethnic Pluralism and Ethnicity in Nigeria* (Ibadan: Shanesson, 1990).
4. O. Otite, "Nigerian Peoples and Their Cultures", in H.I. Ajaegbu, et al. (eds.), *Nigeria: A People United, A Future Assured, A Compendium* (Abuja: Federal Ministry of Information, 2000). See Table 1.2.1, Nigeria's Identifiable Ethnic Groups, pp.14-20.
5. Pauline V. Young, *Scientific/Social Survey and Research* (Englewood: Prentice Hall, 1992).
6. O. Ikime, *Niger Delta Rivalry: Itsekiri-Urhobo Relations and European Presence 1881-1936* (London: Longman, 1969).
7. See *The Guardian*, Lagos, March 27, 2003.
8. G. Allport, *The Nature of Prejudice* (Cambridge, Massachusetts: Addison Wesley, 1954).
9. T.A. Imobighe, "Earlier Attempts at Managing the Warri Crisis", in T.A. Imobighe et al., *Conflict and Instability in the Niger Delta: The Warri Case* (Ibadan: Spectrum Books, 2002), p.56.
10. See T.A. Imobighe, "Conflict Management in Nigeria", in I.B. Bello-Imam (ed.), *Governance in Nigeria, Economy, Politics and Society in the Adjustment Years 1985-1995* (Ibadan: Sterling-Horden, 1997), Chapter 18.
11. For details of the various court rulings, see D.A. Tonwe, "Warri Crisis Survey Report", in T.A. Imobighe, et al., *op. cit.*, Appendix 3. See also S.A. Akpotor, "Warri Crisis Survey Report", in *ibid.*, Appendix 2. Also, see J.O.S. Ayomike, *A History of Warri* (Lagos: Ilupeju Press, 1988).
12. For details, see Judith Burden Asuni, "Academic Associates PeaceWorks' Intervention in the Warri Crisis", in T.A. Imobighe, et. al. (2002), *op. cit.*, pp.94-122.
13. See the *Holy Bible*, John, chapter 2, verses 1-9

MAP OF NIGERIA SHOWING THE SOUTH-SOUTH ZONE

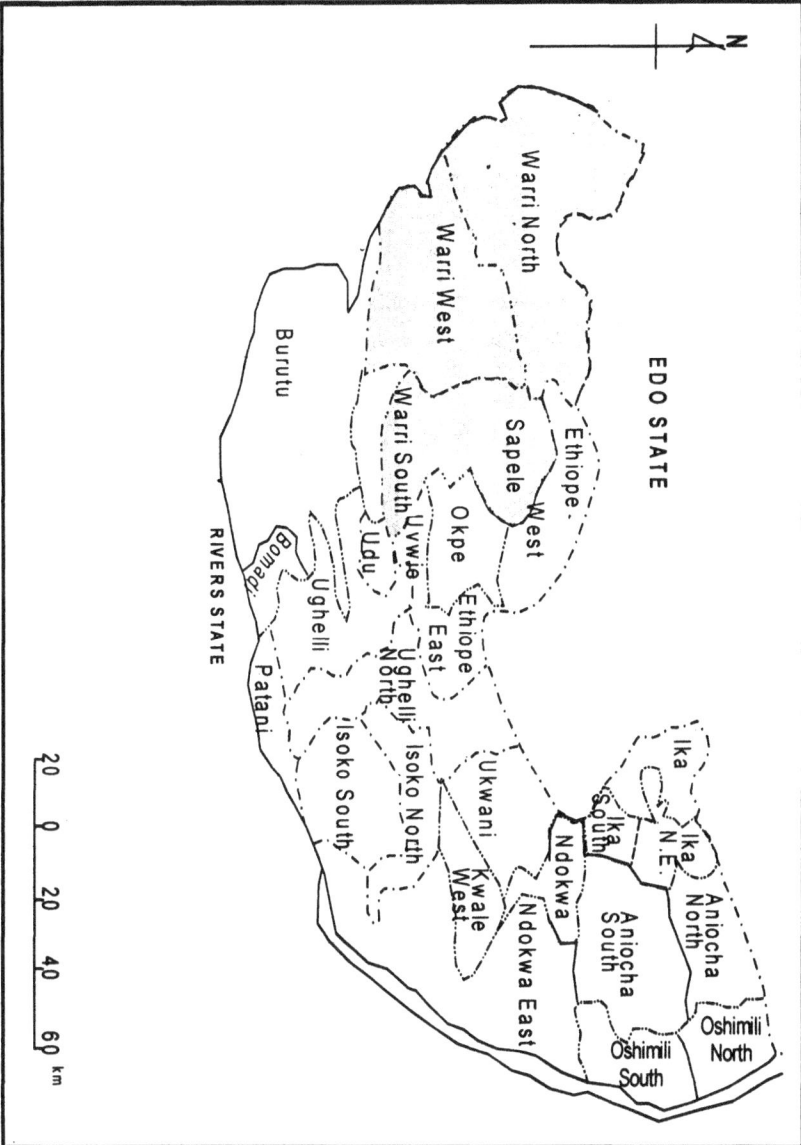

MAP OF DELTA STATE SHOWING THE STUDIED AREAS

PART 3

CIVIL SOCIETY EMPOWERMENT FOR CONFLICT MANAGEMENT

Chapter 10

Organising Civil Society for Ethnic Conflict Management in Nigeria

Ibrahim James

Introduction

Nigeria is a very complex multi-ethnic, multi-linguistic, multi-cultural and multi-religious society. These main variables of Nigeria's diversity index are not necessarily barriers to national cohesion, national integration and national unity. Regrettably, however, Nigeria is replete with ethno-religious conflicts: Gure/Kahugu communal conflicts, 1981; Igbirra/Bassa communal conflicts, 1986, 1997, 1998; Tiv/Alago, 1989, 1993, 2001; Bachama/Hausa, 1989; Zar Saiyawa/Hausa-Fulani, 1991, 2001; Jukun/Tiv, 1993, 1994; Chamba Jukun/Kuteb, 1997; Urhobo/Itsekiri, 1999, 2000; Berom Jarawa Anaguta/Hausa-Fulani, 2001, etc. The above ethno-religious conflicts have placed Nigeria on the verge of becoming "a zone of perpetual and fundamental instability."[1]

Ethnic conflict management in Nigeria should pivot on the three tripods on which the Nigerian society itself rests: the governments, the organised private sector and civil society organisations. The imperative of dialogue, consultations and mutually respectful cooperation among these three principal stakeholders in the Nigerian society is a sine qua non for an effective civil society participation in ethnic conflict management in Nigeria. Tragically, the civil society leg of this tripod supporting society appears the weakest and the most emasculated.

259

However, the above sombre picture is not applicable to the civil society organisations alone when addressing the problem of ethnic conflict management in Nigeria. The governments: federal, state and local government leg of the tripod is as fragile as the civil society leg gleaning through the frequency, scale and intensity of ethnic conflicts in Nigeria.[2] The organised private sector leg of the tripod is even more fragile and more emasculated than its government counterpart to be an effective ethnic conflict management instrument. This is because it is essentially a public sector-led and public sector-driven organised private sector economy.

The lack of autonomy of the Nigerian post-colonial state has had great implication for its mediation in the management of ethno-religious conflicts. The Nigerian state is a modality of class domination saddled with the twin functions of providing the conditions for accumulation and legitimation. However, for a capitalist state to perform these functions efficiently it is a requirement that it enjoys a degree of autonomy such that, "the system of domination is differentiated and dissociated from the ruling class and even the society and appear as an objective force standing alongside society."[3] The absence of this in the Nigerian situation implies that the social formation cannot institutionalize individualism, competition, freedom and equality. The implication of the limited autonomy of the state is that the state is directly immersed in the contradictions of the society, which are defined largely, but not exclusively in terms of ethnic and religious cleavages.[4] The Nigerian state is emasculated and impaired by the internalization of ethnic demands and pressures with severe consequences for state mediation in the management of ethnic and religious contradictions.

Against the backdrop of the emasculation of both the state and the organised private sector in mediating ethnic conflict management, civil society emerges as the only credible and viable leg of the tripod in mediating ethnic conflict management in Nigeria.

The Nigerian Civil Society Landscape

Civil society, narrowly defined, is associational life. This associational life is conceived as a public sphere, above the family, but separate and distinct from the economy, politics and the state. Thus, civil society in this view, consists of autonomous associations which serve as the independent eye of the society and which checks and/or regulates the state in the overall interest of the society.[5] However, civil society defined in the broad sense transcends the narrow associational life. Gramsci, deriving his definition from Karl Marx, sees civil society as constituted by "those intermediary and autonomous organisations, which function and sometimes flourish in the large and loosely bounded zone between organised sovereign authority and the family unit".[6] In the most elementary form, civil society refers to those groups and associative movements outside the realm of the state, but operating in the public (civil) and private spheres of social life. In a more specified sense, it is made up of civil association - voluntary, autonomous, professional or non-professional, which have arisen out of the self-organisational efforts of various social forces.[7]

Civil society encompasses a vast array of organisations, formal and informal. These organisations are subdivided under the following broad groups:

1. Economic (productive and commercial associations and networks).
2. Cultural (religious, ethnic, communal and other institutions and associations that defend collective rights, values, faiths, beliefs and symbols).
3. Informational and educational (devoted to the production and dissemination of public knowledge, ideas, news and information).
4. Interest-based (designed to advance or defend the common functional or material interests of their members; workers veterans, professionals, pensioners).
5. Developmental (organisations that combine individual resources to improve the infrastructure, institutions and quality of life of the community).
6. Issue-oriented (movements for environmental protection, women's rights, consumer protection, etc.)
7. Civic (seeking in non-partisan fashion to improve the political system and make it more democratic through human rights monitoring, voter education and mobilization, poll-watching, anti-corruption efforts, etc.)[8]

The following broad civil society groups characterise the Nigerian civil society landscape:

1.   Voluntary civil society groups;
2.   Autonomous civil society groups;
3.   Non-autonomous civil society groups;
4.   Professional civil society groups; and
5.   Non-professional civil society groups;

The above broad groups can be translated into the following:
   Non-Governmental Organisations (NGOs);
   Community-Based Organisations (CBOs);
   Organised Private Sector Organisation (OPS);
   Informal Private Sector Organisations;
   Religious Bodies and Groups;
   Professional/Occupational Groups;
   Farmers/Peasants Associations;
   Community Development Association Groups;
   Ethnic Development Association Groups;
   Women Association Groups;
   Youth/Students Organisations;
   Age Grades Associations;
   Trade Union Associations;
   Traditional Rulers; and
   Clan and Lineage Heads' Groups.;

Deriving from the above perceptual prisms, civil society in Nigeria is a highly contested public sphere. It is characterized by struggles, crosscutting, overlaps and contradictory alliances in relation to both the economy and the state. Similarly, civil society in Nigeria is neither independently/autonomously juxtaposed against the state, nor inherently democratic, with the overall interest of the larger society at heart.[9] In fact, not all civil society in Nigeria is civil and not all civil society in Nigeria is directly and positively linked to democracy and the democratization process. Indeed, many organisations within the civil society group do not share nor contribute to the diminution of conflict areas, tension zones and crisis spots. On the contrary, these civil society groups maintain and perpetuate systems and structures that generate conflicts.

The Nigerian civil society landscape is characterised by the existence of dual grassroots organisations, namely, those organisations conceived, established and nurtured by decades of authoritarianism: Association for Better Nigeria (ABN), Youth Earnestly Ask for Abacha (YEAA), WAI Brigade, Better Life Groups, Family Support Groups, etc. These were state sponsored, state controlled and state penetrated non-democratic inclined civil society groups which essentially became the voices, agents and organised representation of the authoritarian state within the civil society.[10]

Conversely, the Nigerian civil society landscape is also characterized by the existence of those grassroots organisations that emerged as a response to the exigencies of survival under predatory authoritarian regimes. Although these civil society groups were badly traumatized and brutalized by the authoritarian regimes, they nevertheless exuded resilience by emerging unscathed and vibrant. These include Civil Liberties Organisation (CLO), Constitutional Right Project (CRP), United Action for Democracy (UAD), Joint Action Committee for Nigeria (JACON), Campaign for Democracy and Human Rights (CDHR), Network for Justice (NJ), Campaign for Democracy (CD), Democratic Alliance (DA), Media Rights Agenda (MRA), Women in Nigeria (WIN), Nigerian Medical Association (NMA), National Association of Nigerian Students (NANS), Country Women Association of Nigeria (COWAN), Human Development Initiatives (HDI), Women, Law and Development Centre (WLDC), Women's Right Advancement and Protection Alternatives (WRAPA), Society for Women and Aids in Africa (SWAAN).[11] For these democracy-inclined civil society groups, survival remains a fundamental principle of infinite scope, the achievement of which has meant a way of life distinct from militarism and conflict generation.

While the democracy-inclined civil society organisations have contested the authoritarian and anti people disposition of accentuating conflict areas, tension zones and crisis spots by working towards the diminution of conflicts, state-sponsored, state penetrated and state controlled non democracy-inclined civil society groups have either ignored any pursuit of conflict management mechanism or have clandestinely and actively sought to escalate and exacerbate these conflict areas, tension zones and crisis spots in Nigeria: Bassa/Egbura, Nassarawa State; Tiv/Jukun, Taraba State; Jukun-Chamba/Kuteb, Taraba State; Tiv/Alago, Nassarawa State; Hausa-Fulani/Zar Saiyawa, Bauchi State; Ife/Modakeke, Osun State; Aguleri/Umeleri, Anambra State; Urhobo/Itsekiri, Delta State, etc. Consequently, the contemporary struggle against militarism and for democracy in Nigeria must be characterised by contradictory roles of organised civil society groups.[12] Nigeria's efforts at strengthening civil society are now circumscribed by the consolidation of contradictions in the democratization process.

In order to achieve an effective civil society participation in ethnic conflict management, it is pertinent that pro-democracy groups and democracy-inclined civil society groups should continue to contest and engage the government sponsored and penetrated non-democracy inclined civil society groups, through continued debates, dialogues, constructive engagements and struggles, with the aims of re-orienting and re-directing their focus towards the realisation of the dignity of the human person. Secondly, civil society groups in Nigeria must effect a radical shift from their hitherto urban-bias in organisation and mobilization to rural-based organisations in both their organisation and mobilization.[13] Thirdly, conflict management today requires the mastering of specialized professional skills and conflict management mechanisms. The contemporary approach to conflict management is more as "a matter of fostering *ex-ante-bellum* conflict resolution rather than the hitherto conception of peacemaking in Africa as ex-*post-facto* conflict intercession."[14] The assumption of this primary function of fostering *ex-ante-bellum* conflict resolution as opposed to *ex-post facto* conflict intercession is alien and novel to most civil society groups in Nigeria who lack the requisite professionalism for the application of this proactive, preventive, preemptive *ex-ante-bellum* conflict management strategy. In most instances, it is only the civil society leaders that comprehend these proactive preventive *ex-ante-bellum* conflict resolution mechanism but because most civil society groups lack internal democracy of transparency, probity and accountability themselves, the tendency has been for the leaders to gravitate towards authoritarianism, thus, dominating the groups, stunting the institutional structures, making them brittle and susceptible to disintegration under severe stress or pressure.[15]

Fourthly, civil society groups in Nigeria exhibit some apparent lack of co-ordination and focus. This is manifested in their visible weak linkages and in their dissipation of energies through unnecessary duplication of efforts and petty jealousies, rivalries and quarrels based on exaggerated suspicions.[16] The numerous NGOs, CBOs, church groups, trade groups, occupational groups, ethnic development associations, community development associations, age grades, etc., are narrowly focused or engaged in defending their exclusive turfs rather than respond to conflict management imperative of operating on a broadened and holistic horizon. The weak linkages and low level networking is often contingent upon projects, agendas and rarely based on a socially driven consensus.[17] This lack of coordination and focus generates confusion, which affects civil society groups' capacity to perform, or to sustain programmes over long periods. Such programmes and projects are germane to conflict management mechanism as both require post-completion follow-up action and post-completion monitoring, both of which are problematic to civil society groups that are not well-coordinated and well-focused.

Civil society groups in Nigeria lack adequate or effective civic education programmes and community development programmes which can be mounted as an integral part of the package of *ex-antebellum* ethnic conflict management mechanism. The twin problems of poverty and illiteracy do impose certain serious limitations on the citizenry's participation in NGO work.

The relationship between civil society and successive governments in Nigeria constitutes an impediment to an effective civil society participation in ethnic conflict management. The legal and policy environment for civil society organisations are still ill defined and very unclear. Although regulations do exist for NGOs: CLO, CRP, UAD, JACON, COHR, CAPP, CD, DA, WRAPA, WIN, IGSR, AFRIGOV, PREDA etc., who must register with the Corporate Affairs Commission but CBOs, church groups, trade associations, ethnic development associations, age grades, occupational groups, etc. have very little regulation and are often unregistered bodies.

Since government regulation and control over CBOs has been very limited, government has been very hesitant and at times, reluctant to enter into partnership with the civil society organisations in ethnic conflict management. Moreover, the recent history of antagonism between the military governments of

Mohammadu Buhari, 1983-1985, Ibrahim Babangida, 1985-1993 and Sani Abacha, 1993-1998 and civil society groups, particularly the NGOs, has prevented civil society organisations from fulfilling their potential as a credible partner in the ethnic conflict management initiative. Granted that most civil society groups lack the professionalism required for ethnic conflict management, nevertheless, civil society organisations in Nigeria must create effective space for participation in public affairs. However, not all members of civil society organisations have the same capacity to create this effective space for participation in ethnic conflict management because of the obvious glaring dichotomous interests of civil society groups in the governance debate.

Strengthening the Capacity of Civil Society Groups for Participation In Ethnic Conflict Management
Strengthening the capacity of civil society organisations for participation in ethnic conflict management requires rescuing them from acute constraints and weaknesses, and empowering them with more efficient and effective facilities, skills and methods of operation and functioning. The catalogue and inventory of civil society organisations in Nigeria encompasses the following:

1.   Non-Governmental Organisations (NGOs);
2.   Community-Based Organisations (CBOs);
3.   Organised Private Sector organisations (OPS);
4.   Informal Private Sector Organisations;
5.   Religious Bodies and Groups;
6.   Professional/Occupational Groups;
7.   Trade Unions Associations;
8.   Youth/Students Associations;
9.   Women Associations; and
10.   Farmers/Peasants Associations.

From the above inventory of civil society organisations, it does appear that the CBOs, informal private sector organisations, religious bodies and groups, youth/students associations, women associations and farmers/peasants associations are more amenable instruments of civil society participation in ethnic conflict management. Next to these CBOs and their affiliate associations, are the NGOs of the Profesionalised types, e.g. Academic Associates PeaceWorks (AAPW), Peace Reconciliation and Development Association (PREDA), African Refugees Foundations (ARF), Centre for Development, Support Monitoring and Advocacy (CESMA). Measures for the strengthening and empowerment of the civil society organisations for effective participation in ethnic conflict management in Nigeria should be directed and targeted to CBOs and their affiliates and to NGOs of the professionalised type.

The role played by civil society groups through their intervention programmes in broad areas of conflict management and peace building cannot be ignored. Among others, the Academic Associates PeaceWorks (AAPW), Peace Reconciliation and Development Association (PREDA) Strategic Empowerment and Mediation Agency (SEMA), Peace and Development Organisation (PEDO), Prime Peace Project Limited (PPPL), have established a record of intervention in the area of conflict management and peace-building in the numerous cases of communal violence across the country with relatively high degree of success. These include the Jukun-Tiv conflict in Wukari, the Mughaavul-Ron crisis in Bokkos, Plateau State.[18] But the Nigerian civil society intervention in conflict management portends great prospects of a relapse into violence considering that ethnic conflict management and peace building initiated by civil society groups hardly address the underlying causes of the conflict, normally an issue outside the purview of civil society organisations themselves. Since civil society intervention cannot be a substitute for the responsibility of the state, it becomes pertinent to explore areas of the state-civil society organisations engagement, partnership and collaboration for an enduring basis for peace and harmony. Barbara Hill has identified three phases of the conflict processes as:

1. The "pre-conflict" phase: the sequence of events leading up to the outbreak of hostilities;
2. the "actual conflict" phase: the outbreak and subsequent events of the conflict itself;
3. the "post-conflict" phase: those events beginning with an overt attempt to end hostilities concluding with the resolution of the conflict.[19]

Conflict prevention starts from the pre-conflict phase, while conflict management usually begins from the "actual conflict" phase involving the utilisation of various techniques aimed at freezing and/or de-escalating the conflict. Conflict resolution starts from the post-conflict phase. We want to conceptualize conflict management as a framework which encompasses all the three identifiable phases.

Civil Society Organisation in Partnership with Government
For the Nigerian civil society organisations to be capable of mediating peace operations encompassing these three phases, it must explore areas of state - civil society engagement, partnership and collaboration. In fact, a coalition of civil society organisations, private sector operators and governments at the federal, state and the local governments' levels is considered as ideal to complete the tripod of stakeholders in the creation of an enduring and enabling environment for peace and harmony. Civil society groups must facilitate their entrance into the national, state and local spaces of policy-making thereby strengthening their capacities to understand the policy processes. Some of the measures adopted to strengthen and reinforce the participatory capacities and practice of civil society entities in policy formulation and the process of governance generally is the establishment of a Civil Society Advocacy Group (CSAG) whose primary goal is civil society driven policy advocacy. This is being facilitated by one of the oldest NGO's in Nigeria (CASSAD) (Nigerian Poverty Eradication Forum).

Moreover, the Nigerian Poverty Eradication Forum (PERFORM) has embarked on proactive preventive *ex-ante-bellum* conflict resolution initiatives. This initiative is geared towards the promotion and development of proactive measures, particularly action-oriented studies and programmes on conflicts and conflict-inducing forces and conditions in the society. One of such initiatives has been organised in conjunction with the UN, Food and Agricultural Organisation (FAO) on partnership in the area of Food Security in Nigeria. The initiatives' emphasis is in relation to the necessary advocacy for civil society organisations to be given space to effectively contribute to policy formulation for national food security.

Secondly, the antagonism between the government and civil society organisations particularly the NGO section of civil society appears to be evaporating and receding from the public glare. The consolidation of democracy in Nigeria and the current expansion of the democratic space beyond mere competitive elections to such human freedom index (HFI) like freedom of association and the right to participate in public affairs without restrictions have contributed to a change of an environment, which is cumulatively significant.

Nigeria's nascent democracy has become more tolerant and accommodating to even civil society groups that are autonomous and could likely challenge the state. One index of this tolerance is the gradual recession of uncertainties and inconsistencies in government policies as to the role of civil society organisations in governance. The second index of accommodation is manifested in government tolerance of criticisms and dissent and of its receptivity to policy suggestions emanating from civil society.[20] Civil society organisations have abandoned their tendency to apathy resignation, and outright cynicism characteristic of the civil society under the military regimes and have not only demanded for democratic space but are seizing the democratic space that allows them participate in public affairs. This accounts for the emergence of vigorous and robust civil society organisations that have emerged as critical actors in the discourse on ethnic communal and religious conflicts in Nigeria, for example, AAPW, SEMA, PREDA, PEDO, PPPL, etc.

Thirdly, with the gradual removal of the antagonism between government and the civil society groups, there has been a commensurating gradual retreat of the dualism in grassroots civil-organisations in Nigeria. With the demise of authoritarianism and the nurturing of a nascent democracy in Nigeria, the proliferation of state-sponsored, controlled or penetrated non-democracy-inclined civil society groups appears to have been truncated. As civil society is a highly contested public sphere, characterized by struggles, crosscuttings and contradictory alliance in relation to both the economy and the state, many of the non-democracy inclined civil society groups have collapsed under the pressure of this contest which for them is now devoid of government patronage.

The advent of democracy in Nigeria in 1999 appears to have strengthened the capacity of democracy-inclined civil society organisations and other pro-democracy groups. The proliferation of democracy-inclined civil society organisations in Nigeria particularly the NGOs, which by conservative estimates is put at 10,000,[21] (Akinyele, 1995:5) appears to have decided the highly contested public sphere in favour of the democracy-inclined civil society organisations. Consequently, the antagonism that characterized the relationship between the democracy-inclined civil society organisations and the government-sponsored, controlled and penetrated non-democracy-inclined civil society organisations appears to have been resolved. The very vibrant and robust civil society organisations are expending their democratic space to fill the vacuum created by the state in the performance of its duties in the maintenance of law and order, and in the resolution of conflicts and conflict management.

Measures of Empowering Civil Society Groups
The lack of professionalism alluded to civil society organisations earlier appears an untenable and a contestable proposition in the 21st Century. The number of civil society organisations that have developed expertise in certain definite fields or areas and are even considered leaders in the field of HIV/AIDS (Halt-Aids Group (HAG), Society for Women & Aids in Africa (SWAAN), Journalist Against Aids (JAAIDS)), Human Rights (Civil Liberties Organisation (CLO), Constitutional Right Project (CRP), Campaign for Democracy and Human Rights (CDHR)), Environmental Rights (Human Development/Initiative (HDI), Nigerian Conservation Foundation (NCF), Urban Neighbourhood Development Initiative (UNDI)), Conflict Resolution (Academic Associates Peace Works (AAPW), Peace Reconciliation & Development Association (PREDA), African Strategic and Peace Research Group (AFSTRAG), Strategic Empowerment and Mediation Agency (SEMA), Peace and Development Organisation (PEDO), Prime Peace Project Limited (PPPL)) etc. appears to be on the increase. Civil society organisation's lack of capacity to coordinate programmes effectively is now being surmounted through the establishment of the Nigeria NGO Consultative Forum (NINCOF) to enhance greater coordination of NGO activities and the participation of NGOs in national development by providing a common platform for coordination and collaboration with government (PERFORM, 2000:2).

One outstanding measure of empowerment of civil society remains the extension of the civil society tentacle of professionalism into all the facets of the local variant of the "Complex Emergencies" i.e. humanitarian relief, mediation and conciliation, monitoring of cease fire, demobilization of factional irregular armies, refugees and displaced persons rehabilitations, reconciliation through over-arching joint programmes and projects, formation of an all inclusive local administration, etc.

The seeming lack of coordination and focus of civil society organisation in Nigeria is being surmounted by the establishment of the Nigeria NGO Consultative Forum (NINCOF). NINCOF is expected to promote and improve the level of networking among civil society groups and strengthen their linkages through information sharing. But of immense importance to the strengthening of civil society organisations in Nigeria is NINCOF's commitment to enthrone the best practice in financial and programme accountability in NGO work. The vibrant and robust civil society groups in Nigeria are now subjected and sublimated under this ombudsman umbrella organisation, NINCOF, to function as transparent, accountable and well-managed organisations. This portends a trend towards an effective civil society participation in ethnic conflict management.

One major weakness of the Nigerian civil society organisations has been their urban bias in both organisation and mobilization, whereas, a significant percentage of Nigeria's ethnic conflicts are rural-based. We have identified the CBOs and their affiliate associations, and the NGOs of the professionalised types as the most ideal instruments of the informal method of ethnic conflict management. As most CBOs are community and rural-based, concerted efforts at their mobilisation and recruitment for ethnic conflict management becomes inevitable. Already, governments have recognised their potential as peacemakers and peace-builders, but has failed to harness this potential in any arresting manner. Civil society groups, particularly the NGOs, must break out from their urban-based cocoons and relocate to crisis prone rural areas for effective ethnic conflict management.

The NGOs' breakaway from this urban bias in organisation and mobilization is exemplified by such NGOs as Peace Reconciliation and Development Association (PREDA) that has located its operational headquarters in the crisis prone Kafanchan with its branches in Lagos, etc.

Other measures to strengthen and empower the civil society organisations would entail the training of cadres in grass roots mobilization and advocacy, the training of cadres for the acquisition of leadership and good governance skills and the acquisition of basic facilities and equipment necessary for organisational efficiency, effectiveness and measurable output.[22] The promotion of collaborative/joint programmes of advocacy and mobilisation, which is being mediated by the Nigeria NGO Consultative Forum (NINCOF), has facilitated an effective NGO networking significantly.

Civil society organisations' inadequate funding and their excessive overdependence on foreign aid must be circumvented to accord it sufficient autonomy, neutrality and objectivity as a peace mediation organ. To facilitate, strengthen and promote effective civil society organisations' participation in ethnic conflict management as a neutral arbiter, we recommend the following revenue base diversification mechanisms;

1.   Federal, state and local government special budgetary allocations for ethno-religious conflicts management in Nigeria;
2.   Cost-sharing mechanism between the warring factions and civil society organisation mediating ethnic conflicts;
3.   Absolute cost bearing mechanism by the ethnic groups engaged in the conflicts extractable from their Ethnic Development Coffers; and
4.   Contributions from philanthropic humanitarian organisations and public spirited individual and corporate bodies.

Nigerian NGOs must diversify their sources of funding to creative revenue generation activities in order to reduce their excessive gaze and reliance on foreign grants as their revenue base.

The gender imbalance alluded to as one of the weaknesses of civil society organisations in Nigeria is fast eroding as women NGOs, CBOs, OPS, continue to mushroom in the post-authoritarian Nigeria. The inventory of notable women NGOs in Nigeria is quite impressive: Women in Nigeria (WIN), Community Women and

Development (COWAD), Marked Women Association of Nigeria (MWAN), Medical Women Association of Nigeria (MWAN), Nigerian Association of Women Entrepreneurs (NAWE), Nigerian Federation of Business and Professional Women (BPW), International Federation of Women Lawyers (FIDA), Society for Women and Aids in Africa (SWAAN), Women in Law and Development in Africa (WILDAF), Women in Heath Development (WIHD), Nigerian Association of Women Industrialists (NAWI), Nigerian Association of Women Journalist (NAWOJ), Women's Health and Economic Development Association (WHEDA), Daughters of Abraham Foundation (DAF), Girls Power Initiative, Women in Neighbourhood Ventures (WONEV), Nigeria Women Empowerment Network (NAWENO), National Association of Women in Business (NAWB), Women Living Under Muslim Laws (WLUML) Women Advancement Forum (WAF), Women's Right Advancement and Protection Agency (WRAPA), etc.[23] Women empowerment has taken the centre-stage of the Nigeria civil society debate and the gender imbalance problem has ceased to become a factor militating against civil society participation in ethnic conflict management in Nigeria.

One of the problems and perhaps a major index of the weakness of civil society groups in Nigeria has been its excessive gaze and overemphasis on civil and political rights as opposed to social and economic ones. As a corollary to this, trade unions have traditionally been active in political participation and in lobbying for greater democratic space within the body politics, while CBOs have essentially been more interested in their immediate needs and interests and rarely engaged with wider political issues except if they are directly affected by government institutions and policies. However, in Nigeria's post-authoritarianism, the mushrooming civil society has extended its arena and theatre of contest beyond the civil and political rights into the social and economic spheres. One index of civil society empowerment in Nigeria is the proliferation of NGOs and CBOs in the social and economic spheres: Daughters of Abraham Foundation, Market Women Association of Nigeria (MWAN), Women in Neighbourhood Ventures (WONEV) Operation Farewell to Poverty (OFP), Urban Neighbourhood Development Initiative, Action Group for Research Information and Training on Drug Abuse (AGRITDA), Bountiful Harvest (BH),

Journalists Against Aids (JAAIDS NIGERIA), Girls' Power Initiative Campaign Against Unwanted Pregnancy (CAUP), Gender and Development Action, Country Women Association of Nigeria (COWAN), Society for Women and Aids in Africa (SWAAN).

Nigeria's civil society organisations' vulnerability to the traditional primordial loyalties to ethnic racial, religious, regional cleavages in the macro-society is now receding in the post-authoritarian Nigeria of the 2001. The proliferation and mushrooming of civil society grcups and their distribution across interests appears to be affording Nigerians opportunities to participate in association and informal networks at multiple levels of society thereby crosscutting and transcending the traditional primordial barriers of ethnicity, religion and regions. The future portends a trend suggesting that a richly pluralistic civil society of Nigeria will generate a wide-range of interests that may crosscut, and so mitigate, the principal polarities of political conflict. As new class-based organisations and issue-oriented movements arise, they may draw together new constituencies that cut across long standing regional, religious, ethnic or partisan cleavages.[24]

Finally, it is important to foster a spirit of partnership between NGOs, CBOs, civil society, local authorities, the organised private sector that would replace the mistrust, ambivalence and conflict with an alliance that would promote peoples' participation in setting strategies and mobilizing collective support for ethnic conflict management.

The Nigerian civil society should approach ethnic conflict management from the following perceptual prisms:

1. the social organisation and structural patterns of interaction;
2. the modes of violence employed;
3. the values of the parties in conflict (both values declared and the values actually pursued);
4. the changes in the hierarchy of values to become more specific or more diffused;
5. the degree of incompatibility of goals;
6. the genesis of conflicts;
7. the perception of symmetric and asymmetric perception among the conflict parties.
8. symmetries as to power potential and loyalties; and
9. the way in which the conflict is terminated.[25]

The Holistic Civil Society Approach to Ethnic Conflict Management

After a thorough and detailed analysis of the above conceptual conflict profiles, the Nigerian civil society should approach its conflict management from the Multi Component Missions or the Complex Peace-Building Operations paradigm and perspectives. These complex emergency operations have both civilian as well as military components. The frequency, scale and intensity of ethno-communal conflicts in Nigeria which suggests the involvement of mostly local factional irregular forces, recommends itself to the application of the traditional and non-formal methods of managing conflicts in Nigeria.

The local variant of the Complex Emergencies Civil Society Organisation could adopt would involve:

1. Mediation and conciliation;
2. Monitoring of the cease-fire;
3. Measures to re-establish confidence in the warring factions for peaceful co-existence;
4. Providing humanitarian relief;
5. Demobilization of the factional fighting units;
6. Maintenance of law and order;
7. Return of Refugees to their original places;
8. Oversee land reorganisation, redistribution and reform;
9. Re-establish or nurture local institutional structures for reconstruction and administration;
10. Provide human rights overwatch in the conflict area; and
11. Superintend the formation of an all-inclusive local administration.[26]

Gleaning through the complexity of the above local variants of Multi-Component Mission now labelled "Complex Emergencies", any effective civil society participation in ethnic conflict management must be approached from their disparate specialized professional NGOs and CBOs civil society perspectives. The multi-component mission character of conflict management dictates a very diversified multidimensional approach from the part of civil society organisations.

Already, a number of civil society groups have developed

certain professional expertise and are considered leaders in the field of HIV/AIDS: Halt Aids Groups (HAG) and Society for Women & Aids in Africa (SWAAN); Human Rights Issues: Civil Liberties Organisation (CLO) and Campaign for Democracy and Human Rights (CDHR); Environmental Issues: Urban-Neighbourhood Development Initiative (UNDI) and Human Development Initiative (HDI); Poverty issues: Operation Farewell to Poverty (OFP), Poverty, Ignorance & Diseases Alleviation Group of Nigeria (PIDAGON) and Bountiful Harvest NGO, (BH); Gender Issues: Women, Law and Development Centre, (WLDC) and Women's Rights Advancement and Protection Alternative (WRAPA); Drugs Issues: Action Group for Research Information and Training on Drug Abuse, (AGRITDA); Grassroots Empowerment: Centre for Development, Support Monitoring and Advocacy, (CDSMA); Peace Issues: Academic Associates Peace Works (AAPW), Peace Reconciliation and Development Association, (PREDA); Governance Issues: African Centre for Democratic Governance, (AFROGOV), Institute of Governance and Social Research (IGSR), Research Centre for Democratic Governance and Social Justice (RECEDEGS), etc.

But for a more effective civil society participation in ethnic conflict management, a more diversified and specialized civil society group to cover the whole range of areas involved in the multi-component operations of ethnic conflict management is essential. Meanwhile, the formation of an NGO umbrella organisation, the Nigerian NGO Consultative Forum (NINCOF), provides the nexus for co-ordination of civil society participation in ethnic conflict management.

But the persistence, scale and intensity of ethnic conflicts in Nigeria suggest that the above formal approaches to ethnic conflict management have either proven ineffective because of the potential prospects of relapses into violence or have not functioned at all in the first instance: Bassa-Egbura conflict in Nassarawa State, 1986, 1997, 1998, 1999, 2000; Tiv-Alago conflict in Nassarawa State, 1989, 1993-1994, 2000-2001, Hausa/Fulani-Sayawa conflict in Bauchi State, 1991, 2001, etc.

The above catalogue of the inadequacy and limitations of the formal approach to ethnic conflict management informs the exploration and promotion of the alternative modes of ethnic conflict management in Nigeria. The traditional and non-formal methods of ethnic conflict management best recommend themselves. The conflict profile of most Nigerian ethnic conflicts and their experiences bring into clear focus the importance of conflict resolution mechanisms which dwell largely on building mutual trust and understanding between groups at conflict. An innovative intervention by civil society is, therefore, necessary, in which the elders' forum, opinion leaders, clan and lineage heads, traditional rulers, religious leaders, community political leaders, women associations, ethnic development association, farmers' association, ex-service men and retirees' association, age grades, youth organisations, students organisations are very important segments the society would participate in.

The above preposition is premised on the assumption that ethnic conflicts are likely to be more amenable to resolution when they are handled by non-formal actors. Traditional and non-formal methods of managing ethnic conflicts in Nigeria have proved more efficacious than the formal approaches to ethnic conflict management. Therefore, civil society organisations: NGOs, CBOs, religious groups, trade associations, age grades, etc., have far greater potential and scope in preventing conflicts and in promoting post-conflict peace-building than the governments.

The contemporary nexus of forces requires that ethnic conflict management be conceived primarily as a matter of fostering *ex-ante-bellum* conflict resolution, as opposed to the past practice of *ex-post-facto* conflict-intercession.[27] The Nigerian civil society should exploit its comparative advantage and relative expertise in the area of conflict prevention to promote and develop pro-active initiatives particularly action-oriented strategies and programmes of informal conflict management.

Civil society groups must be trained to recognize and identify the early warning signs of conflicts in general and of ethnic conflict in particular. These early warning signs are indicators that conflict is brewing and imminent. These early warning signs may be manifested in different forms depending on the nature of conflict but the common denominator to them all is that their appearance survives a definite duration before conflict degenerates to a point of open expression of hostility or violence. In Nigeria, the general early warning signs are often manifested in the following indicators:

1.   Massive unemployment;
2.   Pro and anti-government rallies;
3.   Communal disputes: land, boundary and chieftaincy;
4.   Religious crisis;
5.   Armed robbery;
6.   Fuel scarcity;
7.   Public-personal insecurity;
8.   Public and political apathy; and
9.   Food scarcity;

At the ethnic, tribal or communal levels, the early warning signs are manifested in the following indicators:

1.   Protracted land ownership disputes;
2.   Protracted boundary disputes;
3.   Protracted chieftaincy disputes;
4.   Control of local institutions/administration;
5.   Disputes over the siting and location of public utilities;
6.   Disputes between nomads and peasants;
7,˙   Resentment based on status like the superior/inferior and lord/vassal paradigms;
8.   Famine and food insecurity; and
9.   Massive unemployment.

Similarly, the Nigerian civil society organisations which are better pre-disposed to post-conflict peace-building can maximize this advantage by erecting confidence-building measures for the peaceful co-existence of ethnic and social groups involved in the conflict. Some of the well-tested traditional and informal methods of post-conflict confidence building measures include:

1.   Formation of trans-ethnic or inter-ethnic committees;
2.   Promotion and establishment of mixed-settlements;
3.   Promotion of greater cross-cultural marriages;
4.   Organisation of mutual cultural festivals' celebrations;
5.   Formation of an all inclusive local administration;
6.   Organisation of joint community development projects and programmes;

7.   Establishment of alternate community local market days;
8.   Organisation of inter-community sporting activities;
9.   Establishment of joint measures to protect the environment;
  ·   and
10. Establishment of peace cells, peace units, peace associations, peace bodies and peace centres.

Conclusion

It has been argued in this study that ethnic conflict management in Nigeria should pivot on the three tripods on which the Nigerian society itself hinges—the governments, the organised private sector and civil society organisations. Of the three tripods, the governments (local, state and federal), seem to have been more frequently involved in the management of ethnic conflicts in Nigeria although such involvement has not translated into the effective management of these conflicts. This is obvious from the frequency, scale and intensity of ethnic conflicts in Nigeria. While recognising the fact that the civil society leg of the three tripods has been the weakest link, we have nevertheless shown in this study that civil society groups possess great potentials for being transformed into potent agents of ethnic conflict management in Nigeria. The profusion of civil society groups in Nigeria, as evident in the numerous economic, cultural, educational, interest-based, issue-oriented, developmental and civic groups operating in the country, has provided the stimulating impulse for zeroing in on civil society organisations as potent agents of ethnic conflict management in Nigeria.

An attempt has been made in this chapter to examine the factors militating against the efficacy of civil society organisations as vital instruments of ethnic conflict management. The chapter has also explored various measures for strengthening the capacity of civil society groups for participating in ethnic conflict management. Finally, the chapter examines civil society/government partnership and recommends ways of empowering civil society groups for the effective performance of their vital role in ethnic conflict management. The suggestions proffered range from the broad spectrum of absolute government cost-bearing, through cost-sharing mechanisms, to absolute cost-bearing by ethnic groups engaged in conflict. Also recommended is a holistic civil society approach to ethnic conflict management in which the traditional non-formal methods of managing conflicts best recommend themselves.

References

1. R.L. Sklar & Mark Strege, "Peace Through Freedom: The Resolution of International Conflicts in Sahelian Africa". Paper presented at the Conference on Regional Conflict and Diplomatic Initiatives. The Nigerian Institute of International Affairs (NIIA) Lagos, 1991, p. 1.
2. I. James, I., The Settler Phenomenon in the Middle Belt and the Problem of National Integration in Nigeria (Jos: Midland Press, 2000), pp.115-117.
3. C. Ake, "The Nigerian State: Antimonies of a Periphery Formation" , in C. Ake (ed.) *The Political Economy of Nigeria* (London: Longman, 1985), p.1.
4. S. Egwu, "Ethnic and Religious Violence in Nigeria" (Abuja: The African Centre for Democratic Governance, AFRIGOV, 2000), p. 31-47.
5. J. Keane, (ea.), *Civil Society and the State: New European Perspectives* (London: Verso, 1988), p. 61.
6. N. Bobbio, "Gramsci and the Conception of Civil Society", in C. Mouffe, (ed.) *Gramsci and Marxist Theory* (London: Routledge & Kegon Paul, 1979), pp. 21-24.
7. A. Olukoshi, "Economic Crisis, Multipartism and Opposition Politics in Contemporary Africa", in Adebayo Olukoshi (ed.), *The Politics of Opposition in Contemporary Africa* (Uppsala, Nordiska Afrikainstitute, 1998), p. 474.
8. L. Diamond "Rethinking Civil Society: Toward Democratic Consolidation". Paper presented at USIS Kaduna, Nigeria, 1995, p. 3.
9. A.M. Jega, (1998) "Strengthening the Civil Society in Nigeria". Paper presented at a workshop on the 1995 Constitution, organized by CLO, CRP and NHRC, Abuja, 1998, p.3.
10. *Ibid.*, p.2.
11. I. James, *op. cit.*, p.3.

12. A.M. Jega, *op. cit.*, p.3.
13. *Ibid.*, p.4.
14. C.S. Whitaker, "A New Era of Peacekeeping: The African Stake." Paper presented at the Conference on Regional Conflict and Diplomatic Initiatives, NIIA, Lagos, 1991, p.1.
15. J. Akande, "Civil Society Organisations an Interest Group in Poverty Reduction and Sustainable Human Development." Paper presented at UNDP Workshop, Abuja, 2000, p. 3-4.
16. A.M. Jega, *op. cit.*, p.4.
17. J. Akande, *op. cit.*, p.4.
18. Samuel G. Egwu, *op. cit.*, p.47.
19. B.J. Hill, "An Analysis of Conflict Resolution Techniques: From Problem-solving Workshop to Theory" *Journal of Conflict Resolution*, Vol. 26, No. 1. March, 1982, pp. 109-138.
20. J. Akande, *op. cit.*, p.3.
21. I.O. Akinyele, "Nigerian NGOs: Working Together for Effective National Development". Paper presented at Pre-Launching Workshop of the Nigerian NGO Consultative Forum, p. 5.
22. A.M. Jega, *op cit.*, p.4.
23. C. Mbadugha, "Women-Related Establishments and Non-Governmental Organisations", in H. I. Ajaegbu, B.J. St. Mathew-Daniel O.E. Uya (eds.), *Nigeria: A People United, A Future Assured.* Vol. I, A Compendium (Abuja: Federal Ministry of Information, 2000), pp. 362-364.
24. L. Diamond, *op. cit.*, p.6.
25. B. Hoglund and Jorgen William Wrich (eds.), *1975 Conflict Control and Conflict Resolution Inter-disciplinary Studies from the Scandinavian Summer University*, Vol. 1., (Copenhagen: Munksgaard; New York: Humanities Press, 1975), pp.13-35.
26. E. Betram, "Reinventing Governments: The Promise and Perils of United Nations Peace Building." *Journal of Conflict Resolution,* Vol. 39, No. 3, 1995, pp. 388-389. See also J. Cilliers and Greg Mills (eds.), "From PeaceKeeping to Complex-Emergencies: Peace Support Missions in Africa." The South African Institutes of International Affairs, SAIIA & ISS Pretoria, 1999.
27. C.S. Whitaker, *op. cit.*, p.1.

Chapter 11

Civil Society and Ethnic Conflict Management: Lessons From Other African States

Gane Bang Zamtato

Introduction

Ever since independence, ethnic conflicts in Africa have assumed disturbing proportions. This situation is as a result of what has been observed as the fragility of African states. Most African states present the picture of a construction on poorly erected structure. They appear, in fact, as a shallow building patched from the top to the base without a national conscience and the wish to live together. Many African states are eroded from within by an exacerbation of micro nationalistic peculiarities with the dominating influence of traditional chiefs facing new institutions brought about by universal votes. Added to this, is the proliferation of political parties often corresponding to the ethnic configurations of the affected states. These centrifugal factors are potent threats to peaceful existence of African states.

To eliminate these threats, the state needs everyone's contribution, including especially members of the civil society, comprising opinion leaders, elders from the different communities, traditional rulers, chiefs, religious leaders, women groups, non-governmental organisations, various associations etc. Until now, the methods used by African states to resolve ethnic conflicts have failed to yield the desired results. They have not worked at all, owing to their inadequacies as instruments for the prevention and management of ethnic conflicts in Africa. Consequently, suggestions have been put forward that civil society should take over the mediation of ethnic conflicts from government.

The argument is that civil society is much more fit than the public authority to prevent conflicts because they are closer to the keen aspirations of African communities. Besides, the civil society portrays a picture of neutrality that public authorities do not always have. Therefore, it is much easier for civil society groups, as neutral mediators, to find a solution to ethnic conflicts.

Right or wrong, public authorities are accused of being the root cause of all the ethnic conflicts that are so far existing in Africa. It is believed that, if well mobilized, civil society could offer alternative methods for the management of these conflicts. Given allowance for local peculiarities, ethnic conflicts pose the same problems everywhere in Africa. They have the same causes, the same contexts, and are, therefore, amenable to the same approaches for their settlement from one country to the other.

Nature and Types of Civil Society Groups in Africa
Talking about the effective participation of civil society in the management of ethnic conflicts in Africa is to raise the question of identifying the civil society groups that can play creditable roles in conflict management within the continent. In this chapter, we shall concentrate on civil society groups that are well developed to play active roles in the management of conflicts within their respective societies. These include: opinion leaders; elders from different communities; traditional rulers like village or district heads; associations and non-governmental organisations (NGOs); peace and dialogue committees; and religious leaders. For these civil society groups to function properly as agents in the management of conflicts, it is extremely important that the state creates the necessary conditions for them to function effectively. In the discussion that follows, we shall concentrate on the activities of these groups in three African countries, namely, Chad, Cameroun and Mali.

Civil Society and Conflict Management in Chad

Chad is partially a desert country located at the heart of the African continent. It is bounded by Libya in the north, Sudan in the east, Niger in the west, and Nigeria, Cameroun and the Central African Republic in the south. It covers an area of 1.284.000 square km. It is made up of three climatic zones comprising, from the north to the south, Saharan, Sahelian and Sudan. The Saharan zone records very low rainfalls every year, not exceeding 100mm. The region is adapted to oasis farming and cattle rearing. The Sahelian zone records rainfalls that vary from 100mm to 600mm. It is the livestock zone of the country. Farming of cereals and oil producing plants are the other principal activities of this zone. The Sudan zone, with rainfalls between 700mm and 1200mm, is the farming zone of the country, It is the zone where, in addition to cereals, the country's main export crop, cotton, is produced. The Saharan and Sahelian zones are mostly inhabited by Muslims while the Sudan zone is inhabited mainly by Christians.

Since the time of the drought that occurred in the year 1970, the desert has expanded unceasingly towards the Sudan zone of the country; thus causing an imbalance in the grazing ecosystems both in the Sahelian and Saharan zones. Part of the consequences of this, is the degrading of soil, which in turn, leads to the reduction of pastures. Unlike farming that is the dominant activity of the Sudan zone, cattle rearing remains the dominant activity of the Sahelian zone. Cattle rearing is practised by nomads who formerly came from the Sahelian zone to the Sudan zone to look for green pastures for their animals to graze. Moving about for new pastures had always been a way of life for the herdsmen. This movement from place to place has, however, been intensified due to the effect of desert encroachment caused by drought. The practice entails constant movement of cattle from the dry land or drought-affected areas to zones that are relatively well watered.

Until recently, this movement by herdsmen in search of new pastures was a subject of great joy and familiar occurrence. It provided opportunity for regular commercial transaction between the nomads and farmers. They had a peaceful coexistence as the management of grassland space was under regulation and both the cattle rearers and farmers submitted themselves to the village customs and to the laws of the land.

However, today that peaceful coexistence has been undermined by the failure to abide by the existing regulations. Bloody conflicts have now become the order of the day. The failure by the herdsmen to control their cattle and prevent them from destroying farmlands has led to violent conflicts, which often lead to the destruction of not only farms and herds of cattle, but also lives and properties. Because these conflicts now take place with greater frequency and intensity, they have now become a permanent cause for concern; posing danger not only to the country's socio-political economy and the environment, but also to its fledging democracy.

In terms of their evolution, the conflicts fall under two periods. The first relates to the period before 1979, which was the era of peaceful coexistence between farmers and cattle rearers. The second period dates from the 1980s to the present. This represents the era when the historical-political evolution of Chad was marked by multiple crises and wars as a result of which the social fabric and the hitherto peaceful coexistence between farmers or the settled populations and the nomadic cattle rearers were shattered. The democratic process of the 1990s also influenced the situation as politicians, apart from dragging their feet in finding solutions to the problem, actually exploited the ethnic and intercommunal conflicts to serve their own selfish interests. Other factors, such as the lack of authority from the state, impunity and intolerance on the part of individual citizens also contributed to making the conflicts more serious.

Because the methods used by the state to resolve these conflicts have yielded very little or no results, civil society participation in conflict management has received a boost in the country. The civil society particularly involved are: the traditional rulers (villages heads, districts heads) the peace and dialogue committees, customary council members, associations and non–governmental organisations.

Traditional Chiefs/Rulers
The traditional chieftaincy institution is the unique structure in Chad that has been able to stand the test of time and transcend political regimes. The institution stands today as the rare institutions of reference for the great majority of Chadians. Its presence is felt everywhere in the country. Consequently, the authorities have now

granted it legal and statutory means to carry out conciliatory and related functions, which include traditional police functions and authority in some judicial matters. In civil and customary matters, for instance, these traditional rulers are vested with the power to intervene and effect conciliation between the parties in conflict residing within their own area of jurisdiction. In particular, they have the powers to intervene in the settlement and prevention of conflicts between farmers and cattle rearers. However, they can delegate their power to one or several customary council members of their choice. In case of failure in conciliation at the lower level of chieftaincy, parties may, based on a common agreement, take the matter to the upper hierarchy of power.

If there is any objection from one of the two parties to take the matter before their traditional ruler or in case of a failure to effect conciliation, the litigants are free to take their case to a judge or a competent magistrate as the case may be. If conciliation takes place, the chief conciliator will have a statement issued on the settlement. The traditional ruler, his secretary, the two parties concerned and the customary council members who participated in the conciliation will sign this statement. The statement will stand as a proof for the settlement of conflict between the two parties concerned.

Where law and order issues are concerned, which require their immediate intervention, the traditional rulers, on the receipt of the necessary reports, would proceed to settle the civil aspect with the agreement of the administrative and judicial authorities and within the power of their jurisdiction. Traditional rulers are not allowed to claim fines for their own benefit or on behalf of the state. However, where necessary, they can impose payment to offset damages to pacify the victims.

In conflict between nomads, cattle rearers and settled farmers, there exist a structure whereby traditional rulers (i.e., village and district heads) routinely participate in the management of such conflicts. Under the arrangement, the traditional rulers do not limit themselves to conciliatory efforts; they also carry out enlightenment campaigns and undertake measures to prevent future conflicts. Constant dialogue is encouraged between the head of the farming communities and that of the cattle rearers to ensure that existing guidelines are followed. Because the heads of the two groups are constantly in touch to plan the movement of cattle, reconfirm existing tracks and water outlets for the cattle, as well as delimit pasture and new grazing areas, misunderstanding between the two groups has been greatly minimised. They also set up committees made up of farmers, cattle rearers and some traditional rulers to fight against bush fire. In addition, they hold regular consultations with the country's lawmakers to ensure the incorporation of their local arrangements into the grazing laws passed at the various levels of government.

Peace/Dialogue Committees

In Chad, peace/dialogue committees are set up in each district and other important centres for the purpose of educating and enlightening cattle rearers and farmers on the tenets of good neighbourliness, peaceful coexistence and mutual respect. These committees are made up of representatives of the cattle rearers, farmers, traditional rulers and religious leaders (Muslims and Christians). These committees also carry out conflict settlement and counselling functions. To support the work of the peace committees, branches of human rights associations are created in all the districts.

Associations/ Non-Governmental Organisations (NGOs)

The intervention of associations and non-governmental organisations (NGOs) from the civil society, is mainly in the area of organising seminars and workshops, dissemination of the results of such seminars and workshops, as well as conducting other awareness tours and campaigns throughout the country. These associations and NGOs also encourage the creation of producers' groupings that bring together cattle rearers and farmers to work for the promotion of their joint interests.

Role of Assemblies (Cofono)

In Chad, especially in Toubou society, conflicts often involve entire clans and the escalation of violence in which victims are counted in large numbers. So, when a conflict breaks out, it becomes the responsibility of the entire people in order to ensure that there is meaningful reconciliation. The assembly in which conflicts are settled is called "Cofono". The "Cofono" is a fully representative gathering, which brings together not only the traditional rulers, but also customary council members from the surroundings, all interested men—young and old, as well as women groups of all ages. The "Cofono" plays a very important role in the settlement of conflicts. After hot and excited discussions and long talks, a final verdict is given. The guilty party usually submits to the final verdict.

Although one has concentrated particularly on conflicts between cattle rearers and farming communities in the illustration of the role of civil society groups in ethnic conflict management in Chad, other forms of ethnic conflicts do occur. The concern is to highlight the civil society groups that are particularly active in the management of conflicts in the country. As we shall see in a moment, some of the civil society groups that have been identified as very active in Chad equally exist in some other African countries although they are bound to have some local peculiarities. The important point to note about civil society participation in conflict management in Chad, is the fact that it is given official recognition and incorporated into the country's judicial system.

Civil Society and Conflict Management in Cameroun
In Cameroun, our discussion will concentrate on the concept of "African Palaver", which is widely used in many communities to settle conflicts. In Beti society, located in the capital region of Cameroun, the concept is called *adzo*, which means "to say or to talk". Simply put, therefore, "Palaver" could be described as the practice of talking things over, or the settlement of conflict through dialogue. As practised in Cameroun, it involves the entire community. This means all those who feel concerned are invited to participate in the search for a solution to the conflict. In this sense, the concept is similar to the assembly system in Chad known as "Cofono". The basic difference could be in name rather than in substance. In the same vein, the settlement of conflict through dialogue is one that is practised in many African societies. Perhaps, what makes the concept to stand out in Cameroun relates to the structured manner in which it is practised.

In the Beti society, where the concept seems to have been well developed, the use of palaver in the management of conflict involves three stages. The first is the stage at which parties are persuaded to bring their conflict to the "Palaver". It could take a long process to persuade them to accept palaver. The eventual acceptance of the use of palaver, is a demonstration by the parties of their willingness to find a peaceful solution to their conflict. Such an acceptance is usually regarded as a vote for peace rather than hostilities or war.

The second stage is the speech or hearing phase, during which the parties confront each other and let out their grievances and concerns. This is the stage at which opportunity is given to the elders, who will ultimately settle the conflict to get the full history of the conflict, know the fears and concerns of the parties, as well as the fundamental issue involved in the conflict.

The third and final stage is the point at which the elders, after taking evidence from witnesses and listening to all the contributions from the floor, retire to a secluded place to take a decision on the conflict. As soon as they are ready with their decision, they return to give it and conclude the "Palaver". Normally, the guilty party is made to compensate the other party in a proportional or, at least, in a symbolic manner. The idea behind the use of "Palaver" is to restore harmony within the affected community and not necessarily to punish the guilty party. Hence, the successful restoration of harmonious relationship between the parties is usually celebrated with meals and dances as a victory for the entire community.

Civil Society and Conflict Management in Mali

The Palaver system is also used in Mali as a popular conflict management technique. In Mali, conflicts are settled by those regarded as the "keepers of the word of authority". They are considered as judges or conciliators and they render justice in the name of their ancestors who are believed to have transmitted to them their wisdom through elderly men. When a conflict is brought to them, the process they follow is, first, to listen to the parties, second, listen to the witnesses, and then move into question time in turns, starting from eldest member of the team of local judges. The question time is to clarify issues and get the exact picture about the conflict. As soon as the necessary clarification has been done, they enter into their own proceedings in order to arrive at a verdict. Their verdict is without appeal and the guilty party usually submits himself to the decision taken. The important point to note about the use of "Palaver", is the emphasis on the restoration of social harmony within the community rather than a rigid emphasis on who is right or wrong.

Conclusion

The discussion in this chapter has highlighted the multi-ethnic nature of most African societies and the traditional methods of managing conflict in three selected countries, namely, Chad, Cameroun and Mali. It has been shown that the principle of conflict management that is popular in Africa is the settlement of conflict through dialogue, otherwise referred to in this study as the "African Palaver". We have shown how the various civil society groups identified in this study as agents for the management of conflict in the selected African states apply the logic of the "African Palaver" in the management of conflicts, especially intercommunal or ethnic conflicts.

The emphasis on traditional methods in this study stems from the fact that the methods used by African public authorities in managing ethnic conflicts have failed to achieve the desired results. It is felt that to have mutually satisfying solutions to ethnic conflicts especially, the communities involved should themselves play active roles. In this regard, the concept of the African Palaver becomes handy and useful in facilitating the mobilisation of civil society groups and the local communities to settle their conflicts themselves, using their own age-long rules and customs. Because such rules and customs are rooted in their local values and beliefs, the parties in conflict generally have confidence in the process and seldom go against or question the outcome.

Thus, the first lesson one can learn from this study is that because of the ineffectiveness and unreliability of official conflict management mechanisms, civil society must accept the inevitability of a more assertive role in the management of ethnic conflicts in Africa. The present study has proved that there are a lot of potentialities in exploring new conflict management approaches based on the effective use of the civil society and the reinforcement of traditional modes of conflict management practised within various African communities. As noted earlier, only the ethnic communities themselves organised within the framework of civil society can settle the problems that prevent them from living in peace. To maximise civil society participation in the management of these conflicts, the state should take the initiative and create conditions that will make for the effective participation of civil society groups in conflict management. To this end, each African state should put in place laws to facilitate the routine involvement of civil society in the management of conflicts.

References

1. Antoine Zonga, *OAU and Peace Settlement of Differences* (Paris: ABC Editions, 1987).
2. Jean Pierre Pabanel, *Military Coups in Black Africa* (Paris: Harmattan, 1984).
3. Communication of the Traditional Chiefs Association of Niger, *National Seminar on Conflict between Cattle Rearers and Farmers in Chad*, May 14, 1999.
4. Communication of the Association of Traditional Chiefs in Chad, *Ibid.*
5. Georges Ola Davies, *Afrique Magazine*, No. 174, March, 2000.
6. Georges Ola Davies, *Afrique Magazine*, No.178/179, July-August, 2000.
7. Tunde Fatunde, *Jeune Afrique Economie*, No.294, September 13- October 3, 1999.

Chapter 12

Towards Civil Society/Government Partnership in Ethnic Conflict Management: Integrating the Traditional Democratic Analytical Model into Existing Conflict Management Practice

Thomas A. Imobighe

Conflict Management as an Integrated Multi-Dimensional Exercise

The case studies presented in this volume have conclusively proved that formal methods of conflict management have failed to effectively address the persistence and pervasiveness of Nigeria's ethnic conflicts. Perhaps one of the most important weaknesses of the formal approaches has to do with the fact that government attention is usually attracted to these conflicts at the point of their consummation and not at the brewing stages of such conflicts. What this means is that until these conflicts reach a high point of escalation, at which open hostility is manifested, they do not attract official attention. Essentially, therefore, it would seem the relevant authorities in Nigeria see conflict management as primarily concerned with the suppression of hostility and violence. Because they fail to see conflict management in a comprehensive and integrated manner with multidimensional activities which include, particularly, conflict prevention/peace promotion and conciliatory activities, their responses have always fallen short of achieving the expected comprehensive solution to the affected conflicts.

The integrated conflict management model developed elsewhere by the present writer incorporates three dimensions of activities into an integrated conflict management circle. These comprise conflict prevention/peace promotion, conflict control/ abatement and conflict resolution.[1] In this sense, conflict management goes beyond the suppression of violence and includes measures directed towards eliminating the conditions that create an environment of conflict as well as the development of an "early warning system" to facilitate early response to conflict situations in order to prevent violence. It also includes the putting in place of reconciliation mechanisms to resolve the fundamental issues affecting such conflicts, especially after the suppression of violence through the deployment of security forces as is presently the mode of official response in Nigeria.

The logic of civil society participation in conflict management flows from this comprehensive perception of conflict management. In other words, using the integrated conflict management model, it is easy to identify the areas of weakness and limitations in the use of formal orthodox methods and where innovative civil society role fits into the picture. In the case of Nigeria's ethnic conflicts, it has been suggested that grass roots and community-based organisations are particularly suited to play positive roles in their management. It has also been found that different communities in Nigeria have their various traditional methods of managing conflict through the use of traditional rulers, council of chiefs, council of elders, prominent individuals within the affected society and age-group systems. The task that flows from the above observation is to distil from the various traditional practices some particular conflict management modes that could be harmonised with the formal methods for the management of the numerous ethnic conflicts afflicting the country. In this chapter, we shall discuss what is regarded here as the "traditional democratic analytical model" of conflict resolution, which is quite common among Nigeria's rural communities.[2]

The Traditional Democratic Analytical Model of Conflict Resolution

If one were to draw up an inventory of traditional conflict management practices by Nigeria's multi-ethnic society, it would be seen that some similarities and dissimilarities exist in the conflict management practices by the different communities. It is not the intention here to discuss particular individual practices but identify the common strands existing in these traditional practices, which fit them into the model being discussed here. The traditional democratic analytical model of conflict resolution is a conflict resolution mechanism with the central objective of reconciling the parties in conflict. So it is based on the organisation of reconciliation meetings between the parties. Although the model is essentially a rural or grass roots conflict resolution phenomenon, if properly structured, it can be applied at the levels of the society, including family, village and inter-community or clan levels. In other words, the reconciliation meeting can be organised under the authority of the family head, the village head, or the traditional ruler. What distinguishes the democratic analytical model from other forms of traditional conflict resolution practices is that attendance at the reconciliation meeting is not predetermined. It is open to all interested adults. Even representatives and friends of the parties in conflict are usually involved in the common search for amicable solution to the conflict.

The procedure in a typical reconciliation meeting witnessed by the present writer within a community in Owan Local Government Area of Edo State, is as stated below. It was in respect of a dispute between a settler farmer and an indigene farmland owner. The latter had given the settler a piece of land to farm on the understanding that he would give a specified number of yams to the land owner when the yams are harvested. It turned out that the settler farmer defaulted on the agreement and never supplied the yams. Without further authorisation from the landowner, he went again to prepare the land for planting. This action infuriated the landowner that he had to forcefully drive the settler away from the land, notwithstanding the promise by the latter that he would supply the yams for the two years together at the time of the next harvest. Of course, he gave reasons why he could not meet the terms of the agreement, which the landlord was not prepared to accept.

On the basis of the complaint by the settler farmer that he had been forcibly driven from the land he had prepared to plant, the traditional ruler summoned both parties to his palace for a reconciliation meeting. Present were members of the settler's community and the host communities including the chiefs and elders. The deliberations were opened with the breaking of kolanuts by the traditional ruler and the invocation of the spirit of the ancestors to be at the meeting. After the parties had stated their cases and witnesses addressed the meeting, what followed was not a direct verdict of guilt or innocence but analysis of the conflict process and the attribution of blames where necessary. The younger and less experienced adults start the analysis, which progressively moves to the older and more experienced ones until the final summary is given by the traditional ruler. This final summary, which is a reflection of the general trend of the earlier comments thus represents the collective decision of the reconciliation meeting. It is necessary to highlight the contributions of some of those who commented on the issue to get the general picture of what transpired.

The first person that spoke castigated the behaviour of the settler farmer. He opined that the excuse he gave that he was summoned home to attend to his mother who took ill and later died was not sufficient to deny the landowner his yams. The argument was that he could not convince anybody that it was from the sale of the two lines of yams he was expected to give to the landowner that he was able to raise the money to meet his expenses, and that when he returned from home, he ought to have found ways of getting money to pay the landowner in lieu of the yams the latter was entitled to. He, therefore, concluded that his action was deliberate and, therefore, the landowner was perfectly right to eject him from the land.

The second contributor was from the settler's community. He commended the forthrightness of the first speaker and condemned the action of the settler farmer. He, however, brought into focus the consequences of denying him the use of the land and made the point that as a family man denying him the use of the land after the preparation of the land for planting would amount to sentencing the wives and children to starvation. He, therefore, appealed that the landowner should reconsider his stand for the sake of the settler's dependants.

Subsequent speakers tried in particular to address the issue of the family needs of the settler farmer. There was a general agreement that he did not behave well. Some even felt that he ought to have considered the plight he would put his family before behaving in the manner he did. However, as one of the elderly contributors said, "if you want to use the length of the snake to set the fire to roast it, you might end up setting the whole bush on fire". When it was apparent that no new angle was left to be addressed on the matter, the matter was now left to the traditional ruler to summarise the terms of the reconciliation. Let me point out that within some communities, especially in some complicated conflicts, after the contributions from the floor, a small committee of about five persons could be mandated to deliberate and make recommendation, which would guide the traditional ruler in presenting the final terms of the reconciliation.

In the case in question, the decision that emanated from the reconciliation meeting succeeded in harmonising the needs of the settler farmer with the rights of the landowner. The settler farmer was allowed to use the land. However, for defaulting on the previous terms, he would now contribute five lines of yams to the landowner at the time of the next harvest. The five lines were calculated as follows: two lines for the previous year, which he failed to supply, two for the current year and one to compensate the landowner for his patience and understanding.

Another case of settler/indigene land dispute witnessed by the present writer followed the same procedure, except that in this particular case, some violent action took place resulting in injuries, which complicated the conciliatory process. This was also the case of a settler farmer's attempt to use the land after defaulting on the specified obligation he owed the landowner. The settler dodged all attempts by the landowner to reach an understanding on when and how to fulfil the terms of the agreement. On the day in question, the landowner got information that the settler was in the farm and decided to meet him in the farm to talk things over. On getting to the farm, he met a violent reception. He was attacked, macheted and accused of stealing the settler's yams.

After the incident, the settler went to report his alleged case of theft at the police station, while the landowner went straight to report the incident at the palace of the traditional ruler. By the time the police came to arrest the landowner, they found that the matter was already at the palace and, therefore, decided to allow the traditional efforts to play out before taking any other further necessary action. When the conciliation meeting was finally conveyed at the instance of the traditional ruler, the proceedings took virtually the same process as the first case. As speaker after speaker contributed, it was obvious that the accusation of theft against the landowner was a fabrication. Speakers from both the settler and the host communities agreed that the behaviour of the settler was an action capable of causing a.major conflagration between the settlers and their host community. In the final decision, he was threatened with outright expulsion from the community should a matter of that nature be brought against him in future. Besides, he was ordered to immediately meet all his obligations to those who gave him land to farm. He was also asked to pay the full cost of the landlord's treatment.

It turned out that when the settler reported the matter to the police, the latter had extorted some money from him before they agreed to make any move. He tried unsuccessfully to be allowed to pay only a portion of the cost of treatment in view of the expenses he incurred with the police. The fact that as the complainant, he had to pay some money to the police before they could act, shows the predicament some people have to go through when they choose to utilise the formal processes of conflict management in Nigeria. Obviously, this particular settler had thought he could use money to manipulate the formal processes against the innocent landlord. On this occasion, the timely action taken by the traditional ruler to go into the matter saved the nation of what could have turned into another ethnic mayhem.

This is because the youth in the place were said to have already mobilized for action against the settler community should the police manhandle the innocent landowner by way of arrest and detention. The thought that a settler could abuse the generosity of an innocent landowner and still turn round to use the police to harass the latter was one the youth of the town could not stomach. In this instance, wise counsel prevailed and a major calamity was avoided. The decision by the police to allow the traditional processes to work out turned out to be a wise one as the incident was resolved without further violence or bloodshed.

The point to note is that in Nigeria, local arrangements of this type do exist, especially among the rural dwellers, which could be usefully harmonised with the formal methods of conflict management to save the system the frequent occurrences of intercommunal conflagrations and the consequent destruction of lives and properties. It is felt here that, whatever limitations it might have, the traditional democratic analytical model highlighted in this chapter has some basic characteristics that make it particularly useful as a mechanism not only for tempering the escalation of local conflicts and preventing intercommunal violence, but also for the eventual resolution of intercommunal or ethnic conflicts.

First, the method is democratic and transparent in the sense that participation at the reconciliation meeting is open to all interested adults irrespective of their relationship with the parties in conflict. Besides, the deliberations are carried out in the open glare of everybody present.

Second, the method is analytical in the sense that final decisions are based on a comprehensive review of the entire conflict process in order to bring out where each of the parties to the conflict erred or contributed to the deterioration of relations or the outbreak of hostilities. By tracing the entire conflict process and attributing blames where appropriate, the exercise ensures the sharing of guilt and innocence, thereby bringing into focus an essential point about conflict dynamics, namely, that conflict breeds on the action, reaction and counteraction we take as human beings. In this sense, while the action of one party might cause the conflict, an equally negative reaction or overreaction by the opponent might be responsible for its escalation and the sustenance of the conflict. The essence of the procedure under the proposed traditional democratic analytical model is that at the end of the day, there is no single total "gainer" or total loser.

Third, the method enables the conflict to be examined from the points of view of all the parties, thereby bringing out the fears and concern of the parties involved and proffering solution for them. Thus the method is in tune with the problem-solving approach to conflict resolution, which most experts believe is the best formula for ensuring a mutually satisfactory resolution of conflict.

Fourth, because the speakers at the reconciliation meeting are not selected before hand, the possibility of their being unduly influenced by the parties in conflict is minimised. Besides, the openness of the deliberations makes it easy to fault a biased contribution.

Overall, the traditional democratic analytical model is a straightforward method of conflict management that is devoid of the painful delays that make the resort to existing practices cumbersome and tedious. The model emphasises one basic principle of Africa's traditional method of conflict management, which is reconciliation, done with the primary motive of reinforcing relationship through the harmonisation of the divergent interests of the hostile parties. As Ernest E. Uwazie observed of African traditional conflict management, the leaders or chiefs and their council of elders have a holistic view of their society. So, their primary purpose of conflict management is the maintenance of the social equilibrium in the community. Hence, "dispute management is seen as reconciliation of divergent interests, which preserves the physical existence and the spiritual well-being of the whole society".[3]

Civil Society Empowerment through Integration of Formal and Traditional Conflict Management Methods

The question to ask at this point is: How do we harmonise the traditional democratic analytical model highlighted in this study with the country's existing conflict management methods? Using the integrated conflict management model earlier highlighted in this chapter, it seems obvious that civil society could play useful roles at two levels of the conflict management circle—the conflict prevention/peace promotion level and the level of conflict resolution.

First, the proposed traditional model could be effectively utilised to resolve latent ethnic conflicts before they develop into major conflagrations between whole communities. It is a well known fact that most of the violent ethnic conflicts that have taken place in Nigeria have started from disagreements between individuals who happen to belong to different ethnic groups and that it was always a failure to catch the affected conflicts young, to use Kenneth Boulding's analogy,[4] that led to their exploding into major ethnic mayhem. For instance, the violent ethnic clash in Shagamu between Yoruba residents and Hausa/Fulani residents in July, 1999, which led to reprisal killings in Kano; the conflict between the Tiv and Azara indigenes in Nassarawa State in June, 2001; and the Idi-Araba mayhem in Lagos State between the Hausa resident community and the Yoruba resident in Idi-Araba in February, 2002, initially started as disagreements between individuals from the affected ethnic communities. The reason why the various incidents that triggered off the crises were blown out of proportion was due to the lack of the type of civil society-based mechanism being suggested here to nip the various crises in the bud.

Since the existing practice has been for the government to wait until a conflict develops into open hostilities before taking action to put down the violence, civil society groups should be encouraged and empowered to fill in the gap. This is more so because the police to whom some of the aggrieved parties resort to at the early stages of conflict have not been able to entrench the tradition of reconciling disputants in the manner prescribed in this study. The frequent mode of police operation is arrest, detain and, if they cannot get good settlement, charge the case to court, where the issue is decided on the basis of right or wrong rather than reconciliation. What the present proposed method calls for is the entrenchment of the principle of "try the traditional method first" before resorting to the formal methods. If this principle is entrenched in the country's existing practice, then evidence of the use of the traditional process should be a condition for the use of the existing formal methods. In this sense, if disputants should go to the police without first exhausting the traditional mode of settlement, it should be the rule that the police should advise them accordingly.

To operate the system in urban areas, "elders' forum" could be encouraged in each street or within optimum communities to which cases could be reported. Each local government could be asked to group their areas into such optimum communities for this purpose.

We expect the above arrangement to drastically reduce incidents of violent ethnic conflicts in the country. Where a conflict still escalates and develops into open hostilities to warrant the deployment of security forces, then civil society could play a second-track role of facilitating reconciliation meetings while the security forces stick to their responsibility of maintaining the peace. This second-track civil society role is necessary because the security forces deployed to quell disturbances are not usually trained in the art of facilitating negotiated settlement between the parties in conflict. In the past, the failure to explore this second-track role has often led to the recurrence of hostilities and the unnecessary prolongation of the presence of security forces in the localities affected.

What is called for here is that besides the constant practice of arraigning them before judicial tribunals or commissions of inquiry, the parties in conflict, under their own accredited traditional rulers or leaders, and with a competent civil society group playing a facilitating role, should be rallied into a reconciliation meeting where they can use the proposed traditional democratic analytical process to iron out their differences themselves. They should also be encouraged with the necessary resource support to use the opportunity of the reconciliation meeting to work out the humanitarian needs of those affected by such disturbances and organise the distribution of relief materials and the rehabilitation of victims. If the civil society can be empowered in the manner suggested here, it would be possible to gradually do away with the tendency of having too much government in everything that is done in Nigeria, many of which are not usually done well because government is not just capable of doing everything.

References

1.   T.A. Imobighe, *The OAU (AU) and OAS in Regional Conflict Management: A Comparative Assessment* (Ibadan:.Spectrum Books, 2003), pp.1-3.

2.   The present writer has over the past ten years, as a resident among Nigeria's rural dwellers, gathered data from various rural communities in Edo State and parts of the neighbouring states of Delta, Kogi and Ondo to come up with what has been described here as the traditional democratic analytical model of conflict resolution.

3.   Ernest E. Uwazie, "Social Relations and Peacekeeping Among the Igbo", in I. William Zartman (ed.), *Traditional Cures for Modern Conflicts: African Conflict "Medicine"* (Boulder & London: Lynne Rienner, 2000), p.29.

4.   Kenneth Boulding, *Conflict and Defence: A General Theory* (New York & London: Harper & Row, 1962), p.325.

Chapter 13

Conclusion

Thomas A. Imobighe

This study is a response to the burgeoning problem of ethnic conflict, which since the enthronement of Nigeria's Fourth Republic in May, 1999, has grown in intensity and pervasiveness as to threaten the survival of the country and undermine its progress towards democratic consolidation. The problem has become even more worrisome because of the behaviour of Nigeria's new political elite. Apparently in search of relevance, they have found a new fascination in the concept of "ethnic nationality" as a new frame of reference in the determination of the socio-political and economic affairs of Nigeria. In the process, they have jettisoned the concept of Nigerian nationality and relegated it to the backyard of the country's socio-political landscape. Thus, despite the country's past efforts to check the manifestation of its negative excesses, ethnicity has encapsulated class and other forms of identities and has now become the basis for intense and horrific conflict in Nigeria.

There is no doubt that, based on the data generated from the six case studies documented in this volume (one each from Nigeria's six geo-political zones), the warring ethnic groups had, in the past, enjoyed long histories of fruitful and mutually beneficial relationship between them. Many of them, like Ife and Modakeke, Aguieri and Umuleri, for instance, belong to the same ethnic groups and thus share bonds of blood relationship. Most, if not all, of them have enjoyed long years of social intercourse through inter-marriages and joint celebrations of one another's festivals; so much so, as to undermine the ethnic or sub-ethnic purity of the respective groups. For instance, in virtually all the case studies included in this collection, there is scarcely a situation where you find one family from two warring ethnic groups that does not have relations in the opposing group. Yet, in spite of these apparent integrative developments, ethnic conflicts threaten to tear Nigeria apart and scuttle the ongoing efforts at democratic consolidation in the country. All the above add up to the fact—that the long history of association among Nigeria's different ethnic groups have failed to bring about an organic unity between the country's disparate ethnic communities. In other words, inter-ethnic relations in Nigeria have not gone beyond a mere mechanical association.

As we have remarked in this study, our worry is not that conflict should not occur between the different ethnic groups in Nigeria. Our concern is that when conflict does occur, it should be managed productively. We believe that the escalating intensity and pervasiveness of ethnic conflicts in Nigeria is an indication that these conflicts have not been productively managed. The above threw up some obvious challenges which the collections in this volume have attempted to address. First, what is the exact nature of these conflicts and who are the primary actors involved? What management approaches are currently being used to address them and which organs and agencies are involved? What are the limitations in the current efforts at managing the conflicts? What improvements can be effected to the existing management techniques to ensure maximum effectiveness?

All these and other related questions have been seriously addressed in this volume. One of the major observations made in this study is that the issue of ethnic conflict is not a factor of the country's religious or ethnic pluralism, but the product of the country's prevailing socioeconomic and political circumstances. In particular, it is a product of a long history of an unequal access to power, resources and opportunities among the different ethnic groups in the country. A related factor is the inadequate solution proffered over the years by the country's political elite to demands and protests against ethnic inequality. Vital to the upsurge the problem has assumed under the present democratic dispensation, is the continuation by the new political elite with the dictatorial tendencies, prevalent during the long years of military rule, which impeded the development of true federalism. By continuing with the self-serving policies of their military predecessors, the new political elite have completely lost that democratic sense of responsibility to the electorate. Rather than come up with a national developmental agenda that would address such problems as youth unemployment, education, health and basic infrastructures, they are preoccupied with the sterile debate about how to continue with an ethnic presidency. Instead of the search for a person with the drive, national vision, competence, mental and physical capacity, experience, exposure and commitment, which are among the normal indices for leadership choice, Nigeria's political elite are involved in a political permutation as to whether the president should be an Igbo, Yoruba, Hausa, Fulani, Nupe, Edo, Urhobo, Efik, Idoma, Tiv or any of the other numerous ethnic groups in the country. The danger of such a sterile exercise, as we have indicated in this study, is that at the end of the day, the nation would once again have an ethnic president without a national agenda to implement.

By consciously or unconsciously extolling ethnicity as the supreme political virtue, Nigeria's political elite have created an atmosphere for the flourishing of ethnicity and the general attachment of Nigerians to their respective ethnic groups. It is in this sense, that the present proliferation and use of ethnic militia to promote ethnic group interests or fight for ethnic political champions should be understood. A related angle to the problem is the intensity and pervasiveness of violent ethnic conflicts, in which the youth are primary role players in the prosecution of ethnic wars.

Just as this work was being processed for publication, the nation witnessed another chapter of the bizarre use of armed youth in election malpractices by politicians. The irony of the situation is that it is the same politicians who have looted the treasury and denied the system of developmental resources to meaningfully engage the youth of this country in productive ventures, who now use the looted money to thrust arms into the hands of the jobless youths to subvert the wishes of the electorate. The various case studies in this collection have shown that the country's marginalised and abandoned youths are the main instrument of the violence attendant to all the ethnic conflicts in the country. The youths are not the source of these sophisticated weapons. Highly influential members of the society are responsible for the importation and distribution of these weapons. This has been patently demonstrated during the recent election when those we thought were highly responsible members of the society behaved like gangsters, commanding bands of armed youths with the mission of terrorising innocent voters in order to perpetuate themselves in power.

The question now is: What will happen to the arms, now that the elections are over? Are these sophisticated sub-machine guns, pistols and pomp-guns going to be allowed to swell the flood of weapons already in the hands of ethnic militias? Or are they going to be allowed to swell the armoury of the hoodlums who terrorise innocent citizens in their homes and along the highways? These are serious security threats, which must engage the attention of the country's national security planners. Since the politicians cannot be trusted to disarm their political thugs, the country's security agencies need to meet quickly to work out a plan for disarming political thugs and demilitarising the polity.

It is evident from the case studies that the governments at both the federal and state levels have been the primary agents in the management of Nigeria's ethnic conflicts. Since many of these conflicts result basically from the nature of the distribution of power and resources within the polity, the state bears a primary responsibility as a major source of these conflicts. If the state, that is itself a major factor of these conflicts, should be the major role player in their management, then a basic question of credibility becomes apparent, as to whether the state or its agents can genuinely be favourably disposed to suggestions warranting system re-examination and system correction which are usually found necessary for the lasting resolution of these conflicts. It is in this sense that the limitations in the manner of government responses highlighted in the case studies assembled in this volume ought to be viewed.

As documented in the case studies presented here, government usually waits until the affected conflict erupts into a violent confrontation before intervening. There is nothing in place by way of early warning system to enable government to anticipate conflicts and take preventive measures to avoid the possibility of a violent eruption. Any time there is an outbreak of a major conflagration, government usually responds first, by sending law enforcement agents to put down the violence. The procedure is for the government to send first, ordinary police personnel; then, anti-riot mobile police and military personnel in that order; depending on the gravity of the violence. After putting down the violence, a panel of inquiry is set up, usually headed by judicial personnel. The panel is usually mandated to look into the immediate and remote causes of the conflict and proffer solutions, as well as identify the important actors involved and recommend appropriate measures to be taken against them.

It is evident from the case studies presented here that many reports of these inquiries were never published. This has been the fate of many of such inquiries instituted on the Urhobo-Itsekiri conflict over the ownership of Warri in Delta State. In the few cases where the relevant reports were published with the relevant government white papers, they were never implemented. This was the case with the Nweje Commission of Inquiry that looked into the 1995 eruption of the conflict between Aguleri and Umuleri. It was found that the far-reaching recommendations were not implemented despite the fact that the government had accepted many of them in its White Paper on the report.

It is due to the apparent inadequacy of direct official responses that some of the parties usually, on their own, try to seek legal redress. This resort to judicial methods by the parties involved in these conflicts has not also provided the expected lasting solutions to the relevant problems. This is evident from the numerous court decisions on the Urhobo–Itsekiri and the Aguleri-Umuleri conflicts documented here in this volume. For instance, between 1920 and 1984, twelve cases were instituted in the court in respect of the conflict between Aguleri and Umuleri over Otuocha land. Some of the cases even went as far as the Supreme Court and yet no solution was found. Because the judicial process is hardly interested in the harmonisation of the interests of the parties involved in a conflict, the process usually end up in a win-lose situation with the loser always preoccupied with all sorts of manoeuvres to circumvent or overturn the unfavourable judgement. In this sense, the judicial method does not bring about a mutually beneficial outcome to the parties in conflict. Rather, it usually leaves behind a lot of bitterness between them.

It is because of the apparent inability of government to adequately deal with the problem to the mutual satisfaction of the parties in conflict, that this study has zeroed in on the civil society to see how these non-governmental and community-based organisations can play a creative role in the management of these conflicts. In doing so, the collections in this volume have examined the nature of the civil society in Nigeria, brought out their areas of weakness and strength; the state and level of civil society participation in conflict management in the country and the particular civil society organisations that are best qualified to intervene in particular types of conflict, as well as suggested measures to enhance such participation in the management of the nation's endemic ethnic conflicts.

The role played by civil society in the country's democratisation project is adequately documented in this volume. Also well documented is the flourishing of ethnic-based civil society groups, which since the enthronement of the Fourth Republic have shifted their roles from democratic advocacy to that of agitating against marginalisation and the clamouring for resource control. Despite the apparent limitations of civil society groups in terms of administrative capacity, poor resource base and dependence on foreign donors, etc., it has been found that civil society could be creatively mobilized to move from a conflictual antagonistic relationship with the state into playing a positive role in the efforts to solve the country's numerous ethnic conflicts that are threatening to tear the country apart.

What then are the lessons from the case studies assembled in this volume? Does civil society participation in ethnic conflict management mean a replacement of government efforts with those of the civil society groups? Does it mean the two organs should operate on a parallel basis? And finally, do the pieces of evidence from the case studies point to the direction of a partnership between government and civil society? The suggestion in this study hinges on the need for a partnership between civil society groups and the relevant agencies of government involved in the management of these conflicts.

The common theme that flowed across all the case studies assembled in this volume is the fact of government dominance of conflict management activities in Nigeria and the minimal involvement by civil society groups. The minimal involvement of civil society does not mean that civil society cannot play a robust role in conflict management. The present constrained role of civil society in conflict management in the country is predicated on some basic weaknesses afflicting civil society groups in the country. From the evidence gathered in this study, these include, in addition to the earlier stated ones, their urban location, the lack of administrative capacity and the necessary resource base.

The fact that most of the civil society groups are urban-based further constrained their ability to become effective role-players in ethnic conflicts that are increasingly shifting to the rural areas. It is in this sense, that it has been observed in this study that it is the community-based organisations (CBOs) that are particularly suited to play active roles in ethnic conflict management. Thus, if the urban-based NGOs are to be maximally effective in playing positive roles in the management of ethnic conflicts, they should relocate to the conflict/crisis prone rural areas of the country.

The issue of resource constraint is a major problem afflicting civil society groups operating in Nigeria. The Nigerian governments at the various levels have not appreciated the need to operate any regular budget to subsidise the activities of civil society groups involved in conflict management. Thus, the activities of the leading NGOs that are involved in conflict management, like the Academic Associates PeaceWorks (AAPW) and the Strategic Empowerment and Mediation Agency (SEMA), are predicated on the generous funding from foreign donors. Consequently, certain peace processes initiated by these organisations have often been discontinued with the exhaustion of the funds supplied by these foreign donors. A good example in which the present writer was involved is the AAPW intervention in Warri with funding from the United States Institute of Peace and some additional financial support from USAID. The failure of both the federal and state governments to provide resource support for the peace network established at the conclusion of AAPW's intervention, frustrated the efforts of the parties to sustain the peace process.[1]

In spite of these and other obvious limitations suffered by civil society groups in Nigeria, it has been suggested that civil society groups could play useful roles in the areas of early warning activities; conflict prevention and peace building activities; the administration of relief and humanitarian materials; and in mediation and the facilitation of negotiations between the parties involved in conflict. Civil society groups could also help, through research, in identifying the fundamental issues that need to be addressed in order to effect lasting solution to conflicts. While civil society groups can perform useful roles in these areas, it is not within their competence and responsibility to provide the frustrated needs or allay the fears of the parties involved in conflicts. It is not also the responsibility of civil society groups to enforce whatever agreement they are able to help the parties to negotiate. All these fall within the purview of the state. It is in this sense that a well-articulated regime of government/civil society partnership is inevitable for the effective management of ethnic conflicts in Nigeria. To this end, it has been suggested that measures should be taken to integrate into the official system the traditional democratic analytical model of conflict resolution, which is quite popular with Nigeria's rural communities.

References

1.   For a detailed account of the AAPW intervention in Warri, See T.A. Imobighe et al., *Conflict and Instability in the Niger Delta: The Warri Case* (Ibadan: Spectrum Books, 2002), chapter 5.

Appendix I

Civil Society and Ethnic Conflict Management in Nigeria

Questionnaire

It is expected that the primary data for this study is going to be based on both interviews and questionnaire. In the case of interview, important role players in the zone or in the particular conflict being studied could be identified for interview. Also focused group discussion (FGD) could also be applied.

This questionnaire is designed to cover four areas. These are:
* Data of the person completing the questionnaire;
* Causes and history of the conflict;
* Effects of the conflict; and
* Resolution efforts/alternatives.

A.   DATA

1.   Name of community.....................................

2   Age: (Tick as appropriate.)
Under 20
20—39
40 and above

3.   Sex: Male
Female

4. Occupation: Farmer
Elected Official

Trader
Civil Servant
Artisan
Contractor
Others..

5. Are you a titleholder?   Yes.........   No...........

6. If yes, what is the title? ....

B.   CAUSES AND HISTORY

7.   When did the conflict first occur? ....
8.   When was the last incident? ....
9.   List in order of importance 5 major causes
       a   ....
       b   ....
       c   ....
       d   ....
       e   ....
       f.   Any other ....

10.   What was the main cause(s) of the conflict the first time it
       occurred? ....
11.a. What was the main cause(s) of the conflict the last time it
       occurred? ....
11.b. What roles have your sons and daughters outside the
       community played in the conflict? ....

C.   EFFECTS

12. What are the effects of the conflict on your community?

       a. ....
       b. ....
       c. ....
       d. ....
       e. ....
       f. Any other...

13. Estimate the human and material losses of your community as a result of the conflict.
    a. Deaths ....
    b. Injuries ....
    c. Houses ....
    d. Social facilities ....
    e. Economic well-being ....
    f. Any other ....

14. How were people affected by the conflict cared for?
    ....

15. Who cared for them and how effective were they?
    Not effective   Effective   Very Effective
    a. Fed. govt. ....
    b. State govt. ....
    c. LGA. ....
    d. Religious groups ....
    e. NGOs ....
    f. Elders/traditional council ....
    g. Women groups ....
    h. Youth organisations ....
    i. Individuals/family members. ....
    j. Others (please specify) ....

D.   RESOLUTION

16. Have there been attempts to resolve the conflict?
    Yes .... No ....
17. If yes, who made the attempts? (Tick as appropriate.)
    a. Federal government ....
    b. State government ....
    c. Local government ....
    d. Religious groups ....
    e. NGOs ....
    f. Elders/traditional council ....
    g. Women groups ....
    h. Youth organisations ....
    i. Individuals/family members ....
    j. Others (please specify) ....

18. Specify some of the actions taken (provide additional space where necessary)

    a. ....

    b. ....

    c. ....

    d. ....

    e. ....

19. How effective were these actions?

20. Which government was more effective in managing the conflict? (Tick as appropriate.)
    a.   Military ....   b.   Civilian ....

21. Why do you say so? (Provide more space where necessary.)

    a..

    b..

    c..

    d..

    e..

22. Suggest any other method that could be more effective in managing the conflict apart from the ones used in the past.

    a..

    b..

    c..

    d..

    e..

23. Are there local conflict management methods that you think have not been used adequately in managing the conflict? What are they?

    a..

    b..

    c..

    d..

    e..

24. Do you think that civil society and community organisations like religious, ethnic, social, elders, women, etc. have a role to play in helping to manage the conflict? (Tick as appropriate.)

   a.   Yes   ....   b.   No   ....

25. If yes, what form should this role take?

   ....
   ....
   ....
   ....
   ....

Index

Aba reprisal riot, 25
Abacha, Sani, 266
Abegunrin, Gabriel, 159
Abubakar, A. 51
Abuja Accord, 121
Academic
 – Associates Peace Works
  (AAPW) 160, 249-252, 267,
  269-270, 276, 308
 – Staff Union of Nigerian
  Universities (ASUU), 45
Action Group, 4, 157
 – for Research Information and
  Training on Drug Abuse
  (AGRITDA), 273, 276
Adams, Ganiyu, 61
Adedoyin, Francis (Baale of
  Modakeke), 161
Adelekan Ooni (Olubuse I), 154
Administrative and/or Judicial
Commission of Inquiry
 – institution of, 93-95, 140
Afenifere, 44, 51, 60-61
African
 – Centre for Democratic
 · Governance (AFROGOV),
  276
 – communities, 283, 290
 – Palaver, 288-289
 – political life, 38
 – Refugees Foundation (ARF),
  267
 – societies, 288-289
 – traditional society, 49
Agbakoba, Olisa, 64
Age-based group, 99
 – group system, 293
Aguiyi-Ironsi, J.T.U. 5
Aguleri-Umuleri, 13, 108, 264, 302,
  306
     – conflict, 16,
Akinyele, Alex, 132, 159
Akunraledoye, Oba Adegoke
  (Apetumodu of Ipetumodu),
  156

Alafin of Oyo, 153-154
Alagos of Nassarawa, 16
All Nigerian Peoples Party (ANPP),
  92
Anambra East
 – Council of Traditional
  Rulers and Leaders
  of Thought, 214, 216,
  218
 – Peace Council, 214-216
Anglican
 – Bishops' Synods, 59-60
 – Communion, 51
Animosity conflict, 193, 218
Annan, Kofi, 120
Annulment of presidential election,
  50-51
Anti-
 – colonial struggle, 4
 – sharia demonstration, 84
Aquatic life, 225
Araka
 – Commission/Committee 200,
  205-206, 214-215
Arewa
 – Consultative Forum (ACF), 44,
  51, 60
 – People's Congress (APC), 10,
  15
Association
 – for Better Nigeria (ABN), 263
 – of Democratic Lawyers (ADL),
  50
Associations/Non-Governmental
  Organisation (NGOs), 287
Attah, Mike, 195, 197-198
AVM Usman Muazu Reconciliation
  and Search for Lasting Peace
  Committee (Zango Kataf), 95
Awolowo, Chief, 3, 155, 157

Baale of Modakeke
 – status of, 156-157
Babangida, I. B. 94, 132, 266

Bachama/Hausa, 1989, 259
Bafarawa, Governor, 89
Bagobiri, Rev. 89
Bakassi Boys, 15, 59, 199, 202
Balewa, Abubakar Tafawa, 4, 137
Bassa/Egbura
 – Conflict
  – causes of, 116-117
  – Civil Society interven-
   tion, 120-121
  – Communal conflict, 113-
   123
  – effects of, 117-118
  – government interven-
   tion, 118-119
Bauchi
 – Emirate Council, 131
 – 1991 riots, 96
Bayelsa Youths Federation of
 Nigeria (BYFN), 10
Bello, Mohammed, 207
Beron
  – communities, 31
  – Jarawa Anaguta/Hausa-
  Fulani, 259
Better Life Groups, 263
Biobaku, Saburi, 155
Blood Convent (*iko mme*), 215, 218
Bloody conflicts, 285
Bonds of blood relationship, 302
Boundary
 – adjustment, 205
     – exercise, 168
 – classes, 177
 – conflicts, 173-175, 218
 – demarcation, 203-204
     – exercise, 168
 – disputes, 173, 204
 – /land conflicts, 176
Bountiful Harvest (BH), 273, 276
Buhari, Muhammadu, 88, 266

Campaign
 – Against Unwanted Pregnancy
  (CAUP), 9, 274
 – for Democracy (CD), 45, 50,
  61, 263

Campus politics, 10
Catholic
 – Bishops Conference, 44, 51, 60
 – Church, 60
Centre for
 – Constitutional Rights (CCR),
  61
 – Development, Support
  Monitoring and Advocacy
  (CDSMA), 267, 276
 – Peace in Africa (CPA), 59
 – Peace Initiative and Develop-
  ment (CEPID), 121
Chamba Jukun/Kuteb, Taraba
 State, 13, 259, 264
Chicoco Movement (CM), 15, 62
Chieftaincy
 – disputes, 149, 170
 – matters, 119
Christian Association of Nigeria
 (CAN), 44, 51, 59, 82, 87, 133,
 143
Christian
 – minority groups, 88
 – missionaries, 155
Church
 – Missionary Society (CMS),
  179, 191
Churches
 – role of, 217
Civil
 – association, 261
 – disturbances, 131-132
     – military intervention, 141
 – groups, 48, 56-58, 60-61, 63-64
 – Liberties Organisation (CLO),
  45, 50, 59-60, 263, 270, 276
 – protests, 51
 – rights, 45, 67
     – and liberties group, 50
     – group, 52
 – society, 209, 212
 – Society Advocacy Group
  (CSAG), 268
 – Society and Conflict Management
     – in Cameroun, 288-289

- in Mali, 289
- Society
  - based mechanism, 300
  - categories of, 44-45
  - concept of, 38-44
- definition of, 39, 260-261
- development, roles and
  weaknesses of, 49-53
- groups, 9, 37-38, 41, 48-50, 52,
  59, 61, 63, 66-68, 99-101,
  144, 151, 239, 283, 288-290,
  300, 308-309
  - measure of empowering,
    270-274
  - subdivision of, 261-262
    - broad groups, 262
- meaning of, 8-9
- organisations, 259-260, 266,
  269-272, 279, 307
- role of, 99-102, 142-144, 249-
  253
- unrests, 128
Citizen rights, 46
Citizenship, 107, 155
  - definition of, 112
Civil War, 106
Coleman, James, 4
Collective rights, 142
Comity of nations, 18
Commissions of inquiry, 173, 237,
  300
Committee for the Defence of
  Human Rights (CDHR), 45,
  50, 60, 263, 270, 276
Communal
  - and ethnic groups, 43
  - character (language and
    culture), 16
  - clash, 122
  - competition, 172
  - conflict management, 173
  - conflicts, 65, 93, 106, 142, 144,
    148, 167-168, 172, 180, 182,
    201, 217
  - disputes, 209
  - identity, 181, 183
  - land conflicts, 203

-/religious violence, 109
- violence, 132, 141
- youth, 51
Community and
  - religious leaders, 122
  - religious organisations, 99
  - association, 142
  - Based Organisation (CBOs),
    152, 160, 162-163, 212, 262,
    265-266, 271-275, 277
  - development associations, 51,
    265
  - development groups, 40
  - development programmes,
    265
  - leaders, 142, 184
  - political leaders, 277
Complex Emergencies, 271, 275
Concerned Youth of Oil Producing
  States (CYOPS), 9
Conflict
  - analysis, 28-30
  - causes of, 233-237
  - control and abatement, 247,
    293
  - definition of, 20, 223
  - dynamics, 23, 33, 298
  - effects of 240-243
  - intercession, 264
  - management, 36-70, 99, 119
    - and resolution of, 223,
      244-249
    - circle, 299
    - in Chad, 284-288
    - processes, 123
    - project, 67-68
    - strategies, 36, 209, 218
    - theory, 247
  - monitoring, 68
  - prevention, 69, 268
    - and peace building
      activities, 308
    - and peace promotion,
      247, 293
  - profile
    - North Central Zone, 108-
      112

- South-East Zone, 168-173
- South-South Zone, 225-226
- South-West Zone, 149-150
- quotient (high),225
- resolution, 62, 69, 101, 120, 160, 247, 268, 293, 299
  - initiatives, 268
  - mechanism, 227, 294
  - method of, 99
- settlement, 287
- sources of, 224
- victims, 63
Conflictual relationship, 29, 33
Constituent assemblies' debates, 90
Constitutional
- Rights Project (CRP), 9, 45, 50, 60, 263
Continuous migratory activities, 109
Corporate Affairs Commission, 265
Council of Chiefs, 293
Council of Elders, 293, 299
Counselling functions, 287
Country Women Association of Nigeria (COWAN), 263, 273-274
Crisis Management, 120
                 - strategy, 95
Cross-community bonds, 216
Cultural
- affinities and beliefs, 148
- differences, 217
- diversity, 109
- group, 51
- identity, 108
- or linguistic differences, 167
Customary
- council members, 285-287
- Right of Occupancy, 205
Cycle of Conflicts, 189

Dasuki Committee Report, 111
Daughters of Abraham Foundation (DAF), 273
Delta Peoples Movement for Self Determination and Environmental Protection (DPMSDEP), 10
Democracy dividends, 92
Democratic
- Alliance (DA), 263
- Alternative (DA), 50
Demographic explosion and struggle, 22
Desert encroachment, 23
Development Unions, 44
Donor
- and financial agencies, 43
- funding, 37
Drugs issues, 276
Dung, David, 26, 230, 236

Economic
- and gender-based groups, 50
- pauperization, 225
Edo Opanamakhin project, 7
Edozie, Mike, 198
Egbe Afenifere, 10
Egbema National Congress (ENC), 10
Egbesu Boys of Africa, 62
Egi Youth Federation (EYF), 10
Elders' Forum, 277, 300
Election rigging, 149
Eleme-Okrika, Rivers State, 13
Emirate system, 110
Enahoro, Anthony, 7
Enlightenment campaigns, 286
Environmental
- and resource struggle
                 - oil based, 44
- degradation, 225
- pollution, 225
- Rights, 270
Eri-Brothers Association, 216-217
- ethnography, 186
- Genealogy, 186
Esan Youth Movement, 10
Eso, Kayode, 208
Ethnic
- and inter-communal conflicts, 13-14, 285

– and religious conflicts, 55
– animosity, 132
– backgrounds, 4, 33, 227-232
– based civil society groups, 10
– based organisations, 10
– bonds, 5
– boundaries, 109
– clashes, 61, 299
– communities, 24, 59, 107-109, 175, 227, 290, 303
– compartmentalisation, 24
– components, 4-5
– composition, 168
– configurations, 282
– conflict, 223-224
  – definition of, 22-32
  – management, 259-260
  – Warri
    – historical background, 227-232
– confrontation, 24-25
– consciousness, 32, 182
– crises, 115
– development associations, 265
– differences, 109, 168
– diversity, 8, 18-19, 32
– exclusivity, 27
– heterogeneity, 129, 168
– identities, 168
– inequality, 303
– kingdoms, 7
– measuring of, 18
– militias, 15, 30, 59, 304-305
– minorities, 25, 110
– minority settlers, 169
– nationalism, 66
– nationalities, 32, 108, 112, 302
– or ethno communal conflict, 108
– permutation, 28
– pluralism, 8, 303
– politics, 11, 98
– presidency, 28, 304
– sectarianism, 98
– sentiments, 27
– settlements, 18

– tensions, 114
– units, 3
– wars, 304
Ethnicity
  – definition of, 17
  – meaning of, 16-17
Ethno
  – communal conflicts, 275
  – communal identities, 183
  – religious conflicts, 25, 59, 69, 81-102
    – issues and way out, 97-99
  – religious crisis, 93, 128
Egbesu Boys of Africa, 15
Ezera, Kalu, 4

Family
  – conflict, 29
  – Support Groups, 263
Farmers
  – and pastoralists
    – conflict between 169
  – unions, 44
Farming communities, 286, 288
Fasheun, Frederick, 61
Fawehinmi, Gani, 61
Federal
  – Character, 6, 14
  – Constitution, 4
  – Government Judicial Panel on Kafanchan, Kaduna, Zaria, crises, 95
  – Judicial Commission of Inquiry, 96, 140
  – question, 107, 112
Federalism, 112
Federated Council of Igbo Youths, 10
Federated Niger Delta Izon Communities (FNDIC), 62-63
Fetish practices, 215
Focus Group Discussion (FGD), 241-242, 252
Food and Agricultural Organisation (FAO), 268
Foreign donor agencies, 63, 67

Fulani
- herdsmen and farming
  communities, 22-23
  - conflicts between, 30-31
- Irigwe, Plateau State, 13
Gender
- and Development Action, 274
- issues, 276
Geo-political
- boundaries, 107
- structure, 173
George, Olabode, 160, 162
Girls' Power Initiative, 273-274
Globalisation, 98
Government
- boundaries, 204
- /civil society partnership, 309
- policy and problems of
  implementation, 107
- security agents, 107
Graduate unemployment, 15, 30
Grassroots Empowerment, 276
Gure/Kahugu communal conflicts,
  259

Halt-Aids Group (HAG), 270, 276
Hausa
- /Fulani Sayawa Conflict, 13,
  143, 276
- livestock traders, 18
- settlements, 17
- /Yoruba clashes, 13, 24
Hegemonic/influence conflict, 28
HIV/AIDS, 270
Human
- capacity development, 101
- Development Initiatives
  (HDI), 59, 263, 276
- freedom index (HFI), 269
- right abuses, 51, 58, 60
- Rights, 270
  - abuse of, 99, 101
  - associations, 287
  - Monitor (HRM), 59
  - violation, 101
Ife
- Action Council, 161

- Modakeke Conflict
  - background, 150-152
  - major causes of, 151
Igbira farmers, 18
Igbira/Bassa Communal conflicts,
  259, 264
Igbo
- ethnic group, 168
- Peoples Council, 10
- Redemption Council, 10
- Salvation Front, 10
- Youth Movement, 10
Ige, Bola, 159
Ijaw
- communities, 26
- Elders Forum (IEF), 62
- Ilaje conflict, 13
- /Itsekiri conflict, 25, 230
- National Congress (INC), 10,
  44, 62, 65
- Youth Council (IYC), 10, 15,
  61-63, 65
Ikwerre Youth Movement (IYM), 10
Indigenous
- development associations, 44
- ethnic groups, 84
- ethnic nationalities, 111
- homes, 180
Indirect rule system, 110
Individual rights, 20
Institute of Governance and Social
  Research (IGSR), 276
Integrated
- conflict management-circle, 293
  - model, 293
Inter
- clan clashes, 16
- communal
  - conflicts, 188
  - interactions, 17
  - or ethnic
    conflicts, 290,
    298
  - violence, 13
  - wars, 178
- community violence, 14
- ethnic - conflicts, 14, 55, 150,
  167

- frictions, 18
- hostilities, 149
- interaction, 18
- relations, 98, 303
- religious carnage, 82
- violence, 115
Interest groups, 99
Internal
- communal relations, 84
- refugees, 116
International
- boundaries, 129
- donor agencies, 38
- Federation of Women Lawyers (FIDA), 273
- peace-keeping or peace support operations, 15
- War Crime Tribunal, 60
Intra-ethnic
- communal conflicts, 217
- conflicts, 167, 169, 172
Irikefe, Ayo, 207
Isakole (land rent), 155, 162
Islamic
- fundamentalism, 92
- North, 109
Isoko
- Development Union (IDU), 10
- National Youth Movement (INYM), 10, 62
- Youth Movement, 15
Itsekiri/Ijaw
- conflicts, Warri, 63
- /Urhobo, 13
Itsekiri marginalisation, 26
Izon group, 63

Jama'atu Nasril Islam (JNI), 82, 87, 89, 143
John Shagaya Commission, 94
Joint Action Committee for Democracy (JACON), 9, 263
Jos crisis, 112
Journalist Against Aids (JAAIDS), 270, 274
Judicial
- Commission of Inquiry, 136, 195
- tribunals, 301
Jukun/Tiv, 259, 264
Justice Babalakin Commission of Inquiry, 135, 137
Justice Benedict Okadigbo Special Tribunal (Zango-Kataf crisis), 95
Justice Rahila Cudjoe Commission of Inquiry, 95

Kaduna
- crisis, 96
- mayhem, 25
- riots
    - causes of, 89-90
Kaiama Declaration, 62, 65
Kiriji War, 154

Labour movements, 9
Land
- and resources management, 107
- /boundary conflict, 28
- /boundary dispute, 149
- conflicts, 170, 177, 179, 181
- disputes, 119, 169, 180-181
- ownership, 116, 162, 228-229
Landlord/tenant relationship, 155
Large-sclae conflict, 36
Law enforcement
- agencies, 30
- agents, 96, 224, 239, 241, 243-244, 305-306
    - role of, 137
Leaders of Thought, 214
Linguistic groups, 108
Local governance, 107

Maitatsine incident, 132
Manufacturers Association of Nigeria (MAN), 45, 50
Market
- and trade groupings, 51
- associations, 45, 251
- Women Association of Nigeria (MWAN), 273

Media Rights Agenda (MRA), 263
Middle Belt
  – Forum (MBF), 44, 51, 61
  – region, 108
  – scholars and activists, 109
Middle
  – East crisis, 223
Militant groups, 224
Military authoritarianism, 107, 119
Minority ethnic groups, 4-5
Modakeke
  – Progresive Union, 161
  – status of, 151-156
Movement for the Actualisation of
    the Sovereign State of Biafra
    (MASSOB), 15
Movement for the Survival of Ijaw
    Ethnic Nationalities in the
    Niger Delta (MOSIEND), 62
Movement for the Survival of Izon
    Nationality (MOSIN), 10
Movement for the Survival of
    Ogoni People (MOSOP), 62
Multi
  – Component Missions, 275
  – cultural, 259
  – ethnic
      – composition, 32
      – society, 16, 18, 32-33, 294
          – conflict in, 20-22
  – linguistic, 259
  – party politics, 108
  – regions, 259
Muslim
  – aggression, 63
  – Christian
      – clash, 82
      – Committee, 89
National
  – anthem, 4
  – Association of Nigerian
      Students (NANS), 45, 263
  – Association of Women in
      Business (NAWB), 273
  – Boundary Commission, 204
  – Cohesion, 259
  – Conference, 7-8, 60, 111

  – Conscience Party (NCP), 61
  – Council of Nigeria Citizens
      (NCNC), 4
  – Council of State, 88
  – Council of Women Societies
      (NCWS), 50
  – Democratic Coalition
      (NADECO), 9
  – flag, 4
  – food security, 268
  – integration, 107, 259
  – Liberation Council of Nigeria
      (NALICON), 45
  – Population Commission, 130
  – question, 36, 53, 91, 112, 163
  – Reconciliation Committee
      (NARECOM), 159
  – security, 141
  – symbols, 4
  – unity, 4, 259
      – and stability, 167
  – Youth Service Scheme, 5
Nationalism, 174
Nationalities, 107
Ndigbo Liberation Forum, 10
Network for Justice (NJ), 263
Niger Delta
  – Conflicts, 62, 65-66
  – crisis, 238-239, 249
  – region, 224-253
  – struggle and conflicts, 45
  – Volunteer Force (NDVF), 15,
      62-63
Nigeria Delta Oil Producing
    Communities Development
    Organisation, 62
Nigerian
  – Association of Women
      Entrepreneurs (NAWE),
      273
  – Association of Women
      Industrialists (NAWI), 273
  – Association of Women
      Journalists (NAWOJ), 273
  – Bar Association (NBA), 45
  – citizenship, 4
  – Civil Society Landscape, 260-
      266

– Conservation Foundation (NCF), 270
– Federation of Business and Professional Women (BPW), 273
– Labour Congress (NLC), 45, 59, 64, 67
– Medical Association (NMA), 45, 263
– NGO Consultative Forum (NINCOF), 270-272, 276
– ruling elite, 30
– Union of Journalists (NUJ), 45
– Women Empowerment Network (NAWENO), 273
Nnamani, Augustine, 208
Non-
– formal crisis management strategies, 144
– violent conflict resolution, 122
Northern
– Elders Forum, 51
– People's Congress (NPC), 4
– Poverty Eradication Forum (PERFORM), 268, 270
Nweje Commission of Inquiry, 196-197, 199-202, 205, 213, 306
Nweje, Moses O., 195
Nwodo, J. U., 204, 207

Oath taking (*nghu iyi*), 215-218
Oba Ademiluyi, Ooni, 154
Obasanjo government, 160
Obasanjo, Olusegun, 65, 88, 91, 159, 210
Obaseki, Andrew, 208
Obe, Justice Ibidapo, 159
Occupational
– crisis, 228
– groups, 265
Odi
– crisis, 48
– devastation and massacre, 60, 225
Odua People's Congress (OPC), 10, 15, 48, 59, 61
Oduduwa Liberation Movement, 61

Ogbe-Ijoh/Ogidigben crisis, 236
Ogoni
– coflict, 30
– episode, 225
Ohaneze Ndigbo 1, 10, 44, 51, 60, 210
– Initiative, 213-214
*Ohineze opanda,*113
Ohinoyi of Toto, 113
Otuocha riots, 204
Oil producing communities, 226
Okafor, G.N.A. 207
Olu of
– Itsekiri, 235
– Warri, 27, 229, 235
Olunloyo, Omololu, 159
Onoh, C. 169
Onyali, O. B. 207
Onyiuke, G.C.M. 207
Oodua Youth Movement (OYM), 61
Open Community Meetings, 143
Operation
– Farewell to Poverty (OFP), 273
– *Wetie,* 149
Opinion leaders, 283
Oral tradition, 187-188
Oranmiyan Chieftaincy Declaration, 156
Organisation
– for the Restoration of Actual Rights of Oil Communities (ORAROC), 9
– of the Islamic Conference (OIC), 82, 94
– crisis, 94
Organized Private Sector (OPS), 259-260, 262, 266, 272, 274, 279
Osun State
– Council of Obas, 151, 156
– Council of Traditional Rulers, 159
Oyo Empire, 153
Oyo refugees, 154

Pastoralists and agriculturists
– conflict between, 23-24

Peace
- and Development Organisation
  (PEDO), 267, 269-270
- committee, 159, 206-287
- /Dialogue Committees, 283,
  285, 287
- meetings, 214
- Reconciliation and Development Association
  (PREDA), 266-267, 269-
  271, 276
- /Reconciliatory Fora, 95
  - use of, 140
- resolution, 216
- Treat, 1886, 154, 158-159
Penal code, 88-89
Pentecostal christianity, 92
Pentecostal Fellowships Nigeria
  (PFN), 51, 63
People's Democratic Party (PDP),
  92
Political
- activities, 132
- ambitions, 143
- and economic marginalisation,
  22
- aspiration, 108
- associations, 49
- awareness, 100
- circumstances, 303
- competition, 54
- conflict, 25
  - management, 63
- confrontation, 84
- culture, 29
- differences, 11, 170
- discourse, 13
- domination, 93
- dynamics, 197
- elite, 4, 14, 19, 32, 90, 92, 97,
  302-304
- emancipation, 144
- engineering, 135
- entities/entity, 153, 155, 218
- fiat, 5
- gains, 138
- game, 83

- institutions, 111
- issues, 273
- landscape, 5, 14, 33
- malpractices, 149
- mileage, 121
- mobilization, 172
- opposition, 40
- participation, 107, 273
- parties, 27, 58, 282
- permutation, 304
- positions, 107
- power, 39, 93, 111
- process, 54
- regimes, 285
- relations, 40
- relevance, 131
- settings, 130
- society, 39, 42, 46
- stability, 153
- thugs, 199, 305
- transition, 90
  - programme, 50
- troubles, 152
- units, 173
- virtue, 304
- will, 93-94,120, 140
Post-conflict
- management, 58
- peace building, 69, 121-122,
  152,278
Poverty, 98, 129
- , Ignorance and Diseases
  Alleviation Group of
  Nigeria (PIDAGON), 276
- level, 226
Power sharing arrangements, 90
Presidential Conflict Reconciliation
  Committee, 151, 156, 160-161
Primary associations, 44
Prime Peace Project Limited
  (PPPL), 267, 269-270
Pro-democracy groups, 50, 67
Professional
- associations, 50
- organisations, 9
Public affairs management, 14

Quota system of appointment, 4

Ransome-Kuti, Beko, 61
Reconciliation
- Committee, 136
- mechanism, 293
- meeting, 294-295, 297-298, 300-301
Red Cross, 120
Refugee camps, 85, 88
Refugees, 153, 155
Regional political parties, 4
Relief Committee, 136
Religious
- bodies, 143
- clash, 82
- conflicts, 25, 91
- crisis, 60, 88, 91
- differences, 22
- diversity, 129
- groups, 51, 60, 98, 120, 143, 170, 212
- hostility, 82
- leaders, 134, 271, 282-283, 287
- organisations, 132, 212
- riots, 63
- sentiments, 137
Research Centre for Democratic Governance and Social Justice (RECEDEGS), 276
Resettlement and Compensation Committee, 136
Resettlement Programme, 115, 117, 120
Resource
- and occupational conflicts, 24
- conflict, 28, 193-194, 218
- control, 6, 9, 24, 91, 307
- management, 29
Resources
- allocation of, 107
Richard, Arthur, 3
Role of Assemblies, 287-288
Roman Catholic Mission (RCM), 179, 191, 204
Royal Niger Company, 191, 204, 206-207

Rule of law, 46, 61, 143
Ruling classes, 181-182, 260
Rural
- communal conflicts, 172
- communities, 172-173, 184, 293
- ethnicity, 172
- land conflicts, 218
- multi culturalism, 168
- poverty, 202

Security Agents
- role of, 96-97, 140-142
Self
- determination, 107
- governance, 162, 180
- help groups, 51
Settler versus indigene conflict type, 112
Sex-based group, 97
Shagari, Shehu, 88
Shanumwa, Ibrahim, 135
Sharia
- debate, 90
- episode, 60
- law
  - declaration of, 81
- legal system, 84, 88, 93, 136
- riots, 92
Sijuade, Oba Okunade (Ooni of Ife), 161
Social
- activists
  - detention of, 51
- conflict, 242
- groupings, 41
- harmony, 289
- intercourse, 302
- movements, 45
- oppression,4
Societal conflicts, 56
management of, 36
Society for Women and Aids in Africa (SWAAN), 263, 270, 273-274, 276
Socio-cultural
- and linguistic groups, 4
- symbols, 17

Socio-political
  - conflicts, 56
  - events, 52
  - landscape, 106
Southern Minority States, 225
Southern Solidarity Front, 51
State
  - and local government creation
        - instrument of, 140
  - Boundary Adjustment
        Committee, 196
  - Creation
        - instrument of, 95
  - of anarchy, 83, 88
  - of emergency, 64
  - repression, 51, 54, 58
  - security, 96
        - Service, 138
Statutory Right of Occupancy, 205
Strategic Empowerment Manage-
      ment Agency (SEMA), 121,
      267, 269, 308
Structural adjustment programme
      (SAP), 50-51
Suleiman, Adamu (Emir of
      Bauchi), 134
Supreme Egbesu Assembly (SEA),
      15
System/ideological conflict, 28

Tafawa Balewa
        - crisis, 131, 141
        - disturbances, 140
Tansi, Father Iwene, 217
        - beatification of, 215
Territorial boundaries, 109
Tiv/Alago crisis, 117, 259, 264, 276
Tiv/Jukun conflict, 60
Tiv militias, 15
Tiv Progressive Movement, 65
Town or village unions, 99, 212
Trade
  - groups, 265
  - unions, 99, 273
Traditional
  - civil organisation model, 99
  - conflict management
        practices, 294

  - culture, 148
  - democratic analytical model,
      293-299, 301
  - grazing land, 22-23
  - institutions, 107, 111
  - leaders, 134, 142
  - medicine or charm (Egbesu
      charm)
        - use of, 239
  - methods, 290
  - oath taking, 215
  - power, 135
  - rulers, 143, 277, 282-283, 285-
      287, 293, 295, 297
Transition programme, 51
Tri-regional colonial federalism, 4
Tribal groups, 3
Turks, 15

Ukaegbu, Emmanuel, 197-198, 213
Union of Niger Delta, 44, 51
United Action for Democracy
      (UAD), 45, 50, 64, 263
United Democratic Front of Nigeria
      (UDFN), 50
Unity Party of Nigeria (UPN), 159
Unongo, Paul, 65
Urban Neighbourhood Develop-
      ment Initiative (UNDI), 270,
      273, 276
Urhobo
  - communities, 27
  - Itsekiri conflict, 20, 306
  - /Itsekiri, 259, 264
  - Progressive Union (UPU), 10
  - Youth Movement (UYOMO),
      10
USAID/OTI sponsored conflict
      resolution outfit, 121

Violent
  - clashes
        - use of soldiers to quell,
        95, 140
  - communal cosnflicts, 138-140
  - conflicts, 106, 112, 285
  - ethnic conflicts, 300

WAI Brigade, 263
Warri
  - conflict, 31
  - crisis, 233, 235, 237, 239. 248
  - land dispute, 247
  - Our Land, 250-251
Western
  - donor agencies, 45
  - education, 5
  - liberal ideology, 37
Wild Wild West, 149
Williams, F.R.A., 207
Willink Commission, 94
Women
  - Advancement Forum (WAF), 273
  - associations, 277
  - in Health Development (WIHD), 273
  - in Law and Development in Africa (WILDAF), 273
  - in Neighbourhood Ventures (WONEV), 273
  - in Nigeria (WIN), 45, 50, 61, 263, 272
  - Law and Development Centre (WLDC), 263, 276
  - Living Under Muslim Laws (WLUML), 273
  - organisations and associations, 252
Women's
  - groups, 122, 210, 251-252, 282, 288

  - Health and Economic Development Association (WHEDA), 273
  - organisations, 99
  - Right Advancement and Protection Alternative (WRAPA), 263, 273, 276

Yelwa-Shendam
    - Conflagration, 25
Yerima, Ahmed Sani, 84, 92
Yoruba
  - Council of Elders, 51
  - Hausa community, 13
  - history, 148
  - nation, 153
Youth
  - Earnestly Ask for Abacha (YEAA), 263
  - group, 65, 122
  - mobility, 5
  - organisations, 143, 210, 2112, 224
  - unemployment, 304
Zango-Kàtaf
  - conflict, 20
Zar Cultural Association, 132
Zar Sayawa/Hausa-Fulani, 259, 264
Zar (Sayawa) Youth Association, 136
Zoning system, 109-110

www.ingramcontent.com/pod-product-compliance
Lightning Source LLC
Chambersburg PA
CBHW072049020426
42334CB00017B/1443